Can I borrow it   ?!

C000017289

Voices of the People

translated by
John Moore
edited and presented by
Adrian Rifkin and Roger Thomas

Voices of the People

The Social Life of 'La Sociale'
at the End of the Second Empire

First published in 1988 by
Routledge & Kegan Paul Ltd
11 New Fetter Lane, London EC4P 4EE

Published in the USA by
Routledge & Kegan Paul Inc.
in association with Methuen Inc.
29 West 35th Street, New York, NY 10001

Set in Bembo
by Columns of Reading
and printed in Great Britain
by T.J. Press (Padstow) Ltd.
Padstow, Cornwall.

British Library CIP Data
    Voices of the people: the politics and
    life of 'la sociale' at the end of the
    second Empire. — (History Workshop series).
1. Labor and laboring classes — France
— History — 19th Century.   2. France
— Social life and customs — 19th century.
I. Rifkin, Adrian
II. Thomas, Roger
III. Series.
944.07'0880623
HD8430

Library of Congress Cataloging in Publication Data also available

ISBN 0-7102-13085

Chapters one and two are from *Les Révoltes Logiques, Cahiers
du Centre des Recherches sur les Idéologies de la Révolte*, ed.
Solin, Paris. No. 1, Hiver 1975, pp. 5-22; No. 7,
Printemps-Eté 1978, pp. 25–66.

Chapter three is from Denis Poulot: *Le Sublime, ou le
travailleur comme il est en 1870, et ce qu'il peut être: introduction d'
Alain Cottereau*. Actes et Mémoires du Peuple. Collection
animée par Louis Constant, François Maspéro, Paris, 1980.

Chapters four and five are from Alain Dalotel, Alain Faure,
Jean-Claude Freiermuth: *Aux Origines de la Commune: le
mouvement des réunions publiques à Paris 1868–1870*. Actes et
Mémoires du Peuple. Collection animée par Louis Constant,
François Maspéro, Paris, 1980.

Contents

Editors

John Moore, **Adrian Rifkin** and **Roger Thomas** are senior lecturers at Portsmouth Polytechnic, working in the fields of French literature and history, cultural history and cultural theory.

Contributors

Alain Cottereau (CNRS)
Alain Dalotel (Caisse Autonome Nationale de la Sécurité Sociale dans les Mines)
Alain Faure (University of Paris, Nanterre)
Jean-Claude Freiermuth (Education Counsellor)
Jacques Rancière (University of Paris viii, Vincennes-St. Denis, Collège Internationale de Philosophie)
Patrick Vauday

Preface

With the exception of the two essays in Part One, all the texts translated in this volume originally formed part of a longer work. Alain Cottereau's reading of *Le Sublime* seemed very well able to stand on its own, without the book which it was intended to introduce, and which might only have been of much more specialised interest. The two chapters from *Aux Origines de la Commune* between them give both an original analysis of the overall evolution and significance of the public meetings of 1868–70 and a striking demonstration of their day to day unfolding, offering a new understanding of the social origins of the Paris Commune of 1871. The work of Rancière and Vauday was situated within the particular theoretical and philosophical pre-occupations of *Les Révoltes Logiques*, and have been taken from thematic numbers of that important review. And the second of these two pieces pursues its analysis well beyond the chrono-logical limits of the other essays, up to the impact of the gramophone on popular cultures. However, we are convinced that readers of this collection will find that the overlapping of the focus of attention of the different parts makes for a subtle and complex unity between them – just as the divergent methods of handling their material suggest an important debate on the constitution of the 'popular' and the 'people' as an object of study in the historiography of the nineteenth century. Between the essays, the realisation of the people as a multiplicity of voices, of subjects and of meanings, swings from the unseating of the epistemological certainty of historical categories and sources, to the detailed assertion of a new empirical basis for the visualising of such multiplicity.

Since these texts were first published we ourselves have used them as teaching materials, and have taken them as a starting point for new research and teaching programmes. It is through this extensive use that our admiration for them has grown over the years. Producing a definitive translation of them is thus the overdue fulfilment of our ambition to have them better known.

The introduction is quite deliberately not intended to be a guide to the texts, but stands as an independent analysis of the historiography of the closing years of the Second Empire and the Commune, a *mise en scène* of a set of historical problems of which the significance is too often overlooked. The title of the volume points to an essential element of all the pieces – the importance of the voice in histories of politics and cultures, the voices of people in the city of Paris at the end of the Second Empire.

The translation of the vocabulary of French working class and industrial organisation in this period poses some formidable problems of equivalence and connotation. Words like *union*, *syndical*, *chambres syndicales*, *travail* can be turned into English quite readily, but there would seem to be no single, international standard of fixing a precise inflexion. The inflexion of the difference between a *chambre syndicale* as a bosses' or as a workers' organisation, for example (see Cottereau, Note 47, p. 176); or the difference of meaning in the anglophone world of a movement of *workers'* and a *labour* movement. We have aimed to render this vocabulary with strict reference to its immediate context in the original texts rather than for a more abstract consistency. The translation of each text has been studied in detail with the authors. Some minor elisions have been made, and where direct translation has yielded either opacity or clumsiness, we have agreed some rewrites. In some instances, the authors have taken advantage of the translation to improve their original, and here the essays represent more or less a new edition.

We must, then, thank all of the authors for the time and work that they themselves have devoted to the production of this volume, and for the pleasure that we have had in working with them.

Thanks also to Raphael Samuel for backing the project and to Elizabeth Fidlon and Jill Holmden for their editorial assistance. To the Faculties of Humanities and Environmental Studies at Portsmouth Polytechnic for grants in money and time to assist with its completion. To Anne Sizer, Shanie Thirlwell and Pam Miller for typing the manuscript. To friends and colleagues in Paris for their generosity and hospitality, especially Denis Echard. And, finally, to generations of students who have made the whole undertaking worthwhile.

JCM/ADR/RDT

General introduction

'Paris Libre': historiographical perspectives on the Parisian working class 1830–71

Workers,
The independence of the Commune will mean a freely
discussed social contract that will bring to an end class conflict
and secure social equality.

We have demanded the emancipation of the working class
and the elected Commune will ensure this, for it must provide
all citizens with the means to defend their rights, to control
effectively the actions of representatives entrusted with the care
of their interests, and to determine the gradual application of
social reforms.

(Election poster of the International and the Federation of
Trade Unions, 23 March 1871, Paris)

Year II

The revolutionary potential of Paris and its civil administration,
the Commune, is one of the most fertile and poignant themes to
be found in revolutionary socialist writings. In Year II of the
Great Revolution the Jacobins, Robespierre and Saint-Just,
Herbert, the popular journalist, and Pierre Chaumette, the
prosecutor of the Commune, had all agreed (however momentar-
ily) that Paris was truly the Citadel of Liberty. Seventy years later
a young Blanquist lawyer, Gustave Tridon, assiduously
researched the politics of the Commune, in particular the activities
of the Herbertists. Interested in revolutionary praxis Tridon re-
worked this potent theme: Paris was the heart of the revolution,
the very fabric of the city possessed revolutionary energies, which
if aroused would sweep throughout France overthrowing and
annihilating the revolution's enemies. Of course, Tridon and his
colleagues, Breuillé and Rigault, sought to distance themselves
from the bourgeois Parisians. They linked the Haussmannised city

of the 1860s to the revolutionary epoch by isolating the eighteenth-century revolutionary *faubourgs*, especially Saint Antoine, and linking them with the north-east area of modern Paris, Belleville and Ménilmontant. The newer proletarian streets, bars and flats came to occupy the same spatial ideology as the artisanal *faubourgs*, and contemporary socialist struggles thus acquired a revolutionary perspective. Both the ritualised historicist tradition and the innate idea of the revolution made the workers the true heroes of the struggle, for it was their work skills, their political courage, their simplicity of expression and humanism and their atheism that was the bedrock of a powerful revolutionary movement. However, Tridon, like Robespierre and Saint-Just before him, produced a form of prose that strongly veered towards idealisation and abstraction. The material realities of the workers' way of life were only briefly alluded to. And it wasn't until socialist and trade unionist activists began to write their own expositional autobiographies in the 1880s that this subject matter was brought more prominently into historical narrative.

Perhaps the desire to read a more particularised and materialist analysis of working-class life is itself a creation of modern historiography. Certainly the Parisian *menu peuple* of the Great Revolution have received forceful and evocative characterisations from Richard Cobb and Albert Soboul. The former is all biting anecdote, with a Simenon/Zola delight in the pathetic, the eccentric, the selfish and the silly. Cobb implicitly relies for effect on his literary imagination and his imperious knowledge of primary material. Although he is a good story-teller, he apparently assumes that his readership will have the characteristic English middle-class disdain for politics, and that they will enjoy his Oxbridge jibes at marxists and socialists. Even less convincing are his statements about human nature and common sense. Despite his various misogynous outbursts Richard Cobb's writings are a literary *tour de force*. They remain inventive and interesting even if their political stance lies with the cult of the individual, a vague anarchism, and probably Toryism. The more magisterial and modern writer remains his affectionate and generous friend, Albert Marius Soboul.

The late 'Historien de la Grande Révolution Français' was a master of the communist historical genre. His thousand-page text on the sans-culottes was originally written for a doctoral thesis submitted in 1958. It then became a book, thanks to Clavreuil of Rue Saint Andre. The centre chapters were produced as *Les Sans-culottes en l'an II* and then parts of the texts were popularised, section two (chapters 1–6) appeared in 1968, Editions du Seuil, then an abridged version of parts one and three as *Mouvement populaire et gouvernement révolutionnaire en l'an II 1793–1794*, Flammarion, 1973. Soboul's intention was clear – 'within the framework of Paris and the chronological limits which we have set, it is our concern to demonstrate that the popular movement possessed its own autonomous identity.' Somewhat controversially he made the wry comment in the introduction to the later Flammarion edition that

> during the past fifteen years, scholarly research on the French Revolution has expanded and deepened. Despite certain sterile polemics, we do not consider that our own interpretation of the historical problems treated here have been altered or refuted, either by scientific erudition or by critical thought. And the relevance of their problem endures; it is carried onward by the very movement of history.

The thesis contains an unsurpassed narration of the sans-culottes political fortunes from June 1793 to 9 Thermidor 1794, and their relationship to the Montagnards, Enragés, Cordeliers, Herbertists and in particular, the Revolutionary Government. The book's central analytical chapters explore the sans-culottes' social and political values. Here the significance of the right to existence is brilliantly explored. Soboul realistically portrays the sans-culottes' attitude towards the aristocrats, the bourgeoisie and 'respectable people'. The organisational basis of popular sovereignty is located within the sectional assemblies and committees. Underpinning these were the popular societies and the great *journées*. Finally there is an outline of the sans-culottes' social lifestyle, their dress, family and their corporate attitude to the merchant capitalist, to the landlord and the food hoarders. The whole narrative is sustained by qualitative documentary evidence, while the political and factional struggles of this crucial revolutionary epoch are brilliantly and vividly represented. In fact the book is unsurpassed in terms of its coherence and clarity of presentation. The viewpoint is collectivist. Of course much of the work, as Richard Cobb points out, presents the Parisian artisans in a rather sociological context. For Soboul the sans-culottes revealed a political maturity and an ability to organise that clearly pre-figures the activities of the Parisian working class of the 1840s, although Soboul's own comments on the modern factory working class are reductive – Labroussian orthodoxies and loyalties? For himself, Richard Cobb clearly prefers to stress the fluidity and momentary nature, indeed, the accidental vagaries of the struggles of 1793–4. Individuality is Cobb's creed. He always stresses the inherent weaknesses and vulnerability of the '*menu peuple*'. Somewhat cynically he accuses 'his dear friend' – the 'historian of the mass movement' – of concentrating on artisanal elites, often rather more wealthy than their *égalité* might suggest and political minorities whom Cobb detaches from the plebeian *menu peuple*. These militants are presented as hot-headed, drunken, parochial, unstable, ambitious, and manipulative – truly a 'thermidorian presentation'. But this 'presentation' reveals more of Cobb's hostility to *gauchism* and his basic pessimism about popular democracy. One of Cobb's main achievements has been to municipalise the revolution evoking the social character of Parisian quarters and Lyons back alleys. This geographical affinity is lacking in Soboul's writings. Richard Cobb's most effective comment on the sans-culottes of Year II is 'that the sans-culotte movement should not be stressed in isolation in the purely Year II context'. And so it is Professor Cobb himself who has done so much to provide this wider perspective in territorial and chronological terms, although the more recent work on the Parisian sans-culottes by R.B. Rose and R. Monnier has generally supported Soboul's perspectives rather than Cobb's idiosyncratic interpretations. His earlier historical writings, in particular *Les Armées révolutionnaires* will, however, remain widely admired.

1848

If the Parisian sans-culottes constitute such a weighty prelude to the arrival of working class it has been comparatively easy to construct a consensual approach to the activities of the skilled working class of 1848. Perhaps this has been a fortuitous development, although William Sewell Jnr has obviously closely read Soboul's texts as well as some other prominent modern French historians of the Parisian working class. It is more likely, however, that the skilful North American writers in this field, in particular Christopher Johnson, John Merriman, Joan Scott and William Sewell Jnr, have sought to distance their characterisation of Parisian artisans from Marx's strictures on French socialism and his presentation of French workers as not having arrived at their appointed time in history. Still, Marx was more interested in bourgeois politics; after all, the readership of *Rheinische Zeitung* and *Die Revolution* would appreciate the irony, gossip and witticisms which were directed at kings, king's ministers, financiers and failed politicians. Several writers, probably strongly influenced by E.P. Thompson's radical perspectives on the struggles and activities of the English working class, were able to demonstrate that there were strong links between working-class everyday experience, political struggle and popular consciousness.

The specificities of the working class of 1848 were thus characterised to include the right of existence; the right to education, the right to food and the right to work, while towering above these organic values was the theme of co-operative labour. The workers were the sovereign people because like the plebeian sans-culottes before them they did all the useful work.

In terms of methodological influences North American historians became, from the mid-1970s onwards, interested in the ethnographic work of Maurice Agulhon. This was an important debate about 'culturalism' which also included a critique of the literal importation of anthropological concepts. Agulhon had stressed the vitality of popular politics while in the opinion of one knowledgeable commentator 'the novelty of Agulhon's method lay in the fact that he relegated economic factors to the background and demonstrated the contribution that the specifically cultural and social arguments could make to the continuing debate over popular politization in the nineteenth century.' Vulgar marxism could thus be ignored, while a radical form of historical writings developed strongly influenced by the concept of 'history from below', and in particular the writings of the English marxist E.P. Thompson. Several writers were, however, alert to the need to have an economic dimension to their writing. In fact radical historians generally stressed the workers' struggle with the capitalists and the threat and the reality of the ensuing proletarianisation which was initially most acutely experienced in tailoring and the garment trades. Christopher Johnson in particular constructed a careful outline of the nature and significance of '*confection*' while also sustaining an implicit conceptual interest in the idea of 'worker-control'. In the foreground was the problematic of the dialogue between crafts skills and militant consciousness.

The general problematic was the relationship between workers' pride in their work, their skills and the status of that skill, and their critique of capitalism. Associationalism, with its emphasis upon the co-operative organisation of production, and the social workshop, appeared as the unifying and consensual value, evolving from within the working class in its struggles to resist an encroaching and exploitative capitalism. The significance of 'left politics' and the legacy of popular terrorism has generally been underplayed. However, in an important article, that was clearly indebted in part to C. Johnson, Joan Scott developed an interesting utopian and feminist interpretation. The socialist workers of 1848 could now include the seamstress. The resonances of modernity and utopian feminism were evocatively illustrated through quotations from *La Voix des Femmes*:

Women ought to work, it's better for women to have a trade than a dowry. If men and women both furnish the means of existence, they will help one another and be united.

(28–30 May 1848)

The working woman will contribute to her family income and we, who have demanded the right to work for all, we dare also to believe in equality, the religious and fraternal expression of the two sexes.

(14 June 1848)

Sewell's book *Work and Revolution in France* is especially important because it is a clever synthetic essay which is also a highly effective and stimulating college text book. The sub-title 'The language of labour from the Old Regime to 1848' is somewhat misleading since this is no Saussurian– or Voloshinov–inspired text, neither is it a discussion of Parisian patois or an example of discourse analysis. Instead Sewell has sought to make the attempt to draw 'together the findings of a large number of more specialised studies into a new general interpretation'. He has succeeded in this. The book is an evaluative and reflective thematic outline. Starting with *ancien* corporations and journeymen brotherhoods, Sewell moves on to a discussion of the profound ruptural changes which occurred during the course of the French Revolution. This in turn is followed by a succinct interpretation of industrial society and the distinctive features of artisanal socialism. It is clear that chapters 9, 10 and 11, which deal with the period 1830–48, are strongly indebted to the writings of Alain Faure, Jacques Rancière and Remi Gossez. The book culminated in an unprejudiced narrative of the revolutionary activities of the Parisian artisans in the spring of 1848. Rather surprisingly Sewell chose to restrict provincial perspectives, including his own material upon Marseille. The bulk of the narrative stresses the over-determining influence of Parisian artisans upon national events and the evolution of French working-class socialism. Sewell is clearly fascinated by the great revolutionary upheavals of 1789–94, 1830–4 and 1848–51, believing that such conjunctural moments reveal an authentic artisanal voice. He has sought to provide a subtle and contextual characterisation of the socialist workers of 1848, but has undermined the classical meaning of class struggle. Moreover, his presentation does not reveal the true breadth of popular revolutionary activities. Where are the young bearded men with their red neckerchiefs standing and applauding radical speakers in the clubs, and what about those republican ceremonies of planting the tree of liberty? In February and March of 1848 *Le bonheur* was to be found in the streets. Sewell gives us Gossez on the worker corporations and the Luxembourg commission, which is good. Less good is the appearance of these over respectable artisans, and the fudges the author makes in his conclusion – 'the dialectic of revolution'. One consequence of this approach is that the modernism of the 1848 working class is underplayed and the revolutionary legacy of 1789–94 diluted. His politically restrained artisan appears to have little continuity with those plebeians who gathered round to listen to a fellow terrorist read Hebert's *Père Duchêsne* in a crowded wine bar; neither do they appear to anticipate those workers who went with their comrades to the public debates in 1869 on the exploitation of capital and the forthcoming revolution in the Folies-Belleville.

1968

The Paris of May 1968 was the site of the last revolutionary situation in Western Europe. It began as a student sit-in at Nanterre University. At its climax over nine million workers were out on strike; factories were occupied throughout France. In part it was a revolt against Gaullism – 'On 13th May, nearly one million workers were shouting on the streets "Ten years, that's enough" ' (CFDT comment). But the popular slogans were wide ranging – they spoke of an actuality, and a potentiality:

'Arise ye wretched of Nanterre.'

'Our movement of 22 March is against hegemonies.'

'Abolish alienation.'

'Research through action.'

'Down with a society based on consumerism and the spectacle.'

'It's by stopping our machines together that we'll show them their weakness.'

'The boss needs you – you don't need him.'

'The question of POWER is being posed in the enterprises and in society.'

'This is only the beginning – continue the struggle.'

What had begun at Nanterre University and the Sorbonne briefly became an international movement linked to the anti-imperialist struggle of South Vietnam. Did these events renew revolutionary politics? Certainly the power of capital was weakened, Stalinism was challenged and lampooned. While the PCF and CT sought to restrict the struggle to a matter of trade union economism, the CFDT, the PSU and numerous left groupings prepared to countenance a dialogue between students, young technicians and factory workers – 'If the workers are on strike, we must be conscious that, to a large extent, it is thanks to the students who faced problems that discussions, negotiation and dialogue have been unable to solve. Direct confrontation and repression was necessary, if one was to conceive of a disruption of that society, which all of us, workers as well as students, question' (Rousselin, CFDT official, Renault-Flins, public meeting, 20 May 1968). Amongst the many discourses there was inevitably an inclination to evoke past revolutions – the Enragés, the students' Commune – the Paris Commune, the barricades, cobblestones, the violent clashes with the CRS in the Latin Quarter – *l'insurgé* of the 1830s and 1840s. Perhaps 'contestation' was the central premise from which radicals ought to commence their historical investigations. Certainly one result of the revolt was that a generation of *gauchistes* were profoundly moved by the events and the potentialities implicit in the adventure of May 1968.

The worker's world 1830–51

It was therefore probably no coincidence that Alain Faure submitted a *memoire de maitresse* at Nanterre's Faculty of Letters in 1970. The subject was popular movements and the working-class movement in Paris 1830–34 – did the origin of workers' power lie in the strike waves of 1830–4? Was the society of the rights of man an assembly of 'groupuscules'? More sustained research led to the publication in 1976 of *La Parole ouvrière 1830–1851* by Alain Faure who was joined by Jacques Rancière (not the Alain Faure of 'The public meeting movement').

It remains the most comprehensive modern collection of working-class writings for the period 1830–51. The texts are varied, including brochures, letters, poems, articles and posters. Both authors sought to free the texts from the dead weight of certain historiographical traditions. Jacques Rancière in particular argues that the very words of the workers are themselves part of the struggle, a weapon, which corresponds to a specific move-ment of perception, when workers sought to maintain a dialogue with the bourgeois, and yet to emancipate themselves from bourgeois categories. Instead the words shaped class identity and sustained the discourse with the masters. The texts illustrate a rich historical tradition – the insurrections in Paris and Lyons 1830 and 1834, the great strike waves of 1833 and 1840, the decline in the old form of *compagnonnage*, the appearance of new forms of organisation, the grandeur and decay of secret societies, the diffusion of utopian socialism, the hopes and shootings of 1848, the national workshops and the workers' associations. The words themselves constitute a desire to elevate the workers' experiences; to learn, to discuss, and to argue. The writings are assembled in five loosely chronological themes: the proletarian – between slavery and association, from *compagnonnage* to the federation, working-class expression, a weapon or substitute, the workers' spring, and finally the lessons of 1848. Each theme has an accompanying commentary from both authors, with Alain Faure generally giving the broader historical contextualisation, and Jacques Rancière commenting upon the authors and the various writing modes inherent within the papers, letters, addresses and newspaper articles. The book reveals that working class didn't speak in the form of a cry from a savage mass in a pitiful state. Some workers wanted recognition from the bourgeoisie, others spoke through the force of numbers, while others sought to show that workers were best able to say what was just and reasonable. Theirs was a voice of intelligence. They truly understood the principles of liberty, equality and true fraternity. This collective voice adhered to several central generalised perspectives, but there were also several qualitative distinctions. Controversial questions were that of violence and force, secret societies or open debates, and the form in which to undertake a dialogue with the bourgeoisie. For the majority emancipation meant that they had to have the freedom to associate, and that they would be free from the censor, the police, the boss's fines and the employer's reference. Proletarians were opposed to the state's violence and would defend themselves if necessary. Self-emancipation was explored through class struggle. The various utopian aspirations were mostly a fusion of christianity and socialism. Thus the variety and complexity of working-class discourse is allowed to establish itself. The book is partially a workerist perspective, but it is also free from arid Althusserian theoreticism. In fact it is significantly distinct from writings which have been influenced by E.P. Thompson's experiental approach to the making of the working class. Instead Faure and Rancière have produced a thematic and episodic historical contextualisation, while also including an aspect of working-class subjectivism. Texts no longer reflect, but are active. In 1976 this was a pioneer effort at historical discourse analysis, for *La Parole ouvrière* is a book that is full of meanings. It contains some of the material associated with Gustave Leroy and Pierre-Denis Vinçard, that was developed in Rancière's subsequent writings on the worker-poets. Indeed in his more recent essays, he has probed many of the assumptions made about skilled artisans and their consciousness. This kind of insight is not really developed in *La Parole Ouvrière*, although it is hinted at. The fuller development lies in Rancière's doctoral thesis which is the basis of his *La Nuit des Prolétaires*. Retrospectively he felt that in *La Parole Ouvrière* the presentation of the collective struggle of authentic workers was over-simplified, and that he should have stressed more emphatically that the words themselves were polemical. These were texts that were addressed to the bourgeoisie. The images were what the workers wanted to make. They presented a public characterisation. He would now also attribute a more powerful bourgeois presence within the texts – although one is sceptical that these words could '*reflect* political and ideological positions from the bourgeoisie'. This surely ascribes too much unity and power to the bourgeoisie, who throughout the 1840s were deeply sectionalised. However, clearly the dialogue between artisans and bourgeois is complex. Rancière remains fascinated by those on the margins of the broad social classes. And one can agree with him that the workers involved with *L'Atelier* did oppose the idea of work as a condemnation, and that their response was a realistic way of dealing with the feeling of helplessness that workers periodically expressed. For Rancière *L'Atelier* remains a source of struggle which sought to unite the force of intellectual and militant worker elites around a specific political form, that of republicanism. Although the political stance of that republicanism was surely more ambiguous than he suggests, for while the anonymous writers of *L'Atelier* distanced themselves from street violence and criticised the June days, the negation of crude Jacobinism and terrorism was a powerful undercurrent amongst a wide range of socialist intellectuals and workers. The events of 1848 dissolved many of the boundaries of inherited left-wing political labels.

In *La Parole Ouvrière* and in much of his subsequent work on the artisans of the 1830s and 1840s, Rancière has carefully probed the meanings of the writings of individual members of the working class, arguing that 'work' was a paradox, for ever ambiguous – loathed by some, used as utopian and socialist metaphor by those who wrote to overcome their alienation, and to nullify their depression and own dismal job experiences. *Déclassé* writers neither acquiring the recognisable status of poets or journalists were moving between the interfaces of class. He presents them as a potentially rich and poetic source of revolt. The sufferings of those forced to labour manually might be drugged by fantasy or dreams, but it is more likely that this was but a momentary relief. The lot of many workers was to move from job to job, to turn their hands to what was available, or might become available through the act of buying a small master or chargehand a drink in a *goguette*. Motifs of the 1980s experiences of the manual working class, that of 'flexibilities' and the black economy, also appear to be strikingly appropriate for the Paris of the 1830s and 1840s. Skill and the structure of worker corporations do not appear to possess the stability and organisation strength that modern historians often ascribe to them. Instead the very words of the artisans are more subtle, and less optimistic. As Rancière writes

> between the fumes of larger workshops and the grime of the
> tanneries, between the assaults of poverty and the fury of the
> struggle, between the brilliance of luxury and the conditions of
> the artisans, between the artisans' end-product and the
> confidence of the hymn to work, between the rumblings of the
> crowd and the voices of its representatives, an entire series of
> inferences impose themselves almost naturally and end up
> making us blind to the ruses of numbers and the ruses of words
> and the ruses of relationships.

In Rancière's vocabulary the stratagems associated with 'ruse' and the metaphor 'labyrinth' imply the need to address ourselves directly to the task of unravelling working-class history. The ideology of various historiographical traditions needs deflecting. In reality working life is more confused, contradictory and complex than many would wish for.

In his most recent historical book *La Nuit des Prolétaires*, Rancière is concerned with the few hundred Saint-Simonian, Fourierist, Buchezian, Icarian and republican workers and intellectuals in Paris from 1830 to the early 1850s. There is an element of fantasy and exoticism in the utopias of Fourier, Saint-Simon, Cabet and Enfantin and the journey to Egypt. But Rancière's real subject matter is the workers or perhaps the spiritual sufferings of the worker-intellectuals. The Saint-Simonian worker-poets in particular struggled to endure poverty, low wages, comfortless flats and the ever present threat of hunger. But the special feature of their anguish was the theft of their daily time, as they worked laboriously on wood, metal, cloth or shoes and boots. Their life energies were frittered away in these mundane tasks. Instead, their wish was to undertake artistic and aesthetic work – and this they could only accommodate by working into the night. This double strain of daily and nightly labour inevitably weakened their physical constitution, but the yearning to escape to a better life remained, as did the stratagems to find themselves the space to undertake poetic work. For Rancière the remarkable nature of this movement was that while 'no one needs to tell workers that they are exploited, this they already know. It is something else again for a worker to perceive that he may be destined for something beyond exploitation.' But it is here that the tortuous ambivalence and paradox of this liberation appear for

> the proletarians need to grasp the secret of others in order to define the meaning of their own existence. They did not lack an understanding of exploitation; what they required was an understanding of themselves as beings destined for something other than exploitation, and insight which they could only alleviate through the secret of others – the middle-class intellectuals.

For Jacques Rancière this meeting of the workers and the bourgeoisie is of central importance in the history of the working class.

Work in the archive

An earlier generation of socialist historians, represented here by Eugene Schulkind, argued that 'to probe aspects of collective attitudes and motivation in this particular historical situation (the popular attitudes of Communards) requires informed sensitivity to their complexity, elusiveness and changing nature'. For Eugene Schulkind, and Jacques Rougerie, both historians of the Paris Commune, and Remi Gossez the historian of the working class of 1848, archival research on the working class, was both an urgent and life consuming task. Although all three published books in the era of May 1968 they remained little affected by the variant forms of *gauchisme*. Their own work was the product of singular and concentrated work, work that had been undertaken over a decade or more. It was therefore almost inevitable that their writings were infrequent. Only Remi Gossez was able to complete a monograph – *Les Ouvriers de Paris, livre 1, l'organisation 1848–1851*, Paris 1967. This still remains the best study of worker corporations and trade politics of the Luxembourg Commission. The book contains a wealth of material on the democratic organisation of the general assemblies and delegatory politics of the corporations, and upon the earnest efforts made by workers to achieve a significant advance in their conditions through the adoption of tariffs – unified wages – negotiated at boards (*chambres syndicales*), where the workers and masters of a particular trade met in equal numbers. These agreements were then usually

symbolically signed at the Luxembourg Commission. Because of
the political initiative the working class briefly held in Paris after
the February days they were able to obtain the recognition of their
right to work from the provisional government, and the
Luxembourg Commission began to develop as an industrial
parliament – despite the efforts of Louis Blanc and his immediate
supporters. The cause of democracy lay with the members of the
corporations républicaines and they were resolved to initiate the
social and democratic republic by extending the scope of
associations until capitalism itself was superseded, for 'the
principle of association is a natural right made sacred since the
foundation of our glorious Republique'.

Neither Jacques Rougerie or Eugene Schulkind unfortunately
were able to write the substantive book upon the communard
working class which their knowledge appeared to imply was
always potentially there. Nevertheless both men were able to
complete two important documentary collections of communard
material carefully transcribed from the fragile papers of Ly 11,
Ly 22 and Ly 22 at Vincennes, as well as the more accessible
newspaper articles, political posters and election addresses. In
these works they gave accurate but brief historical contextualisation with regard to individuals, trades, organisations and specific
moments, etc., but they drew back from rash interpretations,
preferring instead to narrow the scope of interpretation while
underplaying political sectarianism.

Schulkind argued that with a complex and controversial topic
like the Paris Commune 'the historian cannot hope to achieve
complete objectivity; the most he can do is to recognise his
limitations and be sincere in his efforts'. And he concluded one of
his essays with the riposte that 'no opinion would be worthwhile
that is not founded upon a close examination of primary sources'.
His inclination was to 'let the documents speak for themselves', in
itself a subtle methodological ruse. But he also made the careful
qualification 'that the reader should not have the illusion that he
has full contact with primary sources, since translation itself
unavoidably limits communication of a distinctive flavour present
in the original language' and 'this is particularly true here because
of the French nineteenth-century rhetorical style in political prose
as well as of the associative values of much of the language used'.
In order to stress this significance of the latter point he always
strongly spoke up for J. Dubois's study *Le Vocabulaire politique et
sociale en France de 1869–1872*, Paris 1962. Schulkind's interest in
documentation, however, held a bias and a justified one, since he
argued that 'for the study of a revolution whose origin and
development was to a great extent the product of spontaneous

popular initiative the documentation emanatory for such groups would seem to merit more attention that has generally been accorded it'. He preferred to emphasise that the socialist current within the Commune was a heterogeneous *mélange* of democratic and socialist ideas. The sectarianism which some Communards exhibited retrospectively was also partially denied; in his view Communards were prepared to unite in difficult circumstances, while the best of them were ever ready to subsume their personal desires to the urgent and historic needs of the working class.

Schulkind's most recent essay 'Socialist Women during the Paris Commune' demonstrates that the Women's Union for the Defence of Paris and Aid to the Wounded was the most influential popular organisation during the Commune, and that it gave expression city-wide to the radical politics of unprecedented numbers of working-class women. Moreover its executive was composed largely of working-class women, including Nathelie Le Mel, a mother of three, of humble Breton origin and a book stitcher by trade, and Blanche Le Ferme who had been a frequent speaker at club meetings and who died on the barricades in *la Semaine Sanglante*. Both the secretary, the Russian emigré, Elisabeth Dmetrieff, and Nathalie Le Mel ensured that the committee was affiliated to the First International. Most importantly, the Union had a reciprocal relationship with the Commission of Labour and Exchange. The Union remained preoccupied with the necessity to immediately establish workshops for women, partly because unemployment, which was already acute during the Prussian siege, had steadily worsened; but also because they believed that producer co-operatives represented the transition to a socialist economy. The Union regarded discrimination against women as a means employed by the privileged class to maintain their position, and sought to abolish all competition between male and female workers.

Jacques Rougerie also researched and wrote on the singular subject of the Paris Commune for over twenty years. Like his friend (Schulkind) he was concerned about the academic requirement of the historian's *métier*, especially in the obligation 'to listen to the sources'. In certain ways he was even more fastidious over the uniqueness of the communard experience, and the various nuances and distinctions of the communard's political discourse. There was also frequently an element of calculated understatement, even reticence, in his work – an article which remains the most detailed presentation of the insurrection of 18 March was modestly entitled 'notes which are useful for a history of the 18th March uprising'. Particular themes and metaphors remain throughout his writings. He was always absorbed by the problems posed by the nature of state power in the spring of 1871. And he consistently argued that 'the Commune had been an insurrection, a social revolution and at least in outline socialist'. However, he was also fixated by the communard image of the red sun – did it signify the socialist dawn, or was it in reality the twilight? At one moment he wrote that the 'Commune is only the last revolution of the xix century, the ultimate point, the final moment in the narrative of the French Revolution of the xix century'. And yet in other essays he shifted his position – there was emphasis upon new meanings struggling to emerge, constrained by old linguistic forms, new meanings which articulated an authentic working-class consciousness. The balance between tradition and innovation remained fine, this dualism remained the guiding principle of his characterisations of the popular Commune.

Rougerie pointed to the powerful resurrection within the Commune of the sans-culottism of 1789, although the weight of the emphasis was upon the terrorist experiences of Year II and the rhetoric of Year III. His presentation of communard sans-culottism does not show a working class consumed by archaic and fossilised values. No, the vitality of calls for direct government, and the demands for further revolutionary energy were positive. The very language of revolutionary vigilance, the distinctive communard atheism and anti-clericalism were best found in the club meetings, and upon the wall posters plastered up all over a free city. The fear of the landlord, the hostility to the rich, the worry over poverty, the right to the essential necessities of life, remain powerful forms of equality; they are surely desires which all socialists have to satiate. Moreover, freedom from destitution, the desire for work with the accompanying security of a regular income and the aspiration for a proper scientific education, are all merely part of the basic right to exist. In the spring of 1871 working-class people wanted respectability, they wanted recognition; the traditional slogans of equality, fraternity and liberty were just one of the avenues through which they could obtain their emancipation. And if the communards were barely able to achieve part of this vision, then Rougerie is justified in drawing the reader's attention to their perpetual enemies, to those who declared war on them, to those who denied them, to those Parisians who possessed and didn't share, to those who had accumulated their capital directly at the expense of the toiling class: down with the monopolist, the food hoarder, the boss who had abandoned his workers and thrown them out of work, down with reactionary clerics, aristocrats and all despotic rulers! The distinctive quality of the communard revolution for Jacques

Rougerie was this peculiar intermingling of the memories and associations of the 'Great Revolution' with the new aspirations of the working class, many of them stemming from the struggles of the Second Empire, which were intimately tied together, and which mingled indissolubly in the hearts and minds of the Parisian proletariat. If the socialism of 1871 was vague and only generally expressed in the election addresses, the Communards were still able to reach new territory. In their struggles to achieve a free city they were impelled to outline 'Paris Libre's' relationship with the rest of France, and since the Commune revolution was federalist, the principle of autonomy had to be respected. In this sense the Commune, as Rougerie explains, was the antithesis of the strongly centralised Empire. But this antithesis was also seen when the standing army was abolished, when the central executive power of the Empire was liquidated, and when the secret police fled from the city. Under the Commune, judges and senior administrators were to be elected, popular juries replaced magistrates, elected representatives were subject to both an immediate recall and a continuous form of accountability to the electors. The Church was displaced from its privileged position. Education became free, accessible to all, and scientific. The kernel of Rougerie's work is the thesis that the very process of the democratisation of the state required that the central power withered away, almost at its very inception – it was not to be reconstituted in an authoritative workers' state. The key to democratic socialism was the Internationalist Communards' ability to delegate aspects of state power; placing the real power in the hands of the eager Communards. This was the principal means along with the extension of civil rights by which civil life was reinvigorated. And all this was done while the Communards were fighting a bloody war that was not of their own choosing. Rougerie's achievement is thus to allow the full stature of the communal revolution to emerge. He has sought to reconstitute the entity of the Commune by a series of montage effects brought to the reader through the documentary extracts which are embedded in his books. He has had the ability to rescue the Communards from both myth and denigration.

One of the most well-known outlines of the new socialist principles for the organisation of work was written by a stone carver to the Commission of Labour and Exchange. His desire was to stimulate the International and to encourage its Parisian supporters to form themselves into co-operatives and to go on to establish branches in each section or *arrondissement*. This aspiration was partly realised in the matter of women's work through the activities of the Union. Both Schulkind and Rougerie were meticulous in their presentation of the appropriate documentation which revealed the centrality of the working class's desire for their economic emancipation from capital. Work was everything – and its organisation was the challenge to which the Commission of Labour and Exchange methodically applied itself. Sufficient documents have survived – in the form of letters, and resolutions from individuals, trade unions, and organisations, principally the Union and the Louvre workshop – for a clear idea of the activities of the working class to be formed. Yet the weakness of Rougerie's approach lies at the level of economics/work, for while the activities of those workers committed to self-emancipation are carefully mapped out, and the process of the 'syndicalisation of the means of production' unravelled, the concept of capitalism that Rougerie uses is too restricted and inhibited. He appears to be tempted to portray the workers and their workshops in traditional terms, in a manner that is rather too closely akin to Soboul's Paris of 1793–4. It seems that Haussmannisation is restricted merely to the question of residential displacement. The profound structural changes which occurred in the capitalism of the Second Empire are not adequately examined. Rougerie's *métier* was concerned with mastering the intricacies of the dispersed primary material of the Paris Commune. Thus modern historians of the Parisian working class needed to discover the relationship between the work-based struggles undertaken in the Second Empire, and especially those from the mid–1860s onwards, when there was a resurgence of worker resistance and worker militancy, with those of the Paris Commune. A parallel inquiry also had to be undertaken in the realm of working-class politics. Clearly both aspects are intertwined. Although Rougerie in his book *Paris libre* had traced the maturation of the idea of the Commune through the weeks and months of September and October 1870 until their full emergence in February and March 1871, the question of the origins of the Commune is more than a matter of nomenclature. The beginnings of the Commune inevitably lie in the experiences of the working class during the Second Empire; and from a collective experience, which was publicly stated in the public meetings of 1868–70.

The cluster of writings selected for this book take as their subject the Parisian working class, more especially their experience of and response to the political economy of the Second Empire. Here the workers achieve a dignity because these writers recognise 'the theoretical fact that only those directly concerned can speak in a practical way on their own behalf'. Thus the workers' discourse is through poems, songs, reports, newspaper articles and the police commissaire's *procès-verbal* of public meetings. The authenticity of their activities is successfully decoded from Denis Poulet's moralisms and strictures. These Parisian workers are able to aspire to self-emancipation, they are knowledgeable on the nature of the boss's power, they have a sense of history, they also dream, and they seek to overcome their alienation and poverty through artistic and political struggle. Alain Cottereau's essay and the collective work on the public meetings – 'the schools of socialism' – both possess a *gauchiste* flavour. Emphasis is rightly placed upon day to day worker resistance, upon sabotage and upon the aspirations of the workers to establish the rules of the egalitarian republic in the workshop, for it is the workshop that is the site of the struggles over supervision, incentive wages and go-slows. Where work gangs were able to achieve inter-solidarity they sought to supplant the power of capital. Cottereau furnishes a brilliant outline of the innovatory and exploitative features of Parisian capitalism. He also brings a bit of 'new realism' to the debate through the acknowledgement 'that workers confront their destiny with an element of resignation, an element of passivity and an element of insubordination'. Outside the workshops, when the opportunities arose, proletarians sought workers' power through secret trade meetings and the popular public meetings. The 800 pages of manuscripts discovered in the Bibliothèque de la Ville de Paris completed from the *procès-verbal* of the police commissaires who sat in on the public meetings of 1868–70 is the documentary basis of an important reassessment of Parisian working-class political activity. The authors' bold thesis is that 'the commune is born under the Empire'.

In general these essays also reveal several of the concerns of the Parisian post–Althusserian radical debate. Various theoretical perspectives selected from *Capital*, volume 1, are used to underpin the analysis of the worker delegates of 1867. However, Marx's *Capital* is now read much more critically than was the practice in the early 1960s when scientificity, the 'epistemological break', anti-humanism, anti-subjectivity, and anti-historicism were fashionable intellectualisms. The problematical relationships between workers, worker-militants and worker-intellectuals which absorbed a great deal of debate and writing in the PCF, the PSU and PS political parties during the mid–1970s also stimulates astute insights into the popular struggles of the Second Empire. Jacques Rancière in particular sought to demonstrate how many socialists misread, and continue to misread, working-class activism. For him the workers usually choose their intellectuals from those *déclassé* figures who flitted across the interfaces of the classes. Rancière, more than any other writer in this collection, is fascinated by ideas which one would regard as Foucaldian in inspiration and vigour; the State appears in a repressive form – welfarism is denied, state power resides in a network of factories, prisons, hospitals, barracks, police stations and municipal offices. A matrix of spies, crooks, censors, economists and administrators are always watching, intervening upon and categorising workers. In fact power relations permeate every aspect of social life. Yet there are also positive gains for the working class despite the negative nature of state power. The chief of police despairs of his task, he frets at the incompetence of his underlings, he fears the innovatory power of the working class, some of whom are able to transform, to invent, and to invert modern cultural forms. The paradox is that every effort the administrators make to liberalise the Empire only leads them to repression, while allowing the working class to realise that they can dispense with all aspects of liberalism, and aspire to self-emancipation, symbolically represented by the social Commune. Throughout his writing Rancière reveals that the working class is not an essence which can be grasped by bourgeois science or workerist intuition. Patient research and erudite knowledge of detail demonstrate that there is something altogether different here; Rancière believes that the working class is a concept that continually takes place in discussions, misunderstandings and conflicts between workers and intellectuals, and between workers and their spokespeople.

The desire for knowledge has been transformed among us into a passion which fears no sacrifices, nothing but its own extinction.

(M. Foucault, *Hommage to Jean Hyppolite*, Paris 1971)

Roger Thomas

Part I

Introduction

The two articles by Jacques Rancière and Patrick Vauday and by Jacques Rancière are taken from *Les Révoltes logiques*, nos 1 and 7. The journal was published from 1975 until 1983, its last two numbers each taking the form of a volume of essays. Sub-titled 'Notebooks of the Centre for Research into Ideologies of Revolt', its publication marked an important phase in the development of an intensely philosophical approach to problems of popular history, women's and feminist history and current political tendencies and events. Typically, as in the two essays translated here, a quite restrained, if nonetheless rich range of archival sources is subjected to a complex and inventive process of readings and questionings, a turning of a body of empirical material about its possibilities of yielding meaning. The title of the journal significantly derives from no text of political theory. It is a phrase from Arthur Rimbaud's *Illuminations*.

Démocratie

Le drapeau va au paysage immonde, et notre patois étouffe le tambour.

Aux centres nous alimenterons la plus cynique prostitution. Nous massacrerons les révoltes logiques.

Aux pays poivrés et détrempés! – au service des plus monstrueuses exploitations industrielles ou militaires.

Au revoir ici, n'importe où. Conscrits du bon vouloir, nous aurons la philosophie féroce; ignorants pour la science, roués pour le confort; la crevaison pour le monde qui va. C'est la vraie marche. En avant, route!

Arthur Rimbaud, *Illuminations* (1873–1875)

Democracy

The Flag flies over the squalid landscape, and our dialect muffles the drumbeats.

In the Centres we will nourish the most cynical forms of prostitution. We will slaughter the *logical revolt*.

The way to rain-drenched, spicey lands! – serving under the most monstrous industrial or military organisations.

Wherever we are, here or there, farewell! Voluntary conscripts, cruelty will be our philosophy; ignorant of knowledge, craft where comfort is concerned; for anyone who moves – death. That's what real progress is. Off we go, best foot forward.

1
Going to the Expo: the worker, his wife and machines

JACQUES RANCIÈRE and PATRICK VAUDAY

In the register of the imaginary of our society, exhibitions are spectacles. A recent play ('*En revenant de l'Expo*' – Coming from the Fair) uses spectacle to remind us of this spectacle: the Universal Exhibition of 1900; the worker – just like the bourgeois – dazzled by the Fairy Electricity, contemplating the marvels of industry, art and science; and – confronted with bourgeois patriotic mythology – correlatively fixed in a certain representation of himself and his future: the mythology of the Social Revolution and the General Strike.

If we start by going back several decades to study the Worker Delegation reports of the 1867 Exhibition, our intention is not to elaborate on the discreet charm of fashionable nostalgia, but rather to revolve the stage so that the constitution of this spectacle may become visible at the moment when the workers first perceived it as the product of their dispossession. The industrial upheaval of the Second Empire offered workers the spectacle of labour alienated from itself: products of working-class industriousness exhibited as employers' products and rewards as such by a non-working-class jury; products which were unworthy of the true principles of working-class artistry through the fault of speculators who were pressing for mass production; the intelligence of working men broken by the division of labour and the sight of its recomposition in machine controlled by the bosses. 1867 was the year when the elite workers in Paris industry took stock of what a book published in Hamburg that very year called 'the separation of the worker and the intellectual forces of production'.

In the reports of the Worker Delegations – delegations elected by the assembly of each corporation – this dispossession is not recorded passively. They answer back on two levels. Firstly in the 'technical' section of the reports, where they take to themselves intellectual control over the new machines and where their judgements of the products of this divided and mechanised labour are frequently less than indulgent, thus setting themselves up as a kind of workers' counter-jury to the official jury from which they were excluded. Secondly in the section devoted to the *requests* that in his kindness His Imperial Majesty allowed them to formulate for the occasion: requests of an immediately political nature, since the dignity of the worker demanded the abolition of workers' *livrets* and of discriminatory articles in the Code, and since worker (trade union) organisations presupposed the right to form associations and to hold meetings. These demands for dignity and organisation were intended as preparation for a future hoped for by each and every delegation: association.

These texts – drawn up in the months following the Exhibition and no doubt made bolder by the increasing strength of the labour movement – are in many ways of a strategic nature. They are *theoretically* strategic in that they appeared at the precise moment when economics, politics and ideology – which learned academics conventionally separate into three stages – cannot be disentangled: a comment about a badly-sewn shoe might be linked directly with certain political demands and with a speech about the future of the workers. They are *politically* strategic in that they mobilised a means of expression granted by the Imperial authorities and made it a weapon of class consciousness: in these reports and in the discussions of the Workers' Commission which then met to supervise their publication we are able to observe the transition from the limitations of corporative thinking – perhaps even of Imperial 'socialism' to the formation of a new working-class revolutionary ideal. The position was trebly strategic in that the ideas put forward by the capitalists about the new agents of production (machines and women) were aimed at the point of interconnection between two power systems: class and the home. At this point we would like to spend some time considering the power systems which were involved here: the power of the capitalists over the workers through machines and female labour; the power of science and technology which the workers had to win back; the power of the worker over his wife.[1]

I

The Universal Exhibition of 1867: the employers invite the trades delegates to marvel at a spectacle of machinery. It is like a stage on which magic is mechanised to offer the image of a power made miraculous by the spell of the steam engine: henceforth it would be possible to make quality products quickly, cheaply and effortlessly. As a stonemasons' delegate remarked, the employers' wish to bewitch the workers was not without malice: they contrasted the spectacle of the machines with 'the permanent exhibition of moral and material poverty' of the workers.

Capitalism was celebrating the exhibition of 'its' machines against the dramatic background of a working-class defeat; the mystery and magic of technical progress was revealed as a bag of mechanical tricks which the employers were using in order to introduce new forms of subservience. Consequently it was a spectacle of dispossession: the machines, capital's new avatar, belonged to the employers; by intensifying the division of labour, mechanisation of production was eliminating the need for skills, and workers were becoming increasingly deprived of the practical means of exercising their right of access to the product of their own labour.

The delegates at the Universal Exhibition were mandated by the trades, which united and organised a highly-skilled workforce. They all saw that the immediate effect of mechanisation would be the demise of professional skills. Before establishing a right to the product of labour, skilled training assured the workers of control over a complex area of practical knowledge made real by the intelligent and dexterous manipulation of materials. If in many trades physical strength was a requirement, only by learning a skill could the worker know how to apply that strength with the maximum effect to the resistant materials before him; skills represented by the conquest of the natural strength of the worker's body by his intelligence:

> Only to men has the task of providing for the needs of the family fallen, and it is their duty to submit to this law of nature; they have been given the necessary intelligence and strength to do so.[2]

Workers were proud of their strength because they were able to use it intelligently. The skills provided by apprenticeships raised a trade to the level of an art and constituted the main asset of the working class.

The first effect of mechanisation was to demolish this working-class patrimony by overturning the structures of the work process in a number of ways. The delegates noted bitterly that the effects of mechanised production could be seen in the quality of articles, and that the careful finish which used to characterise quality products was often lacking. For the cloth printers, mechanised work could produce stuff of a standard equal or superior to that made by poorly-skilled workers, but could not successfully produce articles which needed all the concentrated skill of manual craftsmanship. The artistry of a trade expressed itself through the quality of its products; in this respect mechanisation meant a very appreciable decline in the beneficial results that workers' practical knowledge could achieve.

Mechanisation was not simply the substitution of skilled manual work by machines: by intervening in the various stages of the work process in the form of the absolute necessity for productivity, it reorganised the relationship between the worker and his work. There were a certain number of operations which a machine could do more rapidly: the time thus gained led to a new social norm of production being defined for the workers, which meant that they had to work increasingly faster to earn their wages. Far from making work more skilled by giving workers more time to perfect the finished item, mechanisation became the paradoxical weapon with which skills were reduced. The marble masons record how the destructive impact of this productivity norm on the execution of their trade made any concern for artistry useless and impossible:

> It is not simply the workers who should shoulder the responsibility for the mediocre level to which our sector has sunk, because instead of wanting to do a good job they are now forced to think only about getting things done quickly. The first quality demanded of them is to produce as much as possible; the standard of the work itself comes second: competition has also become so fierce that manual work has inevitably been cut back.

The newspaper printers denounce the new working conditions 'which are physically enervating and mentally degrading' and which, in the words of the cloth printers, made work 'the cause of illnesses'; here the workers' representatives of productive labour are measuring the intolerable extent to which work had become something destructive.

With the coming of mechanisation workers imagined that they would be able to pass on their most physically demanding tasks to the machines, but the reverse was true: as the chairmakers noted with reference to bandsaws: 'These tools were intended to help workers by relieving them of the most exhausting part of their job, but instead they've become yet another means of combat to disadvantage them.'

The division of labour is quoted as the main reason for all the negative effects of mechanisation: it robbed the worker of his mastery over his own labour by chaining him to his machine. In the words of the shoemakers:

> Now that machines have brought their innumerable iron arms

to serve industry, they should be allowing workers more time
to do their jobs properly, but on the contrary by dividing
labour they are turning men themselves into machines, robbing
them of responsibility and intelligence, and all for the sake of
increased productivity, whatever the cost.

The work of men who carried out divided labour, *les ouvriers
spécialistes* (unskilled or 'specialist' workers) as the copper founders
called them, was repetitive and exhausting, and it offered skilled
workers a preview of their own mutilated fate at the hands of the
employers' productivity machine. The following description of
the working conditions for unskilled workers comes from the
leather and hide workers' report:

> Anyone who has witnessed the ravenous activity which
> prevails in unskilled workshops, where the worker is nothing
> more than an automation switched on for ten, eleven or twelve
> hours a day, completely unconscious of the value of the
> product he is handling, quite unable to rectify any mistakes
> made by the previous worker, carrying out his unskilled task
> willy-nilly and passing his product on to the next man, and the
> next, so that it will pass through ten or twelve pairs of hands a
> day before it's finished – anyone who has seen this must ask
> themselves what the consequences of such a system will be for
> the future of the workings.

Workers saw in the division of labour, which robbed them of
the technical advantages machines could have provided, the
constitution of a new employers' power system which was aimed
at achieving the complete servitude of labour. This new power
system had its ideal: to dispossess workers as much as possible of
skilled control over their labour in order to turn them into
veritable 'human machines' (as the copper founders put it) and to
feed their strength for work to the insatiable jaws of profit; what
the employers dreamed of was a vast social machine made up of
working-class bodies. Capitalism was organising labour with the
political aim of subjecting a pacified working class by division and
thwarting any attempt at organised revolt. Thus for the bosses
mechanisation was an anti-strike weapon; it stimulated competition and contradictions between the skilled workforce and the
unskilled workforce and struck at forms of organised resistance
within the framework of the trades. The division of labour was a
war machine for the employers, a private machine which
conquered the collective machines which constituted the work of
all; it was the instrument by which the employer – the machine

owner – gained power: the division of labour assured the owner of absolute control, a situation which the shoemakers attacked: 'Surely machines belong to everyone. Thousands of workers have kept them going. Surely it is contrary to justice and equity that they have become a monopoly and a profit to a few individuals.'

The employers' monopoly over machines was an obstacle for the development of the collective labour force and its acquisition of skills. If at the Universal Exhibition the employers offered everyone the spectacle of their machines in order to suggest an imaginary collective appropriation of the magic of progress, in the workshops they spirited them away as though they were ill-gotten gains. The hatters described this mania for possession which deprived workers of their instrument of labour:

> The sole function of this machine is to serve the interests of an individual or a company. It is put in a small, badly-lit room in the remotest corner of the building and as this precaution is deemed inadequate, it is boarded up with planks like some supposedly holy image which must be hidden from the sight of the crowd and which on a certain day of the year pays out a large sum of money. It's kept under lock and key, just like the cash and the banknotes in the firm's safe, and the people employed to work it hardly ever see it. It has become almost like a symbol for the passion, or rather the religion, of every man for himself, and is kept out of the reach of anyone who might be able to study it and so to rescue it from its state of inferiority.

If skilled workers had so many criticisms to level at mechanisation, it was because it resulted in a division of labour which, by threatening skills, threatened one of the means by which workers could resist the arbitrary nature of the employers' authority. If they did not recognise their own dilemmas in those of the unskilled worker, it was not simply in order to defend their 'privileges' against a proletarianised mass who might flood the market and claim their share. The massive introduction of an unskilled workforce resulted .in competitive wages, enabling employers to reduce them to a minimum while increasing their own profits.

> It is exactly the same thing for the human machines, unskilled workers in other words, who frequently only know a minute part of their trade. This makes them unsuitable for any kind of complete or sustained work and puts them in a situation where it is impossible for them to earn an amount comparable to the

levels established by workers worthy of the name in the profession to which they belong.

The fundamental principle of worker resistance was the establishment of a collective right to equitable remuneration based on work produced and the level of skill involved. To the intellectual and practical control of the work process was added the economic and legal control of the product of labour. The defence of skills would establish the right to a threshold beyond which work tariffs would no longer be negotiable: solidarity by each trade in the practise of this right would remove the price of labour from the dictate of the employers.

To start off with the factory offers workers some temporary advantages, which come above all from the division of labour which increases productivity and helps unskilled workers. But there is an increasingly large number of unskilled workers (and this will always be the case) and so their wages go down to a minimum. Then a competitor comes along with the same means of manufacture, and wages fall; therefore the more powerful the factories are and the more unskilled the workers become, the less they will be able to resist.

Against the background of the division of labour, capitalist mechanisation was attacking a right by which worker autonomy was maintained.

The workers of 1848 had demanded the right to work. The right to work meant the right to live off the product of one's labour; a minimal right which justified demands for a minimum wage, defined with reference to a whole body of socially defined needs: 'Every working individual is entitled to enough wages to meet his needs.'

Although they were far from unanimous in accepting the presence of women in workshops, the workers' reports established the principle that all working women should be entitled to wages equivalent to those of the men they replaced, and the tool cutting mechanicians called for men working in prisons to be paid more or less the same wages as free workers. The demand for a minimum wage would bring solidarity to the workers by uniting them as a class exercising its right to establish those things that an employer could not take away; this consciousness of their rights would make workers aware of any arbitrary decisions on the part of an employer, and would justify the organisation of resistance to any abuses of his authority. The defence of skills would stretch collective entitlement to the product of labour to a maximum: it would be the practical affirmation of the workers' right to claim the maximum from the product of their labour in order to satisfy new needs. This is why the mechanicians refused to support the demand for equal wages for all: 'Workers who demand this form of pay are not up to the progressive ideas of the times.'

On the other hand, workers were not to be fooled into thinking that love for one's craft was more important than the practicalities of defending the right to skills. This is the argument with which the mechanicians answered workers who criticised mechanisation in the name of an 'individual talent' which they saw as an end in itself for skilled workers. For the mechanicians, what counted was not individual talent as such but the power it gave to maximise wages: the only reason for learning a skill was to be able to demand the highest possible pay.

The workers' reports do not present machines as cold-hearted monsters which must be smashed: the time for breaking machines was over. Now it was a question of the capitalist appropriation of machines and the reorganisation of labour to combat a division which had robbed workers of their bodies, their intelligence, their rights and their freedom:

> Suppose for a minute that to satisfy all these old-fashioned
> attitudes we were to smash all the machines, and burn all the
> plans, along with all the draughtsmen and engineers. Does
> anyone believe that such acts of vandalism would solve the
> situation that extremes of individualism and exploitation have
> placed us in?[3]

Was this the sign of a working-class awareness that would at last reject infantile revolt in favour of a mature approach to its real interests? It was above all the growth of an unskilled workforce that obliged skilled workers to invent new forms of resistance. The employers' power system used collective organisation for its own profit, and the workers' reports made this a basis for sketching the possible ways workers could take mechanisation over: smashing the great private machine of Capital by the collective appropriation of machines, and answering the employer-orientated ideology of workers hostile to technical progress by establishing worker control over the process of mechanisation. By seeing machines as collective products of wealth-producing labour, the mechanicians' delegates were not making a distinction between labour and machines, like something living as opposed to something dead; instead they were subordinating machines to the working-class morality of labour perceived as a source of life. For this reason they refused to include armaments as an area worthy of labour: 'Because what they are intended for is so contrary to our principles and our feelings of humanity, we have not been able to consider them as industrial products.'

It was in the name of a moral attitude which established the interests, the rights and the obligations of the working class that the immorality of the employers' power system was denounced, and to consider that this was merely a verbal smokescreen one would have to be blind to the practical effects of resistance to subservience, resistance which, thanks to this moral attitude, became to be perceived as a right. The injustice of private appropriation of machines legitimised their appropriation by the collectivity; the immorality of the capitalist division of labour which made workers slaves to machines stimulated a class awareness of the need for workers to organise labour themselves.

> The system is basically excellent, but fails at the top, and although everyone participates in this great productive effort, only a few profit from it. Therefore we must join forces, answering strength with strength, and, while respecting the positions which have already been won, let us gradually replace it with an economic system which will be more profitable to everyone.[4]

Capitalist mechanisation corrupted the body, debased the mind and abandoned the unskilled worker to degeneracy; the workers' reports imagine how machines might be used socially and morally. The mechanicians speak 'of the eminently moralising side' of mechanisation; by relieving him of physically onerous tasks, machines would allow the worker to concentrate on the aspects of his labour which required the intelligent application of highly-developed skills and would also give him free time to dedicate to study:

> Our aim is to get machines to do all the material work, and to make them in sufficient quantities so that all that will be required will be a few hours supervision each day.

The musical instrument makers saw machines as a means of developing the minds of the working class:

> We should push on with our studies diligently, use our aptitudes vigorously, and assert more than ever that there is still such a thing as a good workman, that good workmen will always be needed, and that one day they'll be in short supply.

For the more industrial science replaces the strength or the
dexterity of the worker with steam power, the more such
marvellous processes will exile manual work, and the more an
intelligent worker will be appreciated if he follows the lead
science has given him and continues the good work initiated by
those who went before him.

As for the mechanicians, they considered that the intensive
mechanisation of labour had opened up the possibility of a new
type of skill in the sense of an increased control of the work
process: in this way they saw a solution to the contradiction
which opposed skilled and unskilled workers:

The day when this talent will have become superfluous because
of the use of machines, the worker will be happy to do without
having to make the effort of acquiring it, and will learn
whatever he needs to in the new conditions in which he will be
placed; he will cultivate his mind, and he will use it in order to
work the machine he has been put in charge of.

Here mechanisation has become the instrument for a worker
initiative aimed at socialising skilled labour.

At the Exhibition, that theatrical stage: the spectacle of
machines; in its wings: workers robbed of their work and their
lives. The workers' reports dismantled the machine of the
employers' power system in order to reassemble a working-class
power system which would be brought about by collective
control of machines. The reactions workers had to mechanisation
give a clear indication of the limits reached by forms of resistance
based upon the defence of rights practised in the context of
traditional trade solidarities. Awareness of the effects of the
division of labour gave working-class initiative a new future. In a
remarkable passage in the mechanicians' report the steam engine is
used to elaborate a wonderful utopia of machines which would
bring with them the working-class idea of association:

You also come across it in the country, looking like a black
charger, with a white cloud like a feathered plume, crossing the
widest plains and the thickest forests as rapid as the wind,
bridging the broadest rivers and the deepest chasms, plunging
into the mountainside, burying itself alive in the depths of the
earth only to reappear in the light of day after an underground
journey which may have lasted several kilometres, drawing in
its wake now materials and merchandise which will activate
business and bring dull-silent places back to life, now men

themselves, summoned to these parts by the call of commerce, and facilitating links between even the most distant communities, links which, by propagating uniform ideas, principles, rights and obligations, will hasten the moment when all peoples will finally understand one another, and by throwing off once and for all the subservience that centuries have imposed upon them, and the yoke of Capital and ignorance, will at last profit in the widest possible way from the serious advantages that machines offer them.

II Man's mirror

We need to make it clear that what we are fighting against is not a sex. It is an instrument for lowering wages, a cut-price worker.

This is how the typographers expressed themselves in their report on the 1862 Exhibition in London. If they felt it was so necessary to say this it was because a little earlier there had been a much-publicised strike of typographers to protest against the introduction of women in the Paul Dupont printing house. It had been a significant strike both because of the determination shown by the workers and the extreme nature of some of their arguments, such as this one from Jean-Baptiste Coutant:

If you looked hard enough you would certainly find a couple of *déclassé* women, the perpetual widow type; but you would never find enough to replace the typesetters with. For a start you need to be able to read, and two thirds of women are completely uneducated. As for the remainder, their knowledge is so limited that it's not worth mentioning.[5]

There are no statements like this in the 1867 reports. It was not simply a question of attitudes having evolved, but that this line of argument brought in a logic other than that of the workers' struggle. It was the bourgeois who manipulated *de facto* inequalities in order to impose lower wages (for women, for weakly or less dexterous workmen). From the workers' point of view inequality could never be a principle. It was always a consequence. The concept of irreducible inferiority came from above. If women were eternally inferior, then would not the workers be so too? At the meeting of the Workers' Commission in charge of publishing the reports, the pontiffs of Proudhonism who went along to prove to the delegates the necessary inferiority of women were to be made aware that the workers were much less 'Proudhonist' than our learned academics would have us believe:

> When M. Dupas tried to prove that women are physically inferior to men, that it was indisputable that they lack certain civic virtues, that it was a good thing for everyone that they did, and that therefore it was logical to keep them out of the workshops, this assertion of inferiority was very badly received by the meeting, and when a little later an extract from a book by Madame Flora Tristan was read out in which it was argued that in that case it was very humiliating for men to owe their lives and their mothers' milk to such an inferior creature, it was evident that the meeting approved these words.[6]

Therefore there was no question of inferiority. If it existed in practice, then it had to be eliminated. In the musical instrument makers' report there is even a passage praising women workers' fighting spirit: 'more energetic than many of the men workers',[7] they had succeeded in foiling an attempt by the authorities to impose workers' *livrets* on them. We should note in passing that this resistance had a very specific significance: *livrets* would have placed women workers in the same category as prostitutes. Their resistance was exemplary in the ways it defended the inherent dignity of women.

'What we are fighting against is not a sex.' What the workers wanted was to pretend that the question was a purely economic one: in the workshop, women's only reality was that of a cut-price worker. What was contested, and it put the typographers in the firing line, as they had been before in the struggle against machines, was the role that female labour held in an employers' strategy which was attempting to smash worker resistance by pressure on wages, and more fundamentally by the threat of eliminating the need for skills. An 'economic' question with simple alternative answers: either women should work without competing with men or else they should be kept out of the workshops. But expressed in this way, the alternative was plainly not really a question of wages, but one of place. Workshops were places for men workers, and could only be the place for women workers on certain conditions. A woman's place was elsewhere: in the home. *It was also a question of power*: the way in which the dual space of the workshop and the home was shared between the worker and his wife formed the basis of a struggle between the bourgeoisie and the proletariat. An *economic* solution would inevitably involve a *moral* dimension.

There was one principle on which virtually everyone agreed: if women had to work then they should get equal pay:

Finally, if it is possible, useful or necessary to get women to do work which hitherto has been done by men, then justice, equity and the interests of society demand that their wages be based upon men's; equality should be based on higher rather than lower levels.[8]

Equal work, equal pay. This was not simply a concession which men workers were offering women. It was the logical basis for their own interests. To accept unequal pay for the same work would be to accept a process which would lead to the general depreciation of wages. The *rapporteurs* countered the classic economist's argument (women have fewer needs) with the old argument of working-class democracy: the equality of need. Some even went so far as to insist that the needs of women were greater than those of men. Once the principle was stated, it remained to define the conditions under which it could be put into practice on the labour market. The tinsmiths' report announced two main ways for effecting this, and they both stemmed from the same principle: women could only be equal to men if they were in a different place:

Many men complain about women doing men's work but not many stop to think that there are a lot of men who do women's work.

Isn't it surprising to see men in the prime of life spending their time measuring out lengths of ribbon and lace in drapers', haberdashers' and hat shops? . . . in our view it is certainly not fitting for young men to be selling togs, and were women to take over from them, it would be a step towards solving the problem. Then, if men's wages were high enough to allow their wives to give up going out to work, the problem would be over. Once it became unusual for women to work then their wages would go up, and this would be to the advantage of women who have no father or husband and who have to work to earn a living.[9]

First solution: a distribution of tasks in accordance with the respective aptitudes of the sexes, and not based upon masculine prejudice. It is in this spirit that the wood turner's report – while defining which trades were specifically suitable for women – suggests that a commission composed uniquely of women workers be set up to offer guidance to women apprentices about

which trades 'are accepted as being specifically for women, such
as dressmaking, floristry, fashions, etc.'[10] Second solution: to
establish the law of supply and demand within the female group.
The economically unimpeachable but ideologically over-
determined result of this would be that equality would be
achieved only if women without fathers or husbands went to
work. Both economic solutions stressed the same moral principle:
the economic *competition* between men and women should be
neutralised by activating their physiological and moral *comple-
mentarity*. Men would do work with wood and metals, women
with needles and housekeeping. For whatever the opinion held
about the realities of women's work, the answer to the question
'are women suitable for workshops' was virtually unanimous.
Without mincing words, the tailors put it thus:

> From the scientific point of view (physiology, hygiene), from
> the economic point of view, from the moral point of view,
> there is nothing to justify employing women as agents of
> production.[11]

Even supposing the economic question were to be resolved (the
organisation of the scarcity of manpower), the dual assertion that
workshops mutilated women's – and mothers' – bodies, and
exposed them to moral corruption by promiscuity with men and
hierarchic pressures, remained. Women should not be in workshops with men; not because they were inferior to men, but *in
order not to be inferior to them*. The debates on this subject by the
Workers' Commission are very significant. We may observe three
standpoints. Two 'extremes' – those presented by the French
delegation at the Lausanne Congress of the First International:
doctrinaire Proudhonists like Fribourg and Dupas, arguing the
physical and moral inferiority of women (only Varlin defended
the rigorous demands of female labour as *a means of emancipation*).
But the majority of delegates took a middle-of-the-road approach.
For them women's position in the workshop was *de facto* one of
the inferiority. Liberating women meant finding them a space of
their own where they could become equal to men. Dupas insisted:

> The more liberated we become, the more women will be free.
> For woman is a mirror which reflects us, and if it is presented
> with the face of an unliberated man, the reflection in the mirror
> will be that of a slave. Therefore we must try to improve our
> standard of behaviour in order to get women out of the
> workshops . . .[12]

Chabaud, the tinsmiths' delegate, replied:

> I don't look like a slave, I am well and truly free, and I believe
> that we all ought to try to do something to make women's lot
> a happier one.[13]

Paradoxically, in practice this 'something' was not any different
from the suggestions of the Proudhonists: it was a question of
maintaining women's place in the home. The difference was all in
the principles, and in the way the function of women was
perceived in the defence of the power of the working class in
opposition to the employers. To define specifically feminine
functions was not necessarily to relegate women to a ringside seat
in the masculine fight between workers and employers. The aim
was to make them more equal than would be possible if they
continued to be employed in workshops. Boulanger, the mechanicians' delegate, proposed the following strategy:

> We should ask the government to close all the crèches, it's
> bound to agree to do so, and then we can concentrate on
> getting higher wages so that our wives can take care of the
> children; women will work at home and will obtain equal
> rights as promised by the principles of 1789.[14]

If we consider the aspirations of the feminist movement for the
last 100 years, this was an outrageous argument. Using the same
premise (men are responsible for the degradation of women) he
drew the opposite conclusion. Men's mistake had been to put
women in a place where they did not belong and where of
necessity they would be made inferior. The only way to liberate
women would be to restore them to their natural vocation.
Although this argument may appear quite outrageous in retrospect, it was not without its advocates in the feminist movements
of the time, where some voices were arguing that women should
play their proper role in society and that their equality should be
based upon the development of specifically feminine aptitudes and
qualities. Women could only be liberated if they occupied a space
which was specifically theirs. Only then would women cease to
be a mirror image of the freedoms which men had obtained. They
would be involved in the upkeep of a space which would be
closed to interference from the employers or the state: the natural
system of the family.

It is a natural system which was obviously too profitable for
men workers for us not to ask questions about it. What exactly
was the significance of this economic and moral node? What were

its fundamental aspects? Was it a means to defend male employment or to maintain a space where the male worker could reassume his authority? An economistic explanation would be like this: the resolute defence of the family, the hymns to the comfort and attentions of hearth and home which are too touching to be honest, these were perhaps nothing more than the ideological point of honour of a fanatical effort to keep manpower scarce on the labour market, the form adopted by working-class Malthus-ianism when faced with women as agents of production (a form which was nevertheless paradoxical when keeping women in the home would inevitably result in a healthy rate of procreation, which would quickly make its presence felt on the labour market). Indeed, when they were not threatened by competition from women, men workers rarely sang songs about the comforts of the home. The sedentary nature of family life was a sorry end for any *compagnon* who had known the joys of friendship on his *tour de France*. From this point of view maybe the working-class family was the successful outcome of the bourgeois attempt to train an undisciplined workforce, to make the nomad sedentary. Persuad-ing couples living together to get married was one of the noble aims of philanthropy,[15] and Catholic philanthropist and repub-lican writer alike – in this case Michelet – were overcome with tender emotions at the sight of the interior which a wife had decorated with cheap printed calico (a machine-made godsend) in order to keep the working man well away from the *cabarets* and their depravities. However, if things were more complex than this, it is firstly because bourgeois practice and discourse were of necessity divided on the issue. Certainly the bourgeois enjoyed moralising workers, but it was also in his interest to exploit their wives. And philanthropists saw nothing but advantages in infants growing up in the clean air and enlightened surroundings of crèches instead of in cramped family hovels with mothers who knew nothing about hygiene. For this reason the understanding of what the benefits of family life were differed from one side of the class barrier to the other. On the bourgeois side, the point was to impose a regularity which would normalise workers' undisci-plined and nomadic habits, and a sense of responsibility which would initiate them into the Universe of Christ by linking their interests with those of the moneyed class. For workers to love their wives and pet their children was very touching to be sure; but for them to save up for the future, putting money in a savings bank or trying to buy their own houses, now that was really being responsible. However it was precisely this kind of responsibility that workers rejected. The scientific detachment with which Le Play or his colleagues who carried out an enquiry about workers observed this face has hints of not a little confusion: be they debauched tailors or happily married carpenters, workers are seen to share both a lack of thrift and an indifference towards the prospect of owning their own houses. The aim had been to establish an analogy between the worker as head of his household and the manager as head of his factory. And if the role of head was invoked, this was surely in order to turn the home into a reserved space which would make the system appear natural rather than a creation of discipline and market forces. But on the working-class side of the barrier, this intensification of family life was aimed at preserving some time and space which would be free from domination.

> We've got to live, so let's live with our families. In the winter when we go to work in the dark, our children are still asleep; when we get home at night, they're already in bed. We drink, eat, sleep and work. Can you call that living? The exploiter is less indulgent with us living machines than he is with his metal ones. For us he will refuse to accept that any time be lost; but for them he is forced to, because if he doesn't give them a break they take one of their own accord. [16]

In the time and space where the strength for work was recouped a new power relationship between employers and workers was being developed, along with the threat of increased exploitation. If wives went out to work then this network of relationships, this organised space in which the reproduction of strength for work also belonged to the workers, would be broken.

> Once a household is split up in this way, you can say goodbye to those first joys of married bliss! Goodbye to the tender emotions of family life! The children are brought up by strangers; husband and wife become indifferent to one another; they only meet to sleep, since they are obliged to have their meals separately. [17]

Tender emotions: the imaginary difference between a space in which the worker is still his own master and a space where he and his wife recoup the strength for work which belongs to the employer, and nothing else. Children brought up by strangers as though they were working-class merchandise, husbands and wives becoming indifferent to one another like so many commodities; increase in the workers' dispossession of the market; elements in a new capitalist strategy which was aimed at enclosing working-class life in its entirety within a disciplinary system which reproduced the market system: a system of indifference and subservience: the world of the crèche, the hospital or the tenement.

The function of the family, that is to say, the wife: to do everything possible to ensure that all that could be rescued from the employers and their systems was so. Firstly children, who could not be free if they were not brought up affectionately by their own mothers. Outside the family the only alternatives were the crèche, where in the words of the painters' delegates 'everything is laid on in a disciplined way', or the mercenary attentions of a wet nurse. If they were just like any other commodity, children were all too perishable.

The next thing which had to be safeguarded from the mercenary disciplinary system was health:

> Hospitals have everything you need in terms of medicine, bed linen, cleanliness; in that respect they leave nothing to be desired. But when it comes to more delicate attentions, then it's another matter. When you're paid to be a hospital nurse, your patient becomes a piece of merchandise; orderlies or nurses can treat you harshly.

This is a more or less standard criticism in workers' statements of the period and is frequently accompanied with tales of bitterness and fear: the hospital/prison, bounded by high walls and where visits are only permitted twice a week; the hospital/factory, where the worker's body is exploited to such an extent by the doctors that families have to pay in order to retrieve a loved one's corpse, just like a piece of merchandise. A manipulation of the human body which runs parallel to the manipulation of the human soul by priests and nuns (and here too the manipulation does not end at death: Tartaret quotes many cases of priests blithely giving the last rites to people who were already dead).

Be it in the crèche, the refuge or the hospital, a power system was being imposed upon children and patients, body and soul, more or less symmetrical with the system which was being imposed upon women in workshops, where they were confronted with physical hardships and dissolute language. Measures were needed to rebuild a space for resistance to the bourgeois stranglehold on the totality of working-class life, such as children being given back to their mothers and a transformation of Public Assistance by replacing hospitalisation with an extensive system of home help. Men would rescue women from the torture chamber of the workshop, and women would rescue men from the system of the crèche and the hospital. The wife became the organising force in this space for resistance. These *attentions*, this *carefulness*, this *tenderness*, she alone could give them to her husband and her children, and they were the domestic equivalent of the professional skills which workers were trying to defend. If woman's place was in the home, it was not merely so that the husband's standard of wages would be maintained; she also had the function of participating in the defence of the workers' stand against the great offensive of capitalist disappropriation. In this power struggle women were the prize – and the hostage.

In the same way the defence of the family was not a link in the chain which bound workers to the defence of the employers' system. This chain had broken at its weakest point: the duplicity of the system which sang the praises of domestic bliss in order to enslave its members separately, which wanted workers to be householders only to ensure their disappropriation and the loss of control over their own labour and private lives. Nothing could be more revealing than the attitude of the Worker Delegations to tenements owned co-operatively or by the employers – that high-minded social architects' vision of the Happy Working-Class Home. The mechanicians' delegates were quick to see through this enterprise:

> There are some companies or industrial societies which appear to have done something in the interests of the workers by building shops where you can buy all kinds of foodstuffs, for example, or soup kitchens, tenements, churches; which leads us to believe that they've fully understood that without sharing living facilities it would be impossible for us to exist because of the low level of wages. While we fully appreciate the value of these things, we are partisans of freedom, and we wish to make it clear that we want to run our own lives, and that all we need is the freedom so to do. . . . Come along then, messieurs, in charge of those companies and industrial establishments, let's have lots more food shops, tenements, and don't forget a little chapel, where the boss can watch us bring our savings (if we've got any left) to put in the collection box. And be quick about it . . .[18]

As for the copper founders, they were aware of the link in the chain of working-class dispossession which the expulsion of the workers from the city centre to its peripheries had just achieved: the whole point of it was:

> . . . to bring back in our lifetime the plebeian quarters that our

grandfathers called *truanderies*, something like the ghetto in
Catholic Rome. We'll say it again, you've got to be totally
insensitive to want to dump the working–class man outside the
centre of social life like this. Isn't he unfortunate enough when
he falls ill or infirm and has to be shut up in one of those
punishment parks they call homes, which for some reason that
escapes us are always surrounded by high walls just like
prisons, to hide all the moral and physical suffering within
from the eyes of the world.[19]

This was a rejection of the dumping of workers, be it under the
boss's supervision or outside of a space which henceforth would
be reserved for the employers. The exile of the working class
from the centre of Paris did not simply mean extra time and
fatigue in the working day: it was also the loss of an equality, of
the right to circulate in the employer's space. The musical
instrument makers, one of the most democratic of all the
corporations, expressed this rejection of the creation of two
Parises most forcibly: 'the Paris of horse-racing and love affairs' as
opposed to the Paris of the poet, the scholar, the artist and the
workers.[20] Theirs is the only report which demanded a political
measure to bring this division to an end, and to halt this exile: the
election of a municipal council. They were to elect one in March
1871: the Commune, a political space of a kind which would be
able to replace the working class at the centre of social life.

The *economic* form of workers' emancipation was called
association. It was of course the only way out of this situation of
dependence against which the movements to keep women in the
home merely represented a defence of the status quo, and a
protection against an increase in bourgeois control over labour
and the totality of workers' lives. The family unit was rather like a
substitute association: an autonomous unit which rejected the
over-obliging attentions of tenements and shops provided by
employers, which turned its back on philanthropic institutions
and which resolved 'to do things by ourselves' at its own level.
But obviously this 'by ourselves' had two implications: it was a
decision made by men but also a service provided by women. If
the male worker was to escape from the constraints of employer-
orientated systems, then women had to agree to recognise him as
their protector.

What would the situation be in the world of associations? The
possession by the workers of the instruments of production would
only be completed if co-operatives could be organised on the level
of the consumer. What would woman's role be here? The workers
knew that she was likely to resist and looked for ways of winning

her over. For the brush makers, if the wife was set in her ways about shopping, then it would be the husband who would have to take the initiative and buy things at the co-operative. Bit by bit the wife would get used to it, and as soon as she did, she would be much quicker than the husband. And why? The answer may be found in the musical instrument makers' report: the wives' resistance would be the result of a defective education. But their 'way with figures' would convince them.

It is an interesting argument, and one which may recall what Lenin had to say about the peasants at a later date: they will rally round when they see that it is in their interests to do so. Does this imply a hierarchy composed of those who carry revolution in their heads and their hearts and those who need convincing that revolution will not harm their wallets?

This does not appear to have been the opinion of the bookbinder's mate who in 1867 was virtually alone in expressing his confidence in women's ability to emancipate themselves by their own methods, and who incidentally also proposed a plan for a system of workers' institutions which would prepare the workers for managing a socialism without hierarchies. Another idea of revolution, shot down with Eugene Varlin?

Notes

1 The texts studied are collected in *Rapports des délégations ouvrières*, under the direction d'Arnould Desvernay, 3 vols, Paris, 1869.
2 Mechanicians' report.
3 *Ibid.*
4 Shoemakers' report.
5 *Du salaire des ouvriers compositeurs* (Typesetters and their Wages), Paris, 1861, pp. 23–4.
6 Statement by Fribourg, in Tartaret, *Procès-verbaux de la Commission ouvrière de 1867* (Minutes of the Workers' Commission of 1867), 1867, p. 231–2.
7 Musical instrument makers' report, p. 61 (vol. 1).
8 Cutting-tool mechanicians' report, p. 5 (vol. 2).
9 Tin embossers' report, p. 25 (vol. 1).
10 Wood turners, p. 36 (vol. 3).
11 Tailors, p. 21 (vol. 3).
12 Tartaret, op. cit., p. 229.
13 *Ibid.*, p. 230.
14 *Ibid.*, p. 231.
15 There was a society specially for this, the Société de Saint-François-Régis.
16 Mechanicians, p. 156 (vol. 2).
17 Cabinetmakers, p. 41 (vol. 1).

18 Mechanicians, pp. 64–5 (vol. 1).
19 Copper founders, p. 20 (vol. 1).
20 Musical instrument makers, pp. 65–6 (vol. 1).

2
Good times or pleasure at the barriers

JACQUES RANCIÈRE

There has been nothing new here, except that *The Magic Flute*
has had eighteen performances and the theatre has been packed
for each one. No one could bear to have it said of them that
they have not seen it. Everyone, from worker to gardener has
gone to see it, as have even the good people of Sachsenhausen,
whose children play the parts of lions and monkeys in the
opera. There has never been anything like it here. They have to
open the doors as early as 4 o'clock, and even then there are
always several hundred people who are turned away from
every performance because all the seats have been sold.
(Mayoress Goethe, 1793, in J. and B. Massin, Mozart)

There is something rather picturesque in this crowd in their
blouses up in the gods of the popular theatres, and maybe what
will be gained in individual well-being and general civilisation
will be lost in gaiety and enthusiasm, but it is a step forward
which good taste would suggest and justice seems to demand.
(Camille Doucet, Head of the Division of Theatres, note to His
Excellency the Minister of State, 30 June 1862)

Work and the *goguette* (Drunken Hearts)

On 17 November 1849 an edict granted legal status to a form of
entertainment which had only been in existence for a few years:
café-concert. This liberal measure was not however without certain
restrictions. Every day before noon programmes had to be
submitted to the police station. Moreover, as one would expect,
'all political or immoral songs' were forbidden, but so too were
'male and female impersonations, dancing, pieces from the
operatic repertoire, choirs and choruses, walk-on parts, noisy
instruments' along with any posters advertising the programmes
in public and 'meetings of outsiders' (untoward meetings?). On
12 August 1850 a decree consecutive to the law of 30 July spelled
out the general principles of this supervised freedom:

45

In future theatre managers and producers of shows, concerts and *cafés-chantants* in Paris and the suburbs will not be permitted to use their posters and programmes to advertise first performances of any dramatic work, play, single scene, cantata, romance, song or *chansonnette, in a word anything which is to be recited, sung or performed in public*, without first having received approval for the script or the scenario from the Minister of the Interior, and without having shown the permit at the police station of the section of Commune in which his establishment is situated.[1]

A police state with total rights over everything to be recited, sung or performed: rarely has the language of repression been spoken in so pure a form as it was during the Legislative Assembly of 1849. But here as elsewhere such decisions by the state authorities may be read primarily either in terms of what they repressed, or in terms of what they produced, and their meaning changes accordingly. Despite the 1830 monarchic Republic's attempts to allay the trauma of June 1848 by inventing increasingly painstaking devices for hunting down whatsoever moved or raised a voice, the Imperial regime, for which it was a rehearsal, was not to stint itself for shows, songs, Exhibitions and entertainments of any kind. Hidden behind the obligatory, ostentatious pomp of the Imperial parade something else was coming into being which was to survive the defeat of 1870 and to develop fully during the Third Republic. From the mundane *café-concert* to the extraordinary Exhibitions, in Haussmann's continual sanitisation and embellishment of the city, in the democratisation of the aristocratic pleasures of Empire society (sports and horse-racing), as in the popularisation of new cultural inventions (cinema and the gramophone) it would appear that a single movement was operating, giving the passions and energies of the working classes the means, the forms and the outlets for a regulated satisfaction and optimal use of their leisure. It would be possible to observe a similar development in the series of attacks made by the entertainments police, which seem to have followed the same curve as the commercial rationalisation of working-class leisure and culture until such time as this new culture could play a role within the interstices of working life of a kind that by its own logic it would render supervision obsolete (it was when cinema and the gramophone became widely available that the Commission of Censors for Fine Arts finally gave up the ghost). If we do we may be tempted to see in this complementary the exercise of a large-scale strategy of power 'in the flavour of the day' by which the rationalisation of the exploitation of labour or the factory discipline of the workforce was paralleled by a moralisation and organisation of workers' leisure.

The nature of the object makes it even more difficult for us to avoid such panoptic totalisation. In fact popular pleasure and its relationship to authority were over-determined by highly-coded systems of imagery. For a long time there was the denunciation by progressives and puritans of a plebian class corrupted by the gladiatorial spectacles the ruling class had organised for it. Nowadays these popular pleasures are seen as a dissipation, an act of resistance to the economical and disciplined recouping of the strength needed for work, the time or place of a reversal of power where, by imitation or derision, the people might become the equal of or the master of their masters. The images of a resistance to a system of labour which traverses the dissipations of the *cabaret*, the carnival or nomadic vagrancy are so well known as to have become trite. In fact, things were rather more complicated. If naive historians may see the *cabaret* as a place where the popular classes indulged in pure dissipation and found their own voice, it was just as much a place where business was discussed; if you bought drinks, it was often in payment for being hired, for getting a job for a relative or friend, for getting into the foreman's good books, for winning support from the workshop seniors or, conversely, for buying the workers' good will. The *cabaret* did not overthrow the authority of the workshop, it was also a place where workshop business was negotiated. If, as an employer, Denis Poulot sided with the militant workers in condemning it, it was not simply with a view to protecting the physical strength and moral dignity of the working man, but also because it was a place for unofficial negotiations about jobs and about the application of the strength needed for work which each social partner considered to be exploited by the other. As for the vagrancy of children in Paris, it was often a case of merely wandering off the beaten track of the set rounds of looking for or carrying out jobs as errand boys, street vendors, etc.[2] It is not so easy to see how the power of the employers and the power of the workers could have functioned together on a common ground which was to be used both as a place for productive discipline and for unproductive dissipation. And that was the main concern of all the philanthropists, missionaries or militants who wished to moralise the workers: the problem lay less in the existence of meeting places for working-class autonomy and indiscipline than in the interconnection between the circuits of work and the circuits of leisure, and in the proliferation of these trajectories – real or ideal – by which the workers were beginning to move around within the space of the bourgeoisie, giving their aspirations free rein. Louis Reybaud, more lucid than his colleagues, when he went to Lyons was not so much concerned with the more or less dreamed-up orgies and conspiracies of the *Voraces* as with a certain tranquillity in the workshops which allowed the routine of work to form a basis for day-dreaming.[3] Work which was so monotonous that it allowed the worker's mind to go roaming while his body went on conscientiously grafting, was no longer the antidote for idleness, that proverbial mother of all vices. If individuals were to be fixed within their social conditions it was not simply a question of using the techniques for corporal discipline which had been developed as a kind of antidote to excessive play and physical exertion. The brothers of Saint-Vincent-de-Paul did not complain that the apprentices in their *patronages* ran about too much but rather they did not use up enough energy. In workshops young apprentices had to rise above the semi-industrous, semi-idle, semi-serious, semi-playful level of behaviour of their little errand boy, match-seller friends. Similarly in the *patronages* they had to rise above the meanderings, restless inactivity and japes of their little friends by learning how to play properly.[4] 'Pray and play' was the motto of the *patronages*, but it would be wrong to think that only quiet games were consonant with prayer. All the *patronage* directions, from the most integrationalist to the most modernist, joined voices in despising those lotto or domino enthusiasts who spent their afternoons glued to their chairs, and in giving absolute priority to 'running games'. Different individuals tended to attribute them with different virtues: abbé Timon-David, the very austere director of the Young Workers' Charitable Organisation of Marseilles, saw them very crudely as the means to send his young charges home of a Sunday evening too exhausted to have enough energy to go dancing.[5] Maurice Maignen, organiser of the Saint-Vincent-de-Paul *patronage* in Paris, developed an ethic of light legs and hearts which made prisoner's base homologous with and complementary to confession.[6] But whether the wish was to tire legs out in order that they be led not into temptation, or to lighten hearts that they might rise more buoyantly towards God, the purpose was identical: the *patronage* was a place where play was learned in the form of organised games, something which would be the complete opposite of errand boys' meanderings and idle daydreams.

The idea that still waters run dangerously deep can be as much a starting point for fantasy as· can *carnaval* orgies. But such fantasies can help us to define a certain uneasiness which was not so much the result of the opposition between a counter-culture from below and a way of thought and a culture from above, than from the real or imaginary shifts permitted by a cultural space which was in the process of increasing the availability of meeting places or means of access between one class and another. For example, the *goguette* was not exactly the drunken place that the exalted nostalgia of certain people would have us believe. In his series of articles in *L'Atelier* denouncing *goguettes* Supernant, the typographer, complained not of the excess of wine drunk, but of its dreadful quality. Nor was the *goguette* really the place of an autonomous working-class culture. The drinking songs and vulgar ditties of the working-class *goguette* were neither more nor less subversive or vitriolic than those which rang out in the *Caveau*, a singing club of 'Monarchical' spirit which had inherited the *douceur de vivre* from before 1789. And the fact that workers went there in *blouses* – they also crammed the gods of the theatres in their *blouses* – meant that the *goguettes* were places where they could get away from the working-class conditions without having to change clothes rather than places of working-class autonomy and communion. The king of the Belleville *chansonniers*, Gustave Leroy, whose songs proclaimed the rights of the *blouses* in 1848, used to go to the *Amis de la Vigne* in a suit. Exactly what was his idea of the dignity of the worker, this illegitimate son of a theatre employee, who enjoyed an aristocratic education in a Versailles boarding school thanks to the protection of an illustrious tightrope dancer? Or to put it another way: what was the relationship between the political training of the working class and the cultural emulation individuals used to rise above it? For first and foremost the *goguette* functioned as a place of emulation. There were 400 *goguettes* in and around Paris, and if people came firstly as spectators, they could also hope to sing there, or have their own songs performed, and this led to a proliferation of people who secretly wanted to become *artistes*. It was doubtless rare that a real career as an *artiste*, like that of the typographer Anatole Lionnet, would be launched in a *goguette*: he was taken by a workshop friend who without his knowledge had him included on the programme, was noticed by Joseph Darcier, a *déclassé* musician who played the piano there, and who subsequently introduced him at Doctor Orfila's fashionable *soirées chantantes*.[7] More often than not the success achieved would simply be that of gaining self-esteem or the esteem of one's peers. But that was enough to make the *goguettes* not so much places where energy was wasted to compensate for the productive system or the working-class community as the starting point for a flight of fancy which would come to rest back in the workshops: and in fact people began to make up verses at work, dreaming of becoming a success that very night, and making the most of their breaks to teach themselves or each other the rudiments of music and versification, so that in the end some of them could express themselves better in verse than in prose.[8] The fact that this co-operative school of worker-poets did not produce anything new on the level of form or radical on the level of content has little importance. For it is possible that any disruption of the prevailing system came less from a specific working-class culture than from these singular apprenticeships in a common culture; it was less a question of an uncivilised culture than of an uncivilised relationship with culture, or, to put it another way, of a culture in disorder (where the prevailing system was in the process of disruption). A worker who had never learned how to write and yet tried to compose verses to suit the taste of his times was perhaps more of a danger to the prevailing ideological order than a worker who performed revolutionary songs. The mere possibility that the *goguette* might produce propagandists like Charles Gille, or networks of militants, goes through this detour, this tendency to promote a minority culture, to open fissures within the productive class. For it is undoubtedly through such fissures that a class could become dangerous, because through them a minority might see a line of escape from work which had become unbearable, but also from the language and behaviour of the workshop, in a word from the unbearable role of the worker-as-such. The *goguette* was one of those places which dynamised a class not by uniting it but by splitting it up and making it produce minorities. The crocodile tears shed by well-meaning bourgeois over the fate of workers such as Jules Mercier and Hégésippe Moreau who died of despair for not having become successful poets serve to underline this rather sore point: perhaps the truly dangerous classes are not so much the uncivilised one thought to undermine society from below, but rather the migrants who move at the borders between classes, individuals and groups who develop capabilities within themselves which are useless for the improvement of their material lives and which in fact are liable to make them despise material concerns. It was minority dreamers like these who were in turn encouraging the masses to dream as they gathered around them in the street, listening to their songs and forgetting the errand which had brought them there, buying the sheet music they sold and taking their choruses back to the workshops. This circulation of workers' songs – which sometimes surprised the workers themselves[9] – was an integral part of a much larger process of acculturation: romantic salon songs about Andalusian – or Albanian – beauties, proud men of the mountains, sailors from Naples, or the enchanted land of childhood, and which offered workers dreams of evasion; clever *boulevard* songs which offered the inquisitive enthusiast picturesque images of carefree rag-and-bone men, poor working girls and drunken revels at the barriers, which the workers reappropriated for themselves.[10] If we add to this all the corrections and transformations that the words and music could undergo in their journeys through the streets, the *goguettes* and the workshops, we may understand how to define this culture in the process of disorder, remote from our received images of culture and counter-culture alike: a spontaneous movement of deprofessionalisation which was establishing a distance between the worker and his trade while abolishing the distance between specialist knowledge and amateur culture, the natural proximity between entertainment and action, 'art' and life, the mundane and the world of dreams. Of course workers like the musically illiterate Saint-Simonians who gave up everything for several months to learn the trumpet so that they could play in the brass band that had been formed to accompany Enfantin when he was in Egypt were probably an extreme case. Much more ordinary were the National Workshop workers in 1848 who used their imposed idleness to try their hands at writing poetry. One of these new poets sent his first attempts at verse to the *Père Duchêne* with a note written with a lead pencil saying 'if you like them, I can write some more'.[11] And much more representative was Victor Renard the foundry worker who escapes from the collapse of National Workshops by becoming a street singer, or again Brunet the shoemaker who, on returning from a job in the navy, rejected his sedentary craft in order to become an acrobat, and then a writer of songs, plays and operettas, despite the fact that he had never been to school.[12] The political insubordination of a *goguette* like *La Ménagerie* which was constantly moving its premises in order to go on performing songs freely or of someone like Charles Gille who thumbed his nose at the repression by peddling his songs in longhand, were part of an on-going process of individual cultural insubordination which bears witness to a working class which was more mobile, less attached to its tools and less sunk in its own poverty and drunkenness than the various traditions usually represent it.

The Théâtre de l'ambigu

If, immediately after 1848, the defenders of public order needed to prosecute *goguettes* and subversive *chansonniers*, to the point that people like Charles Gille and Gustave Leroy were reduced to silence, it was even more necessary for them to resolve the confusion in the cultural network which extended from songs in the workshops to theatre demonstrations, via the reading of newspapers in the wine shops and the crowds attracted by the singers and myriad other entertainments in the streets, and to repress a certain *dramatisation* of what was said, sung or acted in this mixed cultural space of confused interaction between genres, places, practices and classes. In this undesirable space where any kind of drama was likely to unfold, worker participation in the theatre had its role to play. It was not for nothing that in his model confession of a repentant rebel, Jean-Claude Romand blamed his theatre-going in Paris for the wicked passions which grew from the pleasure parties he enjoyed with a naughty maid from a good household, at the expense of and without the knowledge of her mistress. Emotions in the theatre belong to those aristocratic passions which can turn a tailor into the leader of an uprising of *canuts*:★ in other words, the habit of always being somewhere where there is nothing to do but concern oneself with matters which are not one's own business.[13] It was perhaps for that reason that the brothers of Saint-Vincent-de-Paul attempted to satisfy their apprentices' overweening appetite for the theatre by offering them only one-act plays based upon their own everyday experiences. The moral of these plays was probably less important than the fact that any kind of escape route to other worlds or conditions had been effectively withdrawn.[14]

For at this time what we now call 'people's theatre' – that is, theatre intended for people who never go to the theatre – did not exist. Precisely because people *did* go. Of course, this more or less followed a hierarchic line drawn from the theatres of the boulevard du Temple to the Comédie-Française by way of the Porte-Saint-Martin, that empire of melodrama. But they scarcely felt the need for a theatre specifically for themselves. They were content to occupy the gods of the theatres which already existed. It was a passion which was encouraged during the period from 1815 to 1848 by the development of new theatres in response to the gradual breakdown of the Napoleonic system of theatrical privileges. These had codified the separation between 'curiosity' entertainments (circuses, puppet shows, mime, tightrope dancers, horse-riding acts, freak shows, etc.) and theatres as such, which were reduced to eight in number and obliged to restrict themselves to a specific repertoire: a vaudeville in the theatre of that name, melodrama at the Ambigu and two other theatres, the great dramatic repertoire at the Comédie-Française. . .[15] However between 1815 and 1848 'inroads' were made in this system, new privileges being granted to riding instructors, lemonade

★ a reference to the Lyon silk weavers who revolted in 1831.

sellers, physicians, tightrope dancers and mimics eager to get a public for their repertoire. In fact, some of them frequently did not even bother to get permission and gradually turned their acts into melodramas or vaudevilles, plundering the repertoire of genuine theatre, even opera choruses. The boulevard du Temple was the privileged location for these fairground theatres which illegally appropriated the domain of theatrical culture.[16] These abuses, which mixed up the genres and set the privileged members of theatrical culture against its parasites, were to produce yet another: entertainments such as those where the genres were poorly defined were particularly vulnerable to being twisted in ways which put drama itself at risk, like actors improvising and talking to the audience, or the audience itself intervening to ask for songs about current events (and if current events had a political slant, one can imagine the kind of abuses that could result), or militant initiatives like the impromptu Saint-Simonian choirs organised in various theatres by Vinçard. On 8 February 1831 announcements were posted at the authorisation of the prefect of police to the effect that 'no member of the audience may insist that the actors perform songs or verses about current events which have not been advertised on the programme of the day' (AN F21 1045). The practice of inserting songs into vaudevilles and melodramas, and the birth after 1845 of the *cafés-concerts* which were a mixture of songs, dancing, extracts from plays and various exhibitions, resulted in endless methods of control which rarely worked: songs and choruses inserted in plays could frequently be harmless, but they always had the characteristic of all stage music of being 'involving', and even if the spoken interludes between *chansonnettes* were trivial, they would nevertheless be delivered as though addressing the audience directly, thus establishing a feeling of confidentiality that would make them feel more than mere spectators. As for programme changes, they were frequently quite remarkable, as witnessed by the perplexed police officers who faithfully reported that at a matinée for the *Société des Amis de l'Enfance* the actress Rachel put some scenes from *Horace* into her performance of *Bérénice* (F21 1338, 18 March 1846) or that one of the songs inserted without permission at the Salle Saint-Jean was *Le petit chaperon rouge* (Little Red Ridinghood). . . (F21 1158, 22 November 1846).

But even theatres which kept to their repertoire always presented a dangerous kind of entertainment. When we read how some people after 1848 declaimed that the 'anarchist' morality of melodramas was one of the sources of the 'demoralisation' which was dragging the working class down into the kind of excesses which we have all heard about only too often, our first reaction is liable to be one of scepticism. If we read them in the way Marx may have read *Les Mystères de Paris*, it is hard to see their revolutionary implications; adopting the protective/inquisitorial stance of a Rodolphe or the sentimental point of view of a Fleur de Marie, they represent poverty as a fatality and either reprimand the working class for its weakness or praise it for its honesty. In the theatres of 1840, divided as they were between the bourgeois seats in the stalls and the *blouses* seats in the gods, the message was much more ambiguous. What, in fact, was the main interest in melodrama? Poverty as entertainment. But how was it possible to show the reasons for this poverty without courting danger? Was poverty the result of social injustice? – that would be an incitement to rebellion; was it the result of private injustice? – then it would be very difficult not to involve the actions of some lord, minister or magistrate who would be singled out as the target for the people's spitefulness;[17] was it the result of immoral behaviour? – the utility of the punishment was liable to be overshadowed by the titillating presentation of the crime; was it the result of fatality? – if so, any moral would lose its legitimate status. Let us take for example *Les Noceurs ou travail et goguette* (The Gay Dogs; or, Work and the *Goguette*) by Dumersan and Vander-Burch, two polygraphers who were not at all concerned with socialism. It is the drama of a decent worker who reacts to the onset of middle age by letting himself be dragged down by a debauched friend, spending all his money in drinking sessions at the barriers. To save his father's honour, the son lets himself be accused of these misdemeanours, his marriage prospects are ruined and he finds himself in prison. Naturally it all ends happily with the repentance of the drunkard, the reward of the good son and the punishment of the villain. And morality would appear to be all the more satisfied in that it is the worker of the future who gives the worker of the past a lesson in sobriety and honesty. But over and above the always disagreeable disassociation of moral order and the family system, plus the doubtful introduction of a young cousin who has to get drunk with the worthless father in order to keep an eye on him, this hope for the moral regeneration of the working class is contradicted by the model son, who describes his father's weakness as an obligatory stage in workers' lives, and one he knows he will have to go through himself one day. It was not very clear what lesson the audience in the 'cheap seats' could draw from this familiarity between morality and immorality. The same can be said of *La Misère* (Poverty) by F. Dugnet, which drew the attention of the police in 1850. An initial report recognised the 'maxims of socialism' in this play in which the worthy worker refers to degeneration of all kinds – prostitution, theft, drunkenness

From the *Propagateur de l'Aube*, Troyes:

Yesterday evening, as soon as the theatre opened its doors, the crowd rushed up to the gods to get the front seats. Then at the back of the auditorium in the point farthest away from the proscenium arch a fight broke out between two workers determined to enjoy and applaud the melodrama *La Grace de Dieu* (The Grace of God) in comfort. There was only one seat for the two of them, and both insisted on having it; thus, naturally, it was the stronger of the two who got it, and his antagonist was forced to clamber over one of the dividing barriers that they have in the gods. It may have been by accident or on purpose, but just as the young man had his foot on the barrier, the other one gave him such a violent shove that he fell backwards over the edge of the gallery into the auditorium, hitting the second tier and disappearing between the benches of the amphitheatre, after falling about five metres.

(L'Artisan, November 1842)

Theatre column
Gaité – *Les Noceurs* (The Gay Dogs) is still raking it in at the box office; newspaper has reported that the manager has received the following letter, which he insists is authentic:

> Dear Manager,
> Haven't your actors ever seen any real engraving workers. Don't they know that engravers live in the lap of luxury? They think we wear the most absurd clothes. If they don't have the goodness to change them, we're coming along to boo. Messieurs, let us tell you that we are not stonemasons or roofers. They are the kind of people who wear costumes like your actors.
> Signed . . . .

Porte-Saint-Martin – Now *Claudine* is all the rage. The theatre is packed every evening, and there is no shortage of tears shed.

(L'Artisan, October 1842)

– as inevitable consequences of poverty. A second and better-read inspector acknowledged the author's moral intentions, but also their ineffectiveness: it may well be that all the immoral actions are punished, but

> given all their bad instincts the people applaud these actions and the maxims mouthed by the various actors wildly, and when the moment of punishment arrives, it does not bear the fruit the author has promised himself, given that most of the audience are not intelligent enough to apply it to themselves.
> (F21 1045)

It is certainly difficult to make people profit from any moral point when they do not make the analytic link between crime and punishment. But in fact the crux of the matter lies elsewhere: it was more a question of misusing representation, of a way of seeing which fixed upon the image while disregarding its functions. What this public lacked was a knowledge of the distance between image and reality, a knowledge of the ways to read its own image. But this presupposes an atomisation of the collective spectator. At this time the reading of the image was determined by the way in which the auditorium was split into two parts, and a play which established the dire consequences of working-class immorality in a completely unambiguous way would bring few benefits for public order if by encouraging applause from the stalls it were to provoke 'collisions' with the 'cheap seats'. This split was the very source of a disorder which was expressed in a variety of ways: disturbances in the queue and overcrowding in the gods, noisy claques which were frequently composed of tailors who more than anyone else were able to disguise themselves as fashionable men-about-town, disorders of the imagination produced by the drama or by the prestige of the actors.[18] This explains the uneasiness all theatres created: they were places where 'morals for the people' were disintegrated by the material division of the auditorium, but also where a certain mass theatricality which complemented the daydreams of a minority in the process of change was given extra vitality. The months of February and June in 1848 revealed something that was probably more disturbing than the explosive impact of any one opera (*La Muette de Portici* in Brussels or *Nabucco* in Milan): a series of shifts from social reality towards theatrical irreality, and the ability of the masses to act out the *mises en scène* of the representatives of the dangerous minorities more carefully than any opera chorus could ever have done (Pujol in June of 1848).

This is the meaning behind the repressive measures and decrees which were brought to bear on public entertainments between 1848 and 1850. By censoring in advance everything that was to be recited, sung or acted in public, it was hoped that the element of improvisation which the police could only punish after the event would be reduced. At a deeper level they were trying to turn every place of entertainment into somewhere where just texts of music were performed, in other words places where nothing happened, and where the singers or actors were reduced to the function of performers and the audience to the function of consumers. The many bans which were brought to bear upon the *cafés-concerts* (choirs and choruses, male and female impersonations, dancing, walk-on parts, noisy instruments, spoken interludes. . .) were intended not only to satisfy the theatre monopoly but above all to suppress all theatricality in the performance of songs, anything which could result in illusion or in winking complicity with the audience, or provoke it into active participation. A decree from the Ministry of the Interior in September 1852 laid down that repertoires should be limited to '*chansonnettes* and *romances* for one or two singers'. The aim was to limit theatre as a form, and all its variants. And as the danger of complicity with the audience was everywhere, nothing was to be permitted to escape the vigilant eye of the authorities. In 1854 a serious debate began concerning the request for a permit by a certain Théâtre Lafayette. Without success its manager argued that it ought to be possible to call a theatre by the name of its street. The authorities made the following distinction: streets are named after 'the glories of national history', but if a theatre were named after a politician it would become 'a rallying point and a centre for regrettable demonstrations'. If the democratic government were to permit a Théâtre Lafayette in the rue Lafayette today, what would stop the monarchic reaction from opening a Théâtre Bossuet, a Théâtre Bourdaloue or a Théâtre Fénélon in their homonymous street tomorrow? The superintendent for theatres drew this conclusion: 'in my view builders and managers should not be free to choose the names of their theatres. For reasons of moral, political and religious censorship names need to be examined and approved by the Minister.' (AN F21 1157). This is not the only time we will see His Excellency contributing personally in judgements concerning the appropriateness of a production or the alterations to be made to an offending couplet. But of course such preventive measures were useless if they did not go hand in hand with methods of control which would assure that nothing was sung, said or staged that did not conform to the directives of the Division of Fine Arts. We must certainly concede that the inspectors attached to this service must have incurred certain expenses.[19] Above all, we may perceive that the principal of state vigilance derived less from a strategic knowledge of how to discipline the popular classes than from a gigantic lack of knowledge of the things which could provoke disorder and the impossibility of mastering those aleatory and spontaneous reactions which made every place where the working class gathered – and particularly places of stage entertainment – a place of potential disturbances.

The prefect and the philosopher

For it was useless to hope for a drama or a song which would be capable of moralising the working class or of filling them with good social doctrines. But this was probably what the prefect of police was hoping for when, in a confidential letter dated 5 April 1850 he gave the Minister of the Interior a report on the situation of the campaign in eight theatres: 'They're putting on revolutionary plays here, reactionary plays there, and immoral ones everywhere' (F21 1045). At the Théâtre Français, Ponsard's *Charlotte Corday* only used the 'horrible' Marat as a lever in order to win more applause for the 'moderation' of 'that butcher' Danton. At the Porte-Saint-Martin *Camille Désmoulins* was misinterpreted by the working class who applauded Robespierre's 'bloodthirsty maxims'. At the Vaudeville and the Gymnase the bravos were shouted down with royalist slogans. At the Gaîté *L'Affaire Lesurques* (The Lesurques Affair), which dealt with a miscarriage of justice, 'teaches the people to be suspicious of magistrates and sovereign decrees'. Finally let us drape the veil of propriety over the Variétiés, where *Les Chercheuses d'or* (The Golddiggers) 'is just a pretext for putting some pretty actresses on the stage wearing next to nothing', the Théâtre Montansier, where, in *L'Odalisque* (The Odalisque), 'a young Lazarist missionary is dragged along at the heels of a fallen woman', and the Ambigu where 'in the House of God, and virtually before the audience's very eyes, a priest rapes a gypsy girl', which, as the prefect observes, 'is hardly the way to foster respect for religion and its ministers'.

This spread of Legitimist, 'anarchist' and suggestive plays presented a vicious circle to the proponents of moralisation. Certainly they could have encouraged a type of drama which would combat anarchy. But how could that have been achieved without a certain 'political bias'? Probably, the prefect genuinely enjoyed the performance of *Suffrage the First* at the Vaudeville, for he says that 'it is a sharp, bitter, light and witty criticism of the current situation. Socialism is presented as an old, crabbed red zephyr whose winds blow nothing but dryness, destruction and death. . . . So far, so good.' Unfortunately the authors did not leave it at that.

> The inevitable Legitimist couplets appear, along with direct references which turn this well-constructed satire into a party political play. . . . That the authors should criticise the cretinism of certain thinkers, that they should expose the phantom of evil doctrines in all its hideous ugliness – these are fine and noble aims; but they should not be made a panegyric for any particular party. The Empire, the Restoration and the July Government all had their *raison d'être*. All decent people who remember those times should forget their old political affiliations in order to work together to assure the future of the fatherland. We must unite, not divide.
>
> (F21 1045)

As a result *Suffrage the First* was banned. But soon the government of Napoleon III became obliged to extend this censorship of Legitimist plays to Bonapartist works, which were also liable to reawaken old resentments among 'decent people' who still supported past regimes. By this same logic anti-communard songs were censored immediately after the Commune.[20] Similarly, well into the Third Republic the works of Erkmann-Chatrian were banned along with a good many patriotic couplets which were deemed likely to offend 'the feelings of the German Ambassador'.[21] Such diplomatic prudence carried with it an obvious wish to restrict a certain patriotic spirit which, in the wake of 1870, was still of a subversive kind. In a word, it was impossible to imagine an official art for the working class. Any praise of the current authorities would always be liable to produce 'collisions' in audiences which were already split wherever there were good seats and bad seats. The only future solution to the problem of culture for the people would be an entertainment where there would only be good seats and where these seats would be isolated from each other. The insoluble contradictions of the moralisation of the working class foreshadowed home entertainment of the future: television, where the absence of a public will allow without risk the presentation of highly revolutionary works, whereas the boulevard theatres of the nineteenth century could not even present works which celebrated the prevailing order without running the risk of creating disturbances in their audiences. When the sub-prefect of Lisieux was consulted about the possibility of presenting *Hernani* in his town, he seemed to speak for future developments when he replied with the positive argument that 'in Lisieux literature does not have enough influence upon people's minds for any literary work to over-excite their passions' (ANF21 996). Blissful the sub-prefecture which recognised so early the rule of the silent majorities!

In the theatre no politics could be good politics; what was needed was drama without any politics at all, an entertainment purified of all extrinsic excitement, but would not an entertainment which was confined simply to pleasing the senses without exciting the imagination be, by its very nature, outside morality? And would not *cabarets* where people no longer sang songs or talked politics be places where people would do more drinking? (Police surveillance during the Empire corresponded to an increase in the number of establishments.)[22] Was it possible to avoid the passions and divisions of politics without uniting the working class in the cult of depravation? One year after the start of his offensive, the prefect of police remarked upon this evolution;

> I have had reason to note that . . . since plays of a political
> nature no longer attract audiences, theatres appear to want to
> cash in on all kinds of scandals. . . . At this moment the
> Théâtre du Gymnase with the play of *Manon Lescaut* and the
> Porte-Saint-Martin with *Vol à la duchesse* (The Robbery of the
> Duchess) are offering each evening a spectacle where morality
> is disgracefully outraged, where theft, promiscuity, adultery
> and suicide vie for the applause of the audience.
>
> (ANF211 1045)

Even more significant was the evolution of the titles of songs which fell victim to the censor. In 1845 a list was established of those songs which could not be sung either in theatres or in concerts or *cafés-concerts*. Political titles were the most prominent: *L'Aumône du pauvre* (The Pauper's Alms), *Le Crédo républicain* (The Republican Credo), *Le Chant du prolétaire* (The Song of the Proletariat), *Le Christ au peuple* (Christ with the People), *Dieu sur terre* (God on Earth), *La Fraternité*, *La Hongrie*, *La Misère* (Poverty), *L'Ouvrière* (The Working Woman), *La Patrouille républicaine* (The Republican Patrol), *Le Pain de l'ouvrier* (The Worker's Bread), *Le Travail plait à Dieu* (God Likes Work) – a great favourite of Poulot's, *Le Transporté* (The Deportee), etc. These outweighed the more vulgar type of song. By 1868 political songs were rarely censored any more. This was because few political songs were still presented to the censor. In the place of heroic and sentimental titles the censor's scissors had turned to subjects such as: *Comme elles sont toutes* (Girls Are All the Same),

Com'on s'marie cheux nous (How We Get Married Down Our Way), *Comme on fait son lit on se couche* (As You Make Your Bed, So Must You Lie), *La dalle en pente* (The Slippery Slope), *Essayez-en* (You Ought to Try It), *La femme à soldats* (The Woman Who Liked Soldiers), *Je garde ça pour mon mari* (I'm Keeping It For My Husband), *Je voudrais bien en tâter* (I'd Like a Bit of That), *J'risque le paquet* (I'm Risking the Lot), *J'n'os'rai jamais dir'ça d'vant l'monde* (I Wouldn't Say That In Public), *Et l'zit et l'zest et l'rantanplan* (Crash Bang Wallop And Rat-a-tat-tat). . . . Virtuous republicans were quick to conclude that the Imperial authorities were encouraging this vulgar genre in order to uproot the love of republican virtues from the heart of the working class. However the care with which its civil servants sniffed out the slightest indecency in the texts and the slightest unauthorised change in the performances indicates something else. What can be traced within the balance between liberal and repressive measures is rather the will to resolve the confusion in an artistic and moral hierarchy of genres. The abolition of theatrical privileges in 1864 was an attempt to encourage every theatre to improve the standard of its repertoire. At the same time by linking political and pornographic passions the police had created a new genre which was artistically and morally inferior, a genre unworthy of interest to people concerned with the defence of liberties and which even those most opposed to censorship must in all fairness agree should be particularly stringently suppressed. It was rather in this way that censorship and 'immorality' made a pair, breaking the old familiarity between aesthetic and political emotion and between morality and immorality. This distancing was increased by the advent of a new professionalisation which, rather than simply being the occupation of a new gap in the market, was really the logical conclusion of the repression: this – as all revolutionaries know – always professionalises by the imposition of a technicity which brings people to conform to its predictions or to circumvent them. Under the circumstances the administrative process and the calculation of concessions and risks called for an expert in licentiousness.[23] But it was not merely for the sake of principle that every year rejected songs continued to pile up in the files of the Division of Fine Arts. The reason was that a new unit was liable to be reconstituted as a result of this degenerate, vulgar genre, and that different representations of protest and revolt could be stirred up in these troubled waters: protest by using that selfsame unsociability which the *café-concert* attributed to the rabble or the outspokenness with which by casting doubts upon the virtue of wives it could proceed to cast doubts upon the virtue of those in power. An example of the first of these types is *Pas*

toujours les mêmes (Not Always the Same Ones), subtitled
'*Récriminations panachées d'un soiffard qui n'a pas son compte*'
(Assorted Complaints of a Boozer Who's Still Sober), which listed
all the grievances of a worker confronted with a bourgeois's
happy lot in derisive verses which could easily have been
interpreted in other ways:

> There are dandies who try to show off
> By treating themselves to two or three Judies at once,
> Going from a smasher as thin as a rake
> To another as big as a fatted ox,
> And when they're tired of one tart
> They take another they fancy more,
> While for the worker who's only got his old woman
> It's always the same soup and the same stew.
> *Spoken*: Well, me, I've had enough of stew!
> If there's one thing that annoys me it's the landlord
> Who sends his porter round every three months
> And on the pretext that you're his tenant
> Has the nerve to ask for the rent.
> The poor worker gives him his money
> Which he spends on behaving like a braggart.
> They're not happy just to own a house,
> But they have to make money from it to.
> *Spoken*: I've had my fill of landlords!
> *Refrain*: I'm not afraid of *un demi s'tier*
> And I'll tell you straight
> It's not always the same bloke
> Who's going to get the plum job,
> And when my turn comes
> I intend to get as much as I can.[24]

In this broad joke written in 1872 in which clearly the author
shows no sympathy with the cause of the workers' revolution, it
would be difficult not to sense the presence of both the real and
the imaginary targets of the spring of 1871: from the moratorium
on rents to the letter which proclaimed the right of workers to
have bourgeois women.[25] This example shows how the vulgar
genre reconstituted a level of indecision where derision and
protest could always swap roles, conferring a positive quality on
the 'vulgar mob' which Rosa Bordas has glorified during the
Commune.

An example of the second type is another song with spoken
interjections, *Franc comme l'Or* (Bold As Brass), written in 1872. In
it the hero, who 'calls a spade a spade', begins by making fun of

his neighbour, a grocer who has invited him to the christening of his latest child 'which he reckons he's the father of'. After refusing to shake hands with 'a young whore' for fear of dirtying his grimy, honest, worker's hands by contact with her white skin, he concludes with a patriotic verse punctuated with a spoken commentary, in which he lashes out at the treacherous bourgeoisie as 'cowards who deserted the town when it was threatened': 'That lot . . . I don't know what history will call them, but me, bold as brass, I call a spade a spade, and I say that they are cowards or traitors who have betrayed or sold the fatherland.' This patriotic protest was also a communard protest, and the moral view which set dirty hands and the appetite for pleasure of *Pas toujours les mêmes* in opposition was in fact to bring them together in the discourse of anarchist songs, which played upon the denunciation of 'white hands' and on the proclamation of 'recuperation'. Here again the revolutionary ideal and its derision were to play a subtle game which was to give anarchists the chance to use many songs intended to make them look ridiculous to their own ends.

Confronted with these tactics, successive governments were not so much complacent as caught in a vicious circle: by censoring political songs, they were encouraging a vulgar genre which they also had to censor in case it were to re-establish the old ambiguities of working–class culture and define new subversive practices. The result was a spiral of repression that censored songs which denounced the immorality they were censoring.[26] There was no such thing as a moralising song, just as there was no such thing as a play that could be politically healthy. On their faraway island of Icarus the last followers of the late Cabet may well have been able to imagine that the 'moral barometer' could be raised by granting entertainment a new role, instigating a three-point programme of 'Work, Education, Relaxation', and urging young women to use all their charms to persuade stubborn young men who refused to join in the pleasures of moralising activities to go dancing.[27] But in an ordinary society, this was unthinkable. Faced with the impossibility of raising the level of 'so low a genre' as the *chansonnette*, the best-intentioned people were in despair. Jules Simon, who was Minister for Public Education after the Commune, confided his discouragement to the prefect of police: it was certainly possible for him to attack 'the orgy of singing' which has occurred during the Commune; he was undertaking a new 'clean-up' of the repertoire in an attempt to eliminate 'what had invaded the *cafés-concerts* and had brought such a low and uninteresting genre down to an even lower level', and, in order to prevent any (unpleasant) surprises during performances, he was having each piece numbered, and insisting that a copy be given to the superintendent. But over and above the fact that the authorities were not ubiquitous, and that the most dangerous songs escaped the board of censors for the simple reason that people refrained from submitting them, the problem had deeper origins:

> No matter how severely we scrutinise the productions intended for these establishments, no matter how strict the surveillance of the Prefecture of Police may be, the evil today lies in the very existence of these places where people smoke and drink, where in a word people get together without any conception of morality or art, simply to spend the evening being vulgar.[28]

All of which led up to the following appeal to the moralising imagination of the prefect of police:

> If I were able to suppress them all, I wouldn't hesitate for one moment. I am forever pre-occupied with the desire to combat hateful music with decent, honest music. I'm always on the look-out. You wouldn't happen to have found any yourself, would you?[29]

Slender hopes in that direction. The chief of police knew the reasons of state better than the minister-cum-philosopher, and wherever public order was maintained he was prepared to abandon the need to educate the working class. He even considered and proposed that the recent habit of smoking in theatres be legalised. When the author of *Le Devoir* (Duty) explained to him that it was not simply a question of safety but also of whether one should allow just anyone to satisfy their coarse passions just anywhere they liked, he was wasting his breath . . .

Puritans at the barriers

Quite obviously Jules Simon ought to have knocked on another door – one which was now barred to the great party of Law and Order's latest recruit: that of the worker elites which he had frequented when he had been an opponent of the Empire and the advisor for worker societies. For traditionally it had been within minorities such as these that concern for working-class morality had been a genuine one, being beyond the sceptical or hypocritical condescension of the bourgeois moralists. The working-class *chansonniers* who expressed their indignation about the filth of the *cafés-concerts* and at the same time offered a model for quality songs, calling on manual workers and intellectuals to forget the recent rifts in order to build the Republic of Labour and Progress,[30] had inherited a working-class cultural tradition which had found its most resolute expression in the workers' newspapers of the July Monarchy and, notably, in *L'Atelier*. One could expect repeated protests against lewd songs, Sunday drinking sessions – and Monday ones – at the barriers, and uncivilised behaviour at *carnaval*, when they came from workers who had recently been won back to religion by *L'Atelier*. But the communists of *La Fraternité* were equally zealous. And the doctrinaire workers of these newspapers were sometimes outflanked by their readers: on 14 July 1847 an *Atelier* subscriber wrote on behalf of his comrades to protest vigorously about the disgusting dances at the Carré Marigny which were a disgrace to the national holiday:

> These dances which it would be impossible to describe are only done by men, most of them social rejects, for even the most degraded women refuse to join in. . . .
> The laborious class strongly demands the suppression of these immoral dances which are not only a sad example to young people but which also can wrongly give a bad impression of the working class, particularly as we condemn them most explicitly.
> Thus in the name of morality we the workers insist that the authorities responsible for public behaviour take the necessary steps to ensure that in future these dances be banned and remain so.
> Pray forgive, Messieurs, the liberty I am taking in sending you this demand; but I do so on behalf of many of my comrades, all workers, who are eager via the press to make it known how eagerly they want to see the entertainment in question replaced by something more worthy and above all more moral.
>
> (*L'Atelier*, July 1847)

The Carré Marigny, at the bottom of the Champs-Elysées, was the place where the first *cafés-concerts* sprang up, the place where the first components of the Imperial Festival came into being; it was also the place where, the following spring, unemployed workers gathered to *gouaper* (hang about drinking), much to the outrage of the bourgeois and the editors of *L'Atelier*. It is clear that the latter were not merely speaking for themselves when they urged the authorities to use their powers to stop the singing of coarse jokes in the streets and the 'pernicious and harmful' excesses of *carnaval*. These leisure activities degraded the workers; but less in terms of pure morality than in terms of the bourgeois who moved within the working man's space and cast his glance upon him. Over and above virtuous protests and appeals to Christian morality there were two essential arguments against the excessive freedom of working-class entertainments and festivities: through the cult of pleasure bourgeois materialism and egoism were infiltrating the ranks of the working class like acids, isolating the individual in his search for self-satisfaction and perverting the people from their own collective responsibilities, as in this refrain which *L'Atelier* denounced:

> Hang politics! To write a song
> My carefree muse will sing of booze.
> Long live the gurgle of wine in my glass,
> And the sweet embrace of a lovely lass!
>
> (*L'Atelier*, August 1844)

If the worker borrowed this 'egotistical' debauchery from the bourgeois, he offered in return a spectacle which the latter would use as an argument to justify repression:

> Our heart is heavy when we think that among the deserved or undeserved reproaches that privileged people level at us and use to justify their oppression or indifference, the most frequent one is usually this: 'What can one expect of the working class? Look how they indulge in their own instincts and natural inclinations! Ferocious in passion, cynical in pleasure. For them, good and evil, justice and injustice have no boundaries. Do they know of them? And please do not accuse us of being prejudiced: in today's ideas, rank and social distinctions have become so confused that we have no choice but to talk about it, it's so blatant! We see it every Sunday, when we go through one of the barriers on our way to our place in the country – or when we're doing jury service at the Court of Assizes, etc..'
>
> (*L'Atelier*, May 1844)

Here we may see two themes coming together in a remarkable way: the definition of a *working-class* morality of work and dedication reflecting the will to free working-class initiative from bourgeois supervision; but at the same time the affirmation of the *image of the worker* as the major component of a system of dependence to which the proletariat had been reduced. Workers had to reject the egoism of bourgeois pleasures but also to destroy the image of drunkenness and debauchery which was used to justify paternalism and moralising enterprises. The self-discipline that this entailed linked any declaration of independence and worker control with a need to present the bourgeois with an image of the workers which would prove their respectability as social partners. It is for this reason, rather than an insistence on moralisation in the abstract, that the demands of the workers' elites took a position parallel to that established in the discourse of the state. The common target of both these mental attitudes was the mixed cultural space in which meetings and exchanges between the bourgeoisie and the proletariat took place: the *goguette* where workers aspired to the rank of *artiste* or amateur; the dance halls and *guinguettes* at the barriers where men from good families used to go to help themselves to working-class girls, the melodramas and serialised novels which gave working-class men dreams of living like lords, and working-class women fantasies of becoming languid courtesans. In this half-real, half-fantastic geography of class exchanges, *carnaval* held the central place: it was a celebration of animality (mounds of food, masks and fatted oxen), of impersonation (bourgeois/workers, men/women, men/animals . . .), a celebration where fashionable folk came slumming to enjoy the spectacle – horrifying and reassuring – of the vulgarity of the working class.[31] *La Descente de la Courtille* (coming down to La Courtille), the journey back to the La Courtille barrier after the drunken masqueraders had been thrown out of the Belleville *goguettes* on Ash Wednesday morning, epitomised what was most unbearable for the theoreticians of working-class dignity. In 1854 the typographer Benjamin Gastineau wrote a book about *carnaval* which emphasised the following horrendous vision:

> After being kicked out of the *goguettes*, drunks staggering along, kicking anyone who falls over, women going home with their forage caps askew, a seasoned pipe clenched between their teeth, disguised as whores, pierrots, street urchins, fishwives . . . dishevelled, muddy, in tatters, their faces besotted and exhausted with vice, with green lips, crumpled breasts, stained clothing . . .[32]

Added to this were all the animal noises and the slops thrown from restaurant windows which the drunks would pick up to throw in the faces of the privileged people in their carriages who had come to enjoy the spectacle. That was the crux of the matter, the sore point, and the green-painted lips of the tattered women of the people were its metaphor: the participation of these folk from fashionable society, who were drawn by the example of Milord l'Arsouille ('Lord Ruffian', nickname of Lord Seymour) to experience the emotions of working-class orgies and with whom the working class maintained a dual relationship of obliging exhibitionism and aggressivity which reproduced the old relationship between the rich and the poor which working-class political militants were trying to break, in order to establish a new way of organising the relationship between labour and property. *Carnaval* had exactly the same structure as philanthropy: an exchange of services where the pauper paid for the charity of the bourgeois-voyeur by exposing his poverty or debauchery in all its nakedness. The generic name for this exchange – the name which the virtuous editors of *L'Atelier* were to pass on to that more shameless individual, Karl Marx – was *prostitution* (and both these mental attitudes came together when they denounced that book about popular exhibitionism/prostitution: *Les Mystères de Paris*). For the worker, the mixed space of cultural exchanges between the bourgeoisie and the working class could only be a place of prostitution. When Benjamin Gastineau quoted prostitution and suicide as the inevitable consequences of *carnaval*, he was speaking metaphorically rather than literally. Perhaps one should say prostitution *or* suicide. It followed logically that people who did not prostitute themselves as paupers could always commit suicide as workers. This was precisely the case with the *goguettier* or the worker-poet. Someone who sought the acclaim of his brothers in *goguettes* or who tried to forget the rigours of work through poetry could not be accused of selling his image to the bourgeoisie. But his desire to escape from his situation would lead him to step outside of his own class in respect of the work he did for a living, making the gap between his dreams and reality – the poverty that those dreams could only exacerbate – unbearable:

> When they are at work, they show no enthusiasm or energy; and if one thinks how pitifully low wages are these days, and if one thinks how a worker can satisfy his basic necessities only by stubborn perseverance and an obstinate use of his time, his unique and precious capital, then one will easily understand how deeply disturbed the situation of people whose minds are forever turned to preoccupations other than what their work must be.
>
> (*L'Atelier*, October 1844)

It was not even a question of saying that workers should not spend their time writing verses; it was enough to observe that they *could* not, that any activity which deflected them from the work which barely provided them with a living was suicidal. But the argument was double-edged, and the impossibility in terms of fact masked an opposition in terms of principle. For did not the author of the article also spend his evenings doing something other than merely recouping his strength, and did not the articles he had to write and the meetings of the editorial board of *L'Atelier* which he had to organise occupy his mind while he was at work? And did not the militant struggles that his newspaper supported expose their participants to the dangers of losing their livelihoods? It was therefore necessary to divide this mortifying use of free time into two categories:

> Nevertheless among the workers there are certain men of energy and conviction who generously sacrifice several hours each day and bravely face the crises which must arise as a result of any interruption in their day-to-day work in order to achieve those improvements and strive towards those reforms which the situation forced upon the laborious classes nowadays urgently imposes; but what an enormous difference there is between men who, seeing things from the lofty point of view of salvation and emancipation for all, take a few instants out of their thirteen hours of labour to dedicate themselves to a common cause, and idiots whose distractions only serve to satisfy their own egotistical and sterile vanity. In a situation where unremitting effort means the difference between life and death for a worker, so to speak, the moral preoccupations of the former mean dedications, those of the latter mean suicide.
>
> (*Ibid.*)

Any gesture which went beyond the use and the reproduction of the strength needed for work was a gesture in the direction of death. But that death could be a sacrifice or a suicide. And perhaps the opposition between the *goguettier* and the militant – those antagonistic figures of the working-class minority – was made to seem clear cut merely to avoid the disturbing realisation that they were closely related. Was it simply the accomplishment of a duty to write a workers' newspaper, to participate in the organisation of a guild, a republican society or a utopistic chapel, to spend one's evenings discussing the best way to organise labour or preparing the means to transport the political and social system which stood in its way? Was it not also a promotion which took the worker out of the mundaneness of the workshop, raising him above his comrades and allowing him to speak the same language as the guardians or reformers of the bourgeois system? Did not the emphasis placed upon his dedication to serving his brothers disguise the possibility that the wish to escape or to pass over to the other side of the cultural barrier may have played a part in this dedication? Did not this concern for a pure morality of class deny the consciousness of minority which motivated workshop poet and militant alike? The typographer Charles Supernant, the author of the article, was himself a (temporarily) repentant *goguettier*, and had once appeared on the trestle stage of the Seveste Brothers' travelling theatre. After collaborating with Proudhon, the typographer Benjamin Gastineau, critic of *carnaval*, became a 'man of letters' himself. And the way of thinking they both developed was clearly a product of that grouping of workers who spent their time rubbing elbows with writers and journalists. It is hardly surprising that the people who were most eager to defend a pure ethic of worker-militancy were the ones who, through their working activity, found themselves constantly at a barrier which was more of a point of passage between two classes made up of hierarchies and minorities than a fence between two rigidly separated spaces. All they needed was to recognise the original twisting of the working-class militant ideal, the need for the fraction which was maintained at the limits of the other camp to reassure themselves of their position by using the most intransigent class discourse, and to deny the process of *minorisation*, which had put them where they were by being up to the *having-to-be-a-worker*. Their moral indignation at the orgiastic exchanges and pleasures they witnessed at the barriers was less the result of an inculcation by 'the dominant ideology' than the metaphorisation of their uncertainty about their own position, a deliberate about-turn in the wish to escape which was sweeping working-class minorities across to the other side of the cultural barrier.

The Belleville Battalion

This was the start of a game of hide-and-seek between working-class moralism and reasons of state. For this working-class call for stricter policing was always made as a form of denunciation couched in the discourse of the opposition. In 1844 Supernant suspected that the authorities were allowing the filth they were supposed to be suppressing to spread in order to degrade the working class even further. This is the point of view which informed republican protests against the 'gay Paris' of the Second Empire, either by setting the 'Paris of working people, scholars and artists' against the 'Paris of horse-racing and love affairs',[33] or by castigating the degrading entertainment with which the authorities were trying to corrupt the people. The *cafés-concerts* were the prime target for this denunciation. A united front grew up to oppose their rise in popularity, in which the former critics of the *goguettes* fraternised with the selfsame *goguettiers* they had recently denounced. Now nostalgic visions emphasised the moralising virtues of the old *goguettes* where the wine had not been adulterated, where in any case it was only the music which went to one's head, and where you could bring the family in full confidence that you would only hear high quality music. For, as a result of the hierarchisation instigated by the repression, it was not the concept of quality which defined the artistic and moral dignity of the songs of yesteryear. The austere Supernant was now placed alongside Edouard Hachin, the author of trash like *Allons Javotte/Frippe ta cotte* (Come On Gert/Tuck Up Your Skirt), *Gertrude n'est pas prude* (Gertrude's No Prude), etc., in the pantheon of popular, artistic – and progressive – songs. Songs, it was said, 'must always have elbow room',[34] and suddenly the bawdy of the good old days became part of the patrimony of the progressive movement. It was a reconciliation which had a parallel elsewhere: *La Lice chansonnière* (The List of Song), a society of republican *chansonniers*, was delighted to observe that its old monarchist adversaries of *Caveau* were moving in their direction. In 1878 they were to join forces to found *La Chanson*.

For the situation was not good. The fact that the Republic had taken over from the Empire seemed to have had no effect upon the corruption with which the latter had been impregnated. So these representatives of the true tradition proposed a type of song that would be worthy of the post-1871 consolidated Republic, exalting work, progress, education and class reconciliation, and of which *La Bataillon de Belleville* (The Belleville Battalion) was one of the best examples.[35]

But if the Republic showed little inclination to support their struggle against the *cafés-concerts*, this was perhaps because their analysis of the corruption of the Second Empire was rather deficient. Various remarks that they made in passing suggest that they themselves were well aware that something had happened which went beyond classic 'circus games' and which explained their reduction to an *arrière-garde* role. Few people attended the monthly banquet of the *Lice* held on 1 May 1878, and those who were there only half listened on account of the fireworks and din from the nearby Universal Exhibition. At the *Caveau*'s banquet in August, said *La Chanson*, there were 'not many people and not much silence'. It blames two things: 'on the one hand, the summer holidays, and on the other the obsession with talking politics'.

These examples are significant: if the death-throes of the *goguette* coincided with the moment the Republic began using the refrains of yesteryear to strengthen its position, then it means that a certain link between festive gaiety and political seriousness had been dissolved. What had been the cultural space of working-class minorities was now split between a political game with well-coded acts and discourse and the constitution of working-class leisure activities as such as spectacle. It is not surprising that in this respect the Universal Exhibitions are very revealing. Since 1869 Exhibitions were the real or symbolic place where a worker could see both art and industry becoming something separated from his own work. And yet when faced with this circumstance our *goguettiers* shared none of the concern the workers of 1867 expressed when they confronted the reality of work which had been divided and alienated from them.[36] On 1 May 1878, after one of their company had just sung *La Fête du travail* (Labour Day),[37] they brought their meeting to a close in order to admire the lights of this triumph of industry the image of which coincided henceforth in their minds with that of the Republic of Labour (rechristened the *industrial* Republic). But in doing so they showed neither rancour nor regret:

> Fully appreciating the situation, the chairman of the *Lice* brought the meeting to a close earlier than usual and everyone went to enjoy the magical sight of the Exhibition all lit up. Within ourselves we all knew that the mighty clamour of a people eager to join the peaceful struggle of labour and progress was as good as any song could be.[38]

Clearly, when our *chansonniers* wanted to show their appreciation of the Harmonies of Industry, not even a Toussaint Turelure could rival them. And moreover their newspaper was pleased to welcome advertisements for *La Dentellière*, a limited company which produced real hand-made lace by machine.

Strangely they seem to have been unaware of a certain number of suspicious factors: that an era which could use machines to produce *real* hand-made lace could naturally also mass-produce *real* working-class songs; that it was precisely their inability to tell real hand-made lace that gave them the status of impotent judges of what were real songs; and that maybe the shameful industry of the *cafés-concert*, much more than their old-fashioned craftsmanship, was giving the Industrial Republic the music it deserved. Was not their crusade for good songs a means of avoiding the question: hadn't this magical spectacle of industry something to do with the 'baseness' of this new entertainment and leisure industry, itself a product of a concomitant waste of working-class hands and voices?

It was not that the learning of professional skills may have represented the obligatory focal point of a working-class culture, as is frequently asserted. It is possible rather than this culture was an attempt at deprofessionalisation. But when 'deprofessionalisation' takes on the form of an imposed reduction in skills, then the ways of escape when not at work are also affected. And what the individual hand and mind would lose in favour of the materiality of organisation and tools, so would the individual voice in favour of song as entertainment. To start with, there would be less singing in the workshops, and less coming-and-going between the workshops and the streets where singing took place; on the other hand the transformation of urban space, where in many respects the organisation of the city was moulded on that of Exhibitions, tended to unravel the confusion of a space where bourgeois and workers, workmen on errands (or on the binge) and street performers all moved together, and to direct its entertainments towards specific places.[39] The reduction in workers' skills and the modernisation of the city came together with the rationalisation of state surveillance in order to professionalise song, turning a very small minority of those who could no longer sing at work into artistes, and the vast majority into spectators. In this respect the biographies of the first *café-concert* artistes are very interesting. Victor Renard was the former iron-foundry worker we mentioned earlier who used to sing on the *tour de France* or for his workmates. After his success as a street singer in 1848 he went on tour several times with his guitar before taking up his trade again in Rheims. He joined an amateur theatrical company, where he was discovered by the Rheims Opera House, which gave him a job. From there he moved to the Paris Opera until voice problems brought him back down to the intermediary level of the *café-concert*, where he became a leading name.[40] The career of Theresa (the interpreter of *La Femme à barbe* (The Bearded Lady), *La Venus du boeuf gras* (The Venus of the Fatted Ox), or *Rien n'est sacre pour un sapeur* (Nothing's Sacred For a Sapper)) whom the old *goguettiers* despised so much, was more direct but equally significant. A milliner's apprentice, she was dismissed because her singing stopped the girls from working. 'It seemed obvious to me,' she remarks, 'that singing was like eating, it was like a call of nature.'[41] When her next mistress sent her to deliver a note to an *artiste*, she stayed to listen to her and was once more dismissed. One day, after working for eighteen firms in two years, she happened to go into a courtyard to sing, something she was not allowed to do in the workshop, and that is how her professional career began. Professionalisation: henceforth it was something that would be nurtured by the cult of stardom, helped along with well-orchestrated scandals, by the writing of memoirs by (or for) every new celebrity, and by the development of its own specialised press. As Theresa herself put it in one of her songs: 'You've got to give people their money's worth'.

It was a process of professionalisation which those who felt nostalgia for the *goguette* refused to consider as such. Their criticism of Theresa and her colleagues worked on two levels, which were to become increasingly combined: an aesthetic defence of quality and the moral denunciation of corruption. But the first of these criticisms only succeeded in confirming the hierarchy which as we have seen was induced by the repression itself by isolating the sector of 'high quality' songs from the riff-raff of the songs of the *cafés-concerts*. Therefore these criticisms played along with the game of professionalisation. And if the second of these criticisms took up the denunciation of the 'image of working-class people' fabricated by the bourgeoisie, it was only to impose it upon the working class itself:

> Refined people would go into raptures when they heard works which were travesties of the spirit and form of working-class poetry, and the short-sighted masses would applaud the caricatures which in high places were presented as good likenesses.[42]

But now the very evidence of this demonstration seems dubious. In the *Tableau de Paris* (The Portrait of Paris) which Vallès composed on his return from exile he pays homage to Theresa, opposing the timidity of the republican *chansonniers* with the audacity of that queen of the Second Empire *café-concert*:

> One day into this age of men with sealed lips and limp arms came a woman with the voice and gestures of a real man. She cried: 'But you've got to give people their money's worth!' And people understood, applauded and helped to make this singer of *Le Sapeur*, who undermined the Empire by laughing at it, rich and famous.'[43]

Vallès's eulogy is itself ambiguous. Was not the vehemence of this voice he praised made up precisely of other people's silence; firstly of those whom the repression had hounded until some – like Charles Gille – even committed suicide; then more generally of those who could no longer sing in the streets, the workshops and the *goguettes* and who now went to listen to artists, peddling a culture composed of the sounds of brilliant voices and all the hubbub that went with them? This is why Jules Vallès, with all the populist complicity of an angry young undergraduate, did not come up with any points of view different from those of the self-taught workers who were defending morality and quality. If he rehabilitated the *café-concert*, it was within the strict framework of the right of decent folk to their share of relaxation and dreams as compensation for the hardships of the workshop:

> Sometimes it's nice to get away from home where you can't burn the candle at both ends and to go somewhere where the gas burns brightly and there's gold everywhere. For a few *sous* you can gaze at the luxury of millionaires.
>
> And then, even though these songs may be stupid, they help you to forget the boss's harsh words or the bank manager's veiled threats.
>
> It may not be a victory over the enemy, but at least it's something.[44]

In this context, Vallès's reference to Theresa, the star of the *cafés-concerts* of the 1860s, in his general discourse on his return from exile in 1880, takes on the same nostalgic function that the pre–1848 *goguette* had for others: a plea that French song rediscover its lost virility:

> In place of stupid bacarolles, the chirping of sparrows, insipid farces, dusty hymns fit only for doves or monkeys to sing, we would offer the new Muse the great wine of the peasants and the workers, a poetry of cloud and sunshine, the paradise of nature, the hell of the workshop. . . . Come on, my old *beuglant* (*café-chantant*), it's no good sitting there bleating like a sheep; we've got to rebel and have our revolution like our comrades did before us. Anyone who leaves the Gallic lark – French song – in the snares of the enemy is a traitor.[45]

The former Communard seems to have divided his discourse in an exemplary way between a nostalgia for the republican Muse with her songs of workers, peasants and wine growers, and which extended the ideology of the *goguettiers*, and a modernism which did justice to the entrepreneurs and the stars who gave people their money's worth of dreams. In any event he made the same change of position, calling henceforth not on the workshop poet and his relationship with his brothers, but on the performer and his responsibilities towards his popular audience.

By rehabilitating the *café-concert*, Vallès was sanctioning a certain shift, by which the question of the way workers used their free time became involved in the defence of the consumer. In

Vallès's view the tepid milk which the *cafés-concerts* were pouring into people's ears should be replaced by a wine which would warm the heart. But the entrepreneurs of the new entertainment had a ready answer to this demand for quality which both producer and consumer were making. To those who accused them on politico-moral grounds of giving people mindless entertainment the partisans of the *cafés-concerts* replied by claiming that their business was of a civilising nature, a claim similar to the one used to justify Haussmann's demolitions. The latter had eliminated the old haunts of immorality and sedition, the former were attempting to purify the vulgar pleasures of the working class which in years gone by had been above all a street entertainment. Marc Constantin, a *chansonnier* who had been won over by this new art form, expressed his delight in the fact that the *cafés-concerts* were gradually abandoning 'the old-fashioned and vulgar ways' of attracting 'gawks' which at first they had borrowed from fairground tradition: bird-men, one-legged dancers, clowns with violins and various other phenomena, all those 'heterogeneous elements' which they had tolerated in the first years of their existence and which were now gradually disappearing. This improvement was also helped by comfortable surroundings which discouraged vulgarity of speech and behaviour. In the same way the tradition of pass the hat round disappeared and was only to be found in 'Paris *caboulot* concerts, travelling fairs, and shady gambling dens in garrison towns and seaports'. By fighting all these manifestations of bad taste the *cafés-concerts* would end up by eliminating their 'original sin', conferring on the working–class pleasures the 'dignity' that the austere representatives of the working-class demanded. And if the latter persisted in their recriminations, there was always the supplementary proof of hard-working dignity offered by the Mutual Aid Society of *Café-Concert* Singers which was founded in 1865.[46]

A seat at the Châtelet

At the moment when the discourse of the republican moralisers was retreating to its standpoint of 'quality' the entertainment entrepreneurs and the property developers of the new city had a different 'morality' with which to respond. They countered the aristocratic morality of the working–class cultural minorities with the contention that the noble aspect of the new streets or the elegant comforts of the new places of popular entertainment would have the practical result of purifying working-class behaviour of its vulgarity. This improvement in manners, which was nothing more than an improvement in the surroundings of everyday life – or leisure – would surely be more effective than all the efforts at moralising and regulation-making. The 'barriers' which had withstood being anathematised would not resist the integration of the suburban communes into the city.

The idea of using the embellishment of Paris in order to unravel the confusion – the lack of civilisation – of the old working-class cultural space was expressed in two different directions: incitement to an architectural repression which would banish equivocal residents along with the rickety buildings they lived in; or a search for ways of making the pleasures of the working-class population more comfortable and hence more civilised. An example of the former is the petition drawn up by the landowners of the Chateau d'Eau quarter just before the 1855 Exhibition, which updated the old aesthetic protest against the vulgarity of working-class leisure activities in the context of the City-as-Exhibition:

On December 18th last an impressive number of the most prominent inhabitants of the (old) 5th and 6th *arrondissements* met to protest against the deplorable state of the stretch of land in the rue de Bondy between no. 2 and the rue de la Douane behind the water tower, which fronts on the boulevard Saint-Martin. Where the rue de Bondy and the new boulevard du Nord have been widened there is a rash of filthy cobblers' stalls, chip shops, etc. . . . made of loose planks and unlit at night, a *café-concert* with a sordid strip of canvas for a door and where there is a side-show of giants, a public dance hall of the lowest type with broken-down walls which looks unbelievably dreadful and about to collapse on all sides.

This state of affairs, which has been disgracing the quarter for more than seven years, encourages immorality and endangers security.

But now that this place is to become the link between three boulevards, the boulevard du Temple, the boulevard Saint-Martin and the boulevard du Nord, created on the initiative of his majesty the Emperor, it is impossible to allow this situation which is paralyzing the prosperity of the building industry to continue, since the magnificent position of the site makes it naturally suited to large building projects which would bring light and prosperity to the quarter.

The Universal Exhibition will throw Paris open to the rest of France and to foreign countries, and the authorities cannot allow people who come to admire the water tower to see the disgusting spectacle of these shacks in the background.

(AN F21 1157)

This is an exemplary text in terms of the light it sheds on the formation of modern 'public opinion'. In a superb summary we can observe moral and material security, national prestige and the interests of the building industry – which are also the interests of the working class, as we all know – ganging up on the former disorders of street life, with its small tradesmen and its precarious, half-constructed and unclosed buildings. Wide streets, solid buildings and artistic vistas also meant a balanced spread of population, and the wish for this is made quite apparent at the end of the petition where a proposed *estaminet* with 30 billiard tables is attacked:

> There are already the Café du Hameau, the *café-concert* on the boulevard du Temple, opposite the Opera House, and several dance halls of the most inferior kind. Therefore people in this quarter already have to put up with more than their fair share of this kind of popular establishment, and it would be unjust to make matters worse, not to say imprudent to attract every bohemian in Paris to one single spot.
>
> (*Ibid.*)

There was however an alternative and more positive version of this repressive concept of the transformation of the streets and pleasures of Paris, and which Haussmann himself promoted when he built the two theatres on the place du Châtelet. Along with improvements in heating, lighting and ventilation, he proposed an additional, revolutionary measure: that all seats be numbered and bookable in advance without any supplementary payment. In fact up till then only the best seats had been numbered and a supplement had been payable for advance booking. As a result the 'working classes' who occupied the unnumbered seats in the gods were doubly uncomfortable: first having to queue for three to four hours in all weathers and then having to stand packed like sardines behind the first row of seats in order to see anything at all of the show.

However, Haussmann's kind thoughts had nothing to do with what either the theatre managers or the working-class audience really wanted. Camille Doucet, Head of the Division of Theatres, makes this clear: both seemed satisfied with the system as it was:

> The partisans of the present system say that the fun starts earlier, that queuing is the first part of it, that having to wait actually adds to it and that the gaiety of the queues is the best argument against suppressing them. The theatre managers see the queues as living advertisements; crowds attract more

crowds, and even if anyone gets hurt it still means a success
for the theatre.

(F21 1045)

In one sense the authorities would have been delighted with
this gaiety and patience on the part of the working class, as they
ruled out demonstrations of impatience which might have led to
demonstrations of another kind. But it was precisely this way the
people had of integrating the annoyances of having to wait and
the disorders of queuing into the organisation of their pleasures
which was dubious; what was no longer acceptable was this
capacity to *waste time* and to enjoy doing so:

> The authorities should look at things rather more from on
> high. Having to queue is in itself uncivilised, and if the people
> are happy to put up with it and even enjoy it sometimes, it is
> nevertheless true that from every point of view it would be
> better if they were not forced to. They could easily be doing
> something useful, like getting on with some work, for
> example. It would be healthier and more profitable.

Three or four hours spent standing in front of a theatre would
be more usefully employed in doing some work: there is no
answer to that particular argument. If working-class pleasures
were properly organised then the discomforts of having to wait
and thus having the time to calculate the extent of one's pleasures
and hardships would be eradicated. This was the real object of
Haussmann's proposals: to give everyone their own numbered seat,
to offer everyone a luxury which up till then only privileged
people could afford, and at the same time to suppress the disorder
in the galleries which was linked to the existence of unnumbered
seats with limited visibility.

> If everyone pays, everyone should have a seat. It is only right
> that everyone should be able to sit down and enjoy the show
> properly, and that workers should not be packed like sardines,
> men and women on top of one another, as they are at free
> entertainments.
>   If all the galleries had seats, as they already have at both the
> circuses and at the racecourse, every member of the audience
> would feel at home.

(*Ibid.*)

It is remarkable to see how far this argument reproduces the
classic discourse of the philanthropists on living conditions, even

to the extent of fantasising about sexual promiscuity. Haussmann's proposals for working-class leisure offered exactly the same response to the same problem as his contemporary Godin's for the *Familistère de Guise*: to give the working class *equivalents of wealth*. In particular this meant giving them the taste for a reserved space through the stimulus of comfort. Throughout all the discussions which were held on this proposal theatre seats were like a metaphor for property, and the people who were determined to get the working class to sit comfortably at shows met with exactly the same problems as the Fourier-inspired inventors of social palaces and the philanthropists who brought in the law on the cleaning-up of unsanitary housing. They all came up against the requirements of property: it was impossible to construct comfortable low-rent buildings on urban land and get a profitable return on capital; it was also impossible to force landlords who already had difficulty in collecting their modest rents to carry out the improvements which would be necessary were the law to be strictly applied.[47] The prefect of police mentioned the same obstacle: it was all very well to put in seats and to number them all, but 'if you are going to book seats they must be easily accessible to the audience, who must be able to remain seated during the entire show, and to see and hear the actors'. If this measure were applied to the four main boulevard theatres it would have had the effect of cutting out '750 to 780 cheap places where workers could stand listening and watching but which could not be numbered or divided up since they did not actually exist as such' (*ibid.*). If blind spots were cut out, extra space made for circulation, and booking fees abolished, managers would no longer be able to make their enterprises profitable. And even supposing that architects could come up with an ingenious solution, the practical problem ran the risk of turning into a philosophical one, by giving the working class a taste for property and comfort, was there not a risk of that taste becoming so exaggerated that they might begin to put the old principles of the bourgeois philosophy of property into practice in their own uncivilised way?

> How would one be able to keep booked seats? It's already hard enough now in the stalls and dress circle; what would it be like in the upper circle and the gods where you normally get only uneducated people? They would never understand that the best seats are not to be had on a first-come first-served basis.
>
> (*Ibid.*)

And in despair of finding a statutory solution to the queue

problem all the prefect could come up with was covered shelters (another Fourier-inspired fantasy), although he knew that there would be objections that these would encroach upon the theatres' usable space and put an extra strain on their profitability. As in the case of working-class housing, it was a question of squaring the circle.

It was not that the problem was being seen in a false way. Of course, the bourgeois establishment would be better assured if it were able to guarantee every worker cheap and comfortable housing and entertainment.[48] But the prefects of police were always on hand to defend the bourgeois establishment, and they knew something which both the prospective vision of the philanthropists and the retrospective vision of the genealogists overlooked: that no statutory or architectural measures could confer the principle of necessary sufficient on strategies which were aimed at assuring the subordination or integration of working people within the system of domination or exploitation. Thus cut-price comfort could not be invented nor imposed by decree. To grant it to workers without harming the immediate interests of the propertied class would entail transforming the conditions of production, accelerating the division of labour and the mechanisation which it had already become necessary to impose upon everyone who thought that the promise that by becoming poor as producers they could become rich as consumers was a fool's bargain.[49]

Thus, as far as leisure activities were concerned, the spontaneous reaction initiated by industry was to find bit by bit the solutions which moralists, urbanists, ministers or philanthropists could only imagine. What was to put an end to the 'orgy of singing' was partly the *café-concert* industry and then the record industry, which gave songs a fixed status as merchandise, and partly the transformation of the forms and rhythms of work. And if Haussmann contributed anything towards solving the problem of the working-class presence in theatre audiences, it was above all in the extent to which he sent workers to live outside the space where they existed. The day when working hours became more constricting and the distance between work and home greater would see the problem of working-class/bourgeois coexistence solved of its own accord: with the disappearance of the former. By 1900 this desertion was already well under way, simplified by a phenomenon of specialisation which offered workers more comfortable premises[50] and transformed the theatre repertoire. As theatre audiences became increasingly narrow socially so the repertoire became more intimist and psychological – which in turn helped the narrowing process even further. Aware of this phenomenon, the state planned the construction of four large popular theatres, to be built in the outlying quarters, which would present a range of historical, spectacular and social entertainments ('the great general scientific and social concepts clothed in the most alluring graces of wit and poetry'[51]) adapted to suit popular needs and desires. Now the era of 'popular theatre' could begin. Henceforth *artistes* and masters of ceremonies would work tirelessly to bring the treasures of culture to the working class, helping them in their struggles or teaching their children the language of the theatre, while dreaming of the time when theatre had been 'popular' because the people's living moments (getting a job, work, shopping, reading the paper, spoken protests and active demonstrations) had been spontaneously theatrical.

Les temps des cerises (cherry time)

Now suppose we compare two texts, the one written sixty years after the other, which turned the entertainments they described into instant myths.

In 1854 Victor Fournel, the historian of street life and entertainments in Paris, described the sights and sounds of the *quais*: where the voice of 'melancholy mountebanks' or ruined ex-orchestral conductors became street singers mixed with the ranting performances of people selling indelible ink, hair-restorer or stain-remover. One of the latter besieges a member of the *Académie* as he comes out of the building and tries to demonstrate his product on his suit. That the honourable learned gentleman is defeated by the merchant's gibes is evidence of the power of a working-class culture which is still part of everyday life and work. As he wanders alone, Victor Fournel marvels at the crowd which gathers and vibrates around this open-air theatre with its ranters and its music-makers: a theatre of audience participation which he explains as a consequence of an active relationship with culture – and with music in particular:

> The people are essentially music lovers. . . . Every doorkeeper, no matter how fierce and sour-tempered, has at the very least her precious accordion which has been passed down from generation to generation, and which is preserved in the palladium of her lodge; every respectable concierge has a piano for her daughter, who is an eminent scholar at the Conservatoire; many workers relax by playing the clarinet or the flageolet for hours on end. And you should see the number of people who usually gather around even the least accomplished singer.[52]

Maybe this vision is somewhat idyllic, the bourgeois journalist smugly presenting his readers with the spectacle of a plebs which found in its own culture the compensation of being able to make fun of its masters; but even if it is exaggerated it would still not have been possible had it not a real basis in a relationship between music and the working class which many other accounts confirm. Sixty years later another writer interested in the transformations of working-class life, Luçien Desçaves, wrote *Philémon, vieux de la vieille* (Philémon the Old Trooper). Colomès, his hero, is a former jeweller's mate who has been exiled after the Commune. He evokes the time when songs were not separated from everyday activities:

> The division of labour and the development of mechanisation had not yet reduced workers to a new condition of slavery as they have now. A worker could still greet the product of his own hands with a song. His voice wasn't drowned by the noise of a machine. Why should I want to sing when there's a steel monster that never stops cutting things up or drilling holes staring me in the face? Try setting words to music like that. The movement of the flywheels and the connecting rods would ram them back down your throat.[53]

Of course Colomès-Philémon repeats the polemic of the old *goguettiers* against the stupidity of the new *chansonnette*. And he enjoys recalling the scene he made on his return from exile, when he heard some young men in a *guinguette* in Châtillon singing the latest ditty *Josephine, elle est malade* (Josephine is Poorly). To 'shut them up' he stood up and started singing Pierre Dupont's *Les Cerises* (Cherries):

> I was like a standard bearer for the songs of the people, the trusty, the true, the best of all songs! I would have died for them! Their Josephine wasn't poorly any more, she was dead! They stopped singing about her and listened to me, quite intimidated. When I'd sung the last verse, they applauded me, rushed into the garden and asked for more – of the same thing.[54]

This success proves to Colomès that the working class is sensitive to beauty and that opposition to the cretinising enterprises of people who claim to come down to its level can be possible. But one Sunday when Philémon and his wife are 'leaning at the casement, warbling a cavatina congruent with the clemency of the weather', another adversary makes his appearance:

Suddenly from an invisible loudspeaker came a voice like that
of a buffoon with a stuffed-up nose, the caricature of a voice,
which eructated a kind of announcement. Then came the
popular melody *Viens poupoule!* (Come On Ducky!) . . . every
single verse of it, sounding like something coming to the boil
over a spluttering fire. But that wasn't all. The street song was
followed by a polka with a trombone solo, a monologue, the
aria from *Faust*: 'Gloire immortelle' . . . and a band of hunting
horns, all of it dished up on a plate with a metal mouth-bowl,
like a dentist's basin.

   In conclusion we listened to a pot-pourri of military and
dramatic music which mixed the *Charge* with the *Marseillaise*,
accompanied by the crackle of gunfire, the shouts of the
soldiers as they attacked, even bells ringing: Cease fire! To the
flag! Quick march, etc.[55]

Philémon and his confidant witness the unbelievable speed with
which the gramophone invasion spreads:

Other vomitoria appeared at other windows, horns, trumpets,
wastepipes and lavatory cisterns which spewed out a mishmash
of *café-concert* songs, brass bands and the lavender water of the
opéra-comique like so much liquid manure. It was like having a
bar and a marketplace in your own living room, silence raped
by the most tyrannical of noises. The ogre seemed to swallow
records and disgorge them again like a frog giving change for
the counters in a game of *tonneau*.[56]

Henceforth it would be impossible to silence the voice of
'progress' as he had done in the *guinguette* in Châtillon. The
narrator remarks: 'You had the advantage over some young men
whom you have taken by surprise and managed to convince of the
error of their ways . . . but I defy you to silence this supreme
mechanism'.

'Of course!' replies the hero. 'Yet another result of excessive
mechanisation. After getting rid of the human arm, it's now
subjugating the human voice! Now it's in captivity, and you
can only hear it filtered through a muffler.'[57]

Of course both the disillusioned tone given to the former
Communard and the wonder-struck language of the journalist of
1854 create myths simply by their choice of images. The
workshops, the streets and the slums of 1854 were not exactly like
the decor of a bohemian song-making Victor Fournel describes.

At the same time in 1913 the streets had not been deserted by their singers and speech-making peddlers; and self-educated workers had a variety of ways of getting round or deflecting the new techniques of culture diffusion. What merits our attention is the actual formation of this semi-real, semi-imaginary representation of songs as 'things of the past', and the shift in perspective such judgements – positive or negative – about these enchanted or disenchanted worlds imply. For example the transfer from the bustle of the street to the invasion of the household is significant. On this point the nostalgic old Communard defines the place of the gramophone in much the same way as its apologists did. In the armoury of new culture inventions, the gramophone, despite being less of a spectacle, was perhaps more effective than cinema in introducing what was to become the great twentieth century revolution in the industry – and the politics – of leisure: the master's voice in the home. For all that, even if in terms of pedagogic discourse they had different functions – concerts in the home or in the democratic spectacle of the future – both the gramophone and the cinema were often thought of in similar terms as an instrument/teacher with a universal vocation. 'Cinema,' declared Pathé, 'will be the theatre, the newspaper and the school of the future.' The ambition of the gramophone to be the absolute teacher, 'the instrument which unites everything, which interprets everything', was the equivalent of this. Both were authoritative instruments capable of achieving the purification of working-class pleasures which well-thinking politicians were determined to bring about and which the entertainment entrepreneurs professed to have achieved. Cinema followed the same curve as theatre or sport, taking off from a beginning as fairground entertainment. It too conformed to the taste for 'living torsos' and other fairground freak shows before winning all the attributes of the new respectability: introduction of seating between 1905 and 1910, comfort and luxury which made Haussmann's impossible dream a reality, development of friendly relations with local authorities and the police, who were eager to avoid any new 'reactions' this new type of entertainment might produce. Henceforth it was ready to affirm its pedagogic vocation. As for the gramophone, it proved without difficulty that it offered the best in education: the model interpretation by the artist-as-star. It carried 'His Master's Voice' to the listener, symbolised by the famous dog. In future the successors of the typographer tenors of yesteryear would probably have been well advised to avoid trying to sing any of the *bel canto* melodies which the famous Caruso had just recorded. In its own way cinema produced a similar effect. Naturally what it produced was not something incomparable, but it was nevertheless a spectacle which was closed upon itself, non-reiterative. Perhaps what was abolished by the new means of technical reproduction was the possibility of appropriation, of untrained reproduction, rather than the 'aura' of the unique work of art.[58] They gave the technical means to realise the pious dreams of the repression of 1850: an entertainment where audiences were merely consumers – precisely because they no longer had any links with its production. Of all these pilot inventions for a consumer culture, the gramophone was the most exemplary in that it immediately installed this passivity within the home. And from this point of view it is interesting to observe the fantastic insistence upon the theme of the home given in the *Compagnie du Gramophone*'s advertising magazine. Be they presented by anecdotes or poems, the various uses of the wonderful instrument are always identified with the role of leader, guardian or representative of the home. Here is the evocation of a warm summer evening:

> On one of the floors they're playing their gramophone, and everyone is listening to it. People who aren't in the know imagine that an admirable artistic and musical evening is being held. In fact it is impossible to imagine that these superb sounds are not issuing forth from a human breast, from a human throat. Life in the entire building is suspended – to listen; maids forget to wash the dishes, children refuse to go to bed, delighted to hear such beautiful sounds. In the distance the confused murmur of other gramophones can be heard. It is true to say that you will not hear a piano played any more, for it has been replaced by this complete instrument which unites everything, which interprets everything. . . . And it is the triumph of the Gramophone displayed for all to see . . .[59]

Despite suggestions of incitement to laziness and disobedience, it is above all the function of silence which is of paramount importance here. But this domestic paradise needs to be protected, and the symbolic dog now takes its place at the other end of the horn:

> We're done for: the crooks are about to break the door down,
> The children are terrified, the wife is almost dead with fear.
> But suddenly a sound rises and rings through the air,
> Then another: a real concert frightens the three crooks away,
> For they think the building is full of excellent performers . . .
> It was the divine Gramophone which came to the rescue![60]

Guardian of the home, the gramophone becomes the home itself, transportable to the very depths of the desert where, according to the house poet, an exhausted Arab is walking in the burning sun:

In the Desert

And the traveller, pensive and full of melancholy,
His soul resigned and fatalistic,
Feels nostalgia flood into his heart:
Home is so far away, and the journey so long!

And yet he smiles, for among his luggage
There is a box – oh mysterious gift!
Songs which soothe the most savage breast
Will bring joy and hope back into his eyes!

In the middle of the desert the divine Gramophone,
By evoking the pleasures of the dear country left behind
And repeating clearly to the resounding echoes
All these songs he had loved, makes the present less hard.

Delighted, the Arab on his distant journey
Scoffs at all his cares; he can well scorn them
Now that the Gramophone with its heavenly voice
Brings the song of the home to the harsh desert.[61]

Let us leave the poets of the gramophone to their panacoustic fantasies. What strikes us here is the emergence of a new figure of entertainment that enters neither into the mode of the ancient theatre, that centre of the collectivity of the popular gaze: nor into its opposite, delineated by the panoptic imagination, the circular gaze of the centralised observer on isolated individuals. But now it may be that the formation of modern public opinion underwent a third phase: a central spectacle seen by all individuals separately. In its naive advertisements the *Gramophone* magazine gives a good definition of what television was to become: the transmitter of entertainment transformed into a piece of furniture. In order for the entertainment of the future to work, it was not so much individuals themselves who had to be domesticated as power itself; it was to be an entertainment which would bring the whole world into the home, omitting only its own production, an unanswerable entertainment, confined within the house, not the instrument of 'cretinisation' or levelling described by some, but rather the summit and the intensification of a hierarchy of leisure which would give everyone their appropriate type of entertainment: a universal enactment which would replace the multifarious gestures of social theatricality.

Was 'cherry time' gone forever? In 1900 Jean-Baptiste Clément, author of that song and President of the *Caveau* in Saint-Etienne, attended a singer's congress at the Universal Exhibition – as ever a significant site. All the congress members shared the same concern: how to combat 'the increasing invasion of our opera houses by the nauseating products of pseudo-*chansonniers* who without regard for literature, art or morality, or for the respect due to the public and their own dignity, use the very filth and squalor they wallow in to write with'.[62] For Clément it seemed futile to expect even a renewal of 'artistic *cabarets*' on the lines of Bruant's '*Chat noir*', 'where everything connected with progress, justice and humanity is made a laughing stock, and where on the pretext of realism the poor are made to speak like whores at the barriers and the working class talk like pimps'. Prostitution and the barriers: Clément, a former Communard, stumbles against the same obsessions as Senator Corbon. But even more radical than Corbon, he suggested that the great struggle of morality against immorality and of quality against stupidity only made sense in the context of an exclusion of the working class:

> They no longer need songs because they no longer sing songs, they merely hum mindlessly. They hum what they hear at *cafés-concerts*. . . . We might as well admit it, the working class doesn't sing any more. . . . This is why the place for songs is more than ever in literature, like other poems and prestigious Iliads. . . . In happier days songs were for singing; with the creation of the monologue songs have become something to be read.[63]

It was because of the feeling that the working class no longer sang songs that the work of real and imitation *chansonniers* became increasingly and absurdly polarised around either literature or sexual stimulation. Against the background of such an exclusion two aims became apparent: firstly to educate the working class in a way which would require the mobilisation of all the pedagogic and cultural authorities.

> The Minister for Public Education must give schoolteachers every facility to organise singing sessions during periods of adult education so that the most popular and the most moral songs may be taught. . . . Societies for working-class education (the Teachers' League, the Philotechnic Association, etc.) must encourage and facilitate these moral and patriotic

songs by offering prizes. . . . The *Académie française* must deign to reserve one or two prizes for authors of the most moral songs.[64]

To assure that songs had a more lasting place 'they must be brought into working-class education. A selection of the best songs, updated every five years, should be circulated to primary schools.'[65]

The second aim was the combined defence of the moral and material interests of the *chansonniers* and the interests of the public their songs were intended to educate. This aim was to be assured by a trade union capable of defending its members' interests and, with the help of the state, of making the managers of the *cafés-concerts* introduce quality songs. If we disregard the specific preoccupation with moralisation which was to disappear completely as the marketing of culture placed increasing importance on quality, we will see a major preoccupation which henceforth was to occupy all working-class culture enterprises: in a situation where the working class no longer sang songs or went to the theatre, the state had to intervene more and more in order to assure that working-class entertainments were of high quality and that high-quality entertainments were attended by the working class. State education and the unions of any *artistes* worth their salt had to redeem the working-class public from the vulgarity of the market.

Soon, this trade union began to show signs of prosperity. On 26 February 1903 a certain A. Bargas wrote to the Head of the Division of Fine Arts to explain his problem. He wanted to join the union in order to get his songs performed on stage; but in order to join the union you had to belong to the SACEM (Société des Auteurs, Compositeurs et Editeurs de Musique), and to belong to the SACEM you had to have published six songs, but to get anything published you needed to have it performed on stage beforehand. . . . And to prove that he was a victim of a new monopoly, the dispirited song-writer sent an article which had appeared in the union journal and which emphasised the need to protect the militant profession of song-writing against infiltration by non-militant amateurs:

> The profession of *chansonnier* is burdened with people who cannot really be called professionals. They hinder progress because their momentary intrusion in our prosperous organisation halts its free movement. Things are slowed up and our profession, already hard enough as it is . . . becomes even harder because the true militants have to fight against other people who aren't militants at all.

It was right and proper that serious *chansonniers* for whom songwriting is a profession should unite and organise themselves. They do not exclude anyone through prejudice, but before they accept someone they must be given every guarantee. In this way *chansonniers* will keep their position and will defend their lives from the threat of intruders who were blocking the way forward.[66]

It was the end of a certain evolution: it was no longer important to regret the passing of the working-class choruses of yesteryear nor even to defend the right of working-class consumers to quality and decency. It was no longer a question of complaining about what people no longer sang but of being concerned about the fact that too many people were singing. Now there was a new type of barrier which completely reversed the activities which had taken place around the old ones: the amateur singer was no longer guilty of neglecting his work but of intruding upon the work of other people. Work and fight, but only within your own specialised area. But running parallel to this compartmentalisation which was rigidifying the free play of the old cultural minorities by enclosing people within their specific productive skills rather than placing them within the globality of having-to-be-a-worker, was a new and radical confusion: *professional* and *militant* had now become interchangeable terms. To produce and to struggle had become one and the same thing.

Of course this was merely a norm – and as always norms were for getting round or deflecting. . . . It did not mean that the ambiguous tactics of cultural promotion and class consciousness were going to disappear. The example offered by the biographies of many members of future labour parties will suffice to indicate that the cultural-promotional role of worker militancy had not died. The new forms for occupying free time (pedagogic, commercial, professional . . .) and for developing individuals and mass culture were opening a perspective of new contradictions between ways of escape and the conscience and organisation of class.

Notes

1 AN (Archives Nationales) F21 1338 (my italics).
2 Cf. A. Cottereau's article in *Autrement*, 'Dans la ville des enfants'.
3 Louis Reybaud: *Rapport sur la condition matérielle et morale des ouvriers qui vivent due travail de la soie* (Report on the material and moral condition of workers in the silk industry), Paris, 1860.
4 Cf. *Almanach de l'apprenti* (The Apprentice's Almanac), 1855.

5 Cf. on the Marseilles charity organisation *Le jeune ouvrier* (The Young Worker), 1856.

6 Cf. M. Le Prévost, *Chroniques du patronage*, Paris, 1862.

7 *Souvenirs des frères Lionnet*, Paris, 1886.

8 Such is the case of Louis Vinçard, *Mémoires épisodiques d'un vieux chansonnier saint-simonien* (Episodic Memoirs of an old Saint-Simonian *chansonnier*), Paris, 1878. As for *L'Atelier*, it asks in 1844: 'What town however small, what public profession however minute, what workshop however obscure has not its verse-monger and its scribbler?'

9 The day Gustave Leroy decided to make a living from his songs and had *La Lionne* lithographed, he distributed more than 20,000.

10 Cf. Gourdon de Genouillac, *Les refrains de la rue* (Melodies of the street), Paris, 1879.

11 Historic archives of the War Ministry, A 3669.

12 Cf. Marc Constantin, *Les cafés-concerts en 1866* (for Renard) and *L'echo des concerts*, August 1866 (for Brunet).

13 Jean-Claude Romand, *Confessions d'un malheureux* (Confessions of an Unfortunate Man), Paris, 1846.

14 Cf. the one-act plays collected in *L'Almanach de l'apprenti* and M. Le Prévost's various collections.

15 'Each theatre will be assigned a type of entertainment to which it will be obliged to restrict itself.' Decree of 8 June 1806, article 5.

16 For example, the Café d'Apollon which, as early as 1816, advertised vaudevilles and melodramas or in 1830 the Théâtre Lazari where live actors took over from puppets, and the *Funambules* which moved from tightrope dancing to vaudeville, etc. (Cf. Th. Faucher, *Histoire du boulevard du Temple depuis son origine jusqu'a sa démolition* (History of the boulevard du Temple from its Origins to its Demolition), Paris, 1836.

17 This was the case in *Marianne*, performed in October 1850, in which 'it was noticed that the authors blame the judiciary for a mistake which results in the heroine of the play being given a life sentence. Although the action refers to magistrates in a foreign country, it is nevertheless of a kind liable to present the judiciary in general as subject to error and consequently to diminish the respect one should have for its decisions.' F21 1045.

18 The Lionnet brothers say that they saw Frederick Lamaître in *Ruy Blas* 49 times. *Souvenirs des frères Lionnet*, Paris, 1886.

19 Cf. the note from the Head of the Department of Theatres, 4 December 1861: 'it is already very difficult for the inspectors to carry out their daily and nightly duties; nevertheless I shall try to ensure that now and again they visit suspect theatres and improve their surveillance. But it would be only right for them to be granted expenses for their cab fares.' F21 1045.

20 Cf. AN F18 1681.

21 F21 1331.

22 Cf. Levasseur, *Histoire des classes ouvrières et laborienses en France de 1789 à 1870* (History of the Working Classes from 1789 to 1870), vol. 2, p. 767.

23 The way this very mechanism of hierarchisation and specialisation has worked recently for pornography, for example, is well known.
24 AN F18 1681.
25 Cf. J. Rougerie, *Procès des communards*, ed. Julliard, 1964, p. 197.
26 This is why *L'Esprit du jour* (The Spirit of the Times) was censored in 1868. It denounces 'the noisy slang of posh people who show off/Doing the splits, dancing and having slap-up meals' and contrasts the age of the fatted ox and the bearded lady to the golden age 'when our grandfathers sang the *Marseillaise*'. F18 1680.
27 Cf. Beluze, *Lettres icariennes*, Paris, 1859.
28 F21 1338.
29 *Ibid.*
30 Cf. the songs of Eugene Baillet, *Le bataillon de l'avenir* (The Battalion of the Future) or *Place aux déshérités'* (Make Room For the Deprived), F18, 1861).
31 Cf. Alain Faure, *Paris, carême-prenant*, Hachette, 1977.
32 B. Gastineau, *Le Carnaval*, Paris, 1854.
33 Report by the musical instrument makers, Universal Exhibition of 1867.
34 *La chanson*, June 1878.
35 We are the lads from Belleville.
   People malign us by inventing
   Fantastic exploits
   Which usually make us laugh.
   We can walk with our heads held high.
   What is the aim of our phalanx?
   Sons of the chisel and the hammer,
   We have emblazoned on our flag:
   Long live industrial France!
   Peace and glory to the human race!
   With our hands we shatter the sword that kills.
   Freedom on its pedestal
   Takes the plough as emblem.
   Beneath the tricolour
   Let us drink, safe from strife.
   With flowers and corn in her hair
   The Republic is waiting for brave men
   To join her fraternal agapes.

   Refrain
   With the strength, determination and courage
   March onwards to progress, useful phalanx!
   There it was born, there it lives and there it will die,
   The Belleville Battalion.
                La Bataillon de Belleville, words by J. J. Evrard, 1879.
36 Cf. J. Rancière and P. Vauday, 'L'ouvrier sa femme et les machines' (The Worker, His Wife and Machines) in *Révoltés logiques*, no. 1, and the present collection, pp. 23–44.
37 In the hive where tomorrow
   The marvels of your labour will shine,

O workers, dear bees,
Bring new tools.
When we all make an effort
We can constantly create new things,
So let us replace every deadly gadget by a tool.
Up with everything productive – down with all that kills.
A rich, strong people is a working people.

Ernest Chébroux. *La Fête du travail.*

38 *La Chanson*, June 1878.

39 Here, for example, is how Jules Vallès talks about the fate of the popular street singer Théodore Leclerc and his fellows: 'They used to perform along the Champs-Elysées, where they paid 12.50 francs a month for the right to do so. That right has been withdrawn, and now they are only allowed to appear in *cafés-concerts*. They are employed for a season. For a fixed rate of . . . they have to appear, and they are also given the takings.'

40 Cf. Marc-Constantin, *Les Cafés-Concerts en 1866.*

41 *Mémoires de Theresa*, p. 14.

42 *La Chanson*, 29 May 1880.

43 *Le Tableau de Paris*, Paris 1932, no. 200.

44 *Ibid.*, p. 199.

45 *Ibid.*, p. 201.

46 Marc Constantin, *Les cafés-concerts à Paris en 1866.* It is clear: the promoters of the new leisure had an answer to this very 'circus games' argument. Their logic may seem to have been devised to suit the occasion, but as the new arts and leisures developed, widening the gap which separated them from their fairground or suburban origins, it became part and parcel of their prescribed propaganda. Before the days of cinema, this happened with sports. The beginning of the popularisation of sport, when Jules Simon's apparent discovery of the philosopher's stone of moral entertainment permitted him to link hands with Paschal Grousset the ex-Communard and the Marquis de Coubertin, were made possible on the basis of an aristocratic purification of working-class gestures. The paradigm of this gentrification was French boxing, effected by such masters as the Lecour brothers, who wrenched it from the fists of dockers and pimps to make it the pleasure of the nobility and the literate classes: 'M. Charles Lecour has turned this fencing for crooks, this *court de miracles* fisticuffs into an art, in one go he has elevated it to the level of English boxing. He has revised and improved these vulgar gestures, giving them elegance and grace.' This certificate of gentrification was granted in 1847 by Téophile (sic) Gautier, one of Lecour's best customers. Lecour (sic) was a singer of romances, and still belonged to the mixed culture, as did people like Bruneau, who worked in the slaughter-houses and who sang romances in between giving boxing lessons, or Auguste Masse, who sang Pierre Dupont songs while lifting 25 kg weights in either hand. This is the kind of exhibition which was to be disowned in the future in the name of the dignity of sport, as were cycling races in the context of fairgrounds, etc. This was to become

the meaning behind the struggle for *amateurism*. Charlemont, *La Boxe française*, Paris 1899.

47 Cf. Daniele Rancière, in *Politiques de l'habitat*, Corda, Paris, 1977.

48 However not all wealthy people were unanimously in favour of this eventuality, and more than one would have agreed with the sensible words of Darien's philanthropist: 'Nearly every miner in the Loire Basin has the little house and garden you've mentioned. Monsieur, no one could be more greedy or tyrannical than they are towards their employers. . . . On the other hand the miners in the north live in squalid hovels, eat rotten potatoes and fester in the most abject poverty; well, they never complain, or if they do it's so timidly that it's laughable.' *Le Voleur* (The Thief), 10/18, p. 203.

49 Cf. the discussions on this theme during Exhibitions and particularly the shoemakers' report at the 1862 Exhibition where their criticism of cut-price production – the working-class consumer included – and their defence of 'perfect shoemaking' takes on the proportions of a hymn to eternal beauty.

50 'People no longer looked forward to a Saturday night in the timeworn gods of the Théâtre de Belleville. Instead they would wander down to the cafe terrace on the corner of the *faubourg* du Temple and the avenue Parmentier where, for four sous each, they could have a drink and a smoke, watching and listening to the passing crowd.' R. Bizet, 'L'Age du zinc' (The Age of the Bar), *Le Touche-à-tout*, February 1911.

51 'Les théâtres populaires', *La Cité*, 6 April 1907.

52 Victor Fournel, *Ce qu'on voit dans les rues de Paris* (The Sights of the Paris Streets), Paris, 1958, p. 87.

53 *Philémon vieux de la vieille* (Philemon the Old Trooper), p. 87.

54 *Ibid.*, p. 118.

55 *Ibid.*, p. 114.

56 *Ibid.*, p. 115.

57 *Ibid.*, p. 119.

58 Cf. W. Benjamin, 'The Work of Art in the Age of Mechanical Reproduction' in *Illuminations*, Fontana, 1973.

59 *Gramophone Nouvelles*, August 1904.

60 *Ibid.*, March 1904.

61 *Ibid.*, June 1904.

62 Universal Exhibition of 1900, minutes of the proceedings of the *Congrès de la chanson*.

63 *Ibid.*

64 *Ibid.*

65 *Ibid.*

66 *Le Nouvelliste de concerts* (Concert Diary), 30 January 1903 (AN F21 1331).

Part II

Introduction

Alain Cottereau's preliminary study on Denis Poulot's *Le Sublime* takes a text whose quotation has become something of an unquestioning habit of French labour history, a ready source of easy categorisations, and reads it to produce both a knowledge of working-class life on the one hand, and an understanding of the constitutive elements and symptoms of bourgeois fantasies about the nature of that life. It was produced within the context of trade union education in France at the end of the 1970s, and edited in collaboration with some groups of workers. Like the first two texts, it disrupts the nostrums of the traditional left representations of working class virtues, suggesting that they are both specifically parodistic, politically unproductive and historically inadequate. It is probable that in the political conditions that have developed since its publication, its questioning has become, if anything, less acceptable. However two unexpected results of the publication were a sharp rise in the price of original editions of *Le Sublime*, from 40 francs to over 600 francs, and the renaming of a section of the place Léon Blum, in the heart of the 11th *arrondissement*, as the square Denis Poulot.

3
Denis Poulot's 'Le Sublime' – a preliminary study daily life and workers' resistance in Paris in 1870

ALAIN COTTEREAU

'Le Sublime' – a book with two meanings

Published a year before the Commune, Denis Poulot's book presents the manners of the Parisian workers of his time from an employer's point of view. At first sight it is an anti-worker pamphlet in which an ex-foreman who has set himself up in business denounces what he sees as the spread of workers' disobedience in Parisian industry. Workers who were allergic to the authority of their employers often ironically called themselves *sublime* workers. In their own words, the Sublime was 'a fine fellow, posh and always ready for action'. But according to Poulot, the Sublime was nothing more than 'a layabout, a ruffian, a drunkard' who leeched off 'the orderly, well-behaved worker'.

Poulot was not a writer, nor was he an economist or a theorist of 'philanthropy'. Far from adopting the pontificating tone and learned distance of the fashionable bourgeois thinkers of his time, he displays his experiences as foreman and company manager in a down-to-earth way, telling what he considers to be the most characteristic anecdotes, with a liberal sprinkling of invective and moralising epithets.

However, Poulot's aim was not simply to denounce, and he himself explains his intentions in the forewords to make the three successive editions of his book. He wishes to make a 'pathological diagnosis' of the 'question of labour and the workforce', using the workers in the Parisian mechanical engineering industry as examples. Thanks to his direct observations as a 'social empiricist', he claims to have revealed the main ill, 'Sublimism', and its main pathogenic factor, the 'Sublime', that is to say the worker who disobeys his employer and flaunts family morality. He prescribes a treatment based upon democratic reforms and the development of workers' associations.

If the book's interest was limited to the first-hand observations and the political programme of a 'left-wing' Parisian employer, it would constitute an historical document of certain interest to the

97

specialist and amateur historian, but of much more limited interest to other readers. It would have its place in the abundant literature of bourgeois and political memoirs, but one would be perfectly entitled to question how it comes to have strayed into a collection of *Actes et Mémoires du Peuple*.★

In fact, Denis Poulot's *Le Sublime* has another importance, well beyond that which its author intended to give it. When Poulot denounces his apprentices' insolence, when he collects details about undermining methods in his workshops, when he sketches domestic conflicts, he unwittingly reveals to us a whole universe of practices of working-class resistance which few documents permit us to see today.

Workshops and everyday working-class life in 1870: barely accessible realities

What is known nowadays of life inside workshops at the end of the Second Empire? What is known of methods of recruitment, of day-to-day confrontations, of internal discipline? What is known of the emotional and family life of working class women and men? The forewords of books about the Commune or the workers' movement often contain many details, but these are used merely to set the scene before proceeding to supposedly more serious considerations: Paris is said to lag behind in the domain of heavy industry, and is presented as a city of domestic and traditional light industries. This is used to explain a 'workers' mentality' typified by pride in craftsmanship, a spirit of independence, unruly workshops, self-taught culture and a tone of mockery; from it a certain 'Jacobin' style, attributed to the Paris Commune, also emerges.

But on what are these kind of considerations based? In fact, even today the historiography of the Parisian worker is in a paradoxical situation. We all know what an important place the Commune has in histories of the workers' movement. One might therefore suppose that there would be a great many studies on the everyday life of the period, the relations of industrial organisation, its labour market, its overall living conditions. But this is not so. We know much more about working-class life in London at that time. In France, most of our knowledge of working-class life still derives from the great social investigations undertaken by moralists, philanthropists and official economists. The only more recent work is G. Duveau's classic book *La Vie ouvrière en France sous le Second Empire*, published in 1946. But it is still very close to

★ A series of working-class writings edited by Maspéro/La Découverte.

the academic and bourgeois investigations carried out in the nineteenth century, and indeed it takes up their results, giving them a thematic classification. As for L. Chevalier's book *Classes laborieuses et classes dangereuses à Paris pendant la première moitié du XIXe siècle*, the police chiefs and moralists of that period would have felt quite at home with it.

On the other hand, when present-day workers ask for information, when, for example, militants on union or political training schemes seek a clearer understanding of the flesh-and-blood workers behind the epic of the Commune, historians and researchers have virtually no answers to give. Our information about such elementary questions as working methods, pay structures, the internal divisions and solidarities of different working-class milieux, the workers' own vision of their lives and destinies, is desperately scanty. This gives rise to a very natural doubt: can anything valid be said about the workers' movement or militant activities when no knowledge exists of their relationships with more 'ordinary' people?

It would be logical to address oneself to what workers themselves said at the end of the Second Empire, and indeed, a great many eye-witness accounts and collective texts have yet to be rescued from oblivion: newspapers, reports by workers' delegations, accounts of public meetings, etc. It is indispensable and urgent that these texts be brought to light, for they would certainly fill in many blank spaces. Nevertheless, they could not offer a complete answer; contemporary working-class texts were interested in necessary social transformations, and presented immediate demands. But more often than not they did not feel the need to offer detailed explanations of the concrete situations of the time, nor of the real motives which had led to the formulation of those immediate demands. All that was taken for granted. For example, no one has discovered a detailed description by a worker of pay scales. How was payment for work calculated? What function did modes of pay have? What rates of production did they demand and what divisions did they create? How did work gangs react, and how did they avoid the possible traps?

This is where the exceptional interest of Poulot's book lies: it introduces us to a level of reality which is difficult to approach by any other means. Through it we may glimpse the many trials of strength in everyday life, in and out of work time, which placed the working-class milieu in conflict with the rules of the economic game, the employers, the public authorities, and religious and 'moralising' forces.

We will return later to these daily trials of strength, completing them with additional information. But to begin with it will be

helpful to clarify how we may use Poulot's observations in order
to gain access to these day-to-day practices. We have already
remarked that his book has two meanings: on the one hand the
conscious meaning that Poulot the employer has put into it, and
on the other the workers' point of view and the methods of
resistance which become apparent behind the anti-worker polemic.

This second meaning develops through many pathways which
intersect and substantiate each other. Here we will concentrate
upon two, which strike us as being the most important:

1 Irony towards the employers' authority
2 Working-class practices concealed behind moral judgements in
   Poulot's typology of workers.

If they so desire, then readers can continue this deciphering for
themselves, in particular by following a third pathway – namely
the slang used by the Sublimes. Clearly, the manufacturer's voice
of slang terms is not an innocent one. The way this living
language is structured, the choice of images, the rules of usage, all
suggest a world view, a sense of distance from events, power,
destiny and death. Thus further analysis of this slang should lead
us to consider what the specific world of imagination and dreams
of the workers' milieu could have been.[1]

Irony towards the employers' authority

In hindsight, *Le Sublime* becomes a work full of more or less
involuntary humour. Every time Poulot appeals to the reader,
every time he deplores the injustice and ingratitude of the workers
towards the unfortunate employers, he unwittingly reveals
something quite different: confronted by workers' resistance,
most of the attempts at 'moralising the people' had become a vast
ironic, mockery. At times even Poulot himself admits the irony of
certain situations, as in this anecdote in the chapter on apprentices:

> An employer had entrusted the task of making a mortise in a
> long thin pulley to a young apprentice who was an avid
> theatre-goer. Thinking no doubt of the last scene in *Antony*,
> which he had seen the previous evening, he broke the fragile
> pulley, and the employer, extremely annoyed, admonished him
> roundly. The lad took a step backwards and said in a tragic
> voice: 'She resisted me, so I killed her.' The employer could
> not help laughing.

But more often than not it is Poulot who adopts the tragic
tone, and quite without humour, to accumulate claims of the
employers' impotence in many working and non-working

situations. Immediately after the anecdote quoted above, he goes on to say:

> It is alright when they are amusing. But just listen to this apprentice's conversation. . . .
> Doesn't it remind you of someone who has just been let out of the Toulon hulks?. . . . It is impossible to expect any other results in Paris when you know that sixty per cent of workers are Sublimes.
> Sublimism is a graft which always takes well on young subjects. It is like a fluid, it will always penetrate no matter how careful certain conscientious employers may be; in the end the apprentices nearly always contract this leprosy.

Thus the workers' irony towards their employers can sometimes be quite transparent in the text. In the chapter on 'Sublimes and Their Tricks', for example, there is a direct description of collective tactics in the workshop. We can still almost hear the successful workers laughing at their 'monkey' over Poulot's shoulders, so to speak. Take the case of the description of 'undermining' methods, for example. Poulot begins by presenting himself as the victim, and calls upon the reader's sense of justice:

> Just listen to these blackmailing tricks, and tell me if you call it justice.
> You agree with several *compagnons* on the price for the making or the assembly of a machine or several parts. Everything is agreed, and the work may be three-quarters finished, but if you are dealing with Sublimes who want to exploit the situation, this is how they will do it.
> If they know, for example, that you are late for delivery and have received a formal demand to supply the work, the next day half the work gang will not turn up.

And Poulot explains that the employer has no alternative but to agree in writing to a pay rise. The epilogue to all this is intended to make the reader even more indignant: 'After that they have a prize booze-up in the "monkey's" honour, and stuff themselves sick. In the *assommoirs* they are considered wicked and plucky.'
With such evident irony at the employers' authority, the simplest and most direct thing to do would seem to be to interpret this publication in terms of daily trials of strength. The book is peppered with anecdotes of this kind.

The reconstitution of working-class practices through Poulot's moral judgements

But generally the dual meaning is not so clear, and working-class practices are not immediately apparent. The overall text is dominated by Poulot's moral judgements, and this is as far as many readers will have penetrated the book. It sketches good and bad types of workers. On the good side, there are varieties of 'Workers' as such, who conform to Poulot's desires. On the bad side, there are varieties of 'Sublimes'. Such a portrait gallery could well seem very traditional. To draw characters and types and to proceed to calculate their degrees of conformity with 'the' moral norm is one of the most ancient procedures known. Literature about the working classes has not avoided this genre, quite the reverse. Since the sixteenth century at least, judgements on workers have established their system of moral measurement by individual profiles or by profession, using the same yardstick as Poulot:

— the degree of drunkenness or sobriety
— the degree of laziness or industriousness
— the degree of conformity to the bourgeois family model
— the degree of violence between *compagnons*.[2]

Naturally, in these moralist and philosophical enquiries the same types always get the same good or bad assessments: the industrious worker is always sober, respectful of family morality and uninvolved with worker agitation. On the other hand, all the 'vices' are systematically attributed to the bad types. Needless to say, in every case these enquiries into the 'working-class conditions' tell us more about the imaginary vision of the philanthropists than about the actual life of the workers.

A superficial reading of the types as presented by Poulot reveals the same moral simplism. Levasseur, who is recognised as being the most competent historian of nineteenth-century working-class life, saw *Le Sublime* as nothing more than a denunciation of the laziness and immorality of the majority of Parisian workers. He found it exaggerated, and used his own experience of investigating several Parisian workshops to present a counter-argument: 'I too visited some workshops in Paris at that time, and I could not agree that the Sublimes constituted more than fifty per cent of the wage-earning classes in Paris.'[3] (Poulot says sixty per cent.)

At a later date G. Duveau takes up and expands Levasseur's documentation, but in turn he becomes involved in a dialogue with economists, philanthropists and bureaucrats of the time, and if he devotes an important place to *Le Sublime*, it is on the basis of a uni-dimensional, single reading of the text. It is significant that he presents its typology in the sub-chapter on alcoholism. The perfect type, the 'True Worker' is supposedly characterised by his sobriety. The leaders of the Sublimes 'were not lacking in education or learning'. As for the more average type of Sublime, for these he uses Poulot's terminology, describing them as manifesting 'dirty, brutal, coarse, ignorant, instinctive and bestial Sublimism'.[4]

Poulot versus the social sciences of his time: the labouring classes and the 'dangerous classes' are not synonymous

However, even on the level of a superficial reading of Poulot, Duveau should have noticed an important point on which this left-wing employer diverges from philanthropic and criminological tradition, namely that he is careful not to confuse the labour classes with the 'dangerous' classes. In academic tradition, the ritual question about manners was to ask what were the crimes committed by workers, by different trades, and by the poor in general. Inevitably this question degenerated through a series of sophistries into a consideration of the 'vicious' or 'pathological' nature of the milieux in which the crimes were committed. This mechanism was fed by administrative statistics on crimes and misdemeanours. The line of reasoning was based on the assumption that apprehended crimes represented the total number of crimes committed. Defence and prosecution speeches in the criminal courts were echoed by the media (newspapers, novels, songs, theatres and tavern entertainments), thus maintaining a permanent statement of anti-worker racism, by attributing individual crimes to a scapegoat group singled out by dominant prejudices. Thus 'criminality' was seen as a kind of natural characteristic of this specific group. Instead of asking why the police repression was directed towards certain social categories rather than others, criminologists asked why certain social groups attacked 'honest people' more than other groups did. Naturally, particularly in towns, the working classes were the main target of police surveillance, and therefore they appeared to be the most dangerous group.[5]

While from 1867–70 onwards the newspapers of the 'friend of law and order' were disseminating widely the equation between the working classes and the criminal, dissolute and infectious classes, Poulot joined forces with the militant socialists to denounce this technique of confusion, be it by the use of police in certain milieux for anti-worker provocation, or through the miserablist pleas of lawyers attributing crimes to the fatality of the working-class condition.

For Poulot, the Parisian manufacturer, the use of statistics on 'criminality' to prove a supposed urban pathology was also without foundation, since an explanation should have been sought in the differences between the system of repression in large cities

Characteristics of Parisian workers according to Poulot's

	True Workers	Workers	Mixed Workers
'Laziness' or 'Industriousness'	*According to Poulot, they are 'the best types of all, the elite, conscientious in their work'* Skilful workers, but not always as capable as Sublimes. They put up with anything from their employers to get promoted. 'If it's night work, some repair job, nothing will hold him back, neither his mates, his relatives nor his friends.' They are willing to work Sundays, and always come in on Mondays.	*In Poulot's estimation, 'very hard-working. You can tell he likes to graft.'* An acceptable level of skill, no more than that. They are willing to work Sundays, and always come in on Mondays. Principal incentive: making money.	*In Poulot's eyes 'he is weaker' than the first two types. 'He is led too easily by others.'* They are the least skilful, and could never act as chargehand. They take part in undermine if the rest of the gang does. Sometimes they 'observe Holy Monday' with the rest of their gang.
Alcohol and 'Drunkenness'	*They are of exemplary sobriety.* They never get drunk. When faced with problems 'he resigns himself to his misfortune. He finds consolation in his work.' They stand aloof from the camaraderie of the workshop, and are rejected by their peers.	*'A sound fellow, but rather less careful than the True Worker.'* They might have a few drinks at home of a Sunday, but they rarely go drinking with their fellow guild members from the workshop, as their wives forbid it.	A weak character, easily led on by his compagnons. They have a drink more frequently, both at family celebrations and out with their *compagnons* from the workshop. They get drunk on Saturday pay days, Monday mornings and at workshop celebrations (marriages, funerals, successful pay claims).

descriptions. (Poulot's moral judgements are in italic.)

Simple Sublimes	True Sublimes	Sons of God	Sublime of Sublimes
'*Sublimes inevitably sink to a life of drinking in wine shops, led on by laziness and intemperance.*' Skilful workers, capable of being chargehands. 'Undermining the boss is not just a habit, it's a duty. As long as a Sublime has any money, he won't bother working.' They leave the workshop rather than submit to over-strict regulations. They have from three to five different employers per year. They refuse to do night work or to work on Sundays, and always observe Holy Monday.	'*He takes a disgustingly cynical pride in his vice and immorality. Laziness, showing-off and piss-artistry are all they're good for.*' They have been top workers, exceptionally skilful. They are still indispensable, which enables them to defy their employer without fear of retaliation. They earn their living by doing a three-and-a-half day week. 'You won't catch him dying of hard work.'	'*A very good worker.*' The one thing Poulot deplores is their political fervour. These are the best equipped workers for being chargehand. They have 'a big influence on the others; you might say he is the soul of the workshop.' They organise collective resistance to the employers. They organise undermine operations. They can go so far as to get signed on simply to get even with a foreman or perhaps to 'put the monkey (boss) in his place'.	'*The elite category.*' But in Poulot's view '*he won't sacrifice himself in order to succeed*'. In the engineering industry they work on the clerical side; in other industries they are found above all doing outwork. They cannot bear being supervised by an employer. They are the 'prophets' of resistance in the workshops, but they only confront the employers through the intermediary of the Sons of God.
'*The Sublime inevitably sinks to a life of drinking in wine shops, led on by laziness and intemperance.*' They get drunk at least once a fortnight, of a Saturday, a Monday or on a 'binge' with their mates from the workshop. They usually spend Sundays at home.	*Poulot sees these as drunkards wallowing in degradation. 'He does more work at the bar than in the workshop.*' The only real alcoholics in the typology. Both in and out of work, they survive on neat spirits.	*Poulot considers that they have sunk as low as the True Sublimes, not through a passion for alcohol, but through political fervour.* They rarely get drunk, except at family celebrations or among friends. They have a drink in the company of their fellows only in order to participate in collective discussions. So at the very most they get tipsy with their mates from work or at a political 'senate'.	

continued

	True Workers	Workers	Mixed Workers
Reconstruction of family relationships			
Before regular cohabitation	They 'prefer street-walkers – (professional prostitutes) – to teaming up on a regular basis. They wouldn't like to debauch any nice young innocent girls and that way they have a clean conscience'.	They team up with laundry maids, chambermaids, children's nannies . . . In this way the woman avoids the restrictions of living in at work or paying a lot of money for lodgings.	Bachelors living in furnished accommodation. Sometimes they buy their own furniture, but this is a big financial gamble. They make do with 'having affairs'.
Settled down	They get married without having previously cohabited.	They finally abandon their sleeping companion and set out to find a good housewife back home.	Alternatively they marry a firm-handed housewife, or pass on into Sublimism.
Relative extent of couple's resources	The most comfortably off. They have savings, and belong to friendly societies, from which they expel the Sublimes: the wife is often a small shopkeeper or works as a *concierge*.	They often have a little money in advance and are able to pay their debts. The wife is often a small shopkeeper or works as a *concierge*.	They have permanent difficulty in making ends meet.
Relationships between couples	They are the head of the household. For them, women are naturally inferior: 'You're like an old woman.' They keep their private lives and their lives in the workshop strictly separate. They are jealous and make sure their wives keep well away from the men they work with.	The wife holds the domestic purse-strings. Called the 'bourgeoisie', and is usually from the country. Sublimes say that 'she has turned the Civil Code inside-out'. If need be she lectures her husband, and blames him for everything. She mixes with her husband's fellow	The 'bourgeoisie' is 'an old battleaxe' who intimidates her husband. She 'holds the purse strings'. Her dominant position prevents the Mixed Worker from passing over into Sublimism.

Simple Sublimes	True Sublimes	Sons of God	Sublime of Sublimes
Either they are bachelors 'living in squalid lodgings. They like it, because nobody preaches to them', or they live with someone.	They remain emotionally unattached, whether they live alone or with a woman.	They play at don Juan until the age of thirty-five or forty. 'A family would be too much of a tie.' They are skilled at seducing the wives and daughters of the men in their gang.	They play at don Juan until the age of thirty-five or forty. They seduce women from all walks of life.
They set up home and often get married to raise a family and provide for old age.	They set up home, with or without getting married, to raise a family and provide for old age.	They settle down late, to raise a family and provide for old age. The woman has a job. The couple frequently remain unmarried.	They settle down very late to raise a family and provide for old age. The wife is a cook, a *concierge*, etc. The couple do not get married.
Permanent problems. Budget balanced from day to day. Frequently in debt. Not paying up is seen as a virtue. The companion usually has a job.	Always 'stony broke'. Resources always below the minimum needed for the up-keep of a family. The companion usually has a job.	They have fewer financial problems than Sublimes, but it is a matter of principle to them to avoid paying their debts to shopkeepers and landlords.	(No problems indicated).
If the wife is the 'bourgeoise' in the household, and has no paid employment, then periodically conflicts erupt: sometimes a Sublime will beat his wife, or get beaten up by her, and every so often when he notices the poverty of the household he feels guilty about not earning enough. If the wife has come	If the companion is not a 'Sublime' then there are permanent dramas and trials of strength. She is frequently battered by her drunken, jealous husband. 'If it weren't for the children, she'd leave him.' If the companion is a 'Sublime' then the couple manage to get along together. Fights on pay-days are not serious. If		Once they are past their prime, their wives take over and 'wear the trousers'.

continued

	True Workers	Workers	Mixed Workers
		compagnons from the workshop on Saturday pay-days, so as to keep him under control.	
Relationships with children	The fathers educate the children themselves. They want their sons to become good workers, with or without the mothers' approval.	The mother educates the children, along the lines of dominant morality. The father is supportive.	'He loves his children, but it's his "bourgeoisie" who takes care of them; he hasn't the time, and in any case, he can't be bothered.'

Links with the political scene

	True Workers	Workers	Mixed Workers
Opinions and political role	'Real democrats'. Read the newspapers of the (bourgeois) republican opposition. They are against the Empire and against socialism. They share with Proudhon the 'reasonable hope	They 'don't really understand' the socialist speeches at public meetings, and disapprove of the most advanced ideas.	They follow the political ideas of the 'Sons of God' and read what the 'Sons of God' recommend. 'If you (the employer) are arguing with one of them, and he gets lost for words, he will say

Simple Sublimes	True Sublimes	Sons of God	Sublime of Sublimes
straight up from the country and has no income, she is often a 'martyr' to her husband, relying on charitable organisations. If the companion goes out to work, she is often a 'Sublime': she is united with her husband in his resistance to exploitation. They both mix with each other's work mates.	questioned by an employer, the companion will say 'Oh, it's nothing, we just had a bit of a fight last night'. Sometimes when there is no food in the house, the companion goes 'soliciting', especially when the rent is due. Everyone may look down on her for doing so, but she is proud to be able to feed her children, her aged parents or any dependant invalided by a work accident from the pocket of an exploiter or small employer.		
The father encourages the children's freedom with or without the mother's approval, and this includes sexual freedom.	The mother takes care of the children. When there is a disagreement, they use the children's interests as an argument against those of the father.	The parents encourage their children to be free and independent. They urge them to take part in 'the emancipation of the working classes'.	
'On Saturday pay-days they make socialist remarks . . . "Yea, it's true, they exploit us like cattle." Their tyrants are the boss and the landlord – exploiters and thieves.'	'The True Sublime rarely talks politics, and rarely reads, except for trivial items in the newspaper; on the other hand they listen carefully when read to, and are particularly attentive when	'They read the paper every day and comment upon the political scene. They are nearly always public speakers . . . with a deep, meditative, inspired air. . . . When they talk	They are 'more circumspect', they 'are men of principle; they produce theories, political theories, economic theories, social theories . . . They are the great leaders of the working-class, and

continued

	True Workers	Workers	Mixed Workers
	of property' and look favourably on the association of capital and labour.		"Look, so-and-so, a Sublime of Sublimes, will explain what I mean".'
Public meetings	They rarely go to public meetings. 'They dislike Utopias.' They see them as working-class demagogy.	Go 'fairly frequently to public meetings and applaud the tribunes.'	He 'rarely misses' public meetings and applauds the tribunes.
If there were a social explosion . . .	If the Republic were attacked by the socialists, they would fight for it		

If every worker were like these three types – we could avoid the upheavals which the future threatens. But the way things are, the Workers and the Mixed Workers follow the socialists.

Simple Sublimes	True Sublimes	Sons of God	Sublime of Sublimes
	'their old campaign comrade, a Son of God, has some comments to make.'	politics, the others listen as though to an oracle. They always seem to be dreaming up solutions to socialist problems'. They have read all the socialists but dislike Proudhon. In the labour movement, they are the 'executives' of working-class power.	mix with politicians and influential people. . . . They are introduced in parliament. They are prophets, scientists, and they legislate the social problems.'
They go to public meetings 'now and again'. 'They sit next to their friends, the Sons of God.'	He 'never goes to public meetings. "It's nothing to do with me." '	They 'never miss public meetings or hustings.'	In public meetings, their speeches gain the widest attention.
		'The Son of God has the makings of a martyr.'	They study the 'social commune'. If there was a republican government, they would attack it.

En masse the Sublimes are as likely to produce heroes as the Vandals were.

and the rest of the country, and in the movements of individuals from one to the other brought about by these differences.

According to him, there were no more criminals 'mixed in with the work force' than there were within other classes of society. What was needed was a differential way of calculating individual repression. Rejecting the equations of the philanthropists and the conservative journalists, he attacked the presence of outlaws in workshops 'because thefts committed in workshops cast unjust suspicions upon the workers and the Sublimes of the workshops'. In opposition to anti-worker racism he in fact adopted an individual racism against the 'born criminal' or the perverted delinquent who had been socially blighted, and those who, by their first offence, had been clothed with a second nature. This line of reasoning results from a defence mechanism which Poulot shared with the working-class milieu, and which has by no means disappeared.

The real practices hidden behind judgements of 'laziness' and 'drunkenness'

Let us turn then to the seven other types of worker, who are also judged as being either good or bad. But, to go beyond these moral judgements, we need a method with which to decipher them. The principle is simple: to identify carefully the behaviour patterns of the workers which Poulot uses to back up his judgements. From that point on we will perceive completely new dimensions which will allow us to contradict the book's explicit judgements.

For example, take the judgements of laziness or industriousness. For the True Worker, endowed with every quality, Poulot is full of praise: he is the 'best type of all', the 'honourable type', 'conscientious in his work' and 'who never gets drunk'. But let us set aside the good points in order to retrieve the real information about the conduct of the True Worker in terms of his work and drinking habits. He works for three hundred days a year, which is not much more than the average for Paris. He makes a good chargehand, but he is not always as skilful as the Sublimes. On the other hand his work rates are much faster. He is willing to do night work and come in on Sundays when his employer asks him. 'If it's night work, some repair job, nothing will hold him back, neither his mates, his relatives nor his friends'. Outside of the hours he is paid to work, he still finds time to invent things.

Thus, when we collate all the concrete information scattered throughout the book, the profile we observe, rather than being 'industrious', is much more that of a veritable 'workaholic'. This attitude would scarcely be comprehensible if Poulot himself did not happen to give an explanation for it. The True Worker knows 'that it is to his advantage to win the confidence of a conscientious employer who will appreciate his efforts and trust him'. In other words the True Workers are aspiring foremen, and are the equivalent of what present-day factory workers might call 'arse-lickers'. If they are willing to work themselves to death it is in the hope of having to work less later, if the employer so wills it.

It is obvious here that Poulot is remembering his own beginnings in the Gouin company (one of the largest mechanical engineering firms in Paris). He mentions the twenty other chargehands in that firm who became foremen and then managers. He himself drew up these statistics (and in fact the numbers are very small in proportion to the total work force of several thousand) and he frequently used them as examples during his period of office as President of the Friendly Association of Former Students of the Schools of Arts and Crafts.

Once we have identified some of the actual behaviour patterns of the True Workers we can begin to establish an exact translation of them from a worker's point of view. Here, for example, is how the True Workers 'flatter' the foreman or become foremen themselves, as described by the nailmakers' delegation at the 1867 Universal Exhibition in a collective text addressed both to their workshop *compagnons* and the public authorities.

> The contractor . . . recruits the help of foremen who forget that they come from the great family of the workers and hide their laziness behind a title which unfortunately attracts flatterers, who grovel to win their favour and who drag us down even farther into poverty; we say forthwith that these flatterers are despicable, unworthy of any consideration whatsoever, and that we ought to throw them out of our workshops and never permit them to set foot in them again. They are completely devoted to the interests of their bosses. They impose pay cuts on their subordinates so that they are almost working for nothing. We might accept it if these pay cuts were only temporary and only for as long as the circumstances demanded; but they've become established as the norm.

The True Workers' exemplary sobriety also takes on a new meaning when we decipher it in this way. In the case of misfortune, illness or accident, when the True Worker finds himself in dire economic straits, rather than turning to drink he 'swallows down his sadness': 'He is not the kind to make a fuss

about his misfortunes'. He neither wants nor can count on any help
from his *compagnons*, because unlike most workers he rarely makes
social links 'he has few friends', and he is rejected for being a
'bootlicker'. And so 'he finds consolation for the bitterness of his
situation in work'. In other words, for the True Worker, work
has become a drug, a substitute for alcohol. He is a bonus for
those employers who are crafty enough to channel the energy of
suffering, and to exploit the alternating forces of joy and anger in
their employees. Moreover, unlike alcohol in the *compagnon* gangs,
the True Worker's labours are an a-social drug, a drug of loneliness
which rejects communication and results in self-punishment.

This deciphering of judgements about industriousness at work
can also be applied to the six other types of worker. We have
summed up and collated the results in the table. At the top of
each, Poulot's moral judgements, and, thereafter, the corres-
ponding behaviour patterns, reorganised from the information
scattered throughout the book.

In every case, these patterns of behaviour alter the meaning of
Poulot's moral judgements completely. The degree of 'laziness'
reveals several distinct dimensions. Above all the typology can be
seen as a means of grading the degree of disobedience shown to
employers. After the True Worker, all too rare in Poulot's
estimation, we are presented with a progression of types who are
not always prepared to do what they are told, the Worker and the
Mixed Worker. From that point disobedience escalates. The
Simple Sublimes are like the infantry of resistance: for them
'undermining the boss is a duty' and they only give in
provisionally when they are 'stony broke'. The True Sublime's
resistance makes him like an individualistic *franc tireur*, skilful and
invulnerable.

Finally we have what the police and employers call 'the
ringleaders'. These are termed Sublimes of God and fall into two
categories: Sons of God and Sublimes of Sublimes. In fact, these
are the people that the labour movement was just beginning to
call 'militants'. But the word 'militant' should not mislead us. At
the present time, rightly or wrongly, it connotes a politicised
splinter group within a larger organisation whose aim is to
'enlighten' or 'agitate' the masses. Poulot's description implies
relationships of a quite different nature.

Of course the employers themselves would certainly have liked
to think that the ringleaders were different from the majority, and
that it was possible to bring this majority, which it was thought
had been led on and misled by propagandists, back to 'a decent
attitude'. But to Poulot's despair he knows that the relationship

goes much deeper than this. The Sublimes of God share a way of being common to the working-class milieu as a whole. They merely carry out a specific function, within certain *collective practices of resistance*. If they are sacked, others will be found in the workshop to take their place. Despite the rancorous accusations which Poulot accumulates against the Sons of God and the Sublimes of Sublimes in the two chapters about them, the situations described throughout the book leave us in no doubt about it. The Sons of God form the executive of the worker counter-power within the workshop. The Sublimes of Sublimes are the 'prophets' of resistance and the destiny of the working class. In them most workers recognise an expression of their own attitudes. They are more eloquent than most, and are designated as 'spokesmen', in the most literal meaning of the word. Poulot admits that even the Mixed Workers see them as having this function: 'If you are arguing with one of them,' he says, 'and he gets lost for words, he will say "Look, so-and-so, a Sublime of Sublimes, will explain what I mean." '

The extent of resistance is based upon the skilfulness of specific professions and individuals. The Sublimes are always the most skilful. Only an ideal True Worker could rival the Sons of God. But in practice the latter are much better as chargehands. In Poulot's eyes it is self-evident that 'having a skill' is not a specific thing, or a characteristic which could be put on an individual's card. It is the expression of a power relationship within the labour market.

On a superficial and moralist reading of *Le Sublime*, drunkenness is the book's major concern. But a deciphering of the real drinking practices will show up the emptiness of this idea, even if we keep strictly to the descriptions given. The only real alcoholics are the True Sublimes. For them, alcohol is part of their life rhythm, both in and out of the workshop. In describing them, Poulot had above all foundry workers in mind. For this work, alcohol could provide the main statement for the intense, spasmodic efforts needed to keep up the rhythm of the casting or smelting processes. Poulot himself gives examples of the kind of metabolic bond between the furnace and the energy of the founder. Similar analyses could have been made of glass-workers and indeed of all workers who were driven to take alcohol by the specific organisation of their work.[6]

Apart from this, the question of alcohol is only meaningful in the minds of the bourgeoisie and the social reformers as a form of anti-working racism. But in the lives of the workers of the time no such question could be posed. Alcohol simply accompanied a series of different practices of very different meanings. It could be a basic form of nourishment. It was a part of family celebrations. It helped to combat physical fatigue and to stimulate bursts of energy, be they for work or sexual activity. It accompanied discussions amongst *compagnons*. It was taken to celebrate subcontract agreements, recruitment for jobs, or workshop outings.

If we still wish to discover a common ground for the question of alcohol, we may only do so in the negative, by opposition to the demands of the employers. The real target was not new, and is still with us today: in order to gain the maximum profit from the work force, employers must monopolise their workers' energy output. They must stop them from mobilising their energy in other directions. Outside the workshop, keeping body and family together are the only types of effort to be tolerated. But, beyond the workshop and family commitment, the employers cannot allow more than a minimal amount of time for rest and recuperation. This is the real source of the employers' anti-alcohol stance. Alcohol in itself is not attacked. The criterion is elsewhere. In *Le Sublime*, immorality is measured in exact proportion to the amount of time the workers take away from their paid employment and their family commitments. This leads to the adoption of the anti-alcohol stance. It is tolerated at home of a Sunday, 'at the lass's first communion' and at similar family celebrations. But 'Holy Mondays' and its libations is a challenge to the orderly working of industry. It is a kind of intermittent mutiny at which, to the despair of the employers, the workers recharge their batteries.

Workers' companions caught between pressures from the employers and pressures from their man

Through personal experience Poulot had few problems in knowing and understanding the life of male workers. But when it comes to his workers' wives, and their household lifestyles, it becomes much more problematic to decipher the message. Poulot adopts a completely misogynistic stance. He shares the accepted bourgeois view of the 'natural' vocation of 'womankind': wife and mother, the decorative little housewife. More specifically in the context of the working-class milieu, his portrait of the True Worker reveals his idealised conception of man-woman relationships. The True Worker is resplendent with all those domestic virtues which Poulot would like to see shared by the workforce as a whole. Certainly, the True Worker 'loves his wife and respects her', but we need to realise what this respect conceals. If an important decision needs to be taken the husband need only say 'you're only a woman' for his view to prevail. And in case the reader is still in the dark, Poulot attributes the True Worker with an observation whose 'common sense' contradicts theories circulated at public meetings: 'And just think that some men actually claim that women are as intelligent as men!'

Pressures from the employers on their workers' 'bourgeoises'

If it were only Poulot's misogyny which confused the issue, the behaviour patterns of the working-class couple would not be too difficult to reconstruct, and present-day feminism has begun to stimulate a certain awareness in that direction. But his book observes another much more discreet logic: Paris employers were committed to a strategy of alliance with workers' wives against their men. This basic principle, which is too frequently over-looked, is the key to an understanding of family life at that time.

With the development of an industrial wage-earning class, the interests of the employer and of the housewife might be seen to converge. We could sum up the dominant pressure as follows: *the more a working husband regularly devotes most of his time to subjecting himself to the production of value, the more he will be of value to his wife*. From that point on employers can play upon conflict between couples for their own profit. Should a husband wish to take a rest, to cut down on work or resist the discipline of the workshop, an employer can rely on the housewife to employ 'the disciplines of hunger' in order to force her husband to devote all his energy towards earning the family wages.[7]

Nevertheless, to talk of an employers' strategy does not imply that this strategy worked successfully. The attempts to form alliances between employers and workers' wives gave rise to counter-pressures from the working-class milieu. This reaction is a familiar one in strike situations. When there is a conflict between the bosses and the male employees, the result depends in part on the wives, and whether they urge their men to go back to work to avoid an empty larder, or whether the movement can give them the means to take up battle alongside the strikers.

But counter-pressures from the working-class milieu can also operate, in a less perceptible manner, in everyday life. Poulot's habit of letting his pen run freely gives us a useful if involuntary example of this. First he describes one of the tricks used by employers, which he finds exemplary. Then he reveals the way in which the working-class milieu is liable to turn it to his own advantage.

In several well-organised businesses, a worker's pay is
accompanied by a little payslip with his name, the date and the

amount earned. His wife is aware of the procedure, and will ask for the payslip, which will often have been lost or altered. If so, she will treat him like a naughty boy, confiscating his money for the next fortnight.

(More explicitly, the wives' blackmail could be translated thus: 'When you give me your pay, I want an unspoiled payslip, otherwise I'll keep every penny of it.')

If the example ended there, we would have an illustration of a successful alliance between the employers and their employees' 'bourgeoises'. The men would have found themselves caught between pressures from both sides to force them to observe discipline and regularity at work. But without regard for coherence, Poulot continues as follows:

And so when she has all the pay, she accompanies her man to the wine shop, along with the children, and they have a meal and spend the evening there. She hears him slagging the boss, the foreman and his crowd, or speaking up for a friend who happens to be there. In point of fact, the wine shops are full of families like that of a Saturday evening.

Thus everything is back in the melting pot, and the weapon provided by the payslip has been turned back against the people who invented it. By enticing wives to join in on workshop outings of guild members of a Saturday night, employers intended to exploit domestic conflicts to their own profit. Instead they encouraged a 'familiarity' between their workers' families. In the wine shops on pay days, even the women and children would be made to see the boss as nothing more than an exploiter. And the greatest irony of this is that everyone would drink, sacrificing the first fruit of work, flouting the requirement to maintain the family. In this day and age, such an affirmation of freedom – spending one's money how and when one pleases – would scarcely be tolerated on the part of 'economically weak' families. Such behaviour would be considered unacceptable to many welfare officers, and might well result in a care order.

The strategy adopted by Paris employers towards working-class households implies a very restricting view of family relationships. Bosses tended to consider their employees' wives as the victims of individuals they themselves were unable to get the better of. Their own contacts with the wives in their role as employers or administrators of welfare organisations helped to promote this view, since it always presented them with penniless mothers who came pleading for charity. To be judged 'worthy of

attention' the wives' most effective tactic would be to act as
though their husbands had victimised them, regardless of what
they really felt. The employers were only too happy to believe
them: it served to reinforce and legitimise their own behaviour.
Furthermore, in the case of an industrial accident, it was cheaper
to give a wife some money out of charity than to be ordered
legally to pay damages and interest. It was of no consequence to
them if subsequently the wives laughed at them and spread tales
about how they took the mickey out of them.

It is remarkable that the employers of that time should adopt
two conflicting responses to what the social authorities call
'malingering'. In the case of accidents at work, the employers,
along with their insurance companies and their doctors, will
always suspect a put-up job to extract money from them (Poulot
himself participates in this indoctrination in the chapter 'the
sublimes and their tricks', where he tells an anecdote about a fake
accident, but fails to discuss genuine accidents as such). On the
other hand, when wives come to plead with employers, then their
attitude changes completely, and any suspicion of malingering
becomes unacceptable. In their practical writings, employers and
charitable organisations are no longer prepared to doubt the
sincerity of the feelings which they see paraded. It is as though the
only important thing is to get the wives to condemn the male
workers' behaviour, and to show 'decent feelings' towards the
'firm's men'.

On the surface, the explicit comments made in *Le Sublime* offer
us a faithful reflection of this attitude on the part of the employers.
The men are presented as being guilty of all the shortcomings in
their household, of loss of earnings, violence and drunkenness.
Apparently their wives are innocent victims, upholding the
virtues of order, thrift and cleanliness. In particular, Sublimes'
wives are seen as having the following alternative: either to spend
their lives protecting their domestic virtue, or, after a more or less
lengthy struggle, to succumb and become 'sublimised' themselves. In this way an inversion of the myth of original sin is used
to describe working–class couples: the worker is the first to taste
the fruits of resistance to the capitalist system. Then he drags his
wife down with him. We can sum up this bourgeois perception of
relationship within the proletarian household as follows: *woman as
martyr to the worker*.

'Bourgeoise' wives and 'Sublime' wives: different ways of getting by

If, however, we disregard the question of moral guilt and
concentrate on the employers' strategy and the way it was

derided, our deciphering of domestic life will reveal another meaning. The fate of wives is much more complex than it would seem at first, and a host of contradictory details may be observed.

To begin with, workers' companions were not as helpless as the employers, in their eagerness to bring moral support, would have liked to believe. Probably there really were women martyrised by drunken husbands, just like the ones so smugly described by the employers and philanthropists and there is no point in denying it. But we should not reduce every single drama, conflict and family 'scene' to this one model. Throughout the book, situations are sketched which suggest that women had a range of effective means of defence. The sexual strike is referred to several times, under the cover of argot, as a by no means unusual weapon. In household fights, the man will not always be the unconditional victor. And in any case, can we really accept that the aim of these fights was always to martyrise the female partner? Would it not be more accurate to say that these bourgeois and philanthropic perceptions of violent scenes are the sadistic fantasies of bourgeois *voyeurs*? In point of fact, in the proletarian milieu, violence was one of the techniques used to resolve quarrels, and was practised in a variety of circumstances. It was codified, controlled and graded according to rules the subtlety of which could not even be imagined by the philanthropic investigators.

It is probable that when he tried to play the good Samaritan by offering to help the supposed victim of one of the Sublimes, Poulot himself was often sent packing. Talking about Sublimes' companions, he observes:

> If she gets a black eye she answers any questions by saying 'Oh, it's nothing, we just had a bit of a fight last night, that's all'. It is obvious that the 'oh, it's nothing' is intended to tell people to mind their own business, but, more precisely, is it not also a way for workers' wives to establish their right to resolve their quarrels without being treated like souls 'in distress' by bosses, policemen and social workers?

Poulot himself admits to being puzzled by the behaviour of Sublimes' wives, and his inability to understand them gives us a number of keys to certain realities which an employer would be loath to accept, as in the revealing chapter on 'The Working-Class Wife':

> The Sublimes, or a lot of them at any rate, have rubbed off on their wives . . . If you point out to a Sublime's wife that she is

working her fingers to the bone for a lazy coward who beats her up, and that she shouldn't, she'll merely reply that 'he's a good lad really; if he's not working at the moment, it's because there's not much work going', or better still, 'he's sprained his back. And to tell the truth, I'm really sweet on him'. That's the real explanation. It takes all sorts to make a world.

It is therefore probable that most Sublimes' wives were Sublimes themselves, and all the more so given that this would contradict the view of reality that the bourgeoisie wanted. These other meanings appear time and time again throughout the book, rising to the surface only to be repressed by its author:
– absenteeism, called 'laziness' by the employers, is above all the result of physical exhaustion through work;
– most workers' companions refuse to accuse their man of being 'work shy' (except during a domestic argument).
More often than not couples stick together against exploitation at work. It is this very solidarity which leads Poulot to say that many of the wives are themselves Sublimes.

When he describes the supposed laziness of Paris workers, and the hope that their companions will accuse them of being 'bone idle', Poulot omits to mention how exhausting work can be. And yet in an aside at the end of the chapter entitled 'The Worker', he crudely admits how widespread this exhaustion is in Paris. In particular he writes:

> Paris is the city where people worker harder than anywhere else in the world. . . . When workers come up to Paris from the provinces, they don't always stay, because so much graft is needed to earn a living. . . . In Paris, there are certain trades which function by piece-work, where after twenty years the worker is crippled and worn out, that is if he's still alive.

Once we have clarified the strategy used by the employers to deal with couples, and once we have deciphered the reaction of the workers to this pressure, we are forced to see the typology of *Le Sublime* in a different light: instead of a typology of male workers, we have a series of profiles of couples.

For a Sublime's wife to become a Sublime herself, the most decisive factor would be for her to become a wage-earner. Poulot never says this directly, but once more we may read between the lines of certain of his detailed descriptions. But first of all we must point out that Workers' wives earn a secondary income just as frequently as Sublimes' wives do. Poulot mentions this at various points in his book, but applies differing moral judgements according to whether he is discussing Sublimes or Workers.

If the couple be True Workers or Workers, and if both partners work outside the home, then he refers to them as 'industrious' (the chapter entitled 'The Worker').

> There are many True Workers and Workers who set their wives up in a dairy, a grocery store, a wine shop or a laundry. Many of them, most of them in fact, are successful. Their partner's wages go into the business, whereas in the case of the Sublime, his parasitism undermines it.
>
> The worker is very industrious; he is always working on the side to increase his earnings. Some are caretakers, and their wives take care of the lodge while they themselves see to any heavy jobs and anything they can do before or after work.

On the other hand, when a Sublime's companion takes a job, Poulot would have us believe that she is being forced into it by a 'lazy coward' (the chapter entitled 'The Working-Class Wife').

> Among the wives of Sublimes there are many who are very active and hard-working, who really graft and wear themselves out to support a family in which the lazy coward is just a liability. Some do laundry, deliver bread, or work as street vendors; others work in factories or at home.

This list of companions' activities reveals the true nature of the 'sublimatisation' of female workers: on the one hand women Sublimes are employed as wage-earners. On the other, the wives of those few workers who conform to their employers' desires become small shopkeepers, or concierges in the service of the landlords.

How couples lived: a series of phases to be resituated in the context of workers' destinies

We could go on deciphering in this way, sifting every detail about the lives of working-class couples. But we have chosen a few key examples, although there are many other aspects that lend themselves to the same treatment:
– bachelorhood, cohabitation and marriage;
– relationships between parents, children and grandparents;
– the question of 'jealousy' and 'familiarity' between working-class couples.

In order to sum up the deciphering and to assemble a few landmarks, we have cross-checked the typology of the couple and reorganised it in tabulated form (see the table on pages 104–11). By these means, in place of a juxtaposition of psychological characters or a kind of picturesque portrait gallery, we obtain a dynamic vision of an entire milieu. It is the bringing together of the whole which imparts meaning to each individual pattern of behaviour.

Each type of couple represents a 'way of life', a *modus vivendi*, a particular manner of dealing with those problems which confront the working-class milieu as a whole.

Bachelorhood, cohabitation and settling down, with or without legal marriage, cannot be interpreted simply as the acceptance or the rejection of a dominant 'family model', or as simple 'illegalisms'. The 'family model' only prevails within the meagre imagination of large-scale philanthropic investigations, or in the minds of those of their contemporaries who would emulate them.

The different social positions of couples will be much more convincingly understood if we see them in the context of *workers' destinies*. More precisely, each form of conjugal union should be understood as exemplifying a way of dealing with working-class existence. The life of each type of couple is situated in a series of phases, and each series has its own coherence. It will always involve a certain amount of resignation, of drifting and of rejection of the working-class condition, both by the man and the woman.

A minority wants to 'pull through' by getting promoted to foreman or owning a shop. Others take up methods of individual or collective resistance, but at the same time this confronts them with more or less unresolvable contradictions at the heart of their domestic relationships.

All types of male and female workers in Paris at the time of the Commune have two phases in common:
– a long phase where stable cohabitation is rejected or deemed impossible, resulting in bachelorhood or 'affairs';
– then, a more stable relationship, with or without getting married, in order to raise a family and provide as best as possible against waning strength and economic resources.

These phases are governed by an ever-present constraint: the variation of income in accordance with age, and debilitation through work. Poulot is careful not to linger over this point, but nevertheless he occasionally lets some sufficiently instructive details slip through. One particularly characteristic trait of working-class income, then as now, is the coincidence of wage levels and the decline of physical capacities: once a worker passes thirty-five his wages will normally begin to diminish. The fate of women workers is subordinate to that of men. Many young girls, earning secondary incomes (only half as much as men), cannot stay single and independent. But, whether or not they have any children, most of them will not be able to set up a stable home until their man reaches a critical age and feels it necessary to do so: unions take place when workers can no longer rely on money or personal charm to pay for domestic services, when they need to rely on extra income from women and children, and when their physical decline increases the risk of illness and unemployment.

Viewed from this angle, the employers' strategy of alliance with workers' wives must be seen in the context of the combined interests of working men and women, at different stages of life. At no point do these interests have a simple one-to-one relationship. Obviously, before couples set up a stable home, the bosses can scarcely exploit the oppositions between them, which may explain their open hostility to 'free love'. Similarly we can explain workers' preference for free love as a ruse to avoid the demands of family life in order to develop a more effective resistance in the workshops. But employers must have profited from the intensive exploitation of single male and female workers, otherwise they would not have found work so easily.

Once couples have settled down, the employers' strategy can become more oppressive. A working-class argot word symbolises the pressure of the dominant class upon their lives: the working-class wife who can make the most of the family budget and balance the books without having to go out to work is known as the 'bourgeoise'.

But on deciphering the relationships between couples we observe that the alliance produces contradictory reactions, without ever being completely successful. It is at its most effective in the case of Workers and Mixed Workers, but here we must point out that the couples' financial weakness probably governs the extent to which they are willing to submit to the demands of the labour market.

On the other hand, male Sublimism produces a variety of reactions in the housewife which can be acted out in several different ways. When she herself is not a Sublime, she will be permanently in conflict with her husband, becoming a 'martyr' or a 'bourgeoise' according to how well she is equipped. In such situations, an alliance with her companion's employer or with charitable organisations becomes an effective weapon for defending herself.

But in the majority of cases, where the woman herself is a working Sublime, family conflicts change meaning when the employer confronts them. The man, physically debilitated through work, is no longer the head of the household, but the employers cannot recuperate the wife's earnings. The profit gain from the workers is obtained on another level. Old age becomes a tragedy. Working women whose companions are worn out, more or less ill, disabled or out of work, become more and more dependent upon having paid employment themselves. They are forced to undergo an increasingly cynical and intensive exploitation, which will reach its climax when they are finally widowed. Maybe it is because such situations are precisely indefensible even in terms of bourgeois morality that when Poulot attempts to portray old age in Sublime of Sublime households, his tone becomes aggressive and unconvincing: he endows them with the mentality of embittered, unsuccessful *petits-bourgeois* tortured with remorse for not having made it into the bourgeoisie in spite of supposedly having had the possibility of doing so.

Such combinations of the exploitation of labour and conflicts between men and women will encourage us to disregard some of the false problems which are posed nowadays: it is not a question of the class struggle on one hand and the battle of the sexes on the other. The opposition between the sexes is exploited as much as cultural, racial and national conflicts are. And every case has historically original repercussions which cannot be summed up by simplistic 'class against class' or 'sex against sex' explanations.

As it is, (at the time of the Commune), the conditions of workers' wives could best be summed up in the words attributed to Flora Tristan: 'Proletarians of the Proletariat', as long as we understand the term proletarian in its most historically loaded sense. This evokes a dual exploitation, but also a dual defence on the level of everyday life. In so far as available perspectives isolate 'woman' on the one side and 'working class' on the other, it must be at this unspectacular level of everyday life that such struggles take place.

In Poulot's time there were certain feminist movements which, by allowing only the opposition between the sexes to define their struggle and unite women from all walks of life, became restricted to a kind of bourgeois or petit-bourgeois feminism. When women from the bourgeois or petit-bourgeois classes attacked their husbands' authority, challenging their position as masters of their money, their bodies, their time, the possibilities of liberation were real enough. But what could their campaigns have meant to working-class wives? They were urged to demand the reform of the marriage laws. But, in Sublime argot, most of them had already 'turned the Civil Code inside out': they were already in charge of the household finances, and possibly regarded their men's lack of domestic responsibility as a desirable thing.

Reconstruction of the probable reality of workers' practices as shown in 'Le Sublime'

The coherence of the practices of each of the seven types has been examined here in the context of the couple, but it is to be found in every aspect of daily life: the workshop, emotional life, the family, leisure, politics. And this coherence cannot be reduced to a list of more or less matching modes, more or less subject to mechanisms of integrations and authority. Rebelliousness has no absolute law beyond which revolt or rebellion are inevitable, and no demarcation line exists between a supposedly passive majority of the workforce and militant minorities. The points we have made in relation to the way couples lived are also valid over the entire area of everyday behaviour: *each way in which working-class men and women confront their destiny will always contain an element of resignation, an element of drifting and an element of rejection.*

To visualise this coherence it is helpful to glance through the preceding tables and consider the behaviour patterns of each of the types in differing contexts of everyday life. To complete the picture we have added a section which presents the links with the political scene, and which presents few problems of deciphering. We will return later to the question of the context of Paris which makes 'Public Meetings' so important and which at the beginning of 1870 must clearly have made the hypothesis of a 'social commune' feasible. Other comparisons, of housing, clothing, street behaviour, activities at celebrations, parties or on Sundays, are also possible.

The coherence between political life and other everyday practices is an area of study in its own right. If we accept this coherence, we will upset a number of intellectual habits, for it calls into question the idea of a dualism between ordinary working-class life on the one hand and the 'labour movement' on the other, which informs the social sciences, just as much as it does journalism, and studies produced under the aegis of labour organisations.

What, for example, can the idea of 'consciousness' mean when used to describe the supposed transition from ordinary life to militant activity? Can we talk of a lack of 'awareness' in the case of a woman worker who has to defend herself on two fronts every day – against her boss and against her husband? Where can we situate the 'consciousness' of a True Sublime who can protect his living conditions more effectively by individual resistance than by collective activities?

As we decipher *Le Sublime* we become conscious of how authentic its material is. It would be absurd to question whether it is sufficiently objective to be an acceptable 'source' of historical facts. Poulot struggles with several contradictions. He wants to denounce the methods his workers use to obstruct him, and at the same time he is unwilling to admit they exist. These contradictions are the most telling aspect of the book. The way he parades his partiality and inconsistencies makes his account all the more authentic and verifiable.

But each time we reconstruct workers' practices, no matter how authentically, we will inevitably give rise to new questions: what other means have we to verify the real extent of the day-to-day trials of strength suggested by Poulot's book? Once again we are forced to note the paucity of general information which we referred to at the beginning of this introduction. We can but hope that the new edition of *Le Sublime* will draw attention to research in this field.

In point of fact, everyday practices are not inaccessible. Given that this is only an introduction, we will limit ourselves to a few examples drawn from current research. The most important task is to reconstruct methods of subcontracting labour, wage systems and modes of exploitation. In this way we can unearth the roots of Sublimism in the workshops. On these bases it becomes easier to understand what the targets were in these day-to-day trials of strength, both in and out of the workshop. At the same time, the labour movement can be reconsidered within the context of the concrete targets of the period, thus achieving a more universal dimension.

Denis Poulot: a democratic capitalist

But first of all we must examine what we have been able to piece together of Denis Poulot's life in order to evoke his own experience, which will enable us to situate the methods of combating Sublimism which he proposes in the last third of his book. At the beginning of the Third Republic, some of the democratic 'new social strata' actually used many of these methods.

In fact, as a person, Denis Poulot brought together – often in as an exaggerated a manner as his own descriptions of Sublimes – the characteristics of an entire species of Parisian employer engaged in the struggle against Sublimism, using democracy and industrial 'progress' as his weapons. A distinguished member of the employers' class, he was one of a generation of men, opponents of the Empire regime and more or less 'radical' democrats, who became wealthy through their activities in industry. Always ready to quote their own success as an example, they were convinced that only a democracy based upon merit and equal opportunities could re-establish peaceful relationships between the employers and the workers.

Denis Poulot's family: provincial bourgeois, social climbers thanks to their education

Denis Poulot was born into a modest bourgeois family from the Franche-Comté. His father became wealthy and well known in Gray, in Haute Saône, the canton of the Franche-Comté where he was born. At the end of the First Empire he began a military career, then, after reaching the rank of captain, he retired in 1815 to become an iron merchant. At that time the town of Gray had a prosperous river trade, based on the commerce of raw materials.

When Denis Poulot was born (March 3 1832, at Gray-la-Ville, a small village near Gray), his father had been living for several years with a common-law wife who is referred to in the birth certificate as being of 'independent means'. Together with four older brothers and sisters, Denis-Joseph became legitimate when his parents married in the following year. They were to have a total of eight children. At this time the Poulots were at the height of their economic prosperity, and held an important position in the local community. The father was made a commander in the canton National Guard. The government had singled him out from the other officers because of his high level of education. He sent his children to *grandes écoles* and was in a position to give them sufficient capital to set up businesses. At least three brothers went through the military *grandes écoles* and took up careers as senior officers. Two other brothers went to the School of Arts and Crafts in Chalons, becoming civil engineers and subsequently mechanical engineering contractors.

Denis-Joseph was also sent to the school in Chalons, from which he graduated at the age of fifteen. As soon as he left school, he began work for his brother Etienne-Alfred, who ran a mechanical engineering business in Paris. Because he was too young to take up a managerial position, he worked as a chief fitter, the highest grade of skilled worker.

If we are to believe the personal references he makes in *Le Sublime* (the digressions to be found in the chapters entitled 'The Worker' and 'The Mixed Worker'), he was trained by foremen, who were True Workers. Hostile to the 1848 revolutionary movement, they disassociated themselves from those attempts to establish production associations which were aimed at uniting and 'emancipating' the totality of each 'craft grouping'. They believed that only an elite should create associations.

The chief fitter's first love affairs were unsuccessful. He attempted to court girls from bourgeois families. He even tried to bluff away the callouses on his hands to disguise his manual employment, but to no avail. Despite his attractive appearance and the care he took to behave in a cultivated manner, he was never to win the hand of any rich Parisian heiresses.

At the age of twenty he was promoted to the rank of foreman at the Gouin factory, and there are numerous anecdotes about the most archaic form of Sublimism, that of the *grosses culottes*, which stem from this period of his life. The *grosses culottes* (thick trousers) were an elite group of subcontracted workers who were able to make both the heaviest and the most delicate components using the simplest manual tools. There are good descriptions of their methods in the chapters 'The *Grosses Culottes*' and 'A Meeting of the Senate'. The key to their power is simple: they were indispensable and without their knowledge and skills, the professional engineers could not have coped. If one gang started work on an order, it could not be completed by another. As for arranging the work gang, the *grosses culottes* were more like theatrical agents than like a petty officer preparing for manoeuvres.

The book explains how the Sublimism of the *gross culottes* was killed off by machine tools. In Paris, the crucial period in the manufacture of locomotives and heavy arms was the start of the Second Empire, the very time that Denis Poulot was a foreman at Gouin's. It is perhaps this experience which helped to define the grand design of his career: to combat Sublimism both on a political and on a technological level.

Poulot's first industrial successes: a technology of combat against skilled workers

At twenty-five Poulot followed in the footsteps of his elder brother, who was a company manager and who invented machine tools: he started his own business, in partnership with one of his brothers-in-law. With a capital investment of fifteen thousand francs each, the two partners assigned their collective partnership to 'the manufacture of bolts, rivets and other parts for the mechanical engineering industry, as well as the buying and selling of such parts, including metal'. The capital outlay came from family inheritances.

While his brother-in-law dealt with the management side, Poulot immediately set about the task of renovating the manufacturing processes in the engineering department in order to rid it of Sublimist practices. In effect engineering was one of the areas in which Sublimes formed an overwhelming majority:

Poulot estimates that 85 per cent of his bolt makers were Sublimes. From the workers' point of view 'it was liberty hall': neither workshop regulations nor discipline from outside could hinder their own collective control over subcontracting.

A close examination of technological inventions in the context of labour relations would result in a totally different picture to that found in the usual histories of technology: while these are happy to chart the supposed linear progress of tools of production, a detailed examination reveals quite different dimensions: there was rivalry between various types of invention, and 'technical requirements' can never be considered by themselves without reference to opposition to workers' control. We may use the example of bolt making to give a brief illustration of this fact, and to spotlight Poulot's observation that 'in our opinion, nothing has a more moralising influence than a machine'.

Poulot's technical writings explain how, in order to satisfy manufacturers, 'good' machine tools should fulfil three conditions simultaneously:
– to increase precision (in made-to-measure or ready-made)
– to improve the technical conditions for speed of production
– to decrease the free will of the workers.[8]

Right until the 1860s, no method for the manufacture of bolts had been considered satisfactory. The first two conditions could be satisfied, but not the third. In the case of purely manual production, there was a regular improvement both in tools and in the level of precision of the product (wards, moulds, removal of bolts). But the employers considered themselves to be much too dependent upon the gangs of bolt makers and beaters, which were specialised variants of the gangs of *gross culotte* founders and beaters.[9]

In the field of machine tools there was a long series of highly automated inventions and complex models, but they failed to satisfy the industrialists. Poulot analyses their main defect: automation may well have made work easier for bolt makers and beaters, but the maintenance of the machines was a delicate operation, and depended too much on the machine operators themselves. In other words, these machines could create new opportunities for skilfulness and control open to the workforce as a whole throughout that branch of production. They might open the way to new forms of Sublimism. And so most of these prototypes were scrapped. As for the rare machine tools in use at the beginning of the 1860s, they did not change the fundamental need for skilled workers. For a long time reserve gangs were kept in the large boiler-making workshops to produce made-to-measure bolts. They were recognised as so indispensable and skilful in their specialised field that they could not be employed for any other task.

Machine tools became a necessary feature of the bolt industry only when this tendency was checked, and when bolt making became unskilled. This is the precise point at which Poulot made his industrial breakthrough, making small specialised taps for 'ring-shaped threads' and 'spherical left-hand threads'. The specialised nature of these tools was intended to save time, and to give rise, in the factories that bought them, to a group of workers specialised only in their maintenance. In this way it would be possible to prevent workers from taking short breaks: until now they had used their own tools, which were much too adaptable for Poulot's taste, and if they broke, which happened frequently, then employers had no alternative but to let the workers repair them themselves.

Next the firm of Poulot-Bricaire went on to heavy machine tools for stamping rivets and bolts, and for the tapping of the latter. Its success rested upon one simple principle: the development of increasingly specialised machine tools for rapid mass-production. With this aim in mind, contractors disregarded the technical virtuosity of certain automated inventions. In Poulot's words, their ideal was achieved when production could be carried out 'by an intelligent workforce trained in a few weeks', and when the individual norms of production could be established in terms of the characteristics of the machine, and not in terms of the aptitude of the worker, as they had been in the past.

Commercial success vindicated this choice. 'Denis Poulot Tapping Machines' began to make a name for themselves on the French market. By the time of the 1867 Universal Exhibition, more than a thousand of the heaviest models had been sold. The spokesman for the international jury commented, not without a touch of jealousy, that the machines which Poulot had put on show were 'even more specialised' than those of his English competitors, and that they had become 'more or less official' because 'they are even used in government workshops' (in the dockyards). In the movement towards a standard screw thread, Poulot had managed to impose the use of the 'Denis Poulot thread' in naval dockyards (ministerial circular, 15 December 1863). In short, Poulot's struggle against Sublimism had resulted in the invention of what are now called O.S. (*ouvriers spécialisés* i.e. semi- or unskilled workers) for his particular sector of production, or at least, had created the necessary technical conditions for them. For a boss like Poulot, who faced the everyday resistance of the workers, it was essential and necessary to elaborate technologies of combat, but far from sufficient.

*Poulot's democratic project: the re-adjustment of class relations,
with the 'new social strata' as pivot*

On the political scene, Poulot was only of second-rate importance. He never managed to take the final step that would have
made him a Paris councillor, a deputy or a senator. For this reason
he is all the more representative of the thousands of important
professional figures in the margins of the political scene who
formed a network of very effective local power.

He took his first steps in public life within the Society of Old
French Students of the (Imperial) Schools of Art and Crafts,
which he joined in 1851. In 1864 he joined the management
committee to promote a campaign to attract foremen and
engineers away from the army and into private industry. His hope
was to reassert the value of manual work in the eyes of the sons of
the bourgeoisie. At the end of his chapter on apprentices Poulot
gives an account of how he envisages the social vocation of this
type of association. In reality the Society of Former Students
became a kind of freemasonry for managers, technicians and
engineers in the private sector. It was very influential and offered a
market-place for the exchange of favours and information about
vacancies, techniques and policies within specific businesses.
Later, in 1882, Poulot worked hard to increase the number of
contacts, meetings and publications. According to his figures,
when he retired from public and industrial life in 1899, the society
had more than six thousand members.

In 1861, the same year in which he began to promote the new
social strata, he also gave up his ambition to marry into the
Parisian grand bourgeoisie, and he returned to Vesoul, in his
native province, to wed a young bourgeoise of private means,
with assets worth rather more than forty thousand francs, a
fortune more or less equal to his own. Without having actually
'made a fortune', the couple were immediately able to move in
well-to-do bourgeois circles. They had four sons, all of whom
were sent to the Chalons School of Arts and Crafts to study civil
engineering.

The publication of *Le Sublime* in April 1870 won Poulot a
noticeable entry onto the political scene. Nevertheless he remained
anonymous until the second edition, fearing retaliation in his
workshops from the Sons of Gods. The book was reviewed in at
least fifteen newspapers. Most of them, while praising the author
for his 'pictorial' and 'photographic' artistry, reduced it to the
usual picturesque and moralising level of the time. The proposals
for reform the book contained were very much connected with
the immediate political context. They belonged to the radical

republican opposition, and if they incorporated the programme proposed by Gambetta, they also took inspiration from the work of the worker delegations set up for the 1867 Universal Exhibition.

Their originality lies above all in the grand political design which underpins them. Focusing on the problems of Paris, Poulot aims to create a class alliance between a democratic bourgeoisie, the new social strata of engineers, managers and technicians, the petit-bourgeois (craftworkers, small tradesmen, clerical workers), and a labour elite which was to be fostered and singled out from the mass by the three other social forces. This alliance would gain strength and cohesion from the common struggle against aristocracies of money, privilege, large-scale monopolies, and against their faithful servants: cassock, sabre, wig and red tape. A common ideology would unite them: equal opportunities, open participation in public affairs, opposition to state control, democratic integration of the workforce.

No record has been found of Poulot's political activities during the Commune, but we can read about his position in a pamphlet published four months after Bloody week, with the evocative title: 'Manifesto of a Democratic Bourgeois' and signed with the initial D.P. In it Poulot adopts a bombastic tone in order to put into words the horror he feels at the repression, a feeling shared by many Paris industrialists, and to set out his scheme for a class alliance. While expressing his solidarity with Gambetta, he nevertheless disassociates himself from the butchery of Versailles more vigorously than his political friends, and goes on to explain the reasons for this bold gesture:

> Three or four thousand citizens on trial, that's a big job; court martial can't do everything; and so people like Bazaine, Trochu and other top brass and cowards who surrendered Metz, Paris and France go free. There's no hint of heresy about those chaps, and when it comes to social injustice their lips are sealed.
>
> But what about the thousands of innocent people who are rotting in the hulks with thieves and arsonists and that whole quagmire which dishonours whatever it touches; what about those victims from the ranks of the poverty-stricken who have been crying out for justice for the last four months? Is nothing to be done?
>
> Oh great party of law and order, how your slowness terrifies me! Could it be that you are afraid of using the firing squad to get it over with? This heap of corpses, this lake of blood (deep enough to drown the lot of you) worries your consciences . . . the martyrdom of your victims makes them saints in our eyes;

and in the name of justice and appeasement a fearful cataclysm is brewing which will claim us, the bourgeoisie, as its first victims. In the name of our security and of that justice which has been trampled underfoot, we execrate and pillory you.[10]

Written in the condescending style of a father disciplining a child, this manifesto could only discourage the workers. But in political circles the labour wing of the Gambettists, with Barberet, attached great importance to the pamphlet, a year before Gambetta's famous call to the 'new social strata'.[11]

A few extracts from the manifesto will summarise its contents better than a lengthy commentary:

TO THE PEOPLE,

Panic-stricken after so many disasters and mistakes, you denounce the bourgeoisie for having abandoned and betrayed you. They have failed to follow you or back you up, and in your hidden anger you condemn them all to the implacable hatred of the workers. You say that these bourgeois egotists are all enemies of the people. . . . But . . . there are bourgeois and bourgeois, just as there are republicans and republicans. You know only the story, surely . . .

Here you see a democratic bourgeois, a feak perhaps, but who has come to show the way. The path may be strewn with stones, and large ones, but we will not stumble. We, and we alone, must carry out the task. We have had enough of being propped up.

Do you know what you need to be able to own the instruments of labour? Well, you've got to be big enough to attain them unaided, and not to expect the Providential State to give them to you. And before you start shouting that it's impossible just take a look at the English (to give just one example). The Associated Society of Engineers has four million five hundred thousand francs in liquid assets; it uses them to supplement wages until such time as the great social purge comes which will sweep its country clean of aristocratic castes and rid the legal system of laws of privilege which forbid it to use its funds for co-operative production and appropriation of the whole project . . .[12]

Bowed and humiliated by the corruption and mindlessness that those in charge have cultivated in order to dominate you, you must stand up, and this is how. For fifty years they have shouted 'Get rich!' Your bourgeois answers 'Let us become citizens' . . .

Manual workers, clerks, painters, intellectuals, small shop

keepers and tradesmen, small manufacturers and everyone who has any generous feelings in their hearts, let us unite in the great political arena, let us unite in attack; we want to become citizens in the broadest and largest meaning of the word.

A synthesis of the most radical of Republican programmes follows: public freedoms, free state education at all levels, free legal costs, election of magistrates, suppression of the permanent army, etc.

It is not Monsieur Capital who must be struck down, but social plagues, the main ones being: the sabre, the cassock, the wig and red tape . . .

Let Monsieur Capital alone; at present he can't help you; but when you've proved yourself, he'll give you his daughter's hand in marriage.

In Paris there are a hundred thousand petit-bourgeois, clerks, people with small incomes, workers, who are rallying to the programme you have just read; instead of shutting yourself up in your own pipe dreams and wasting all that famous popular energy in useless anger, you must step into the open arena to join them, and then within twenty years we will have pierced a path as big as the Mont Blanc Tunnel through our difficulties.

The first step is to apply democratic principles in order to solve the great social problem.

To realise it we must use the law to defeat our common enemies; for victory to be ours, we must be united, and above all disciplined. Away with dreams, cosmopolitanism, phantoms: we need pragmatism, nationalism, reality; that is the price of success.

If you heed this summons, the Democratic Republic will be firmly established for all time. The democratic bourgeoisie awaits you to affirm this triumph.

Meanwhile Poulot was continuing his industrial career, and the fact that he was a democratic bourgeois did not stop him from becoming wealthy. In 1868 he gave up his partnership in Poulot-Bricaire, which was then at the height of its prosperity, to devote himself to new inventions and to marketing his old ones, while awaiting the right moment to start his own business. His partnership, which had cost him fifteen thousand francs eleven years earlier, went for fifty-five thousand.

His chance came a year after the Commune. Having invented a new moulding process, Poulot started a business manufacturing machine tools in this sector, based on aims analogous to his first business venture: to conquer a quasi-monopoly in a gap in a highly technically-developed and specialised market, and to exploit this monopoly while keeping his factory at a modest size. Profiting from the fall in land prices, he bought a 990-square-metre plot on the avenue Philippe-Auguste on the edge of the main built-up area, where he built a three-storey residential block facing the avenue, and two parallel industrial buildings facing the inner courtyard. On the ground floor some shops and a porte-cochère gave out onto the street. The 200-square-metre first floor was equipped as a ten-room apartment for Poulot himself. In all, including the land, his investments comprised fifty-three thousand francs for the residential block and forty-five thousand francs for the factory (37 per cent for the land itself, 22 per cent for the factory buildings and 41 per cent for the permanent machinery).

Real estate deals were very typical procedures for the average industrialist of the time. In 1872 alone, five other factories with a residential block facing the street and a first-floor apartment for the owner were built on the same avenue, and all with family capital. From the radical-republican point of view, such deals were very moral when compared to the speculations of the 'financial aristocracy' during the Empire, since both land and buildings functioned immediately as instruments of productive capital instead of being monopolised by the large property companies in order to 'get a ransom from the user', as the Parisian radicals of the day put it.

The factory functioned with only from ten to fourteen workmen. Poulot maintained his supremacy in the highly specialised area of large artificial grindstones. At opportune moments he renewed his machine tool prototypes. At every large exhibition his models were always among the best, and were awarded medals. He became quite wealthy, and when he died in 1905, while not being exceptionally so, he was nevertheless one of the richest bourgeois in Paris, leaving an estimated 4,100,000 francs, the equivalent of an annual revenue of more than 120,000 francs. Five hundred thousand francs of this came from apartment blocks, the remainder from financial securities. His capital revenues were fifty times greater than the wages of a skilled mechanic of the period.

When historians talk of the supposed 'semi-domestic industry' character of small Parisian businesses and ramble on about the supposedly close relationships between the employers and their workforce, they would do well to bear this example in mind. If Poulot's workers could rub elbows with him every day, surely this would be yet another reason for making the social distance between them all the more obvious. What conclusions could they have come to, for example, when they knew that if the revenues of the 'small' employer and his workforce were to be averaged out, every worker's wage would have gone up more than four times?

A political notable in search of impossible working-class aristocracy

The establishment of the Third Republic gave Poulot the opportunity to carry out his programme. The reforms proposed by *Le Sublime* and *Le Manifeste* . . . make him a precursor. Nevertheless, like quite a few of his Parisian colleagues, he remained in the shadow of the politicians with radical policies for overt action. Similarly he remained in the shadow of leading figures in the workers' movement when it was necessary to bring pressure on labour organisations. He played a discreet part in the struggles of the syndico-political 'Barberettist' clan in favour of reformist trades unionism (with supportive articles in the press and at public meetings). He supported the overt action of ex-militant workers who had become local councillors or members of parliament (like Nadaud, Tolain and Corbon) in favour of the creation of worker production associations.

He took his first step towards a political career in 1879 when Gambetta arranged for his nomination as mayor of the 11th arrondissement. For three years his activities were typical of radical public figures in working-class districts: support for peoples' education and resistance to clericalism, promotion of primary, professional and 'adult' education (the latter followed mostly by adolescents and young workers). He increased the number of lay-state 'charities': municipal nurseries, infants' schools, peoples' libraries, physical training schools, local music societies. These good works were run with the active participation of the self-same 'petit-bourgeois' clerks, factory manager and shop-keepers whose participation in public life he had preached ten years previously.

Similarly the nuns were thrown out of the social assistance organisations along with the patronesses, and were replaced by staff and procedures which a worried article in the *Figaro* referred to as a *bon zig* style ('jolly good fellow'). Petits-bourgeois – local authority employees or amateurs – began giving out public aid in accordance with material resource criteria, forbidding any moralising or religious blackmail. And these *bons zigs* – to use the *Figaro* expression – went so far in the direction of democracy as actually to 'have a drink at the bar with the pauper they were giving aid to, just to cheer him up'. (In Paris more than 10 per cent of all working-class households were on local authority assistance every year). In Poulot's eyes it was an effective way of making the regime popular, and perhaps it was one of the civic actions in which his strategy was at its most relevant, since the workers could appreciate very real and tangible increases in freedom.

Contrary to the idea which superficial historiography has sometimes bequeathed, anti-clericalism was a natural thing for many capitalists. The reason is simple: the ecclesiastical apparatus was rejected whenever it was unable to contribute to the submission of the workers. Moreover, in Paris, many industrialists deplored the fact that 'the cassock', with its claims to the most ostentatious and humiliating forms of authority, was a permanent incitement to class hatred. Furthermore, popular Parisian anti-clericalism was stronger and more violent than ever since the perpetrators of the Versailles massacre had been blessed by the clergy.

Therefore Poulot had good political reasons for using anti-clericalism and liberalism to attack the working-class practice of living together. In 1881 he founded the 'Society for civil marriage' as a non-religious rival to the overly clerical 'Society of Saint-François-Régis'. He defined its aims in the following manner:

> To facilitate the marriage for people who are unable to afford the costs or observe the formalities demanded by the law, as a result of their needy condition.

The *bon zig* style is in evidence here in that the proposition is aimed simply at making the administrative formalities easier and alleviating the heavy costs of a religious ceremony. This would only affect couples who made a point of claiming financial aid, whereas the Society of Saint-François-Régis systematically canvassed every irregular relationship it could uncover, submitting the couples to moralising blackmail. In 1904 the Society for civil marriage could boast of having encouraged 18,280 marriages and thus of being responsible for the legitimisation of 7,880 children (9–10 per cent of the total number of legitimisations through marriage in Paris).

Here is a sample of the aggressive style of the period. It is an extract from a short speech Poulot made in his town hall in 1881 (a text which was rediscovered among his personal papers, left in the town hall of the 11th arrondissement):

> Newly-weds,
> . . .
> you have just created a republican family, since by rejecting

ceremonies which are not even believed in by nine-tenths of the people who go through them, your first act has been one of freedom and independence.

Above all I want to offer my sincerest congratulations to you, madame, because these acts of independence would be more frequent if the finances did not nearly always insist upon this out-dated ceremony.

You are entering social life with the cult of the family, humanity and fatherland; and that's a religion which does not teach young women to abandon the joys and duties of motherhood for a ridiculous mysticism.

No; you are protected from that school for cowards; you will become a mother, you will experience all the joys a mother's love can bring.

If I have a few bitter words, it's because I've just heard something that has upset me.

I know a young girl, beautiful and intelligent. I watched her grow up. She has just left her mother, her father, her brothers and sisters in order to join a convent. Today Mademoiselle Louise has become Sister Raphaela.

She was seduced by the monstrous theory that it is nobler to spend one's life praying than to raise a family and bring happiness to a husband.

I know that you reject such abhorrent doctrines and I am overjoyed that you are undertaking a serious way of life, guided by those principles of which good citizens are made.

Poulot became intoxicated with the changes which were taking place in local political life. Confident of success, he felt he was in the forefront of history. In the preface to the third edition of *Le Sublime* (1887), his tone is triumphant. The eruption of the 'new social strata' into public life was a success. With these new strata, political power had achieved a less bourgeois appearance. Poulot considered that from then on the aspirations of the working class could be channelled by the democratic regime. In his view, the first sign of this progress was the decline of Sublimism. To demonstrate this alleged decline he came up with two series of arguments which he put forward in his preface:

– the disappearance of external signs of Sublimism in the streets of Paris;
– the development within unions and other democratic labour institutions of a working-class elite hostile to Sublimism.

In fact, the first point corresponded to reality, and this is readily verifiable. In the street, bourgeois arrogance was no longer answered by arrogance on the part of the working class. Working clothes were no longer flaunted as a symbol of proud defiance. But to go on to see this as a sign that the working class had become integrated within bourgeois democratic society is a step Poulot took much too blithely. His argument had scarcely more weight than any of the considerations about working-class *embourgeoisement* which have appeared regularly ever since.

It is extremely questionable that any elite hostile to Sublimism developed within workers' organisations. Without entering into a discussion of the fundamental problem – which would entail a critical scrutiny of an entire phase of the Paris workers' movement – we will simply offer one useful example, taken from an intervention Poulot made to the workers' unions.

Poulot was one of the most active founders of the 'Central Popular Deposit, Labour and Savings Bank'. The purpose of this operation was to promote a vast movement of new workers' production associations with a collection from people's savings. In its report to the Board of Directors n 1883, the Central Bank defined its aims in the following way:

> When thousands of workers each have a share in a People's Bank, when they have put their savings in one, when they have come to appreciate the value of its methods of management, accounting, information and credit, when a certain number of them have made it clear to their bank that they are thrifty workers capable of keeping vigilant control of their modest fortune, they will discover that the Central People's Bank will be ready to offer all the necessary support for them to set up a business either personally or in association.
>
> In this way the elite of the working-class population will have its chance of following the path to wealth and freedom and will at last acquire its rightful share of France's industrial and commercial assets.

However, contemporary reactions to the offers of the Popular Bank reveal a complete allergy on the part of the workers' movement to the proposed dynamics. At the beginning Poulot's friends may have been labouring under several illusions. When it was started in 1879/80, backed by Gambettist deputies, Paris councillors, leading Freemasons and left-wing industrialists in a wave of publicity, the deal was favourably received not only by the small shopkeepers' and clerical workers' unions, but also within the reformist circles of labour unionism. The project got the quasi-official backing of the Federation of French Labour Unions, an assembly of reformist unions which had regrouped after a split at the Le Havre National Labour Congress in 1880.

The leaders of this trades union became deeply involved in the deal. At the very time the split took place (and Poulot seems to have played a large part in it) they were secretly getting the financial backing of the Central Bank for their newspapers. Many of them bought shares in the bank which they ceded to their own union members. Regular meetings of workers who held shares took place at the Federation head office. In accordance with the wishes of its backers, two leaders from the Federation were elected to administrative posts at the Central Bank.

This strange marriage had to be officially justified by the creation of production associations. In fact twenty or so production co-operatives were created during its first three years (1880–2). But there was an immediate deterioration of internal relations within the Federation, and the business went into a decline even before the economic crisis of 1883–6.

At first glance this deterioration would seem to have been the result of financial corruption on the part of the Federation leaders.[13] However, corruption is only the visible tip of a much deeper phenomenon. By trying to introduce the logic of capitalist management into the unions, left-wing politicians and capitalists showed that they had completely misunderstood the dynamics of the labour movement at that time. The reactions of the workers, including those belonging to 'moderate' unions, were significant. Not one active union actually joined in the collective savings game. The largest members of the Federation, such as the Union of Builders and Decorators, withdrew immediately and expelled their representatives because of their double dealing in 'cabinet meetings' and in the Central Bank. In smaller unions where the leaders did not withdraw, membership soon became limited to groups of administrative staff interested in the public tender of work or the setting up of small businesses.

In its managerial methods the Federation rejected the principles of representation and election observed by capitalist businesses. The Union's treasurer, J. B. Gruhier, a member of the Board of Directors of the Central Bank, was publicly denounced as Denis Poulot's puppet. His Trades Union colleagues refused to let him behave like a bourgeois administrator. They would have liked to have introduced the usual methods of worker democracy into the 'popular bank': enforced mandates, delegates at all times answerable to and dismissable by the Worker Assemblies.

Even within reformist labour groups, the demands for production associations did not have the same meaning as they did for the left-wing employers. In the Paris Labour Movement Association it implied the collective 'emancipation' of the entire working class, in other words, the suppression of the bosses. The only question was the ways and means of achieving it.

For their part, Denis Poulot and his friends dreamed of a working-class aristocracy composed of association and union executives, able to introduce the discipline of collective savings. They reckoned that these new elites would be eager to promote the prosperity of their associations, and would thus be well placed to repress Sublimist go-slow tactics at work and to introduce a productivist morale. But in the Paris of the period nothing like this actually happened: the few prosperous workers' associations that there were could only exist by applying the rules of capitalism, and were immediately seen by the working-class milieu as associations of exploiters.

Following this failure, Poulot's political career became compromised.[14] In the general election of 1885, on the occasion of a joint operation set up by some leading employers and some members of the Federation, Poulot's name appeared on the list of opportunist candidates supporting Senator Tolain. Their committee wished to impose 'candidates from commerce and industry' to fight against 'the policies of the politicians'. But neither Poulot nor any other of the candidates accepted on the opportunist list gained the necessary number of votes.[15]

So Poulot returned to activities more classically consonant with his position as a leading employer, having only little influence on social relations. He was seen as a great specialist in questions of apprenticeships, and as such he was given several official assignments simultaneously, in particular a regional inspectorship of technical education, membership on international exhibition juries and on the Higher Labour Council. But if the author of *Le Sublime* spent his life preaching in favour of professional schools which would rid the workshops of apprentices, in practice these things were different. The policy of apprenticeships was shaped by other demands. The Ministry for State Education only ever seemed to produce specialists in the humanities, and at the Ministry of Commerce, employers like Poulot gave advice which differed significantly from their public statements. They admitted that the managers were trying to halt the learning of skilled trades by the masses. All they demanded of the collectivity was the formation of training schemes for middle and higher technical personnel. This policy of the employers was successful, and in official circumstances Poulot was one of its principal spokesmen. Nothing serious was done to develop apprenticeships for the masses, and only schools for engineers, technicians and foremen were created.

The roots of Sublimism in workshops: 'We are rebelling against the work we love'

A preliminary question: what were the social relations behind the imagery of Parisian 'domestic industry' and 'small businesses'?

If we are to begin to comprehend the reality of working-class life at the time of *Le Sublime*, our first step must be to dispel several current myths which prevent any kind of understanding of the social relations involved. A set of 'Industrial Revolution' images, repeated like a catechism for the last century, would have us believe that only large-scale factory production and the use of the steam engine resulted in real 'typical' industrial capitalism and its by-product, the real 'typical' working class. In consequence, descriptions of the situation in Paris refer only to these stereotypes. Production in Paris had supposedly remained separated from large-scale industry, retaining for the most part its 'traditional' nature, preserved in the old forms of domestic industries and small businesses. 'Luxury' industries (goldsmiths, 'articles from Paris', fashionable clothes) and the main body of consumer industries are thought to have produced a particular working-class profile which differed greatly from that of the proletariat the Industrial Revolution had created. A powerful 'working-class aristocracy' had supposedly grown up, highly skilled, jealous of its independence and with a libertarian attitude rooted in former values. This tendency would have been reinforced by the large-scale immigration of rural craftworkers.

In point of fact our scrutiny of workers' own analyses of concrete work relations reveals a universe in which such images are totally alien. To begin with domestic industries and small luxury workshops do not necessarily imply 'craftworkers' and 'luxury workers'. As an example, let us take the most 'traditional' and 'luxurious' sector of all, the goldsmith trade. This is how the workers' delegation of goldsmiths, which the employers considered to be one of the most moderate of the time, put its views at the 1867 Universal Exhibition:

> In 1789 our fathers crushed their wardens and masters; by destroying privilege and proclaiming every freedom, they believed that henceforth justice and equity would control the relations between capital and labour. But the misfortunes which confront us now are taking these freedoms away from us, leaving us defenceless and unable to protest, and at the mercy of an insatiable capitalism – even worse, perhaps, than

privilege, which we certainly do not want again.

Never has this evil been so obvious and so destructive as in those large centres of manufacture where accumulated capital, enjoying every freedom, becomes a kind of legalised oppression, regulating labour and parcelling work out so as to create more specialised jobs which dispense with the need for workers: this is the English system which is threatening to take us all over by turning the worker into a labourer, subjected to mindless production which brings him no personal benefits, and leads him to forget everything he has learned, since it has become useless. We draw your attention to this as the most dangerous of all present evils, and we think that despite all its false advantages, which are intended to dazzle us, the recruitment and centralisation of labour constitute a major attack of workers' personal freedom, since these firms absorb everything in increasingly large proportions, and soon the only choice left will be either to work in factories for lower wages or find another trade.

We are faced with an overwhelming energy: the centralisation and division of labour, which is diminishing the intrinsic value of the worker, striking a blow at our present interests and destroying the future workforce by suppressing the will to work together which characterises and explains the excellence of French workers. These are facts which are threatening us all, and we must resist them.

The evils denounced by the goldsmiths are repeated in most working-class grievances of the time: an ever-increasing dependence upon centralised capital, and the breaking down of work into individual, unskilled operations which rendered skilled training unnecessary. In the second part of their report the goldsmiths denounced the increasing competitiveness of workers as a result of the reduction in tariff barriers, which produced pressure to bring wages down. Unless they began organised resistance, workers had no choice but to make up their losses by doing increasingly longer hours.

This is a far cry from the imagery of 'traditional' independent craftworkers. Already, at the time *Le Sublime* was written, Zola had experienced the impact of this contrast: when visiting a goldsmith as preparation for his novel *L'Assommoir*, he discovered a home-based craftworker whose situation recalled the imagery of the 'Poor Weaver' rather than that of luxury craftworkers. The description of his visit shows us a couple in a minute dwelling specialising in the fabrication of gold chains for a merchant. Careful not to waste a single minute, the two 'craftworkers' had been repeating the same gestures since childhood just to earn enough to survive. At 30 and 31 respectively, the man and woman already looked aged.[16]

The most frequent misinterpretations become crystallised around the notion of 'domestic industries'. Even in history theses, one still finds general commentaries on 'domestic industries' or 'small businesses' in nineteenth-century Paris, as though they were homogeneous entities. However, nothing could be more dangerous than this notion of domestic industries, since it can obscure the existence of totally heterogeneous social relations. Today, many political and trades union militants also imagine that the communards were somehow different from the 'typical' working class, because they do not conform to current representations of the industrial proletariat. And yet contemporaries saw things quite differently. Present-day marxist-inspired analyses are also frequently contaminated. Therefore it would seem appropriate at this juncture to recall the way Marx indicates the progress of modern capitalism under the cover of 'traditional domestic industry' and 'outwork'.

The following summary from *Capital* situates and sums up the tendencies denounced by the goldsmiths' delegation:

> Along with the development of the factory system and of the revolution in agriculture that accompanies it, production in all the other branches of industry not only extends, but alters its character. . . . This is the case not only with all production on a large scale, whether employing machinery or not, but also with the so-called domestic industry, whether carried on in the houses of the workpeople or in small workshops. This modern so-called domestic industry has nothing except the name, in common with the old-fashioned domestic industry, the existence of which pre-supposes independent urban handicrafts, independent peasant farming, and above all, a dwelling-house for the labourer and his family. That old-fashioned industry has now been converted into an outside department of the factory, the manufactory, or the warehouse. Besides the factory operatives, the manufacturing workmen and the handicraftsworkers, whom it concentrates in large masses at one spot, and directly commands, capital also sets in motion, by means of invisible threads, another army: that of the workers in domestic industries, who dwell in the large towns and are also scattered all over the face of the country.[17]

These invisible threads have been analysed in detail in hundreds of Paris workers' collective texts contemporary to *Capital*. The mechanics of exploitation which reduced most independent 'domestic industries' and 'small workshops' to pure facade have also been demonstrated by De Maroussem of the Le Play school. It is not enough simply to say that 'domestic industry' became more and more dependent. If we are to understand the dynamics of the social relations involved, we must reconstruct the units and real systems of production of which these pseudo-craftsworkers were merely fragments.

The most obvious cases are the making up of customers' own material as outwork or in small workshops: the agents received the basic materials from a customer for whom they had to carry out such and such a task in return for a 'making-up price'. This making-up price was often only a piece rate. Therefore it follows that making-up workers belonged to much larger units of production. From 1848 until the end of the century in Paris there was an increase in the number of 'outworkers', most of whom were making-up workers. Generally, in industry their total numbers have been under-estimated. In round figures these rose to 80,000 in 1847–8 (23 per cent of the working population in these industries) and to 164,000 in 1901 (25 per cent of the working population). This rise can be almost totally attributed to female employment.

But frequently units and systems of production were much more complex and concealed. They were a combination of national or international commerce, department stories, factories, small workshops and outwork, which were scattered throughout Paris and the provinces. Du Maroussem has singled out units of this kind which were formed in the clothing industry between 1860 and 1890. Sometimes several hundred pseudo-craftworkers and a couple of dozen small workshops were nothing more than the terminal antennae of large clothing interests each with several thousand employees, managed by merchants, industrialists or department stores.[18]

Just like isolated domestic industries, the small workshop itself can look so deceptively simple that the fact that it belongs to one type of unit of production or another is concealed. The linking of 'small workshops' to the real units of production can be summarised in three ways:

1 Of course, genuine small firms, limited to small workshops, really did exist: we have seen two examples in the mechanical engineering industry with Poulot's two successive firms.

2 Another type of genuine small firm was the economic unit managed by a small capitalist subcontractor, in other words by a

small employer, who owned all the means of production and accumulated capital while at the same time depending upon regular custom with one or more other firms. This type of establishment was particularly vulnerable to Sublimism, and was frequently to be found in mechanical engineering, cabinetmaking, the bronze industry, work in precious metals, and clothing. Several building firms also worked on a similar basis.

3 But a great many workshops belonged to very different systems of production. In everyday life they could produce relations of the kind suggested by Poulot's descriptions of sublime employers. More or less short-lived workshops held the legal ownership of a capital sum, but their bosses did not have any real control over them: they could not regulate their means of production (it was impossible, for example, to finance stocks of basic materials or finished products, and there was not enough capital to order complete cycles for the production of merchandise). There was no internal stockpiling. In reality these apparent firms were nothing more than a worker team leader, acting as middleman with the sleeping partners. Such pseudo-firms were to be found throughout every branch of Parisian industry. They were numerous in the cabinetmaking sector, and prolific in building and clothing. We must be aware of this kind of structure before we can understand the implications of Poulot's chapter on 'Sublime employers'.

Frequently the managers of this type of pseudo-firm were originally workers themselves. Inevitably a great many of them went bankrupt. Many economists and ideologues close to the employers' outlook have blown up this strange population of entrepreneurs out of all proportion, erecting impressive philosophical theories on the ease of access for workers to the status of employer, and drawing conclusions about 'working-class psychology' in France.

Once we deduct all the false domestic industries and small firms, we are left with a minimal number of genuine independent artisans in Paris in the second half of the nineteenth century.[19]

Sublimism in the workshop: a war against the expropriation of time to live

Taking shape in the background to methods of day-to-day resistance is something quite different than the defence of a disappearing domestic industry. It was against the stranglehold of capital on everyday life and against its 'invisible threads' that the day-to-day trials of strength were aimed. The targets aimed for were derived from the capitalist industrial revolution, and had little in common with the former corporative and domestic industry trades. The life of workers in Paris was in a state of permanent upheaval. The foundations for the division of labour were transformed. They were no longer based upon a division by craft which could be handed down from father to son, from master to apprentice. The nodes of capitalist organisation, international commerce, department stores and industrialists were constantly redistributing work, reorganising their operations in order to place as many of them as possible in the hands of a workforce without any recognised skills: labourers, women, children and old people.

It was not only technology that was affected by the ubiquitous race for productivity. Legal practices and modes of remuneration were constantly being destabilised. Both in Paris and the provinces, different types of firms were made to compete with one another: factories, workshops, outwork.

In this context, workers had long since stopped dreaming of regaining some paradise lost of domestic industry. Only small minorities could still share the feelings of a Proudhon. For everyone else, the overall prospects served to prolong daily collective practices: forced by the insatiable stranglehold of capital into a position of permanent counter-pressure, they constantly used their meetings and their group texts in order to establish a collective counter-power as an alternative to capital.

This permanent confrontation is described with exceptional lucidity in a text by J. P. Drevet, a mechanic, a militant, and a former delegate from Cail's (one of the biggest firms in Paris). He examines in the simplest terms how a lack of interest in work developed. But rather than blaming this on some kind of Parisian folklore, he shows how resistance methods in workshops derived from the very pressures created by modern capitalism. In this respect, as A. Faure and J. Rancière pointed out when they rediscovered it, his text offers, nineteen years in advance, a kind of a working-class reply to Poulot's book.[20] Here are a few significant extracts:

> Do you want to know why workers are becoming alienated from work? It is not the work itself, but the length of time they are condemned to be imprisoned every day. They all love work; but whenever men and women are condemned to become the prisoners of work they will rise up even against the work they love; no man is prepared to lose his most cherished possession, his independence, for without it he is nothing but a

machine. And it is true that workers who are shut up from the moment they get up until the moment they go back to bed are not free men and women, but veritable slaves, machines whose only movements are those required to carry out their master's work . . .

. . . For example, take tailors, shoemakers, cloth weavers, silk weavers, lacemakers, etc., all those industries (frequently outwork) which give out piecework and where, because competition is so stiff, people are forced to work eighteen hours to earn from one and a half to two and a half francs. And not forgetting the women who work eighteen or twenty hours to earn from seventy-five centimes to a franc.

Such a set-up is a crime of lese-humanity, for it condemns those who serve society the most to becoming beasts of burden; it sentences us to death at fifty, without having ever known happiness.

If we do not produce as much as we could, if we fail to be as careful with the raw materials and our work tools as we could, it is because we have no interest in the boss's prosperity; he pays us as little as he can, we work as little as we can; he spends an hour arguing with us about our pay, and so we spend an entire day working as little as possible.

When we turn up at the workshop, it is not in order to work hard, but simply to earn the amount that the boss has agreed to pay us. How many times a day do we ask ourselves: What's the time? If that had been the bell, how happy we would have been to go home! I feel like I'm doing hard labour! I'm so bored! I'm fed up with grafting! Those are the kind of things we say while we're at work. If we see one of our mates damaging the raw material or a tool, we couldn't care less, when we see someone working clumsily we even laugh.

. . . If we help to invent or perfect a new machine, as soon as it is finished the boss will say: 'There's no more work for you.' In vain we reply: 'Our wives and children will go hungry. . . . This very machine which is replacing us, which is taking the bread from our mouths, we invented and built most of it ourselves.' . . .

All these protests are in vain, and the boss turns a deaf ear to them. He replies: 'Other people's problems are nothing to do with me; if there's a machine to replace you, as far as I'm concerned you no longer exist.'

Captivity at work was not the result of strict supervision.

Drevet equates (unsupervised) outwork and work in factories. If large firms were frequently referred to as 'penal colonies', outworkers and workers in small workshops and building sites felt just as trapped in a convict-like existence. *In fact, everyone was bound hand and foot by the same 'invisible threads': subcontracting, piecework and productivity-linked wages. Using such wage systems, the capitalist stranglehold was established in secret, without the imposition of a tyrannical hierarchy.*[21]

In the background of Drevet's text, and in the background of Poulot's, a permanent battle between employers' productivity incentives and workers' go-slow counter-offensive was being waged. While working at the Cail factory in Paris, Drevet himself had experienced the first attempts at imposing productivity-linked wages against which many Sublimist methods were to be directed. The system adopted at Cail's in about 1840, perfected at Le Creusot and subsequently put into practice throughout the engineering industry in Paris, was summed up by J. Euverte, an engineer and former manager at Le Creusot, in the following manner:[22]

Given an apparatus to build, a permanent fixed machine, an engine, a boiler etc., the design office does a complete blueprint of the ensemble and the details.

When the engineer has given the machine its final shape and when all the details have been completely agreed, precise names are given to all the parts which will go into the apparatus under construction. These names, along with the blueprints, are passed on to the foreman, who uses them as a basis for subcontracting the workers.

In well-organised workshops, all the parts of a machine, without exception, are given to the workers to build at an agreed price.

A workman is generally in charge of the same parts, or similar ones, so that as he always does the same job his skill is developed to the maximum. Therein lies one of the essential principles of the division of labour.

As soon as the workers and the manager have settled an agreed price, a document is drawn up stating that the man named X . . ., metal-worker, turner, or whatever trade, started working on such-and-such a day at such-and-such a time on a part with the number . . . on the blueprint, intended for such-and-such a machine, and that he will receive such-and-such a price. This document is given to the workman who hands it in when the part is completed, so that the agreed amount may be paid.

Later, at Le Creusot in the 1850s, Euverte perfected the piecework subcontracting system developed in the Cail factories:[22b]

> It was at that time that we got the idea of organising our accounts so that every day the workers could know the results of what they had done. Moreover we thought it was essential to introduce a 'progressive' principle into work prices (bonuses for rapid work, reductions for slowness) in order to stimulate and develop in our workers all of their faculties, and also to remunerate in a way we judged equitable the exceptional efforts we were demanding, efforts which in the final analysis would accrue to the benefit of the industry.

Euverte goes on to explain this 'benefit to the industry' at Creusot: rates of production were doubled, while, during the initial period, wages increased by 50 to 60 per cent.

This form of subcontracting, with productivity-linked wages, was an attempt to overcome worker resistance to the simpler forms of subcontracting. Therefore we must start by considering simple subcontracting and the way it was more or less thwarted. The subcontractors, veritable sub-entrepreneurs, took care of orders from merchants and industrialists, and competed for the lowest prices. They organised the work, and recruited and paid the workmen. Above all they profited from the pressure to reduce wages, since they pocketed the difference. One way the subcontractor could achieve a reduction in wages was to cut back on actual time worked as against the estimated time. From the 1820s and 1830s onwards, this simple subcontracting became general practice in Paris industry. It was the most transparent form of 'man's exploitation of man' against which many unions took up arms in 1848.[23]

Already implicit in simple subcontracting was a certain race for productivity resulting from competition between subcontracted groups: to maintain a certain level of wages the worker had to produce more and more, and faster. But the workers were able to organise various forms of counter-offensive, the most organised of which was the imposition of general branch rates to avoid Dutch auctions. But many other less collectively developed forms were elaborated and put into practice by tacit complicity, and these figure among the Sublimist methods denounced by Poulot. The most effective of these was probably a working-class counter-ethic of solidarity within work gangs to eliminate inter-exploitation: workers with different levels of skill refused to compete with each other. They harmonised their rates of productions and established more or less egalitarian rules for the sharing-out of subcontracted wages. Frequently the subcontractors themselves played along with this. Sometimes they took charge of a workers' counter-subcontracting system on an egalitarian basis. In the phraseology of the time this is called 'going into association'.[24]

Another Sublimist method was practised frequently in the 'luxury' industries most connected with fashion. In order to avoid long months of seasonal unemployment workers in fancy goods would systematically undermine urgent orders so that production could be more evenly spread. With the same end in mind they would limit the working week to three or four days, while still managing to earn enough to live on for the entire week. Bourgeois outside observers noticed this practice, but instead of understanding it as a contingency against being laid off, they used it as a basis for more or less picturesque stereotypes, be it the folkloric high-living worker or the deplorable improvident type. As early as the mid-1830s we read this description by a social aid officer which prefigures the moralistic reading of *Le Sublime*:

> Thrown in their tender youth into the midst of older workers who take a barbaric delight in perverting their minds and corrupting their morals, these men quickly develop an attitude of effrontery and depravity which they will never be able to lose. They are skilful and intelligent, working mostly in the more lucrative industries, and when times are good they can earn enough in three or four days to spend several more in idleness and debauchery, and then no matter how much they are needed it is impossible to get them to do any work at all.[25]

To overcome resistance to simple subcontracting, the owners of many branches in Paris went in for real productivity-linked wages.[26] In this way the power of the subcontractors was reduced, giving the employers and heads of workshops more control. The only responsibility left to the subcontractors was to make sure that the work got done. As for the employers and the workshop heads, they would obtain a quotation for each operation ('cost price' instead of 'price agreed by negotiation'). They would keep a record in books or on cards of all work done, and decide the payment. Variations of these productivity-linked wage systems were put into operation in large businesses as well as in small workshops, and applied also to outworkers and building site workers.

The principle behind the change was a simple one: rather than getting paid in exact proportion to the quantity they produced, workers now only received a bonus for extra work carried out during a specified time, while if they produced things slower than the norm they were liable to a penalty deductible from their normal wages. This is the very principle of 'differential rates' preached by Taylor half a century later: bonuses for faster work, penalties for everyone who fails to keep up the pace. From the employers' point of view, wages became material incentives. From the workers' point of view, it was an institutionalised swindle: a slowdown in production would automatically mean a reduction in wages, and this reduction would be proportionally greater than the drop in production itself. The system produced a vicious circle: increase in the rates of work – decrease in basic rates of pay – new increase in rates of production, etc. It would inevitably have killed everyone off had it not by its very nature sparked off a go-slow reaction on the part of the workforce.[27]

Older methods of resistance against simple subcontracting were still useful in the struggle against productivity-linked wages, but they did not go far enough. It became difficult not to join in the race for productivity. The cost of being able to regulate production and the number of working days individually or as a small team was a high one. As its dependence increased unchecked, the entire workforce became obliged one way or another to deepen its reaction.

In the workshops, such reactions could still have an indivi-dualised dimension, like, for example, refusing to keep a record of work subcontracted, or by disputing and disorganising the employers' records and accounts.[28] One of the collective reactions in workshops was to undermine, and this was used to regulate rates of productivity and to establish a position that would be the exact opposite of the employers' system of bonuses. But above all the workers' groups had to agree to impose very strict collective counter-discipline if they were to keep the initiative in the face of the threat of productivity-linked wages. From that moment on, workshop regulations about the start of shifts and the possibilities for talking, moving around and getting together became an important source of latent and overt conflicts.[29]

Sometimes workers would resort to violence in order to assure that the collective counter-disciplines were observed. Every workshop had to prevent any over-zealous colleague from shortening the normal time of production and thus allowing a fall in the official rates.

In their enquiries in 1872 and 1875, the employers' unions in Paris denounced a wide range of such resistance methods in workshops, linking them with non-conformity in family life, and suggesting how that recently they had become widespread. But rather than admit to the working-class counter-offensive against the race for productivity, they preferred to direct their attacks towards a certain 'immorality', an 'improvidence' and an 'idleness' in their workforce. The Paris Chamber of Commerce summed up the attitude of many employers' union reports when they sent these lines to the Minister of Commerce:

> Workers in Paris expect everything from association: they dream of working less and being paid more; they consider the employer as the worker's natural enemy. They mistrust the foreman; the workers police the workshop; if one of them is seen working in a way which they think is too skilful or too industrious, they denounce him to the committee as a traitor, and bring hidden pressures to bear upon him until he leaves or submits to the rules imposed upon him. The workers' aim is to rule the workshop and to lay down the law to their bosses.[30]

Family Life and Bourgeois Voyeurism

Thus, without wishing to admit it, most of the employers' unions in Paris were attacking the same forms of resistance that are denounced in *Le Sublime*. There is no doubt that in the Paris of the 1870s Sublimism at places of work was widespread. It had not that much to do with some kind of a folkloric tradition.[31] Quite the contrary, it came into being by contact with the most up-to-date mechanisms of exploitation. If one had to generalise the notion of Sublimism at work, eliminating its moralistic elements, one could define it above all as a dynamic. In a word, Sublimism was at one and the same time a race and a pursuit between modern mechanisms of exploitation on the one hand and working-class subterfuge to resist every system of ascendancy on the other.

Pressures to increase rates of productivity called the totality of daily life into question, both in and out of the workshop. This is one of the secrets of the coherence between different working-class profiles. Faced with these pressures, the working class was forced to react in one way or another, and resistance was inevitably bound to throw every aspect of daily life into the balance.

But it is even more difficult to decipher daily life as a coherent entity than life seen simply in the context of work. In fact, while resistance at work placed workers in conflict with pressures which converged, the struggle to have control over the overall pace of living was against pressures which were dispersed, and often contradictory.

Let us take the case of family policy in Paris during Poulot's time. Our previous deciphering of the different types of Sublime revealed the employers' strategy of alliance with their workers' 'bourgeoises', a strategy which implied a pressure in favour of legitimate marriage and procreation. But this is only one example, and we should not be fooled by it. In this case the employers could be compared to firemen who are also arsonists, since while progressing to fight bachelorhood and living together, they were also largely responsible for promoting them.

In fact the policies concerning the workforce and new techniques of exploiting it carried with them anti-family dimensions, the most obvious of which was the policy of immigration and of labour mobility. But there were many other aspects of employment which had analogous effects, and these were on the increase.

For this reason at the end of the Second Empire workers had to fight on two fronts: to demand the right to the kind of family life denied them by the new labour market, and to combat the methods of capitalist control which were developing as part of the campaign for the family 'bond'. If we had to sum up the various discussions on the 'family question' held at Workers' Assemblies from the end of the Second Empire to the first years of the Third Republic, we might well modify Drevet's remarks about work, and say 'We love the family against which we rebel'.

Recent histories of family policy have often neglected their anti-family aspects. However, if these dimensions are not taken into account, the behaviour of the working class as described by Poulot is in danger of being misunderstood or misinterpreted. It may be tempting to see Sublimist methods simply as a reaction against family constraints, and so echoing contemporary ideologies. But in fact the reality is not so simplistic. As a warning against such omissions, we will limit ourselves to one fact, a fact which in turn poses a whole range of questions. Oddly, the majority of observers have failed to notice it: *at the end of the nineteenth century in France, the majority of working men and women were not married.*[32] Given this fact, how can some recent studies allege without batting an eyelid that throughout the nineteenth century public authorities and employers carried out a 'strategy of familiarisation'? Even if we assumed that such a converging strategy had really been in action, then one question above all would need to be answered: why did the 'strategy of familiarisation' work so badly?

Beyond the question of family policy our deciphering of *Le Sublime* reveals an emotional life and a family life which are far from being directly accessible to modern ways of understanding, and to follow up a debate of the questions raised would take us beyond the scope of this introduction. But it is important to stress

several requirements. For the deciphering of *Le Sublime* implies a
questioning of the very way we are to understand working-class
lives from a reading of their 'memoirs' and the more or less
'bourgeois' transcriptions of them.

In their written accounts, workers of the time tend to be very
discreet about their so-called 'private' lives. And so our present
knowledge is based more often than not upon external accounts:
big 'social' enquiries into working-class life carried out by
doctors, economists, moralists and philanthropists; legal trials and
investigations; official studies by parliamentary deputies and
administrative demographers; accounts by journalists and novelists.
In fact to a large degree all these points of view tend to converge,
and yet they also lead systematically towards the same mistakes.
Frequently they are unconsciously haunted by the problems of
bourgeois 'private' life.

Zola's use of Poulot's book for the writing of *L'Assommoir*
gives us a first-class example of this.[33] He probably read *Le
Sublime* when it first appeared in 1870. Perhaps when he first
thought of describing a *ménage à trois* and using it as a symbol for
a supposed degradation in Parisian working-class morals, he was
inspired by it. In his first draft of *L'Assommoir* in September 1875
the intentions of the novel were clearly stated:

> To show the milieu of the people and to explain through that
> milieu the morals of the people; how in Paris drunkenness, the
> breakdown of family life, violence, and acceptance of every
> possible shame and misfortune are the result of the conditions
> of working-class life themselves, the graft, the promiscuities,
> the slovenliness, etc. In a word, a very exact picture of the life
> of the people with its filth, its moral laxity, its vulgar language,
> etc. An appalling picture which will carry its own moral
> lesson.[34]

It was in this frame of mind that he read *Le Sublime* for a
second time, but in a way that was revealingly selective. Right
from the start his notes ignore methods of resistance in
workshops. Only remarks on the degrees of 'laziness' of the
various types are noted. In Zola's book, if a worker quits, it will
be through lack of will-power. From that point on, the coherence
of the profiles in *Le Sublime* is shattered. There is no longer any
link between life in the workshop and life outside of work, unless
it be in the degree of conformity with the employers' needs. Zola
does not seem to imagine that the various types of worker
suggested by Poulot could react against their destiny, and organise
a certain art of living.[35]

This thinning down is at its most extreme in the way the female characters are conceived. Gervaise, the main protagonist, will be constructed with the characteristics of an innocent young bourgeoise, a 'white goose', martyred by the proletarian male. The fact that she is unable to hold her own against men will make her all the more touching. Thus she incorporates the dual role of 'woman' and 'woman worker' as seen through the eyes of a man of the bourgeoisie.[36]

Zola's shaping of sketches, portraits and situations from his research into working-class morality is unconsciously captured by those taboos of bourgeois family life which were recognised to be transgressed in the 'popular milieu'. For example, he can only see the frequent working-class practice of married couples and single people living together in the same house as a 'promiscuity', where in fact it was often a simple act of solidarity. The lack of communication between two different worlds stands out clearly in this one distinction. Poulot and Zola's perceptions are trapped in the same polarisations as those of a multitude of health, social or architectural enquiries into working-class housing conditions: because intimate parts of bourgeois life were partitioned off, social investigators into working-class housing conditions could only see the absence of their own moral barriers. These absences would fascinate the frustrated mind, and terrify the moralists and social workers. The next step was to 'imagine things' . . . But they forgot to ask themselves whether other rules of living together, specific to the working class, might exist. And yet the taboo of incest existed long before norms of 'social housing' came along to impose it!

Literary critics have often praised the 'pictorial' or 'photographic' artistry of *L'Assommoir*. But this metaphor must be taken at the level of its literal implications, and we must ask ourselves what are the processes by which Zola allows the films of his mind to be exposed, and how the resultant image is projected onto the mind of the reader.

In fact Zola's reading of *Le Sublime* is characteristic of a *bourgeois voyeurism* which is already latent in Poulot and which is apparent in a great many social observers.[37] Unconsciously bound by this voyeurism, most major social enquiries into working-class morality are walled up within their authors' representations of their own world. Peering through keyholes, the investigators see only their own fantasies.

Bourgeois voyeurism is a frequent way of representing working-class morality. But it is still only one of a range of ways, and belongs to a much wider mechanism: the formulation of every observation in terms of the deviance it establishes vis-à-vis dominant social rules. To see a different social code as immorality. To see the rules of a parallel milieu as criminality. To see social pathology simply in terms of an inverse model of a 'healthy' society. To see life styles which diverged from a recognised nucleus as marginality. To see unsuspected discipline as 'illegalism'. To see one's own imprisonment in a certain idea of progress as 'traditional'. To see moral behaviour which 'civilisation' could not understand as 'savage'. The list is endless.

The transcription of working-class behaviour has been sub-merged beneath all these mechanisms, and can be compared to the way Western colonisations perceived 'savages'. In ethnological studies of non-Western peoples, this phenomenon has long been elucidated and denounced as 'ethnocentric'. In the same way, if we are to use the documentation of the dominant culture in order to decipher working-class behaviour, *bourgeois ethnocentrism* must be exposed and thwarted.

'Let us get together and organise our own exploitation.' A capitalist collective project against workers' collective practices

Today Poulot's expression 'we should exploit our own resources' may seem to offer a cruelly ironic definition of the vague outlines of 'self-management'. There was no irony about it in 1870, but the same ambiguities were there: should exploitation be abolished or self-administered?

In his proposals for reform, Poulot lays out a very rigorous plan for the foundations of a democratic system within a developed capitalist society which was successful on the world market, in place of a cynical, costly and increasingly ineffective domination over the working class, he proposes a new dynamics of power relations on every level of society. He illustrates his theory by a technical image:

> The social question may be compared to an engine comprising a generator and a machine; the aspirations of the workers represent the steam, which must be distributed in the machine to produce a strength, a result, a product. But if you stop (and in politics to stop is to retreat) . . . the steam will escape through the safety valves; since the noise will irritate you, you will put two forty-kilo weights on them to keep them quiet and get some peace. Then one fine day . . . you will be startled by a huge explosion. You will not be able to start the machine up again, and it will be too late. People who block up safety valves are imprudent and clumsy. The machine must be kept

working at all times. When its every part has been perfected, the safety valves will stop belly-aching.[38]

Instead of repressing the aspirations of the workers and running the risk of a social explosion, the various authorities should learn to allow the labour movement to develop so that its energies could be recuperated or craftily deviated without ever being directly obstructed. This is the force of meaning behind the support that a large number of capitalists gave to demands for working-class freedoms.

After the explosion of 1871, several great channelling mechanisms along the lines of this new system preached by Poulot were in fact established. Above all it was a question of separating and coupling two overflows for conflicts, 'politics' on the one hand, and 'economics' on the other. These two areas, with their desynchronised rhythms, could easily turn out to neutralise each other, and even to enter into confrontation. At the end of the Second Empire, the political regime alone was beginning to move towards this duality, whereas within the labour movement struggles over wages and the constitution of workers' power were still indissolubly linked.

The system of diversion also worked on the level of day-to-day trials of strength, but with much less satisfactory results for the employers. It is well known that for a long time the workers' unions refused to play along with this separation of the two areas. This refusal was not limited to union hierarchies. No matter how it was formulated on an official level, it was in real terms the expression of modes of day-to-day worker resistance.

Poulot's political project did not limit itself to the democracy which was effectively put into operation by the Third Republic. It also contained a utopia which combined collectivism and capitalism in a way which may seem strange to modern eyes. Thus utopia must be understood in the context of 1868–70. At that time the dynamism of the Paris labour movement seemed irresistible, and unlike the 'party for law and order', Poulot was not prepared to rely on the provinces to repress it. To avoid the social explosion which many people felt was imminent, this capitalist offered a solution which was both peaceful and radical: the transition to a system of capitalist collectivism.

The propositions in the third part of this book make it clear that the expression 'organise our own exploitation' is not merely a paradoxical turn of phrase. Poulot was suggesting that every worker should have access to collective ownership of capital, and that worker production associations should be given the means to obtain it.[39] He reckoned that the essentials of capitalism would be maintained, and that after collectivisation, capitalism would not undergo any fundamental change of nature. The only real change would be in the way the accumulation of wealth was managed, whereas capital itself would merely undergo a modification of legal status.

Together all the producers would democratically elect managers who would be better placed than the 'money aristocrats' to get their men to work and to subdue the Sublimes. It was in this spirit, for example, that workers' *livrets* were to be retained. It would no longer be the responsibility of the police to supervise them, but of the official trade unions. In other respects widespread mechanisation, piecework and productivity-linked wages would smash go-slow practices and would bring about the defeat of Sublimism. To put it in certain Marxist terms, Poulot's proposal would safeguard the production of the dominant capitalist classes by playing the game of elective recruitment within a 'formal' workers' democracy.

To demonstrate the validity of his proposals, Poulot invoked the experience of the workers' production associations at the end of the Second Empire. Frequently the elected worker executives behaved like virtual employers' collectives. To back up his thesis, Poulot quotes some workers' association rule books which were so stringent that if any employer-organised workshops had dared to apply them they would probably have been blacklisted. In fact, by the end of the 1860s, there had been numerous optimistic attempts to organise workers' collectives inside every trade which were to be denounced as 'exploiters' associations'. In Poulot's view this experience could well be put into general use by a workers' democracy: the executives of collective labour would be placed in the position of the dominant class, guardians and guarantors of capitalist accumulation in the name of the productive class. Moreover, workers' disciplines would be much more strictly maintained than under the previous system.

Poulot's reaction to the Paris labour movement reveals both a detailed knowledge of its methods and a refusal to fully comprehend its underlying motivations. For example, if one believed that exploiters' associations ought to become widespread, one must have assumed that the nature of management must inevitably be capitalist both in periods of transition and after the establishment of collective ownership.

It was certainly possible to observe such a tendency, and in hindsight it is difficult not to make connections with attempts at socialism in Eastern Europe. But the methods of organisation practised by Paris workers just before the Commune could also have produced a quite different view of things. Most trades were aware of the dangers of self-exploitation. The various apparently byzantine discussions about statutes were in fact attempts to subvert the rules of the game of accumulation and management of capital. At the time when 'workers societies' (mutual aid associations, resistance funds, production associations, unions) were being set up, the worker collectives were playing the game according to quite different rules. They were not seeking compatibility with the social system, but on the contrary were promoting rules to oppose the dominant society (while at the same time not excluding compromises in accordance with the gradual consolidation of collective power).[40]

Within the most elaborate organisations it became the practice to widen the scope of the subterfuge and collective inventive capabilities developed during the course of day-to-day trials of strength. The six years preceding the publication of *Le Sublime* had witnessed an extraordinary dynamism which was so powerful that it surprised the workers themselves as much as it did the more observant employers. The workers' collectives took advantage of the liberal overtures of the imperial regime and accepted the institutional offers which had been put forward in order to hold the movement in check (toleration of strikes, reform of mutual aid associations, toleration of production associations, general assemblies of the crafts and unions, authorisation of public meetings). But in every case they managed to avoid the traps and go beyond the working rules.

In 1864, with the toleration of strikes, came the signal for this escalation. The measure had been intended to facilitate the amicable conciliation of disputes in all factories. But as early as January 1865 a police report made a preliminary assessment expressing dismay at unexpected social practices hitherto unknown and with no recognised analogy with the behaviour patterns of the groups which were usually kept under surveillance: attempts at unity within each trade; an increasing reduction of conflicts of interest with each new success; an absence of careerist attitudes and noisy rivalries among the enthusiasts for 'coalitions'. The cohesion was so incomprehensible, even as far as actual tactical details were concerned, that the Paris police headquarters suspected a secret dictatorship. The report analysed sixty-nine strikes which took place in Paris during the first eight months of tolerance, and noted that not one of the Workers' Commissions which had been set up to co-ordinate each movement had been disowned by the workers within the professions concerned. Not even the Commissions which had been set up secretly by tacit agreement and without official designation:

Some of the coalitions have been organised by ringleaders who have formed Commissions and imposed their decisions upon their comrades without consulting them. But the spirit of solidarity among the workers is so strong, and their fear of the ringleaders is so acute, that they have gone on strike and behaved as though they were in complete agreement.[41]

Here police intelligence was coming up against a fundamental dimension of the labour movement which was equally to stymie every category of 'common sense' produced by dominant culture: workers' *collective practices* cannot be reduced to the dynamics of the groups within bourgeois society. Here bourgeois ethnocentrism is evincing the same blindness as when it describes family 'immorality': it can only see the disparities with its own rules of behaviour, and is unable really to admit that different rules are possible.

The final third of *Le Sublime* offers an attempt at putting these practices back on the 'right' lines, and any deciphering of this part of the book will inevitably lead to an understanding of the internal dynamics of the labour movement.

Several years earlier, Corbon had already pointed out very clearly the presence among workers of certain disconcerting collective practices which were not reducible to the usual categories of dominant thinking. In the introduction to his book *Le Secret du peuple de Paris*, he warns against the short-sightedness of the bourgeois moralists and economists, the individual of testimonies of educated workers (the ones who have been . . . too good an example) and the populism of 'the truth that resides in the heart of the people':

It would be a serious mistake to believe it possible to discover the secret of the people by studying a few individual characteristics rather than the totality. Although the Paris worker is very forthcoming and easy to see through, I have many reasons for believing that the secret of the collective persona cannot be found in observations about individuals. There are some extremely important phenomena which only occur in the mass heart, which cannot be grasped except in the heart of the masses, which individuals are not completely aware of. Consequently their impression of them is more or less weakened . . .

Sometimes, to back up in passing some fashionable idea or other, publicists come up with the old saying: 'The voice of the people is the voice of God', but few are really being serious. It is a general rule that publicists who talk about the social sciences never look to popular feeling for their inspiration: and this is why on so many counts the people are still a mystery.

My point is therefore that those workers who have managed to accrue some general knowledge and enjoy spreading it within the milieu in which they live are liable to share the prejudices of the educated classes, and consequently they do not have the necessary frame of mind to offer any revelations about the instinctive tendencies of the popular masses . . .

. . . I want to emphasise this point: it is above all the collective persona which should be studied in its totality, and from a distance. I would add that it will be very difficult to see into the people's soul if one essential condition is not observed, namely that one should have been intimately involved over a long period of time in the unrest of the masses, so that afterwards one may find within oneself, and in hindsight, impressions and personal memories which will be so many points of reference.[42]

These 'extremely important phenomena which only occur in the heart of the masses' can influence the development of ideas themselves among the working classes. At the precise moment when Poulot was writing *Le Sublime* life in Paris was being shaken up by an extraordinary experiment of this kind, and which is still not fully understood today. Over a period of two years tens of thousands of workers were holding regular public meetings to discuss the 'social question'.[43]

Between June 1868 and May 1870 933 public meetings were held; at their peak, there could be 15,000 to 25,000 people at meetings on any one evening. The first meetings had been organised like kinds of people's universities. Economists, liberals, Catholics and social reformers gave lectures which attempted to enlighten the people pedagogically by passing on knowledge. But most of these meetings rapidly changed character, since the workers imposed their own methods of discussion. From that point on there were no more doctrines, pedagogues or learned personalities. The meetings had taken the character of a workers' 'co-operative school'.* Ideas about society, its history and its future were put to the test on the public platform, and were instantly approved or disapproved by the audience with applause or boos.

This method of reception bewildered bourgeois observers. Little interest was shown in the origins of ideas and even less in eloquence of style. The theories defended were treated in the same

* *école mutuelle* – eds.

way as the development of common policies in trades confabula-
tions, by going beyond internal oppositions and rejecting each
formulation progressively until such time as a real agreement
could be reached on the nature of the situation and the means of
changing it. To this aim it was customary to express approval or
disapproval for as long as was necessary. Speakers were in the
firing line of a kind of demanding and permanent scrutiny, and
the meeting places, with their hundreds of thousands of workers,
were like permanent juries.

Everyone was astounded by the speed of this evolution. For a
militant as informed and prudent as Varlin, the surprise was a
particularly happy one. In an article he wrote in March 1869 and
which he sent to the office of the IWMA he says:

> One thing that these eight months of public discussions have
> revealed is that the majority of workers actively interested in
> reform is communist . . .
>   . . . The social question came up all of a sudden, which upset
> the people in power and the high-livers . . . although it is still
> very vague, the communist system is more and more favoured
> by people who are working themselves to death in workshops,
> and whose only wage is the struggle against hunger.[44]

Poulot's entire book is a passionate protest against this
evolution. He sizes up his different types of worker politically
according to the way they participate at Public Meetings. He takes
his models for the Sublimes of Sublimes from speakers who
received popular approval during these meetings. He, the boss,
notes with deep regret the decline of Proudhonist ideas and the
advance of the vision of a 'social commune' based upon different
perspectives.[45]

Here again we need to decipher the caricatural way in which
public meetings are presented in *Le Sublime*. The long theatrical
sentences which Poulot ridicules were the product of an interplay
between speakers and audience. The apparently terrorist attitude
of the audience towards the speakers followed a precise logic.
They were expressing their dissatisfaction with every form of
institutionalised knowledge and with the deficiencies of available
ideologies. If anything was frightening, it was the high level of
demands they made.[46]

If we were to attempt a complete deciphering of Poulot's
various reform proposals we would need to reconstitute in a
similar fashion all the concrete practices developed in 'worker'
organisations between 1864 and 1870, when they emerged from a
phase of clandestinity. Through talking on every overture the

liberals made, the movement was able to elude all the traps set to harness it. Rather than being halted by them, it used the weight of each institution it confronted as though they were so many trampolines, springing forward in leaps and bounds. Strictly speaking, the establishment of trades unions was not in itself a working-class conquest. What was achieved was its diversion to the profit of the labour movement.[47]

The continuity between daily life and the labour movement

In *Le Sublime*, with its intuitions, its contradictions and its indignation, Poulot provokes us to knot beneath its surface the strands of its unavowed coherence: working-class subterfuge and derision of the authority of the employers had their own logic which informed daily life and thus the labour movement would be established.

Reduced to its most common level, this logic can be summed up very simply: it is the result of a dynamism of liberation. But in concrete social situations its complex progress, coupled as it was with contradictory reactions, was nearly always obliterated by dominant ways of thinking.

The example of public meetings is a good illustration of the obscurantist reflex reaction of a society faced with such a dynamism. Just as in Poulot's book, reports of them had concentrated on a supposed anti-intellectual terrorism and a picturesque *grand guignol* style, both declamatory and empty. In hindsight these debates were interpreted as having pre-figured the confused and bombastic style of many of the sessions held in the Hôtel de Ville by the delegates of the Commune. But such records and recollections failed to capture whatever it was that had made them such an extraordinary experience which many had felt to be very constructive.[48]

However it was more than the spectacle of disorganised discussions that made tens of thousands of workers give up their Sunday afternoons or evenings after work for two consecutive years in order to participate in debates and meetings about society. The observations in *Le Sublime* suggest a key for understanding the reasons why they had such a mobilising effect. Poulot describes a variety of practices which allowed for collective small-group discussion both in and out of the workshop. Amongst other things he complains indignantly about how newspapers were read collectively in the wine shops. We do not need to dig very deep to realise that what he is objecting to is the practice of criticising the press collectively, including the radical democratic press.

Once this is taken into account, the dynamism of the Public Meetings becomes easier to explain. They brought the need for alternative models of social relations which was discussed on a daily basis in workshops and wine shops out in the open. Conversely, these large-scale meetings encouraged small-group discussions and made *ad hoc* discussions easier. With results such as these, it is hardly surprising that the most assiduous of the workers' meeting places were swayed by a certain feeling of jubilation. They were like theatres in which everyone had a part to play, and where speakers and working-class audience alike managed to communicate in a triumphant complicity expressed by frequent laughter and derisive gestures directed towards the authorities.

The republican press of the day knew what it was doing when it joined its voice to the concerted attacks aimed at denigrating and despising meetings which drew working-class audiences, and if it did not go so far as to actually launch an attack upon the rabble, it nevertheless challenged the modes of expressions the Paris workers had introduced. For the mass media found themselves more and more doubled by forms of reinterpretation and circuits of interaction that contested their hold, and their method of representing social and political life.

Poulot had tried to explain the continuity between daily life and the labour movement by presenting Sublimism as a unique, contagious disease and the source of all forms of resistance. Although this idea may seem clumsy and moralistic, it nevertheless breaks through the barrier which is always present in today's intellectual attitudes. For Poulot, the labour movement was not an 'emergence' above a certain waterline of everyday apathy, and he made no distinction between the organised on the one hand and the so-called 'spontaneous' and 'non-structured' on the other.

A second symmetrical partition is demolished by his book: ordinary 'working-class life' is not seen as something routine and isolated, separated from movements of resistance to the dominant social order. Poulot was a man of action, and it was obvious to him that working-class behaviour could not be compartmentalised into a folklore of popular traditions. Only bourgeois voyeurism could be captivated by such a folkloric vision.

In the same way Poulot's intuitions go beyond the limits of his own portraits of workers' types. The milieu he describes is not summed up by a series of juxtaposed characters, psychologies or 'mentalities', fixed for all time. Our earlier deciphering of some aspects of his typology revealed how each type takes its meaning from its relation to a larger set of relations, and how a much more dynamic vision can be observed at work within this gallery –

every sketch of a couple representing a certain way of organising how to live and how to react against a social destiny. Taking this set of relations as a whole, we were able to imagine from it how ways of living were able to develop and diversify in different stages. For this deciphering to be complete, we must take one more step and consider collective practices in their ensemble.

Indeed the typology conceals the diversity of roles and functions at any given time. But individuals can change position. They are not irrevocably fixed in the direction that a system of domination may draw for them, and, when he talks about Sublimism as an eminently contagious disease, Poulot is well aware of this. It is precisely because they allow everyone to escape from the rut of the status quo that collective labour practices are so powerful. The dynamism of liberation is frequently surprising: it is able to multiply possibilities and redistribute them throughout a given working-class group.

Poulot lets this dynamic aspect appear when he suggests how each type might behave in a hypothetical social revolution. 'As a body Sublimes would produce as many heroes as they would vandals.' Workers and Mixed Workers would abandon their leaders to follow the Sublimes. 'The Sons of God have the makings of martyrs.'[49]

He based his predictions upon the trials of strength he observed every day. Be they heroes or vandals, the Sublimes were in constant conflict with the exploitation of their daily lives. Their destruction of productivity and savings of time and money was 'prophetic'. Their actions were understood by virtually the entire working-class milieu.

Even more unbearable for the democratic employers was perhaps the way in which there lay behind the derision of their power the derision of state repression itself. The Sublimes of Sublimes and Sons of God were not reckless adventurers, and their tactical skill in confronting years of provocation bears witness to this. Nevertheless as a whole the Paris working-class milieu showed that it was prepared to take greater and greater risks as alternative power opened up the perspective of another society.

Confronted with threats of repression, the movement was constantly improving its control over the use of violence. Derision of authority stemmed from a practice which was the opposite of provocation. Far from sparking off violence, the movement's prophetic challenges reinforced working-class complicity and brought it out into the open. Through them tactical opposition to police machinery grew to a fine art, as did methods of concealment, to take the initiative in unexpected areas.

From the gestures of daily life to massive street demonstrations the workers of Paris seemed to laugh at the repressive blackmail of the State apparatus. Every challenge seemed to say: 'even if we try not to get ourselves killed, we won't save our lives for the profit of capital'. The 'argot' itself, as Poulot situates it, plays out fate and destiny on the level of words. For the workers of Paris in the years preceding the Commune the sister of their derision of authority was the derision of death.

Notes

1 The following extract is from Poulot's preamble to his book:

> We were running a business establishment in Belleville (that Sublimist centre *par excellence*); two True Sublimes, formerly *grosses culottes* had got tired of propping the bar up, and had set out to look for work; after three or four rounds of 'vitriol' to steady themselves, they came to see us.
> One of them said:
> 'You the foreman of this place?'
> 'Yes, citizen.'
> 'They taking people on?'
> 'We don't need anyone right now.'
> The other said rather insolently:
> 'Fancy a jar?'
> 'No thank you, we never drink between meals.'
> 'Come on, we'll have a good one – none of your draught stuff.'
> 'There's no point, we're not thirsty.'
> The first turned on him angrily, crying
> 'You idiot! offer him a coffee with brandy!'
> 'For the last time, we don't want a drink and if we did it wouldn't be with drunks.'
> Our reply provoked a stream of abuse:
> 'What a twerp you are, it wasn't you who shat the column, good-for-nothing *aristo*, buzz off, you scrimping scrap of metal. You dumb oaf, don't you realise that what pleases God is the SUBLIME worker.' [Literal translation‾ eds]
> His tone and dramatic gestures made us burst into noisy laughter which brought the conversation to a close. We said to ourselves: typical SUBLIME workers.
> People no longer refer to orderly, well-behaved workers as 'good workers' and to lazy, violent and drunken ones as 'bad workers', they simply call the former *Workers* and the latter *Sublimes*.
> Hence *Sublimism*, that deadly plague that is eating the laborious classes away; we would add that this dreadful illness is spreading throughout the whole of society.
> With their mocking argot Parisian workers had not needed the

help of any brilliant thinker to come up with these two philosophical operations:

(a) to adopt the vision of Man-makes-God proposed elsewhere in Hegelian thinking;

(b) to claim an historic salvation for the working class by substituting 'man' by the productive class ('We are the productive class, and it's up to us to safeguard ourselves'). As a result of such metaphysical somersaults, the 'Sublime Worker' assumes the position and the function of God the creator.

2 A fifth criterion usually associated with the genre is the only one that Poulot does not use: the criterion of 'theft', since with the evolution of systems of production, it is not very relevant to Paris. By 'theft' was meant the practice of appropriating basic materials for one's own use and exploitation, whenever the modes of manufacture and commercialisation permitted, be it in the home, the workshop or the factory.

3 E. Lavasseur, *Histoire des classes ouvrières et de l'industrie en France de 1789 à 1870*, A. Rousseau, second ed., vol. 2, p. 774.

4 G. Duveau, *La Vie ouvrière en France sous le Second Empire*, Gallimard, Paris, 1946, pp. 492 and 519–20.

5 Just after the Commune, a learned scientific article entitled 'Essay on the comparative morality of various classes of the population, and principally the working classes' (by E. Bertrand, a Paris Appeal Court councillor) appeared in the *Journal de la Société de statistique de Paris*, no. 10, October 1872, using this idea to justify equating urban workers with the *canaille* (rabble). By manipulating the fact that effectively the workers experienced a stronger police repression than any other group, it demonstrated that workers in urban industries held the record for 'criminality'. Generally speaking most of the texts on 'urban pathology' churned out during the nineteenth century use this type of reasoning, which is often repeated even nowadays.

6 In Paris many workers in the sugar refineries would have fallen into this category. During a general meeting of strikers in April 1870, one participant replied to the accusation of immorality made by the bourgeois press (as reported by the newspaper *La Marseillaise* on 31 April 1870, that is to say ten days after the publication of *Le Sublime*. The speaker could well have had Poulot's book in mind):

Next, another worker . . . gave a deeply emotional, depressing and accurate account of the plight of sugar refiners who have to work constantly in temperatures averaging between 40 and 60 degrees.

'Piece-work is killing us and runing us; that's why we drink, and then we're accused of drunkenness, and when we're ill and exhausted we get laid off for two days. If we are to survive, it's imperative that we work a little less and earn a little more'.

7 In this decipherment we have not paid particular attention to living standards, which is something Poulot skates over rather too easily. The typology of workers corresponds to differing resource levels (see the Table: 'relative extent of couples' resources' column). Here it is important to remember that if since 1848 the question of famine and

food shortages is no longer posed directly on a scale of global consumption, the whole issue of hunger still confronts most workers in less spectacular guises. Poulot refers to it several times when discussing 'unemployment', by which he means seasonal laying-off. As a general rule, with the quantitative improvement of resources, problems of subsistences are eliminated during periods of employment for the young and healthy workers, but they are still present in other cases. They are more discreet, because their rhythms are more individualised. Moreover, given the abundance of commercialised foodstuffs and the improvements in transportation, workers could always buy damaged produce, just as more and more there were second-hand clothes for them to purchase. Few people died of hunger any more, but rather of food poisoning, contagious disease or accidents at work.

8 See the list of Poulot's writings at the end of this introduction, in particular nos 1, 2, 4 and 6. (French edition, not the present one)

9 As preparation for his novel *L'Assommoir*, Zola read Le Sublime, and we shall discuss its influence upon him later. He also read an article by Poulot on the bolt industry ('Work in metals . . .' no. 4). The contents of his manuscript notes reveal that he visited a bolt factory as well. The result is the precise description of manual operations using simple tools to be found in chapter six of *L'Assommoir*.

10 'Manifesto . . .' pp. 28–9.

11 We scarcely need to point out that in present-day political speeches and analyses of class relations which put forward new policies, engineers, management and technicians are always referred to as the 'new social strata', whereas in fact this kind of discourse or strategy is more than a hundred years old.

12 A reference to the legal impossibility of transforming trades unions into production associations.

13 There was a permanent in-fighting between union officials to get appointed to lucrative administrative posts in the Central Bank or in one of its intermediaries. Union treasurers became stockbrokers, earning commission and other rewards, and sometimes getting involved in crooked deals. In this way they were following the example set by the Bank's management: the main founder member, the financial group Donon, used shareholders' money to pay for the political 'publicity expenses' of Gambettist deputies. Production associations were set up simply as money-making deals between small professional cliques. They developed mainly in places where Paris councillors and parliamentary deputies could pull enough strings to obtain public orders for work.

By following Poulot's political action in this way (using business archives and police archives open to the public) we were able to unearth a little-known episode in the history of the labour organisations: the first attempt to unite the reformist trades unions nearly had its own little 'Panama Scandal' when it adopted the behaviour of parliamentary opportunists. The conditions under which this Union was created were even more suspicious than its revolutionary-orientated adversaries supposed. They denounced its shady dealings on the political scene, and dubbed its board meetings 'cabinet meetings'. In fact, the Federation also backed the aspirations of a small number of employers. Its treasurer, who was a sleeping partner in the newspaper *Le Moniteur des syndicats*, passed the accounts directly on to Denis Poulot. Seen in such a context Poulot's panegyric of the Federation and *Le Moniteur des syndicats* in the preface to the third edition of *Le Sublime* appears in a new light.

14 Poulot does not appear to have become involved in the legal irregularities of the Central Bank. He had probably been taken advantage of. It was possible to liquidate the Central Bank without a scandal. From 1884 a large reduction in capital made it possible to discreetly reduce the constitutional irregularities. In 1893 it was finally liquidated.

15 Alongside D. Poulot appeared notably the name of V. Delahaye, president of the Professional Society of Mechanicians. This labour federation, part of a split in the large Union of Mechanicians of the Seine, was based on the English model. It was well thought of by small employers. But when it tried to introduce production co-operatives it too collapsed completely, and disappeared in 1888.

16 The working conditions of the Lorilleux couple are described in minute detail in chapter two of *L'Assommoir*.

17 Marx, *Capital*, vol. 1, part IV, chapter 15 – *Machinery and Modern Industry*: Section 8b. L and W London 1970, pp. 461–2. What is really surprising is that there has been an intellectual regression in the way the labour relations in Paris have been analysed. During the second half of the nineteenth century, and right up until 1914, much more satisfactory intellectual methods were being developed, but now they seem to have been forgotten. Apart from Marx's analyses – impoverished by the prism of the 'Industrial Revolution' – the most interesting analysis is certainly that of the Le Play school, a group of Catholic-inspired reformers. Its methods were to examine precise case studies, resulting in the definition of a body of theory around the notion of 'fabrique collective'. Meeting up here with Marx's analysis, they emphasised the fact that in many large cities and rural areas the real units of production were vast ensembles under the direction of big capitalists, and that the so called 'independent artisans' who were bound to them by a variety of exploitative links were nothing more than ordinary labourers whose jobs were parcelled out.

18 Ministry of Commerce, of Industry . . . Labour Office, *La Petite Industrie*, vol. 2, *Le Vêtement à Paris*, by Du Maroussem, Paris, Imprimerie nationale, 1896.

19 Strictly speaking, by genuine 'independent artisans' we mean small producers living mainly on their manual work, and 'independent'. 'Independent' means dependent upon the market but not falling within the orbit of capitalist sleeping partners. By cross-checking censuses and fiscal statistics, and extrapolating from branch mono-graphs, we may arrive at approximate global figures. These are no more than ceiling figures, calculated from the total workforce of

obvious small employers, excluding all the integrated subcontractors, making-up workers and other identifiable 'independent artisans'. The real total workforce could have been smaller than these maximum numbers. Thus for the active industrial population (excluding transport and commerce) we arrive at the following figures:

in 1847 a maximum of 5.1 per cent of genuine craftworkers
in 1860 a maximum of 3 per cent of genuine craftworkers
in 1901 a maximum of 1.9 per cent of genuine craftworkers

20 *La Parole ouvrière* . . . texts assembled by A. Faure and J. Rancière, UGE, coll. 10/18, Paris, 1976, pp. 396–426.

21 The only detailed study of wage systems currently available is B. Mottez's *Systèmes de salaires et politiques patronales*, CNRS, Paris, 1966. The remarks which follow are taken from this book, and also from my own personal research into daily life in workshops and in the home.

When defining modes of control over the workers, Poulot's image of 'intertwining' has the same function as Marx's image of 'invisible threads'.

22 J. Euverte, 'On the organisation of the workforce in large industries', *Journal des économistes*, September 1870, pp. 363–4.

22(b) J. Euverte, *op. cit.*, p. 369.

23 Here, simple subcontracting is described in an obviously schematic manner. On subcontracting and workers' claims see B. Gossez, *Les Ouvriers de Paris*, livre 1, Paris, 1967.

24 In *Le Sublime* Poulot refers several times to a well-known example which bothered him, namely the carpenters. At the end of the Second Empire that had a 'free field', and subcontracting was thwarted by a corporative daily wage rate and collective control of rates of production. Their practices did not fit in to the usual patterns profiled in *Le Sublime*. In fact, the high level of resistance to inter-exploitation did not mean that there was not a marked degree of moralism in the execution of subcontracted work and in family life. In order to ridicule this good behaviour, Sublimes in the mechanical engineering industry called them 'Holy Joes', a reference to the holy Catholic family. (This expression, *bons josephs*, is still in use today in 1978 in the navy, where ship's carpenters are called it by the stokers.) But the 'good moral behaviour' of the carpenters, recognised by employers at the end of the Second Empire, did not last. Directly after the Commune the building industry began to slow down, and the labour market became less strained, enabling the employers to take the initiative. The inter-exploitation of subcontracting became widespread once more. As an effective method of defence, moralism had relied upon the *compagnonnages* and when they went into decline it disappeared completely. Thus carpenters' day-to-day resistance finally took the classic road of Sublimism, while their organised resistance relied upon the trades union movement.

25 H. Vée, *Bureaux de bienfaisance et secours à domicile*, undated pamphlet (circa 1834–5), printed by Crapelet, 110 pp.

26 Writing in a less limpid style than Euverte, Poulot advocates the same
wages system in his chapter 'Associations'. But he is more progressive
than the director of Creusot, and is quite prepared to accept the setting
up of union rates of pay, as long as they do not interfere with
differential piece-work payments. For a prosperous employer, union
rates would also have eliminated the lame ducks who used simple
subcontracting to carry out dumping on the workforce. Later, at the
Higher Council for Labour, Poulot was to defend the principles of
piece-work payments with bonuses and differential rates of pay much
more explicitly.

Historiographers frequently misunderstand wage systems, since the
relevant terminology has never been clarified. This is because systems
of exploitation always develop very rapidly, empirically, sector by
sector, without necessarily changing their vocabulary. Thus Euverte's
system was called simply 'piece-work wages'. Moreover the distinction between 'piece-work wages' and 'time-work wages' as used in
debates between lawyers and economists has no real meaning in itself.
Every time one of these terms is used we need to identify the concrete
relations they conceal. In particular when certain sectors abandoned
paying wages simply in proportion to the amount of work in favour
of incentive productivity-linked wages, the change could operate just
as much under the label of 'time-work wages' as 'piece-work wages'.

27 From the start of the 1870s, especially in Paris, employers began to
boast of the success of productivity-linked wages. Like Poulot, many
Parisian employers' unions considered that rates of work and
productivity had 'increased and were faster in Paris than in the
provinces. There is a paradoxical contrast between this self-satisfaction
in a high productivity and the tone of catastrophe they adopted to
complain about workers' go-slow practices. But it is only a superficial
paradox, and indeed it can often be observed in this day and age. In
practice it is quite possible for heavy pressure from the employers to
increase rates of production and intense worker counter-pressures to
develop simultaneously, while the level of production remains high.
From the standpoint of the workers, the mechanical engineers'
delegation at the Vienna Universal Exhibition of 1873 referred to the
increase in productivity-linked wage schemes by the term 'piece-work
wages'. They denounced the way they functioned:

> Apart from a few rare exceptions, the substitution of piece-work
> for hourly work has not improved the lot of the working class,
> because only the industrialists have profited from it. . . . The price
> for this type of work is nearly always decided by the employer
> alone and in such a way that productivity needs to be doubled to
> earn a fifth, a quarter or a third surplus value on the ordinary daily
> wage. We all know only too well that this increase in value can
> only be achieved at the expense of great effort, and above all,
> intelligence. . . . The methods of abbreviation (reduction in hourly
> norms) which have been introduced and perfected recently were
> invented by piece-workers. . . . As soon as a new method of
> abbreviation comes into being, resulting in a new increase in value

    as quoted above, then a rapid fall in pay (for the unit to be
    produced in a given time) merely reduces the workers' effort to
    nothing.
28 When he stresses the fact that the True Worker keeps a regular record
    of his subcontracting, Poulot is making an oblique reference to these
    methods.
29 We must have this context in mind if we are to understand Poulot's
    chapter on *conseils de prud'hommes* (elected tribunals). When ruling on
    individual disputes, *conseils de prud'hommes* followed the procedures of
    common practice in the trades whenever no written workshop
    regulations existed. In point of fact common practice was more
    favourable to workers than were the new regulations. In practice there
    could be rates of pay based upon time worked whenever there were
    no written specifications to the contrary. But Poulot advocates much
    stricter models for workshop regulations, which should be approved
    by a *conseils de prud'hommes*. He considers that industrial tribunals
    should also be in favour of employers monitoring work speeds, and
    that they should permit the payment of productivity-linked subcon-
    tracted work, etc.
30 'Letter addressed to the Minister for Commerce and Agriculture by
    the Paris Chamber of Commerce, 12 March 1872', produced, among
    others, in *Enquête sur les conditions de travail en France pendant l'année
    1872*, Chambre de commerce, Paris, 1875.
31 This is not to say that Sublimism did not make use of former
    traditions. But this was not a case of surviving practices which were
    dying out like so many melting icebergs. Old habits were reprocessed
    in the struggles of day-to-day existence, and this changed their
    meaning. For example, it was fairly common to 'observe Good
    Monday' throughout the eighteenth century. But in those days it was
    part of a series of trades guild strategies to control labour markets,
    whereas at the time of productivity-linked wages it became both a
    practical and symbolic way of regaining a certain control over the pace
    of living.
32 It is true to say that statisticians and demographers of that period seem
    not to have noticed the importance of this phenomenon.
33 Henri Mitterand has revealed the role of Zola's reading of *Le Sublime*
    in the book's development (study on *L'Assommoir* in *Les Rougon-
    Macquart*, re-edited by Gallimard, Bibliothèque de la Pleiade, vol. 2).
    In particular he uses the preparatory manuscripts for *L'Assommoir* in
    the Bibliothèque nationale. Among these are twelve pages of notes on
    Le Sublime taken with the explicit intention of using Poulot's
    observations in the novel. There are innumerable borrowings, starting
    with the title itself. But its inspiration goes even farther: the whole
    novel seems to have been born from this reading of *Le Sublime*.
34 Quoted by Henri Mitterand, *op. cit.*, p. 1544.
35 The masculine characters in *L'Assommoir* have thus been given moral
    profiles from *Le Sublime*, but the real practices of various groups have
    been weeded out so as to represent only good and evil. Coupeau
    descends the moral ladder from being a Worker to being a withered

old Sublime. Goujet is given the morality of the True Worker, and Lantier symbolises the immorality of the Son of God. When they fail to fit into the moral scheme underpinning the novel's composition, even some of Poulot's most explicit observations are ignored. One particularly revealing fact is that in *L'Assommoir* Zola's Sublimes do not have the work skills which Poulot concedes to them, while the True Worker is given specialised skills which in *Le Sublime* he is shown not to have. And yet, like Poulot, Parisian employers had frequently deplored the fact that work skills often went hand in hand with insubordination.

36 Another commentator of *L'Assommoir*, Jacques Dubois, rightly points out that in many respects the character of Gervaise is a transposition of a bourgeois character into a working-class situation. Her psychological motivations remain fundamentally bourgeois (Introduction to the Garnier-Flammarion edition of *L'Assommoir*, 1969).

37 Zola reduced the argot of *Le Sublime* to the level of a picturesque ingredient to impress his bourgeois readers. When he drew up his list of 'spicy' swear words it was as if he were filling up a cruet with salt to sprinkle on a meal. The whole procedure by-passed the essential dimension: Poulot always places working-class language in a certain situation, and he frequently gives a key to help us to understand from within how workers saw themselves in terms of events, their peers and their own destiny. If Poulot and Zola both share the same voyeurism, *Le Sublime* once more gives us the means to establish a certain distance and to guess at what the workers' points of view might have been.

38 Chapter twenty, 'Political observations'. Corbon, an ex-militant worker who befriended Poulot, also used hydraulic imagery at that time to denounce the 'repression' of the workers. He too proposed a theory of 'diversion' [or 'drifting'; translation of *derivation* – eds], an institutionalisation of the labour movement in order to domesticate its energies. He situated his analysis on both an individual and a collective level in order to advocate something which Freudian psychology was later to call 'sublimation'.

39 When the threat to the dominant order receded after the Commune, Poulot abandoned his ideas about collective capitalism and returned to a much more classic form of political radicalism. The experience of the Central Popular Bank never had the same ambitions, since its only aim was to skim off and use an elite of workers and craftworkers by facilitating the creation of small businesses.

40 The unusual practices in question relate specifically to the Second Empire. Similar collective practices had been developed during the spring of 1848. R. Gossez has pointed out the reaction of surprise on the part of the ruling classes and political authorities of the time. The very term itself 'the movement' – denoted something indefinable for the political and intellectual groups of the period. (R. Gossez, *Les Ouvriers de Paris, livre 1, L'Organisation, 1848–1851*, Paris, 1967, Société d'histoire de la révolution de 1848.)

41 Paris Police Prefecture, which was against the authorisation of general

assemblies of the crafts, made the following conclusion from this analysis: the workers had no need for general meetings of the crafts since sixty craft bodies had already managed to reach agreement in secret on dues and cash levies and shared tactics and risks.

42 Corbon, *op. cit.*, pp. 11–13. Corbon's book is unfortunately confused by a use of moralist language, and its most interesting analyses are not always as clear as the text quoted here. If it were possible to decipher the allusions to the situations and debates of its time, it would form a complement to *Le Sublime*.

43 Thanks to the book on the subject by A. Dalotel, A. Faure and J. C. Freiermuth, *Aux origines de la Commune. Les Réunions publiques à Paris, 1868–1870*, Maspero, Paris, 1980, the importance of the Public Meetings between 1868 and 1870 has been revealed.

44 Letter dated 30 March 1869, quoted in Eugène Varlin, *Pratique militante et ecrits d'un ouvrier communard*, Petite Collection Maspero, 1977, pp. 66–8.

45 The possibility of a 'social commune' had sprung up and taken root during public meetings as the framework within which a socialist revolution could be organised. Poulot appears to have followed its progress very closely, and in his political chapters he offers a point-by-point reply to some socialist articles by Millière which appeared in *La Marseillaise* in December 1869 under the title 'Our Programme'. A month later Millière wrote a detailed summary of the conclusions of a series of public meetings which appeared as a series of articles entitled: 'The Commune, a Social Question'. In them he analyses very realistically the problems which 'social communes' might face after a hypothetical socialist revolution. Among other things he discusses the considerable economic obstacles which would have to be overcome if an alliance between the workers and the peasants were to be achieved. It is possible that when Poulot called his book *Question sociale. Le Sublime* he was deliberately paraphrasing the title of these articles. But Millière's style has little in common with Poulot's caricatures of it. The second article, 'The Commune', has the following to say to its readers: 'We should not fool ourselves, we will not be able to transform our present communes by simply issuing a decree.'

46 Some intellectuals blamed their rough reception on the presence of a vague demagogic obscurantism within these working-class audiences. In fact these meetings revealed the ignorance of established intellectuals, and audiences would demand conditions for a real knowledge of society, as is shown by the frequent votes for social enquiries when discussions broached factual questions (for example, enquiries into female labour).

47 First of all it was the Parisian employers who gained control of the unions' establishment. Between 1867 and 1870, when 'workers societies' began to proliferate, subsuming the term *chambre syndicale* originally used to designate an employer's organisation, there were over sixty of these employers' unions already in existence. When he advocated the election of workers' syndics in order to give employers' syndics representatives whose authority would not be challenged by

the workers as a whole, he was speaking for a large section of employers. In this way Parisian employers hoped to be able to arbitrate in disputes, to regularise wage rates and to promote the joint creation of a certain number of welfare institutions.

48 One exception must be noted, however: the clear and lively account give by Lefrançais in his *Souvenirs d'un révolutionnaire* (republished in 1972 by La Tête de feuilles). In it Lefrançais, one of the leading speakers of the time, gives a more exact description of the atmosphere of these meetings, an impression confirmed in *Aux origines de la Commune* which we have already mentioned.

49 The 'makings of martyrs' of the Sons of God has little in common with contemporary Catholic mysticism. They fought as strongly against self-punishment as they did against self-exploitation. If they 'sacrificed' many things, they did not allow other people to rely on them. Apart from sentiment, it was nonetheless a question of efficacity. Worker counter-power was all the more effective for the fact that workers agreed collectively that they would have to pay the price for it themselves, without relying on the good will of others.

Part III
The origins of the Commune

Introduction

The following two chapters from *Aux Origines de la Commune*, are probably its most crucial elements. In them we find the most systematic and analytical exposition of the material found by the authors in the register under the number NA 155 in the archives of the Library of the History of the City of Paris. The discovery of this unique record of police surveillance made it possible to produce a far more complete knowledge of these meetings than had previously been possible, of their geography and location, of their changing public and of their relation to the elections and the Plebiscite which they came together to discuss.

Chapter Four, the section written up by Alain Faure, insists on the way in which the law governed the forms and modes of public association, revealing both its own inadequacies for its Imperial authors and precipitating a new knowledge of their needs among the popular movements of the City. The overlapping phenomena of the city in physical transformation and the evolution of political ideas suggest a new approach to the study of the sociability of political movements, the complexity of the relations of different rates and processes of change.

Chapter Five, written by Alain Dalotel and Jean-Claude Freiermuth, was conceived more specifically as a reflection on the political debates of the left in France in the period before the breakup of the Common Programme in 1978. Hence the foregrounding of the presence of all kinds of popular and spontaneous militancy and political originality. For the authors this debate on the mass movement had already lost its drive before the book went to print. What remains most significant in their exposition is the remarkable and definitive shifting of our understanding of communard thinking back into closing years of the Second Empire, a complex overlapping of social ideologies that refuses ready categorisations and historical labelling. In the two chapters then, the debate on the Commune as the 'last of the old/first of the new' revolutions is laid to rest.

The public meeting movement in Paris from 1868 to 1870

ALAIN FAURE

Introduction – highly-supervised freedom: its origins and use

> In the meantime we must keep these meetings going, because they are the people's school. The people need to learn. There are some who would be only too happy to stop these meetings. We must not give in unless we are forced to, and that will take some doing.
>
> Sébille, Folies-Belleville, 30 January 1869

A The law of 6 June 1868

The preparation, voting and application of the Law of 6 June 1868 on the freedom of assembly constitutes an important episode in the history of class relations in France during the Second Empire. After 1860 the moneyed classes began to capitalise on the support they had given their saviour of 1851 by demanding the restoration of parliament so that their interests could be better represented. The Emperor's response to these increased threats to the men and the institutions of his regime was to inaugurate a 'social policy' aimed at the urban proletariat. Increased freedom for Paris workers to assemble and elect delegates to the Universal Exhibition in London in 1862 was followed by worker candidates standing in the 1863 and 1864 elections, with the approval of the authorities. This new climate enabled workers to demand the removal of all the legal obstacles to their autonomous organisation and the free defence of their interests, but sincerely or through some ulterior motive – without making any fundamental challenge to the political and social organisation as such. From this moment on a series of prudent but essential reforms were introduced, aimed at gradually integrating workers' organisation within the Imperial state and the working class within bourgeois society.

The Imperial dream of a society pacified by the granting of

moderate freedoms and the intervention of the state as arbitrator between the classes was soon to collapse, taking the law of 6 June along with it. In fact freedom of assembly brought up the whole question of the legality of the unions which were springing up in large numbers at this time in an atmosphere which was increasingly hostile to the regime. Not only did the law miss its target, it also backfired on its authors by offering the enemies of the Empire, and the socialists first of all, the weapon of free speech.

1   A necessary law

The cornerstone of the Imperial policy of opening out the political spectrum was the law on Coalition of 25 May 1864. This law, which was introduced with the greatest of difficulties, being greeted with disbelief by the magistracy and anger by the employers, deleted the articles forbidding agreements (coalition) between workers to force employers to modify working conditions – strike action – from the Penal Code. Of course, the history of strikes does not start in 1864, but nevertheless the workers were to use this brand-new freedom immediately and widely. The police were obliged to let them get on with it, despite the 'intense annoyance' of the employers. But the splendour of the gift was relative: up until now there had always been a large number of strikes which had escaped the repression, and above all the obstacles to the exercise of the new right in real terms remained considerable. In this respect the most serious obstacle was not that all 'violence', 'assault' and 'fradulent schemes' which undermined the 'freedom of labour and industry' continued to be punished, but that Penal Law remained unchanged on two essential points: meetings and association. The right of assembly and the right to organise were still subject to the same regime of strict regimentation and prohibition as in the past. Workers could go on strike as much as they liked, but to do so would be nothing short of miraculous, as they were not permitted to hold discussions among themselves or establish any kind of solidarity. In the eyes of the law a strike remained a collection of accidental individual actions rather than a concerted one.

In fact some fundamental texts on general security were being threatened. Since the French Revolution penal legislation had been haunted by the spectre of organisations of people opposed to order of popular societies, of 'clubs'. Right up until 1901 article 291 of the Napoleonic Code remained the canonical text: the creation of any association of more than twenty people intending to 'deal with religious, literary, political or other matters' was subject to approval by the government 'under such conditions as it may please the public authorities to impose upon the society'. When the *Société des droits de l'homme*, a republican organisation with a predominantly working-class membership, tried to split itself into sections with less than twenty members, a new law of April 1834 extended article 291 to cover all societies with splinter groups. For a long time there was no text to cover occasional meetings, since it was obvious that an illegal association could not hold meetings, and the ban on opposition party meetings was natural, since such meetings would demonstrate a pre-established and permanent link between them. Under this regime, which the bourgeois lawyers called preventive, any meeting which was not held under the auspices of an authorised association was seditious by nature, and obviously guilty of intending to undermine the established order. Only an individual with material independence (property) was deemed free and sufficiently intelligent to manage public affairs and to act. In questions of pay, 'the master is taken on his word' by the courts (article 1781 of the Civil Code); by definition, the wage-earner had no voice. 'Get rich quick' was a moral associated with individual safety which denied the non-wealthy any kind of collective action. Meetings, clubs and coalitions threatened the stability of a society in which the individual who had become rich through his own endeavours was king.

The repression of socialism and the workers' movement during the Second Republic completed the stock of repressive measures against meetings and association. After the 'Great Days' of June, the decree of 28 July 1848 had already imposed certain regulations upon the clubs which were proliferating in Paris: the authorities had to be given prior notice of all meetings and a police superintendent had always to be present, women and children were excluded, delegations to government powers were prohibited. . . . Then came the revolutionary events of 13 June 1849: a law was rapidly voted through authorising the government to suspend 'clubs and other public meetings which were liable to endanger public order'. An emergency regulation, but one in fact that was maintained for the duration of the bourgeois Republic. It was the first time that the expression 'public meeting' had appeared in a legislative text. It may well have been in response to the banquet campaign which immediately preceded the revolution: in an attempt to get around article 291 the republican opposition had come up with the idea of disguising political meetings as innocent feasts. Taken by surprise, the government had been forced to invoke the by-law of 1790, which gave mayors the task of 'maintaining good order in places where a lot of people are gathered', in order to ban a banquet in Paris, and this had led to the outbreak of the revolution. But the main motivation behind the text was surely the urgent need to stem the wave of strikes by prohibiting workers' meetings. In any event, the precise expression used – 'and *other* public meetings' – shows clearly how strongly the repressive mentality linked the two phenomena: clubs were dangerous because they held public meetings, public meetings were dangerous because they could grow into clubs. This was a real headache for the lawyers of the time. Where did meetings end and clubs begin? The men in power had merely wanted to give armed might legal backing, leaving it to the legal commentators to sort out the details. Immediately after 2 December 1852, such niceties were no longer appropriate. The decree of 25 March 1852 repealed the July decree and made article 291 and the law of 1834 applicable to 'public meetings of every description'. The July decree had merely been intended to regulate and supervise clubs: the authorities had had the right to acknowledge their existence (by notification), but not to authorise them. The repeal of the July decree meant that all meetings were purely and simply assimilated with associations, and associations were all regulated by article 291 again (by authorisation). Clarity has always been a virtue of political dictatorships.

All this was upset by the law of 1864. Workers wanting to meet to prepare or conduct a strike had to seek authorisation from the Prefecture of Police; if they failed to do so, or carried on regardless of a ban, then they ran the risk of having the meeting broken up and being sentenced to two months to a year in prison and a fine of 50–1,000 francs, or double that for a second offence (law of 1834, article 2), for being members of an 'unauthorised association'. Workers ran the same risks if more than twenty of them made themselves into a permanent association without the authorisation of the Prefecture, either during a strike or not. In fact, once outside the workshop, coalition had become an offence once again, since all collective activity was paralysed. Therefore policemen and judges found themselves on the horns of a dilemma: whether to make the right to strike a reality by tolerating violations of police law which might have a considerable political significance, or to make the new law a nonsense and show it up as a trick and a joke.

The authorities immediately found themselves with their backs to the wall, for as soon as the law was passed a wave of strikes began in Paris which were larger than anything seen since 1848. Naturally the strikers organised many meetings without bothering to ask for authorisation. . . . The police were quite unable to cope, and had no alternative but to tolerate these illegal meetings, particularly as the new law prevented them from intervening at the root of the problem: the strikes themselves.

Soon, in the struggle to break down the legal barriers which were hindering the workers' movement, words were to take over from actions. We know that as an integral part of their policy of worker formation the authorities organised the election of workers' delegates to the 1867 Universal Exhibition in Paris. There were 316 delegates from Paris, representing 112 trades. They were elected in free general assemblies and for a long period of time they were the most influential and representative workers' group. It was in their reports on the Exhibitions, which were finally published at the beginning of 1868, and in the discussions at their (authorised) meetings held in the passage Raoul for the two years from July 1867 to July 1869 that the principal corporative demands of the working class were formulated for consideration by the Emperor and public opinion. Most of the delegates, while keeping their distance from the regime (very few of them were committed to it), believed that fundamental reforms were possible within the context of the Empire. That was the main thing: therefore it was the Emperor's social policy to listen to the delegates and to grant whatever possible, rather than to see the workers' movement become more radical.

Already the question of legal recognition for co-operatives (production, consumption, credit) had long been a subject for discussion among the men in power. The new law of 25 July 1867 authorised commercial societies under the name of variable capital societies, and thirty-five francs was all that was needed to found a co-operative legally. At a time when every worker was an ardent co-operativist, the measure was an important one; but a much more important issue remained: the right of assembly. The delegates' reports had been unanimous in their demand for its complete and total recognition. Many were prepared to admit that the authorities were good-natured enough and had treated them generously. But how long could this last? 'The government has authorised the delegates to hold meetings, but this authorisation is only temporary and may be withdrawn at any moment.' In fact this tolerance was less than generous:

> Workers meet in the workshop or when taking a stroll, and sometimes when they go to have their meals; no doubt they can talk among themselves, but they cannot hold discussions, and the absence of the right of assembly forces them to consult each other via their delegates.

Therefore 'what we need is not tolerance, but the right of

assembly'. Without this right, the law of 1864 was obviously nothing but a sham.

> Why must it be that when we praise the principles of justice contained in this law we are forced to point out an important omission which robs it of some of its effectiveness by leaving it to the whim of the authorities whether to tolerate meetings or to ban them, despite the fact that they are the workers' only means of reaching agreements about strikes and the ways of effecting them?

It was not merely strikes which were behind this demand, but also association and unions. The permanent links between all the workers. 'If we are to create the workers' societies we've mentioned . . . we shall have to hold frequent meetings to get to know each other and consider each other's needs more effectively.' Meetings, association, coalition, these were but one and the same necessity which had yet to be granted:

> Giving us a right, the right to coalitions, and refusing us the right to association or assembly, is rather like a father giving his children a trumpet and a drum and then saying: 'There you are, children, I promised that you could have these, but remember, don't make a noise.'

All the *rapporteurs* more or less agreed that freedom of assembly was essential if the workers' programme were to be realised: 'Without the right of assembly everything, from professional and mutual education to the development of co-operative associations and societies, as well as any kind of sincere election, is condemned to sterility.' The opticians' delegates pointed out that most of their colleagues were not even aware that their trade had its own production co-operative and mutual credit society. Why was this? 'Because there are never any meetings.' And they added that right of assembly was 'the fundamental basis of all other rights', or, as the pattern-making mechanics put it, 'the consequence of our right to reach an agreement about our closest interests'. After an interview with the Minister of Commerce on 19 January 1868, the delegates wrote a memorandum for their host which began by submitting the principles 'wishes and needs of industry' outlined in their reports for his kind consideration, but which then went on to conclude: 'Without the right of assembly, none of the reforms we have indicated can be usefully achieved without full knowledge of the facts.' For these wise and circumspect spokesmen of the Fourth Estate, meetings were the cornerstone of the future.

'Isolation will kill us, freedom to hold our meetings will give us life.'

2   The spirit of a law

The Emperor was bound to listen to the delegates since a decision of principle had already been taken. In February 1866 he made it known that authorisation of assembly 'would be granted to everyone who wanted to discuss their industrial or commercial interests, outside of politics' and, notably, authorisation to found co-operatives. A few days later, a circular from the Minister of the Interior recommended that prefects should authorise all meetings aimed at 'regulating the economic relations between employers and workers'. The famous letter of 19 July 1867 to Rouher about reform of parliament and the press, which was a rough draft for the future liberal constitution, contained this passage: 'It is also necessary for parliament to regulate the right of assembly by keeping it within the limits demanded by public security.' Chaired by the Emperor, the Council of State drew up a bill which was referred to parliament. In June 1867 the appointed commission presented its report, which was discussed in the Chambers in March 1868. The law on public meetings was proclaimed on 6 June 1868.

Appearing during the period of liberalisation of the regime, contemporary with the law on the press, one year before the general elections of 1868, the modification of the status of meetings is generally regarded as a concession by the regime to its liberal, Orleanist and republican opposition. But as we have seen, this was not the case: the measure was in response to the workers, the new law was a social law. In fact the bourgeois opposition had never asked for such a law. In his speech to the Legislative Body on 'necessary freedoms' Thiers said nothing about meetings. Certainly freedom of assembly figured in the traditional republican programme, but the republicans were the first to be surprised by the gift; for them the press was a much more important issue. Up until then the pink or pale red bigwigs who dominated the republican party from their lofty parliamentary seats had come to terms with the 1852 regime by organising private meetings, closed political groups where, under the cover of the inviolability of the home, the happiness of the working class could be discussed, while the object of those discussions was kept at a distance. In a remarkable speech attacking the bill's shortcomings and explaining why he would vote against it, Camille Pelletan told the Legislative Body:

> Private meetings are perfectly adequate for our needs and are
> worth more than the public meetings you are proposing. These
> public meetings of yours are nothing but a provocation to the
> police courts . . . There's only one thing to do: keep meetings
> private, shut your doors and let discussion stay in the family.

In effect the new law maintained the need for authorisation in the
case of meetings dealing with political issues, with the exception
of legislative election meetings: it is in this final aspect that the law
appears most like a gesture by the Emperor towards his
opposition, and a prelude to the *senatus consulte* of 1869 and 1870
which re-established parliamentarianism. But, over and above the
fact that since 1863 election meetings had been widely tolerated,
the gesture was here again directed to the workers, over the heads
of the republicans: 'Come along to meetings, proclaim how good
I have been to you and silence the opposition trouble-makers.
Remember that it was I who re-established universal suffrage in
its entirety in 1851' – this is what the author of *L'Extinction du
paupérisme* (The Eradication of Pauperism) seemed to be telling
them.

But exactly what did the law specify? Henceforth seven citizens
in possession of all their civil and political rights would be
permitted to organise public meetings in their commune,
excluding all political and religious matters, on the one condition
that at least three days beforehand they notified the authorities of
the place, the day, the time and the subject (articles 1 and 2). The
legal innovation of the law was a double one. On the one hand it
abolished authorisation for non-political meetings and replaced it
by the formality of notification. On the other hand it made a clear
distinction between assembly and association. The upholding of
article 291 and the law of 1834 (specified in the last paragraph of
article 9) meant that the law was intended to make each meeting a
separate entity in itself (one meeting = one authorisation), and
that the link created between individuals who had assembled in
order to discuss a common object would be purely limited to the
length of time of the meeting, and dissolved when the latter was
concluded. As Emile Ollivier put it to the Legislative Body:

> If we suppose that 6, 15 or 20 people got together and met to
> discuss one thing one day and another thing the next, there is
> no doubt that it would be a case to which legally one would
> have to apply the category of club.

In other words, a case for the public prosecutor. On the surface
the law was clear, and intended that reality would accord strictly

with the distinctions that it made, but in the minds of its authors it was another matter. Peyrusse, a *rapporteur*, made the following speech to the deputies:

> Messieurs, let us be realistic. We will never be able to prevent the same people from coming as informants, or agendas from being altered, or audiences always being composed of the same customers. What we want to avoid at all costs is the rebirth of the clubs. And, messieurs, what is a club if not a more or less regular group of public meetings made up of *habitués* who get together to talk politics (by inference: against the prevailing regime)? Political meetings mean the re-establishment of the clubs.

Therefore let us formally forbid politics at meetings, and we will have given all good citizens a moderately progressive law. Peyrusse does not draw this conclusion, but his entire speech was pointing down this slope: a-political citizens would be able to hold regular meetings without being harried, and the associative link which would spring up between them would enjoy the indulgence of the authorities. The latter would respect the freedom of such meetings, and would acknowledge the merit of unions which banished politics from their statutes and the hatred of employers from their minds.

But what is politics? A verbal battle took place in the Legislative Body and the Senate over the precise meaning of the bill. The preamble stated: 'No assemblies would be permitted where at any moment the institutions, acts and members of the government and the administration would be discussed.' A narrow definition of politics with which everyone in the Chambers, or nearly everyone, expressed their agreement, as they did on the point concerning the exclusion of religion: the Church is above ordinary citizens, faith cannot be discussed. The regime was saying: something is first and foremost political if it is against me and against God. But the text drawn up by the Council of State had been at pains to spell out that any subject involving 'social economics' could be discussed freely at public meetings. The parliamentary commission had not followed it on this point, and gave the following reasons in its report:

> To our way of thinking, political systems involve the organisation of society in its entirety, and it is in the nature of things that social questions are in part political questions, for governments are mandated by society, and are instituted by society to protect and defend it.

The political system underpins the social system; to permit the discussion of the latter would be not only to place the former in jeopardy, but to threaten the entire edifice. Rouher, the Minister of State, spoke up in defence of 'social economics':

> Messieurs, we have discussed these words most carefully within the Council of State, in the presence of the Sovereign himself. What are the reasons for our decision not to adopt them? Because we would have appeared to have been placing a ban on the discussion at public meetings of any questions relating to pay, production, the workers' labour, manual work, production by the employer, etc. . . . . We wanted to permit every freedom to all peaceful discussions which are not public political discussions, and to maintain in the form of a law what we have already accepted in the form of authorisation.

He went on to say that of course there were questions of social economics which were intimately related to politics and to the entire organisation of the city: The commission was forced to submit and the reactionary majority was made to swallow this bitter pill of 'social economics'.

> I think that to challenge the very principle of property would be a serious political issue, and there was no question of authorising meetings on that theme, nor on the subject of the family 'in its intimate elements', but everything else was a matter for free discussion.

This dialogue between *grands bourgeois* is truly exemplary. The guardians of institutions are first and foremost and above all the guardians of society, said the members of the commission, and to allow anyone who is not devoted to conserving it or who had been excluded from owning property the right to free speech and action would be to invite the very devil into one's own home and to fling wide the prison gates. Replying for the government, Rouher said that constraint could not always work, and that true wisdom consisted in giving the impoverished the right to govern their own affairs, in the spirit of the principles upon which society was based, and in a manner which would turn them into vigilant guardians of the system. The rifle on one hand, the law on the other: the purpose was the same. Thus co-operation was frequently touched upon during these debates, but only as understood in its bourgeois meaning, namely as a means of access to individual property. Pinard, the Minister of the Interior, who had spoken before the Senate in defence of the bill, had this to say:

'The question is whether the worker who cannot do without having an employer or any capital can become his own boss and earn capital in the form of co-operation'. Capital for all was the solution to the social problem; freedom of assembly was necessary if co-operation was to flourish; therefore, he concluded, the law was a necessary one and would help to 'make the worker conservative'. The authorities had seen nothing in the attitudes of the delegates that might have dissuaded them from granting this long-requested right. On condition that it remained moderate and politically faithful, the working class was being offered a regime of absolute freedom for its strikes and its co-operatives, and an unofficial statute of tolerance for its trade union – or so article 1 of the law suggested.

So much for the 'philosophy' of the text. But there were still the details, the application of the principle, which in the case in point was the essential thing. The rule of a three-day deadline for notification was a detail of some consequence: in terms of a vote to strike, it implied a decision which had been given much thought and which was very unlikely to take an employer by surprise; in truth it meant that notice to strike had to be given. In terms of the conduct of a strike, it put a stop to any immediate and collective reactions to unexpected initiatives on the part of an employer. The delegates would have agreed with this, certainly, but nevertheless would probably have wanted correct behaviour to be a result of their own initiative rather than something imposed on them from above. But that was nothing compared with what came next.

Article 3 stated that the meeting should be held in 'enclosed and covered' premises. Therefore public thoroughfares were ruled out for meetings (for then their name changed and they could only be called demonstrations) and they could not be held anywhere but inside a building. . . . Rather than being intended to keep onlookers away, the law was aimed at limiting the number of participants. Since public address systems and loudspeakers were not available very large meeting places were not at all conceivable.

Naturally the regulations did not stop at the entrance of the premises: the preamble stated that

> no matter how good its intentions may be, every large public meeting needs to be controlled, organised and maintained. Left to its own devices, it would soon become disorderly and a possible danger to public safety. It is therefore important to have people in charge.

People in charge meant a committee: a chairman, two assessors –

three members, therefore, to avoid an equal share of the votes. The principle of authority which had to be imposed on every human community – the family, the workshop, the nation – also prevailed for something as simple as a meeting. According to the terms of the law (article 4), the committee had to keep order in the assembly (in practice it controlled the debates) and to make sure that nothing transpired that infringed the law. This trinity made sure that audiences at meetings were kept under the eye of society. But since the task of making sure people respected the law could not have been delegated to citizens who had no specific mandate, and who at best had been elected by individuals who had assembled precisely to discuss the law itself at some stage, only their public-spiritedness was involved. Their only penal responsibility was to see that the agenda followed the form in which it had been notified: they had to stop any speech which would turn the meeting into a political discussion or a detailed review of all the things the participants were dissatisfied with.

At this point the other essential character introduced by the law made his appearance: the civil servant whom the administration 'could' delegate to every meeting (article 5). Here, as in every public place, authority, in the person of its mandated agents, had freedom of access, but in this case its presence was institutionalised and the duties of its representative well defined. He wrote minutes of the 'items' (article 6, paragraph 3), that is to say he put what he saw and heard into a report to the administration. It was certainly a good way of keeping police files up to date and of facilitating the legal repression of any criminal action. But the civil servant was not simply an observer, he was also a participant: if the committee let a speech slip through that did not figure on the agenda, he would remind them of their duty by pointing out that the law had been broken; if the committee continued to permit the speech or showed itself incapable of keeping the assembly in order, the civil servant could close the meeting (article 6). He was therefore the indirect censor of the speaking and the direct guardian of the committee; supreme judge of whether speeches were within the law, he corrected any mistakes the committee might make by giving them a warning, and took over from them if things became 'disorderly'. It follows that his presence and his right to such graduated interventions must have struck terror everywhere, among the audience, on the speakers' platform and on the chairman's dais. We should also note that the law did not formally oblige the civil servant to give a warning before deciding to close a meeting: as the legal commentators put it, it was simply a 'moral duty, a sign of good will'. In fact, the law subjected the right of assembly to the duty of right thinking:

like a convict let out of prison, speech had been placed under the surveillance of the political police.

Article 9 spells this out even more clearly. To avoid any hesitations of judgement on the part of the civil servant, it gives a precise list of all the possible offenders: informants (i.e. those who had justified the meeting to the authorities), owners of the premises and above all the committee members. It must indeed have been a dangerous honour to chair a public meeting under the rule of the law of June. For example, at what exact point did the penal responsibility of the committee begin? The warning prior to the closing of a meeting did not erase an offence – on the contrary it punished it – but nevertheless the law did not use this warning as formal proof that an offence had been committed. Law courts were to rely principally upon the evidence of the delegated civil servant to decide upon a committee's degree of 'tolerance' or 'non-tolerance'. Finally the law specified that if no committee had been formed, then the responsibility was transferred to 'those organising the meeting'. But who were these 'organisers'? The people who spoke most? The *informants*? What if they were absent? It mattered little . . . the police would know how to recognise its own.

A careful count reveals that this article cites seventeen circumstances liable to result in seventeen different misdemeanours. The article is quite explicit that it was a question of 'misdemeanours' rather than 'offences', in other words, infractions which were normally tried in the police courts. But the penalties provided for (from 100 to 3,000 francs fine and from six days to six months in prison) were far greater than police courts normally imposed (up to five francs and five days). Therefore any infringements of the law of 1868 came under the jurisdiction of the criminal courts, while the penalties retained the characteristics of those normally imposed by the police courts for misdemeanours. For example, an accused person would not be able to argue his good faith: only the facts counted. A landlord who had let his premises to the organisers of an unnotified meeting without realising it would be found guilty. Similarly the judge would be able to pass as many sentences as there were misdemeanours, rather than a single sentence as was the usual practice for offences: thus the members of an over-lax committee who had also given inaccurate notification would each be liable to a prison sentence of from 12 days up to a year. . . . The presence of the civil servant at meetings was certainly not for show.

As we have seen, it was the committee's responsibility to see that the agenda was adhered to. In the Legislative Body, this system had been found preferable to the one originally provided for by the Council of State: the personal responsibility of the speakers. It was argued that the committee members were extremely likely to be the instigators and the real leaders of a meeting, its 'brains'. By prosecuting the committee alone, one would therefore be striking at the head; moreover, by making the committee ensure order was maintained both in the audience and in the speeches, one was also forcing the leaders themselves to give a lesson in good behaviour to their troops; finally, to find them guilty would be an object lesson. But this would be 'without prejudging any prosecutions which may be carried out for all the other crimes or offences committed at public meetings' (article 9, final paragraph), in other words principally the various offences of speech of which speakers were liable to be personally guilty: (attacks on the principle of property, incitement of citizens to mutual hatred, insulting remarks about religion, etc.). As for members of an assembly who refused to obey a civil servant immediately he ordered a meeting to be closed, they were guilty of an offence punishable by a 6,000 franc fine and a year's prison (article 10). There was no need for open rebellion – passive resistance sufficed to constitute an offence.

When proclaiming the right of assembly, the authorities had at the same time given themselves a formidable defence system. The new system of repression was every bit as efficient as the previous system of prevention, and we cannot help thinking that under conditions like these a meeting which was notified, conducted and concluded without any incidents at all ought to have been awarded a badge for conformity and public-spiritedness. One final measure topped it all off: article 13, which gave prefects the right 'to adjourn all meetings . . . which were likely to upset public order and compromise public safety', even if it meant requesting the Minister's signature to transform the adjournment into a pure and simple ban. This power was well and truly discretionary despite what was said in the preamble. Article 7 was already at pains to point out that supervision of meetings fell within the competence of mayors by virtue of their traditional powers (the law of 1790). A simple by-law could adjourn or ban any meeting deemed dangerous. In the case of a crisis, the right of assembly was completely in the hands of the bigwigs and the authorities.

3   A law diverted

Was this the unreserved freedom of assembly called for by the delegates both in their reports and at their monthly gatherings in the passage Raoul? As Thiers had done in the name of the liberal bourgeoisie, so the elected worker representatives had called for the 'freedom needed' for the real existence of their class and their liberty. But what kind of meetings were they offered? Policemen in the auditorium (in Paris, the civil servant mentioned by the law was the local police superintendent, the *quart d'oeil* as he was popularly called), terror in the committee, closure for everyone and prosecution for those responsible for anything disruptive, not to mention the promise of an invitation to stay at home when the reasons of state demanded.

Let us leaf through the list of meetings held between June 1868 and April 1870 while the law of 6 June was operative. How many meetings of the trades do we in fact see? One general assembly of the *Chambre Syndicale* Tailors Union in September 1869, four meetings of painters and decorators in September 1869 on the occasion of a strike, three new unions founded (including the casemakers in 1869 at the Marmite, and the Consumers Co-operative founded by Varlin), a discussion between Mutualists of the 12th *arrondissement* in July 1869 and two assemblies of co-operative members (the Stonemasons' Association, at the Vieux-Chêne, rue Mouffetard). Even when a few more are included, the number of meetings is less than sixteen. 15 out of 933! However, to reduce the Paris workers' movement of 1868–70 to these few meetings would be utterly nonsensical. The conclusion is obvious: the law of 1869 had practically no direct impact on the corporate life of the workers; the people who inspired it were not those who took advantage of it.

When the law came into effect at the beginning of the second half of 1868, the Paris workers' movement had in fact evolved considerably since 1864, and the relations between the authorities and the working class were becoming strained. The powerful movement of strikes in 1864–5 had produced a renewal of unionisation: at the lowest estimate, there were a hundred or so societies between 1868 and 1869 which, accepting Jacques Rougerie's calculation, had an approximate global membership of 40,000. Now during the Empire, workers' unions were never anything more than *de facto* associations, tolerated but not authorised by law. When he made this tolerance official in a notice which appeared in *Le Moniteur* on 18 March 1868, the Minister of Commerce had been at pains to specify that if the unions 'should undermine the freedom of commerce and industry, or . . . deviate from their purpose, however gradually, and become political meetings unauthorised by the law, (the administration) would be obliged to prohibit them'. Therefore the law of 6 June could no longer be relevant to meetings of workers, since these had become a daily event in the life of the unions: as unions, were they likely to accept the imposition of a system of authorisation when their meetings already enjoyed a system of simple notification? It meant the ruin of article 291, that legal backbone of the prevailing political and social system, unless a new law were brought in to create a special right of association for workers, as in fact happened in 1884. . . . But the Empire could not and would not go so far. In January 1870 Varlin described the situation as it had gradually become:

> All our societies are outside the law. They only exist because the administration tolerates them. But this tolerance has become such a habit, and is now so deeply engrained in people's behaviour that it would be impossible for the administration to reverse it. We claim to enjoy the natural right of association. For our General Assembly meetings we simply inform the prefect of police at least twenty-four hours beforehand. He sends a policeman along who makes his report, but that doesn't stop us saying whatever we want to say. Our meetings are neither public nor private, they are individual; our doors are open to everyone, if we so wish it, or closed to outsiders if we so desire, it's entirely up to us.

The law of 1868 was conceived with a well-behaved and fragmented workers' movement in mind, for guilty strikers on the lookout for somewhere to meet and union officials ready to enter into consultations, and so when confronted with a strongly organised, aggressive workers' movement whose political allegiance was becoming increasingly shaky, it became quite inappropriate. The regime's policy of worker formation was shown to be a complete failure: the guest of honour at the grand celebration for the reconciliation of the classes was not behaving as the organisers had expected. If the workers had accepted the Empire's gifts, it was in order to control their own future, beginning with their day-to-day struggles, through strikes and corporative organisation. The initiative for social reforms had gradually changed sides and since 1864 the authorities had always been one law behind.

The failure of the law of 6 June is doubly important: from the point of view of the principle involved, it marked the freeze of the social policy of the Empire, and in terms of chronology, the moment of break between the regime and a large section of the organised working class. Certainly other reforms were to follow: the law of August 1868 abolishing article 1781 of the Civil Code, the law of September on Insurance Banks; several other measures were never discussed because of the war. There was nothing of fundamental importance here, although when we sum up the total 'labour legislation' during the Second Empire, we may well conclude that it was the first attempt at a labour law of any importance, a rough draft for the 'social laws' of the Third Republic. But the spirit of paternalism still had the upper hand among most of the bourgeois concerned about 'pauperism'; their worthy sense of philanthropy blinded them to the fact that if their class was to be preserved, attitudes other than the complacently displayed exercise of well-organised charity would be necessary.

One could never be too emphatic about the exceptional and exemplary character of the months when between the affair of the subscription to the Baudin monument (November 1868) and the third trial of the International (June 1870), Paris witnessed the death throes of the Empire. But this liberal Empire devoid of liberals – even though Emile Ollivier had long since rallied to the government – was not lacking in resourcefulness, and in the spring of 1870 it used all its methods of Imperial authoritarianism to launch a great offensive to uproot the revolutionary opposition (the trials of the First International and Blois's trials of the Blanquists), and to rally the crowds to the throne once more by giving them freedom of speech for just long enough for them to say yes (the Plebiscite of May 1870). Its last hope was to win eternity through the glory of human slaughter (war with Prussia). But sedition had already attacked the Empire at its heart before this burst of Imperial pomp. It was to be found not in the Cataline conspiracies of a Gambetta, nor in the immense popularity of a Henri de Rochefort, democracy's Milord L'Arsouille ('Lord Ruffian', nickname of Lord Seymour) nor in the campaigns conducted by the radical news-sheets, nor even in the disorder of street demonstrations, but in the emergence in broad daylight of a 'socialist' party which was backed by men of action and intransigent political objectives, both inspired by Blanquism, and which had the support of the people and the unions via the worker elites of the Paris workshops. The First International wanted to be the organisation for combat which would unite the corporative struggle with the political struggle, and workers' unions with local sections, to inaugurate a socialist and proletarian republic. The Commune was born during the Empire. From Autumn 1869, in fact, the prize to be won by the battle was perfectly clear: the regime was doomed, the Republic was about to be born. But what Republic? The Bourgeois Republic of a Jules Favre or a Jules Simon? The Old Lag's Republic of 1848? Or the Republic of Labour? For the powers which became involved it was a race against time, for the most aware Internationalists knew perfectly well what would happen if socialism was not strong enough to impose itself as soon as the regime changed: the Paris deputies would take over the government.

In the worker revolt at the end of the Empire an unexpected element was to make its appearance: speech, and it was to speech that we owe what might be called the diverting of the law of 6 June. In effect the Paris socialists changed themselves into public meeting organisers; 'left-wing Proudhonists', Collectivists, Blanquists, revolutionary unionists used the law to create their own platform: the great majority of meetings mentioned in our documentation expressed their ideas. For nearly two years, despite warnings from the police superintendents, closures of meetings and prosecutions, socialism developed its ideas and drew the crowds.

The militants of the First International who had been dispersed by the trials of 1868 were perhaps the first to realise what an extraordinary vehicle for propaganda the law could become. In February of 1869, Combault congratulated himself on the fact that the increase in the number of public meetings meant that 'everyone who thinks and acts among the working-class population of Paris has joined (the First International) both in principle and – though irregularly it is true – in practice'. In effect audiences at the public meetings were always mostly made up of workers, it was to the workers that the speakers addressed themselves first and foremost, and in some halls the entire audience was composed of workers. And what was the speakers' message, repeated over and over again, more and more openly and more and more violently? The Imperial regime had to be overthrown, not simply because it was a political dictatorship, but because it represented the power of the bourgeoisie; political struggle was the necessary and natural continuation of corporate struggle. The fundamental effect of these meetings was to make the idea of a social commune familiar well before it became a reality.

People and events had overtaken the ruling class, which was caught up in the contradictions of its social policy. In retrospect many of them sided with the reactionary majority in the Chambers who had only voted for the law through a sense of duty. The senior official at the Prefecture of Police who wrote a lengthy report which is still extant on the law of 1868 had understood it perfectly when he said that

> from the very first meeting, revolution was a foregone
> conclusion. . . . If the war accelerated the fall of the Empire,
> the government was already doomed because of the clubs, and
> after a period of time which one could calculate in advance, it
> was obviously going to be brought down by a popular
> uprising.

He concluded that the history of this law should reach society's masters that freedom to discuss political and social issues was 'the most powerful and dangerous weapon that could ever be left in the hands of the people'.

B   A tumultuous history

On 18 June 1868 the first public meeting to be held by simple notification opened at eight o'clock in the Vaux-Hall. During several months, the principal meetings were the theatre for an increasingly open conflict between the economists of the society of economic politics and the christian liberals, who had instigated them, and socialists of all persuasions. After January 1869 the former gave in, and except for the period of the elections, the extreme left was to be in control until meetings were discontinued.

At first the administration had recommended that the police superintendents 'be very cautious about intervening', 'temperate with their warnings' and 'above all to avoid resorting to closure of meetings'. Their brief was therefore to be inconspicuous; in point of fact the subjects discussed and most of the speeches were not at all subversive, the audiences were largely bourgeois and the committees themselves called speakers and audience to order if they were in danger of infringing the law. A first warning was indeed given at the Vaux-Hall on 14 July, but at the meeting of 3 August when an indescribable disorder erupted in the hall, the superintendent did not intervene and left it to the committee to close the meeting. If the Prefecture of Police banned the use of posters to advertise meetings, its aim was to avoid excessive numbers (the attendance at all the initial meetings in the Vaux-Hall was more than a thousand) rather than to stop them from being held.

After November, things began to change. The tone of speeches deteriorated, new halls were opened, and there was a sudden rise in the number of meetings: from 11 in October to 23 in November and 37 in December. The forthcoming elections brought the figure even higher, and in March there were as many as 117, a record for that period. On 10 November the prefect of police alerted his superior that meetings were being invaded by 'the followers of Tridon and Blanqui', that yet more meetings were being prepared in the *faubourgs* and that for all the enemies of the Empire, meetings were 'the most effective way of training the workers and preparing for revolution'. On 2 November a short demonstration was held in Montmartre cemetery at the tomb of Baudin; the plan to repeat it on 3 December led to article 13 being applied for the first time: a meeting about city taxes which was to be held in the Reine-Blanche was prohibited.

From that point on the conflict was not between factions within the halls, but between the halls and the public authorities. On 15 January 1869 the first prosecution for an offence of speech began in the Sixth Chamber. Conservative opinion was becoming mobilised, and when the parliamentary session was opened on 19 January 1869, the government was questioned about the police's inability to assure that the person of the sovereign, the dogma of religion and 'the principles upon which society is based' be respected at meetings. On the eleventh, the prefect's office issued the superintendents with new directives: the law of 1868 was being flouted, scandalous theories 'were being exposed at public meetings to the sound of sadly significant applause'. Henceforth, to ensure that complete and irrefutable reports would be available for use in the courts, the superintendents would be accompanied by stenographers. On 16 January a letter from the Minister of the Interior was published in the *Officiel* announcing these measures, and inviting public opinion to see nothing but a sad echo of the age of the club in these 'over-heated debates' and 'dangerous theories'. On the eighteenth, in the Jardin de Paris, just as the crowd was rising to its feet to applaud the speaker for invoking the names of Marat, Robespierre and Saint-Just, the meeting was declared closed, the first time this had happened.

The repressive clamp-down on the meetings and their militants was to prove more or less successful. 17 dissolutions were announced in March (one meeting in eight), 15 in April (one in seven); between January and June 1869 there were not less than 22 criminal prosecutions, in which the judges handed out 84.5 months of prison and 6,575 francs of fines to 39 persons charged. For example, seven people from Puteaux were found guilty of violating the law of 1868 by signing a notification while stripped of their political rights. In effect the administration had become extremely touchy on questions of procedure, and turned down any notifications which were not formulated according to regulations. On 10 March the police threw out the large number of people already gathered in the salle Robert because one of the informants had just admitted to signing a false name. In April they introduced a new tactic which consisted of sitting on notifications of meetings with agendas which had already resulted in closures. For this reason, on 9 April at the Folies-Belleville, the committee had to change the subject of the meeting at the last minute.

In reality this arbitrary measure concealed a totally legalistic preoccupation, and in effect every large hall had a regular agenda which was always organised behind the scenes by the same people. Take for example the Wednesday meetings at the salle Molière, where from 4 November 1868 to October 1869 'monopolies' were discussed; or the Folies-Belleville, where every Friday from January until April 1869 'labour unions' were on the agenda. The Imperial Prosecutor had drawn the government's attention to this as early as November 1868: these meetings, he wrote, 'make up a whole, a continuum, and gradually take on the appearance of regularly organised clubs'. And he was right. The people who had written the law were obviously caught between Scylla and Charybdis: after unions, clubs! The authorities were once again confronted with the eternal problem: meetings led to association just as surely as rivers flowed to the sea; tolerate the one, and you end up with the other. Therefore the measures taken by the Prefecture in April 1869 were intended to avoid this new hazard, in theory only the application of article 291 could have been really effective, but in practice the absence of a constitutional link between the various organisers made prosecutions impossible. In any event, it is to these measures that we owe the meetings with weird agendas where speeches with double meanings were received with gales of laughter: 'Grandeur and Decadence of the Crinoline in France' (27 April), 'The Art of Raising Rabbits and Getting an Income of 300 Francs' (20 April). On every front, the Empire's own obsession with the law was forcing it to fight shadows.

Finally, the last aspect of this anti-meeting offensive before the elections of May-June 1869 was the publication of the famous pamphlet *Les Réunions publiques à Paris* (Public Meetings in Paris). Since the beginning of the year, extracts from minutes had been passed to the pro-Empire newspaper, the *Pays*, but in his pamphlet the fashionable lecturer and paid publicist Auguste Vitu offered bourgeois opinion a copious commentary on texts which were supposed to illustrate the disorderly ideas prevalent in meetings. Atheism, regicide, murder, total abolition of the family and of property were the entire programme of this *cours de Miracles* and its hordes which, if not carefully prevented, would soon spread throughout the city brandishing flaming torches and knives. Once again 93 and June 48 were being openly prepared by these 'dregs of society' agitated by 'unhealthy ambitions'. It was hardly surprising that one of the heroes of these talking shops, Lefrançais, was 'a contractor for emptying cesspools'. Maxime de Camp invented nothing: as if the Commune were already there, *Les Réunions publiques à Paris* was already written with the pen of a Versaillais.

Even at the very outset of the election campaign the pamphlet had had a massive distribution, and was in its third edition. Its purpose was to provoke a holy union within the moneyed class in order to shame the liberal opposition for being against the Empire, and on the same side of the barricades as the socialists. But for us the important thing is what Vitu writes about the law of 6 June: in his estimation, freedom of assembly had sprung fully armed from the Emperor's head – he refers to him as 'that crowned thinker' – so as to open 'the wide avenues of the future to the laborious classes'. And, he adds, 'thanks to this freedom peaceful, co-operative meetings were held every day, blessing the sovereign's name'. But this idyll between the workers and their benefactor had become disturbed by the intrigues of 'socialist demagogy' lurking treacherously behind the law in order to win over simple hearts and pander to the most ignominious passions. This fabric of falsehoods expressed one great truth: Vitu was echoing those men in power who had become angry and worried at the way the meetings were going.

Let us pause to examine this bourgeois view of the meetings. At the time moderate republicans expressed their surprise that the government had waited until February 1869 before taking measures against socialist meetings, when opposition newspapers set up after the new law on the press had immediately been confronted with administrative measures and prosecutions. Some even did more than just suggest that the police had secretly infiltrated the meetings by the use of discreet disguise or speakers in the pay of the Prefecture. The public authorities, in allowing itself to be ventriloquised or in acting as a ventriloquist, must have sought to frighten the bourgeoisie before lending its pen to Auguste Vitu. But the situation was simply that it had taken the government some time to become aware of the real danger posed to the system by the meetings and the progress of socialism, which it had seen nothing more than a problem involving brigands and anti-social elements. At the Council of Ministers on 4 November 1868 it was decided 'to wait before making any prosecutions, until such time as derision should no longer prove to be an effective punishment for these acts of violence and madness'. For these important bourgeois did not believe that, in the working-class milieu, words could be powerful. Nearly all of them had received their business training at the bar, and for them eloquence and a persuasive tongue were the natural monopoly of the educated classes. They were in a much better position to appreciate Gambetta paraphrasing Cicero on the platform of the Sixth Chamber than to understand how much speeches at meetings could affect the masses both in their form and their content, simply by reading their minutes. For a writer like

Rochefort to publish a successful inflammatory pamphlet would seem to them to be much more serious than a couple of thousand proletarians getting together every evening to talk about 'social economics'. Their priority was to attack the opposition press because known enemies wrote for it and it was considered to be particularly formidable. As far as the rumours spread by moderates about the morality of the meetings are concerned, they may be seen as nothing more than attempts at discrediting the extreme Left. It is a time-hallowed practice.

Moreover, the repression started as a result of pressure on the regime from bourgeois opinion. While the liberal press, and sometimes even the radical press, was being very discreet on the subject of the meetings, the reactionary newspapers in Paris talked about them at length, in tones which prefigured Vitu. In the *Pays* in November 1868, Paul de Cassagnac wrote about 'political bawdy houses'. Should a man of government venture 'among the howling mobs', he adds, he would be exposing himself 'to every possible danger, without mentioning how careful he would have to be to protect his pocket-watch from the threat of communism'. The prosecutions and the new prefectorial directives were therefore clearly there in response to the disquiet of the Parisian bourgeoisie.

The period of elections for the new Legislative Body which opened on 4 May 1869 was an important step in the history of the public meetings. It brought to a halt the repressive offensive of the authorities, who, of course, could not treat election meetings in the same way. They had been authorised by the law of 6 June, although under certain conditions (article 8): there were to be no meetings after the fourth day before the ballot, and only candidates and franchised constituency members could attend. The second of these conditions was never observed because of the very large number of meetings and the enormous size of their audiences. In effect, in the nine Paris constituencies, and for both rounds (May 23–24 and June 6–7) exactly 200 were organised, with tens of thousands of participants. The first free election campaign of the Empire had fired public opinion.

Despite the fact that they had only presented the odd candidate here and there, the socialists played a key role in these meetings, both as organisers and participants. The audiences were larger and more diversified, but although 41 per cent of election meetings were held in halls which were usually employed for socialists' gatherings, it was the moderate or radical republicans who sat at the front of the platform, and who received the loudest applause: before winning at the polls, they had already conquered the meetings. Nevertheless the real mobilisation of the people during these elections had introduced the habit of going to meetings, and a powerful new public had been won for them. On 5 June the police noted that 'we have never seen so much activity over so long a period, and of such great intensity, although it's only happening in a few constituencies'. Moreover the street disturbances which were acted out in Paris in May and June had begun on 12 May in the place du Châtelet as people were leaving a meeting. Therefore, after having violently challenged the social system, the public meetings had played their part by checking the political system via the ballot box, and by endangering public order through riots. When the meetings were resumed the return match promised to be a tough one.

But that was not until the end of July, and on the 28th to be precise, in the salle Molière. The ban on meetings which was decreed as a result of the June disturbances was then only lifted thanks to the efforts of a small number of organisers, but in fact it was not until September that they returned to a level comparable to the one that had been previously reached. The slowness of this recovery must be attributed in part to the exhaustion of the socialists and in part to the sense of disappointment the election period had produced: the republican Left had retained all its prestige with the masses, who seemed to have been left largely indifferent despite a year of public meetings on the social question. It was at this time that Benoît Malon, who had organised about twenty meetings in Puteaux between January and April 1869, wrote in disenchanted tones to Albert Richard: 'As far as the attitude in Paris is concerned, I can sum it up in two lines: the minority are militants and revolutionaries, the majority are democratic republicans.'

But to this was added the serious problem of the shortage of meeting places. Halls which up until May had played host to a very large number of meetings both socialist and electoral subsequently disappear from our list: the Pré-aux-Clercs (40 meetings until April 1869), the salle Robert, boulevard de Rochechouart (26 meetings), the Vaux-Hall (20 meetings), just to mention the most important ones. In the case of two others, the Jeune-Gaule, place du Trône (35 meetings) and the salle de la Fraternité, avenue d'Italie (21 meetings), we know the reasons for the slump: their organisers, Budaille the schoolmaster and Nostag the writer respectively, were both socialists. Budaille owned the premises. Nostag was the main tenant. Both had tried to avoid police surveillance by giving out personal invitations to meetings without notifying the Prefecture; in April the criminal court found them both guilty of violating the law, judging that the private nature of their meetings was fictitious. As far as the other disappearances are concerned, police intervention is the only explanation. As early as the end of 1868 some hall proprietors had been summoned to the Prefecture and 'threatened with closure if they continued to tolerate disorderly assemblies on their premises'. In fact most of the largest halls were public *bals* which current regulations placed in the direct control of the Prefecture: they could be closed down temporarily or permanently by simple decree. The salle Robert, for example, was a former barrier *bal* which had just had its permit withdrawn. Thus the premises were empty, and Dr Tony-Moilin rented them. He organised 15 meetings there in March 1869 and 11 in April. The episode is a murky one, but it seems that the police took it upon themselves to lift the ban on the *bal*, only to close it up again in May or June, thus depriving the revolutionaries of an important meeting place. At the time the police regularly used pressures and tactics of this kind in order to hinder the resumption of the meetings.

The almost systematic practice of breaking up meetings betrays this intention. In August, 11 meetings out of 29 were closed by order of the superintendent (two out of five); of the first 15 (July 28–August 20), 10 were broken up. The reopening of the salle de la Belle-Moissonneuse, which had taken over from the salle de la Fraternité, was a difficult one, as it was not until the fifth meeting that the proceedings were allowed to come to a natural conclusion, and it was a miracle that even one escaped being broken up: *L'Extinction du paupérisme* was being read out, and the superintendent was following it with the text. . . . In September, when only 14 meetings out of 83 were broken up, the level of closures had almost returned to 'normal'.

Therefore the police had failed to halt the resumption of the socialist meetings, which had got their second wind and new premises: the Alcazar and the Folies-Bergère in the centre, and above all, a galaxy of halls in the *faubourgs* which were to play an important role, as we shall see later. There were as many public meetings in the second period (July 1868–April 1870) as there had been in the first (June 1868–April 1969): 462 as opposed to 471. But as soon as the meetings had got under way again, in September and October the conflict with the authorities became open warfare. On 10 October there was even a serious confrontation with the police at a meeting at the Folies-Belleville. After the 'clash at Belleville' committees began to issue warnings to agitators more frequently, and several times terminated violent speeches in order to avoid the eventuality of having to break proceedings up: during the 44 meetings held during the last two weeks of the month, superintendents only got to their feet and put on their caps four times to bring proceedings to a close. For a while, armed confrontation with the regime had been postponed.

A few days later the by-election campaign began: after the exercise of options for provincial constituencies, four seats in the Seine had to be filled (the 1st, 3rd, 4th and 8th constituencies). During this breathing space between ballots not less than 110 meetings were held. Only one was broken up (3 November at the Folies-Belleville), as against five in May–June 1869. It should be noted that 20 of these 110 meetings were held in private: organised above all by the socialists, their audiences were every bit as large as at the public meetings (on 19 November there were 4,000 people at the Folies-Belleville). Despite their equivocal legal status, private meetings had been systematically prosecuted by the authorities during the previous year (Forcade's circular of 4 May 1869). After November, although we are unable to give any figures because of the difficulty of discovering them through our sources, many private meetings were held with impunity: convoked by letter of invitation in halls habitually used for meetings, they were nothing more than camouflaged public meetings. This means that the estimated attendance at meetings during this second period must be increased, perhaps by between 10 to 20 per cent.

This election was even more passionate than the previous one, especially in the 1st constituency (Epinettes, Montmartre, la Chapelle, la Villette and Belleville), where there were 42 meetings, 17 more than in May for the election of Gambetta, despite the fact that the withdrawal of the other candidates of the Left meant that Rochefort was bound to win. This time nearly three out of four meetings took place in halls habitually used by the socialists, which meant that moderate or radical republican candidates frequently had a hard time of it. Despite the fact that the latter were victorious in the three other constituencies, the tone of these attacks, the voting of an anti-Left socialist manifesto in some halls and the whole Rochefort phenomenon proved that revolutionary ideas were making progress within the popular masses.

Between December 1869 and April 1870, meetings were intimately linked with the events which punctuated this period like some march towards civil war. In January, as a result of the vast agitation created by the assassination of the *Marseillaise* journalist Victor Noir, meetings were suspended for several days. On 7 February Rochefort was arrested in the wings of the hall which bore his name: the resultant disorders prompted the authorities to close halls between the eighth and the fourteenth. Among those arrested then were many speakers and meeting organisers. The atmosphere in the 96 meetings which were still to be held can be imagined when we learn that the deputy for the 1st constituency was made honorary chairman of 47 of them. . . . But the meetings which had survived two electoral periods came to an end with the Plebiscite campaign, whose meetings, 94 in number, were the last the Empire was to experience: after they had been closed, the authorities suspended the use of the law of 6 June. The arrests which followed the anti-Plebiscite manifesto of the First International (24 April) had already deprived meetings of a number of regular speakers: they foreshadowed the big trials of the men and the organisations of the revolution which were to take place in May and June. At the beginning of June attempts were made to persuade the Minister of the Interior to reopen the halls, but in vain: the floor had been given over to the judges.

In its broad outlines, the general history of the meetings reveals the surprises in store for governments based on political absolutism and social constraint when they grant such and such a liberal law: even the strongest safety railings erected to guarantee its application will be ineffective if determined opponents take control of its essential measures. Despite all the weapons it had granted itself to control meetings the so-called 'liberal' Empire was never able to halt the progress of the socialists once they had made a place for themselves in the halls. When it became impossible to go on permitting free speech, its only solution was arbitrary closures, in other words the implicit repeal of the law. But in the meantime it had given a platform to its worst enemies: the meetings were the veritable spoken newspaper of revolution, the organ through which its multiple ideas were developed, clarified and popularised.

C   Geography of the Paris of the public meetings

Nine hundred and thirty-three so-called 'non-political' meetings, 310 election meetings, 94 Plebiscite meetings, surely this is not insignificant, and in fact not many periods have experienced such a celebration of speech.

Before analysing the content of these meetings, it is necessary to understand their material conditions of existence. The political moment and the attitude of the authorities had a profound influence on the exercising of the right of assembly, which had been contested no sooner than it had been granted. But meetings still had to be held somewhere; prior to the meeting there had to be the hall, some kind of space is implied, and of all the problems faced by the organisers this was by no means the easiest one to resolve. For the question of halls for meetings has always been a particularly persistent one in Paris. From the couvent des Jacobins to the salle de la Mutualité, places of speech have their history, and an important one. To begin with it throws light on the possibilities allowed to working-class organisations to express themselves. On the other hand, knowledge of the places where meetings were held is significant and valuable, for the way urban space was organised always reveals social and political realities. The public meetings at the end of the Empire concern us not simply in so far as they were a victory for freedom of speech in Paris, but also because they were an affirmation of the belief that freedom could be won through speech.

1   The problem of premises

Felix Pyat, who knew what he was talking about, said in one of his novels that the right of assembly expressed itself 'however it can, thanks to *bastringues*, taking turns with *chansonnettes* in the *cafés chantants*'. In effect in the nineteenth century the speech of the working class never had a home of its own, and the places it found shelter in were always rented or commandeered. The meetings were no exception: the 63 halls in which the 933 'non-political' meetings were held can be divided according to their nature in the following way:

dance halls	:	21
cafés-concerts	:	9
theatres	:	4
circuses	:	2
wineshops	:	18
various	:	9

Of course at the time there was no question of setting up automatically in any old premises, since an agreement had to be reached with the proprietor, who had to be paid. Dance halls were by far the main haven (60.6 per cent of meetings). In fact dance halls were among the largest public establishments in Paris: the Vaux-Hall could hold 1,800 people, the Alcazar d'Italie 2,000; the Grand Salon Poissonnière and the salle Lévis 3,000, the Folies-Belleville 6,000. . . . They closed three or four days a week and many proprietors were in the habit of letting their premises out to societies or meeting organisers, particularly when business was bad. The musician's rostrum would be used as the platform and benches were laid out on the dance floor. A simple on-the-spot change, and music and dancing gave way to political speeches.

Certain speakers complained about having to meet in places devoted to frivolity and immorality. Just before Christmas 1868

Ducasse announced from the platform of the Folies-Belleville that: 'Next Friday we will have nowhere to meet, because here they're holding a dance to celebrate the birth of Christ. Obviously on that day we'll have little chance of doing anything serious.' Speaking at the salle Molière about the premises, Durand the shoemaker said that 'on Sundays it's used as a theatre so that people can come and learn the skill of murdering someone with swords, sticks or kicks'.[1] But perhaps these unhappy circumstances were not without their advantages. Outside of the largest *salles de bal* whose fame spread beyond the confines of their *quartier*, most of the 200 which were scattered all over Paris had an entirely local clientele: office clerks and petits-bourgeois on weekday evenings, workers taking Mondays off, entire families on Sundays and public holidays. . . . Going to the *bal* was like going to the cinema would be in years to come. Thus for most of the socialist meetings the venue would be well known. But even better, on evenings when meetings were held, the audience would not be very different than for evenings given over to dancing. Having a good time and politics were not mutually exclusive, particularly where young people were concerned. In Denis Poulot's spiteful yet authentic portrait of the mechanicians of the period, the 'Sons of God' and the 'Sublimes of Sublimes' are just as keen on public meetings as they are on dancing. What better sign for a meeting than the sign that hung outside a *bal*?

In any event, organisers had to make do with what was available and by dint of being undesirable tenants of limited resources they had to face many ups-and-downs of fortune. We do not know what fees the proprietors of the most popular halls charged, but we will get a rough idea from the Reine-Blanche,[2] a large *bal* on the boulevard de Clichy, which was rented out at 80 francs per evening, and the Grand Salon Poissonnière, boulevard de la Chapelle, which went for 200 francs. These fees, which included the hiring of the *bal* and the lighting costs, were paid immediately after the meeting; but as the hall had to be booked several days in advance, they still had to be paid even if the meeting did not take place. Thus at the Redoute on 1 November 1868, disquiet was expressed about the future as a result of non-payment for a hall at which a meeting had been cancelled the previous week; Horn reassured the audience by saying that he had paid 'what was owing' himself. Sometimes, at the start of a series of meetings on a specific topic to be held in one particular hall, a short-term lease would be signed with the proprietor: the hall would be reserved once a week for the organisers for a more or less prolonged period of time (six months at the salle Molière for 'Monopolies', for example) and at a lower rate than for ordinary bookings (in 1869 Millière hired the salle des Martyrs, boulevard de Clichy, for a month). But in that case the fee was payable in advance.

Election committees frequently hired a hall for the duration of the campaign. Thus the committee for Laurier (a radical candidate in the 4th constituency) took out a lease with Desnoyers, the proprietor of the Folies-Belleville, which gave them sole use of the hall for the entire month of November 1869. Following a quarrel with Jules Allix, who had also wanted to hire the premises and who had accepted the concierge's word on it, a 'treaty' was signed between the committee and Allix: the former was recognised as the sole tenant of the hall, and it was agreed that the latter be permitted to use the premises on three nights a week. At the same period, the committee for Alphone Gent, a radical candidate in the 8th constituency, had hired the salle du Concert, passage du Génie; they announced in the press that they were offering the premises 'to be used by all candidates'. The candidates with the most money would obviously be given first choice.

Money was the sinews of meetings, and their financial balance depended firstly on their audiences. As soon as the first meetings began

> it was agreed that the audience should contribute to the cost of hire by means of a voluntary contribution; but despite the diligence of the collectors, the necessary amount was not always forthcoming, and the organisers were forced to make it up themselves.

Many of the audience would slip out discreetly shortly before the end of the meeting or take advantage of the scramble at the exit in order to leave without paying a centime. And there were certain people who challenged the principle of making the audience contribute financially. At the Pré-aux-Clercs in July 1868, when a committee member asked everyone to 'make an offering' of 20 centimes as they left, Abel Peyrouton declared that everyone remained free and that it was up to the 'signatories' to contribute if there wasn't enough money to pay for the hall: 'We must show that being in the faubourg Saint-Germain doesn't mean that we are any the less democratic.' But rules became imposed very quickly: a basket was placed near the door and people would put in their 'obole' on entering or leaving. For ordinary meetings, contributions were still voluntary, but the presence of a policeman or one of the organisers near the basket would remind everyone of their moral obligation to make the financial sacrifice of a few sous. On the other hand at election meetings and at lectures, the public had to pay a compulsory admission fee: 25 or 50 centimes, one franc, sometimes more. In 1869 the funds raised in this way at meetings played an essential role in financing the campaigns of the candidates of the Left. For example, Lefrançais, a candidate in the 4th constituency, paid for his posters with the proceeds from a meeting organised at the Alcazar. As far as lectures, the most bourgeois of the public meetings, were concerned, their high admission fee had the dual aim of rewarding the speaker and selecting the audience.

Were organisers able to recover their expenses? To answer this question one would have to be able to establish the budget for each hall and compare the takings and the outlays, and our sources do not permit this. Let us make do with a few observations. The radical committee in the 3rd constituency (Laferrière), formed in November 1869, published its financial accounts: 4,690.45 francs takings from meetings in the salle Molière, the Redoute and the gymnase Pascaud, 4,956 francs outlay for 'hire' and 'sundries', in other words a deficit of more than 260 francs, 'made up by all the committee members'. Certainly, the outlay detailed here represents the total expenditure for the campaign, but the meetings must have taken the lion's share; therefore takings had not fully covered the hire fees. It is highly likely that in a certain number of cases organisers were forced to make up their takings from their own pocket; it is probable that a considerable proportion of public meetings were held thanks to democratic patronage. Appeals from committees reveal that serious financial difficulties were frequent. In September 1869 at the end of a meeting at the Folies-Belleville the chairman announced a deficit of 20 francs: 'If this continues', he went on, 'we will have to discontinue these meetings.' The organising committee of the Plebiscite meetings in the rue Dieu used the press to warn the public that as the meeting of 2 May 'will be the last one, and as the cost of hiring the hall has not been recouped, we have had to raise the admission fee to 50 centimes'. The Red Clubs were to experience similar vicissitudes during the Siege.

It follows that the wide spread of meetings is explained by their success with the people of Paris. Regular meetings on a single theme could never have run for several weeks, or several months as in some cases, without a devoted or constantly replenished public. But here again we have only fragments of information about the exact composition of this public, its geographical recruitment and its differences from one hall to another. We will examine these later, but in the meantime everything we know about this public indicates that it was on a massive scale, and made up at one and the same time of *habitués* and of people who attended irregularly or occasionally. And it was this public which kept the money permanently flowing into the coffers of the organisers. As we have seen at the Grand Salon Poissonnière, the evening could cost 200 francs. On 30 November 1869 an election meeting with a 20 centimes admission fee attracted 1,600 people: the profits were therefore in the region of 120 francs. Well-attended meetings worked like this: success meant a profit on takings which would cover a possible deficit in the future or allow for the hire of a larger or better-situated hall. An *obole* or admission fee of 10 or 20 centimes was nevertheless something of a sacrifice, since a worker in Paris earned an average of 5 francs. Notwithstanding, as enterprises which functioned both through self-financing and permanent contributions from the public, the meetings put socialism within the reach of everyone's pocket, every evening at the ritual hour of eight o'clock.

But the considerable disadvantages involved in hiring soon became apparent: after ten sessions the economists' meetings which began in the Vaux-Hall had to be transferred to the Redoute 'because of the prize-givings and *bals*', says Horn, their organiser. In December 1868 the meetings on the question of city taxes were not held in the hall that had been hired for them, the Reine-Blanche: as soon as he learned that the session for the third had been banned, the proprietor, 'afraid that he would be deemed responsible in the event of disorder', asked the organisers to find somewhere else to go in future. In effect, relationships with proprietors were to pose a permanent problem for the organisers, sometimes even poisoning the atmosphere of meetings. During the elections refusal of halls or manoeuvres on the part of the candidates of the Right were common occurrences. In May 1869 the committee for the radicals in the 2nd constituency was refused the salle Valentino by its proprietor and had to call upon the electorate of the Palais-Royal *quartier* to go . . . to the gymnase Tryat, avenue Montaigne. The salle Constant, rue de la Gaîté, was 'the only one that Rochefort's supporters had been able to hire at any price and which had been hired by the friends of M. Jules Favre without any difficulty.'

An election meeting in the presence of the main candidates had been announced for 31 May 1869 in the salle des Mille-et-un-Jeux, rue de Lyon: 600 people turned up only to find the doors closed. Losing patience, they appointed a delegation which went to see the proprietor, Père, tracking him down in a furniture shop in the *faubourg* where he told them that the hall had been hired secretly by Garnier-Pages, who had paid in advance but who had no intention of coming, 'as he was indisposed'. We have already seen that there was a serious shortage of halls in mid-1869; at this point we should add that the choice of the Folies-Belleville, the largest hall in the working-class east end of Paris, was in many respects a forced one since the organisers had preferred the large *bal* nearby, but its proprietor Favie had declined to allow socialist meetings on his vast premises.

In fact the political preoccupations of hall proprietors were often quite in evidence, but fear of the law in 1868 and above all of the Prefecture of Police, whose power to withdraw authorisation was an imposing weapon, must have made more than one *bal* proprietor think twice. Not a month went by without the press mentioning rumours about the imminent closure of the large halls because of pressure from the police. And with the possibility of material damage the chance of making a profit became an increasingly tarnished incentive. The proprietor of the Cirque Napoléon demanded a retainer of 15,000 francs for an election meeting on 13 May 1869, the day after a riot. At one meeting in November 1869, when the arrest of Rochefort was announced, pandemonium broke loose: 'The proprietor of the Grand Salon,' writes the tribune in his memoirs, 'told me afterwards that there was such an incredible din of screams, stamping of feet and kicking against the walls that he thought that the entire building would suddenly collapse.' Then on 28 December a meeting in the salle Molière was broken up, but the committee wanted it to continue: 'The boss of the establishment intervened and said that if they persisted in resisting, he would turn off the gas.' One can well believe that the insurance companies of the time would not cover the public meetings.

The absence of appropriate premises for crowded and emotionally-charged meetings was particularly felt during the election campaigns. In May, June and November 1869 the usual places for meetings were never empty: from 1–9 November, for example, there were no less than five meetings at the salle Molière and ten at the Folies-Belleville. On Sunday, 30 May 1870, at the time of the battle against the Plebiscite, both an afternoon and an evening meeting were held in five halls. But ordinary premises were too few in number, and with their limited space they were no longer adequate. A lot of ingenuity was called for. The time of the school playgrounds had not yet arrived.

Candidates may have been all in the same boat, but money and influence gave the government ones a lot of advantages. For his single, ill-starred election meeting, Emile Ollivier took over the Théâtre du Châtelet. Shopkeepers and industrialists often put their vast premises at the disposal of government candidates: a carriage manufacturer offered Pouyer-Quertier's committee a warehouse which could easily hold 3,000 people; the meetings of Allou's

committee were held in a huge store in the rue Dieu which had
been lent to them by some leather merchants. Admission to a
meeting held by Terme, Rochefort's opponent, in the salle de la
Boule-Noire, a large *bal* on the boulevard Rochechouart, was free,
something that was sufficiently unusual to merit our drawing
particular attention to it.

Considerably more crowded and more important, meetings of
the Left not held in any of the large halls always took place in
premises which were always improvised and which were often
unexpected and colourful. Emmanuel Arago had to pay a fortune
to hire a stable for a meeting at Clichy-la-Garenne on 10
November 1869. Rochefort's supporters organised eight meetings
in a leather currier's giant drying shed in the rue des Cordelières-
Saint-Marcel on the banks of the Bièvre. Gent's committee called
the people of Bercy to a meeting on some waste ground in the rue
des Fonds-Verts: a canvas sheet for the audience, some planks for
the committee and some candles to light up the speakers were the
only equipment. Gymnasiums were valuable venues for meetings:
19 were held in them in May–June 1869. The one in the rue de
Vaugirard, for example, 'is really a vast place which will hold
3,000 electors. The wall bars and ropes are hidden by the clusters
of citizens; some sit on the trapezes or perch right up near the
ceiling'. Cité Chaumont, 50 boulevard de la Villette, a warehouse
with an iron framework which had formerly been a workshop,
was the setting for two meetings, at which the electors of the
quartier seemed somewhat lost in the chiaroscuro of the immense
hall. But most extraordinary of all were the meetings held in the
catacombs: a path drawn out by paper lanterns placed on the
ground led to the entrance of a pit with several long galleries
leading to a central point where the platform had been erected; in
November 1869 and again in May 1870, 4,000 people responded
to a series of emotive speeches by making the vaults above them
echo to their resounding and unanimous 'Vive la République!'

After the incident at Reine-Blanche, Horn said that 'since we
are being forced to peregrinate so often, you will follow us
wherever we go'. He was right. In effect, meetings were always
being transferred here, there and everywhere, but always to
precarious and expensive venues which had to be fought for.
Deeply working–class, the meetings never threw down roots.

There were indeed a few exceptions. The most notable was the
salle de la Jeune-Gaule (or salle Budaille).[3] Budaille was an
independent schoolteacher to whom we will have reason to
return, who had converted his gymnasium into a meeting hall: 40
benches with room for 10 people, standing room for 200, a table
covered with red moquette for the committee. On the pediment

was the name of the hall, and a coat of arms with the words: 'Liberté-Vercingétorix-Egalité-Baudin-Fraternité'; lower down, dancing wantons were painted on the wall. Situated on the edge of the *faubourg* Saint-Antoine, two steps from Charonne and Saint-Mandé, this hall was for long the largest in south-east Paris, and when at the height of its splendour, at the beginning of 1869, it could rival the Folies-Belleville. Théophore Budaille had his writings distributed by his pupils, who wore Phrygian caps: 'You can pay what you want as you go out.' His attempts to transform his hall into a private venue for meetings, plus his habit of making subversive statements, resulted in his being prosecuted in April 1869. He arranged for letters of invitation for people to come and 'spend the evening' at his place to be distributed at public meetings and in the vicinity of the hall. In March 1869 six meetings of this type each drew audiences of a thousand. 'We don't have to split up at any set time' he declared at one of them. 'We're at home here. The night is ours.' He was given a year's prison sentence, and as a result the hall was provisionally closed down.

In the 13th *arrondissement* Gaston Buffier, known as Nostag, attempted a similar enterprise. Nostag, an unsuccessful shop owner who had gone into writing, was 24 at the time. Round about March 1869 he hired a warehouse which could hold 4,000 people, 27 avenue d'Italie, leased at 11 francs a day. Baptised Salle de la Fraternité, it was frequented by 'people living in the *quartier* for the most part', and in March and April 1869 twenty one meetings were held as well as several private meetings which also resulted in the proprietor being prosecuted. After the elections, the socialists had to find refuge in neighbourhood *bals*, the Belle-Moissonneuse (which they had already used before the elections) and above all the Alcazar d'Italie. Later in 1875, Chalain and Lefrançais accused Nostag, like Budaille, of being in it for the money. The similarities between the two halls and the two men are in fact rather disturbing: Budaille often came to speak in the 13th *arrondissement* and during the Commune Nostag worked for the First International as secretary for the section gare d'Ivry and Bercy, which overlapped the 12th and the 13th *arrondissements*. Had not Nostag wanted to start some 'courses in adult education' in his premises on the avenue d'Italie. . .?

Thus these abortive attempts to create independent halls were the actions of isolated individuals who had misread the social tendencies of the regime and who had hoped to cash in on their position as important figures at the meetings in order to carve themselves a place in the sun. But not every project was the result of self-interest. On 15 July 1868 a plan was launched from the platform of the Vaux-Hall by the economist Horn: the building of a hall 'where we can be at home' thanks to a sum of money which had been collected. The audience backed the idea, and in August an eleven-member committee was named to find a plot of land and to look into possible statutes for a co-operative building society. In November the commission delivered its report: a landlord in the rue de *faubourg* Saint-Martin had given his approval; with a down payment of 1,500 francs and the immediate setting up of a fund which would allow the work to begin at once with the balance to be paid off in three years, 'democracy' would soon have its own 'edifice'. Our documentation is silent on the ultimate fate of the project: doubtless the elimination of the economists must have effectively buried it. But it rose to the surface again in 1870: the *Marseillaise* of 11 January published an announcement by a commission which had been formed at public meetings 'to set up halls for public and private meetings'. It had just got as far as the final draft for a co-operative society. Once again our information stops there, but it is certain that none of these emancipated halls ever got any farther than the ground plan.

Why these failures? Of course, the first reason was that although there was no shortage of ideas, there was never enough money. Only a fund launched among the audiences at meetings could obtain the unobtainable. But a militant operation of this kind would have had little chance when audiences were floating and unstable, and already paying more than their fair share. At the same moment a massive fund in aid of the tawers who were on strike had been made possible through worker solidarity and the existence of workers' unions, but there was no institutional link to unite the frequently motley gatherings at meetings. Moreover, without rejecting the project in principle, many people refused to bleed themselves dry to see it become a reality: 'When we pay for big places already,' one worker replied to Horn, 'I don't see why we should fork out any more . . .' 'We ought to get the senators to pay,' added someone else. The fact was that there were too many useless mouths and wasted space! 'We pay taxes for them to build palaces, churches for tarts, and to do crooked deals.' Flourens summed up the dominant feeling of the audience when he said prophetically that: 'We'll turn the churches into meeting places for the people.' Everyone thought that before Houses for the People were built, the bourgeois stranglehold on society and thus on the city had to be smashed. A free man in a free city would then be at home everywhere.

2   The large meeting halls

The public meetings of the Second Empire were not immune from the political and social effects of the transformations of Paris. They have a close link with the organisation of space and the labour market of the capital. To explain our maps is to try to understand the reasons for the distribution of the meetings, both in terms of numbers and of halls.

The 'works of Haussmann' represent the Parisian version of the phenomenon of the provisional restructuring which affected nearly every big city in capitalist Europe at about the middle of the nineteenth century. When they first began, the drastic changes imposed on traditional trades by the Industrial Revolution and free enterprise were drawing a new workforce into the already congested city. Its concentration within the city boundaries or *octrois* led to a rapid saturation of space, while *extra muros* suburbs developed, each commune slowly evolving from rural village to dormitory town. The hardening of social relations and living conditions in the old centres produced a permanent threat to the political system: the edifices of bourgeois power (townhalls and *mairies* of the *arrondissements*, prefectures and ministries) were caught up in a mass of workshops and housing; to a large extent working class and bourgeoisie, rich and poor still coexisted in the same *quartiers*, sometimes even in the same houses. It was the era of civil war with the gloves on. Then came the era of the enlightened administrator, Vaisse in Lyon, Richeebe in Lille, Haussmann in Paris, under whose reign the *faubourgs* were annexed and the old *quartiers* bled: henceforth old cities would be renovated and new ones destined for the poorest members of the community would be built alongside them: thus urban space became characterised by a centre and a periphery.

This sketch may be crude, but it is basically accurate, and Paris is a classic illustration of it. The circle of suburbs, already swollen by exoduses produced by demolition and rent rises *intra muros*, and now the obligatory haven of bare-handed immigrants, was annexed in 1859: a periphery (the last 10 *arrondissements*) which was predominantly working-class, a centre (the first 10) which was predominantly bourgeois. The former communes which were now *faubourgs* (Montmartre, Belleville, Grenelle, Charonne, les Batignolles, Bercy, Montrouge) formed a circle around the central *arrondissements* in which the bourgeoisie could spread themselves out comfortably; henceforth the line of the former *octroi* barriers (the second circle of the boulevards) would be the demarcation line of a social division of space within the city as a whole. It would be impossible to understand the public meetings without reference to this increasingly clear-cut opposition between the working-class colonies of the periphery and the parent city.

Everyone at the time remarked upon the speed at which venues for meetings evolved: after the meetings at the Vaux-Hall and the Redoute, writes Vitu, 'came . . . public meetings as such, the ones held in the Vieux-Chêne, at Belleville, Menilmontant, Montparnasse'. Meetings left the *beaux quartiers* for the *faubourgs*, at the same time modifying their agendas and their audiences. Albert Thomas was also struck by this phenomenon, and compares the meetings of the Empire with the People's Universities at the end of the century which experienced the same slide towards the same *quartiers*. To bourgeois thinking the farther away a hall was the more violent its ideas were likely to be. An article in the *Gaulois* provoked the indignation of its readers by situating the salle de la Révolution, rue de la Crimée, 'right next to the Carrières d'Amérique', a habitual haunt of cut-throats in cheap crime novels. But what exactly do the figures tell us? For the entire period (excluding election periods):

	Halls	Meetings
Centre	28	416 (44.6%)
Periphery	37	474 (50.8%)
Suburbs	8	43 (4.5%)
Total	73	933 (99.9%)

As we see, there were more halls and meetings in the periphery than in the centre, particularly if we include meetings in the suburbs. During the period from July 1869 to May 1870 the number of meetings held in the central *arrondissements* was practically the same as during the previous period (209 as against 207); in the *arrondissements* of the periphery they increased by 9.2 per cent (247 as against 227), while in the suburbs they became rare (6 as against 37). The spread of halls in the periphery is an indication of the unstable nature of meetings in the *faubourgs* – be it due to increasingly difficult relations with proprietors or to insufficient funds – but also of an increasingly strong capacity to start from scratch again: after June 1869 fifteen peripheral halls disappeared, and the next month fourteen new ones were inaugurated, as opposed to nine and nine in the centre and six and twelve in the suburbs. Important halls in the centre like the Pré-aux-Clercs or the Vaux-Hall were not strictly speaking replaced, whereas just about everywhere in the periphery new and important halls were opened which each held about twenty meetings during the Plebiscite. We should add that more than three out of four meetings which were broken up took place in the *faubourgs* (80 out of 11). These more difficult conditions of existence in no way stopped the word of socialism from spreading throughout working-class Paris.

But it was in the other Paris of power and wealth that the first meetings took place, in halls which were always among the most important and the best attended. The audiences were always predominantly bourgeoisie, but on occasion they attracted a working-class public, sometimes on a massive scale. For in the centre a number of *quartiers* still had a worker population, which stayed on because of modest rents or the wide availability of jobs locally. Thus the halls in the 5th *arrondissement* were thronged with the people of the Montagne-Sainte-Genevieve: furnished rooms where building workers lived, houses which sheltered the silent labour of out-workers, filthy, dilapidated cottages for people who lived from street trading. . . . The Vieux-Chêne was the epitome of those neighbourhood *bals* where meetings were so frequently happy to find a home: a former *bal champêtre* whose garden had been invaded by workshops, its modest hall welcomed generation upon generation of stonemasons and rag-and-bone men until it was finally closed down in 1882. In the bourgeois guide to the places to go dancing in Paris, it had long enjoyed a high reputation: 'The street is as good as the *bal*, the *bal* is as good as the street.' Its audience? 'Some are Cayenne game, others are game from Saint-Lazare.' On evenings when there were meetings and the crowds thronged the rue Mouffetard, the author could have added game from Sainte-Pélagie. It was here at a meeting in October 1868 that the deputy Darimon, who had rallied with the government, was sent packing by a hostile audience. As one speaker said: 'I like the Vieux-Chêne because you never hear any supporters of the clergy there.'

There is nothing surprising in the fact that Lefrançais recalled having seen 'a few *messieurs*' at the first Vaux-Hall meeting. A stone's throw from the place de la République (place du Chateau d'Eau at the time) in a zone of the old *faubourgs* of Paris which was like a strip of life-giving tissue under the city's skin, the hall in the rue de la Douane (which held approximately 1,500 people) must have attracted many a proletarian in its heyday. But one feels that already the audience there must have been more staid than at the Vieux-Chêne or in the rue Lhomond. At a meeting about female labour, Chemalé was able to say things like: 'Above all treat your maidservants with respect.' It was not long before the organisers

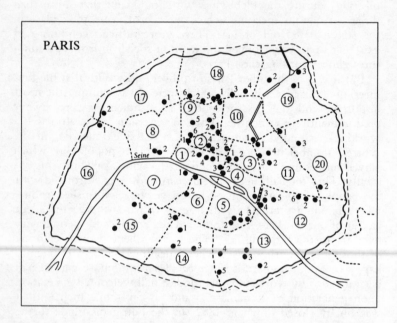

Location and character of Parisian meeting halls

Arrondissement	Type of hall	Number of meetings
1		
1 Salle de la Redoute, 35, rue Jean-Jacques-Rousseau	*Bal* (Dance Hall) (B)	58
2 Salle Valentino, 251, rue Saint-Honoré	B	6
3 Cafés des Halles centrales, 18, rue Saint-Denis	*Café-Concert* (CC)	4
4 Cour d'Aligre, 123, rue Saint-Honoré	?	1
2		
1 Salle des conférences, 39, boulevard des Capucines	?	25
2 186, rue Saint-Denis	?	6
3 6, rue Notre-Dame-des-Victoires	?	1
4 7, rue Vivienne	?	1
3		
1 Salle Molière, 159, rue Saint-Martin	B	164
2 36, rue Michel-Lecomte	?	1

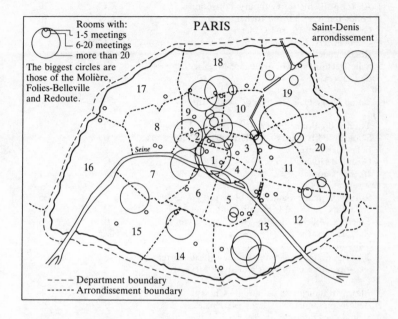

Location and character of Parisian meeting halls

4
1 Elysée des Arts, 13, boulevard Bourdon   B   5
2 Théâtre impérial du Châtelet   *Théâtre* (Th)   1
5
1 Le Vieux-Chêne, 69, rue Mouffetard   B   13
2 Salle du Concert du Châtelet de la rue des Postes,   CC   12
  rue Lhomond
3 Café du Progrès, 36, boulevard de l'Hopital   CC   2
4 La Marmite, 8, rue Larey   ?   1
6
1 Cercle de la Librairie, 1, rue Bonaparte   1
2 3, rue de Sevrès   ?   1
7
1 Pré-aux-Clercs, 83, rue de Bac   B   40
8
1 Cirque d'Eté, Champs-Elysées   *Cirque* (C)   1
2 Théâtre des Folies-Marigny, Champs-Elysées   Th   1

Location and character of Parisian meeting halls

9

1 Alcazar, 10, rue du Faubourg-Poissonnière	CC	26
2 Folies-Bergère, 32, rue Richer	CC	10
3 Grand-Orient, 16, rue Cadet		7
4 Café-concert de la Gaîté, 15, boulevard Rochechouart	CC	2
5 Salle Beethoven (Théâtre Faure-Nicolai), Impasse de l'Opéra	Th	2

10

1 Tivoli Vaux-Hall, 16, rue de la Douane	B	20

11

1 Théâtre du Prince impérial, 46, rue de Malte	Th	9
2 Salon de Paris (ou Folies-Méricourt), 22 rue de la Folie-Méricourt	B	5
3 Cirque d'Hiver	C	2
4 16, rue Gambey	?	1

12

1 Salle de la Jeune-Gaule, 28, place du Trône	?	35
2 Salle du Concert, 24, passage du Génie	CC	15
3 Salle des Mille-et-un-Jeux, 18, rue de Lyon	B	5
4 Cafe Trousseau, 2, place Mazas	CC	4
5 Salle du Bal, 66, rue de Charenton	B	1
6 208, rue de *faubourg* Saint-Antoine (headquarters of a co-operative of masons and stone carvers)		1

13

1 Alcazar d'Italie, 190, avenue de Choisy	B	30
2 Belle-Moissonneuse, 31, rue Nationale	B	28
3 Salle de la Fraternité, 27, avenue d'Italie	?	21
4 51, rue de la Glacière	?	2
5 129, rue de la Glacière	?	1

14

1 Jardin de Paris, 21, rue de la Gaîté	B	30
2 Salle de la Réunion, 10, rue Maison-Dieu	?	8
3 4, place d'Enfer (Denfert-Rochereau)	?	3

15

1 Salle Chaput, Café-concert de l'Etoile, 142, boulevard de Grenelle	CC	29
2 90, rue Javal	?	4
3 Maison Tonnelier	B	3
4 Salle Ragache, 61, rue Lecourbe	?	3

16

1 3, avenue de Neuilly	?	1

17

1 Salle Levis, 8, rue de Lévis	B	4
2 106, route de la Révolte	?	1

18

1 Salle Robert, 54, boulevard de Rochechouart	B	26
2 Salle des Martyrs, 2–4, boulevard de Clichy	MV	21
3 Grand Salon Poissonnière, 124, boulevard de la Chapelle	B	8
4 24, impasse d'Isly	?	4
5 Elysée-Montmartre, 80, boulevard de Rochechouart	B	1

Location and character of Parisian meeting halls

6 Bal de la Reine-Blanche, 88, boulevard de Clichy	B	1
19		
1 Salle de la Révolution, 12, rue de Crimée	ex-CC	17
2 Salle de la Marseillaise, 51, rue de Flandre	?	12
3 Salle de la Bourse du Marché de la Villette	?	1
20		
1 Folies-Belleville, 8, rue de Belleville	B	124
2 Ancien Bal de la Chaumière, 68 boulevard de Charonne	B	8
3 Grand Pavillon Ménilmontant, 27, rue de Ménilmontant	B	5

realised that it was difficult to 'attract workers' to this hall, since 'for many of them the Vaux-Hall was rather a long way away'.

Comments such as we have about the other halls in the centre are often brief, but they suffice to give us an idea of the tone. At a meeting at the Alcazar, rue du Faubourg-Poissonnière, chaired by Lissagaray, 'the *faubourg* element was totally absent'. On 15 May 1869, in the salle Valentino, rue Saint-Honoré, 'the audience was completely different from the other meetings. Here the majority of people are wearing suits.' But for the Pré-aux-Clercs, the former Théâtre des Victoires nationales founded in the Year III, which had been turned into a *bal* of the same name in 1849, there are many accounts, all of them in agreement. 'More hats than caps were to be seen there, more overcoats than *blouses*.' In fact, the hall in the rue du Bac was the preserve of socialist students, a kind of political salle Bullier, also frequented by drapers' assistants and seamstresses 'in more simple attire'. 'There aren't many workers, and then they're not locals,' adds Lefrançais. At the end of the first meeting, the superintendent was sceptical: 'I doubt whether M. Horn will manage to attract as many listeners as on the Right Bank. The *quartier* doesn't have the right elements for this sort of meeting, and it's too far away for people to come who live in the centres where democracy thrives.' But in fact there were to be 39 more meetings, each with several hundred people in attendance, more than a thousand on some evenings. As one of them wrote in his *Mémoires*, the local bourgeois went frequently to 'revel in' meetings on free love or the art of raising rabbits. Even after Catholics and Protestants no longer frequented it, the Pré-aux-Clercs maintained a well-bred brand of socialism: people came out with quotations in Latin, and there was open laughter on the day when Napoléon Gaillard told the platform: 'The children of a widow who had married again can have different fathers. There

ain't nothing excandlous about that.' According to Vitu, gram-
matical mistakes were frequent in the halls of the *faubourgs*, but no
one ever made fun of them there.

But the largest of the halls in the centre, and indeed the largest
in Paris, was the salle Molière. Built in a vacant alley in the rue
Saint-Martin by an unusual entrepreneur, Boursault, a former
member of the Convention who has left his name on another of
his enterprises in the Batignolles *quartier*, it was first a theatre
named the Sans-Culottes and then the Variétés-Nationales et
Etrangères before being converted into a *bal* in 1832 after a series
of ups and downs. The entrance was in the alley of the same name
– the passage Molière – at no. 6, where a long, narrow corridor
led to the hall: decorated in the Italian style, with stucco columns
and elegant balconies.[4] The record of achievement of the hall is
impressive: 167 ordinary meetings, 23 election meetings, 3
Plebiscite meetings. It is evident that its influence went far beyond
its *quartier* (in November 1869 it was used by the electorate of the
9th and 10th arrondissements), but the very active shops and light
industries in the neighbouring streets, plus the proximity of the
Halles, the Temple and the Marais, guaranteed it a permanent
public drawn from the industrious *petite* and *moyenne* bourgeoisie
of the central east end of Paris, mainly 'local manufacturers and
small shopkeepers'. In July 1869 there was a protest when one of
the meetings was broken up: among the signatories we see
journalists, shop assistants, a jeweller, a stationer . . . all resident
in the 1st or 2nd *arrondissements*. The agenda usually corresponded
to the preoccupations of this public of middlemen: 'The
Monopoly of Property Finance', 'Reform of Commercial Law',
'Free Trade and Protectionism'. And yet they were often broken
up (one meeting in ten), although this is a lower than average rate.
Although they were far from being models of good behaviour,
the audiences here were more reserved than in the *faubourgs*, and
calls to order were frequently more effective, like the one
addressed to Mme Désirée, who had noisily called for one of the
speakers to be thrown out, and was requested 'not to turn the salle
Molière into a branch office for her Belleville outbursts'.

Most of the lectures given under the auspices of the law of 1868
(66 out of 110) were also held in the centre, at the salle Molière,
the Redoute, and above all in the special hall on the boulevard des
Capucines. The public lectures held in this hall had developed
from those held in the rue de la Paix, which had been started in
1860 by a group of exiles of 2 December and intellectuals,
including Lissagaray. In 1869 they had emigrated to premises in

the boulevard des Capucines costing 8,000 francs a year, hired in the name of a society whose capital was funded entirely by the republican bourgeoisie. Its literary, scientific, philosophical and historical lectures were aimed at initiating 'the educated public as well as the masses themselves . . . in every area of thought and human curiosity (presented) in a down-to-earth but refined way' by leading intellectuals. They were 'secular sermons' which replaced the 'words of the clergy' by the light of science; by uniting people 'through common tastes and interests' their target was 'to eliminate the miserable class divisions which result either from routine or from Machiavellianism'.[5]

The authorities had always been extremely tolerant of didactic lectures, and they required neither notification nor authorisation. However the Paris deputies and the leading figures in the republican party 'who were unwilling to set foot in meetings (and) yet wanted to appear to be encouraging the movement' adopted the form of lectures for their own meetings: self-confessed meetings which had 'the particular advantage of avoiding any replies or discussion'. This was well illustrated at the lecture given by Etienne Arago in Saint-Denis in November 1869: 'At one point Briosne attempted to speak, but Jules Favre (who was in the chair) pointed out that it wasn't strictly speaking a public meeting, but a lecture, and consequently replies were not allowed.' The cries of 'Give Briosne the platform' did not sway the chairman, who preferred to close the proceedings. In the centre, similar spoilsports were rare.

The spirit of the Capucines' lectures and of the lecture-meetings of the republican leaders was fundamentally the same. In April 1870 Jules Ferry developed his conception of the school of the future: social peace through 'the mingling of rich and poor on the benches of a school'. At the Grand-Orient, rue Cadet, several months earlier, before a 'select audience; dressed up for the occasion, not one *blouse*; a considerable number of lawyers', Jules Favre spoke about 'the inequality of social conditions'. His thesis was that inequality is the natural state of society, but that ambition and greed have created 'artificial inequalities' which throughout history have offended man's innate sense of justice; from Spartacus to the negro cotton picker, it is a history of revolt. To bring this to an end, all ideas should be expressly freely – they would get sorted out of their own accord – 'similar interests' should be given the right to associate. But above all we should educate the people. Knowledge will 'refresh, console, purify and strengthen' the underprivileged; then women will become 'intelligent companions and mothers to free citizens'. Pawing at the portals of power, the future masters of the Republic were thinking aloud about the need to convert bourgeois society. At the Capucines, Victor Lefevre's satirical talks on the 'bourgeois mentality', egotistical and blinkered, were enthusiastically applauded by 'a well-groomed, well-polished, well-gloved and well-varnished audience' which thronged this 'elegant hall in the centre of the most aristocratic *quartier* of Paris' just as the crowds did in Belleville, and which one evening even had the thrill of being at a meeting which was broken up. . . .

The socialists had recourse to lectures as well; they organised a large number in the salle Molière in particular, at the beginning of 1870. They had no intention of letting republican lectures have a monopoly on knowledge, and thought it could help their struggle to present a literary case ('Aristophanes', 'Shakespeare') or an historical example ('Athens'). They were also eager to reach a public which through fear or indifference did not frequent meetings, thus making a little more money. Although the admission fee (generally 50 centimes) was lower than for other lectures (from one to three francs to listen to Jules Simon at the Folies-Bergère) it often resulted in a 200 to 300 francs profit. Moreover, socialist lectures were regularly advertised as being 'in aid of a democratic charity': after December 1869 all profits on receipts and the collection at the end of lectures were paid to the newspaper the *Marseillaise* in aid of political detainees.

But it was still in the halls of the *faubourgs* where the word of socialism was really at home. Their most remarkable feature was the way they were dispersed through space: on the map they trace a wide crescent around the centre of Paris, from Montmartre to Grenelle, while in the centre two thirds of all meetings were held in the first three *arrondissements*; at one time or another every *faubourg* had its own hall. One of these stands out, a kind of pendant in working-class Paris to the salle Molière: the Folies-Belleville.

Founded in 1810, this establishment was one of the principal relics of the old Courtille, that pleasure town of eating and dancing which in days gone by had spread for more than a league along the rue de Paris. Fronting on the boulevard and the rue de Belleville, the ex-Grand Salon Saint-Martin occupied an entire quadrilateral formed with the rue Desnoyers and the rue Lemon at the back. At the time of the first meetings, the new manager, Hyacinthe Dubacq, Alexandra Dumas's secretary, had just organised a large summer concert in the *bal* gardens, and it had been a considerable success. On the same land the cradle of melodrama, the Théâtre de Belleville, had also just reopened its doors after being damaged by fire in 1867. The dance hall itself had not changed: columns supporting a gallery with wooden balustrades which encircled the hall and overlooked the dance floor which was surrounded by tables for people to have something to drink and red velvet seats for the dancers to take a rest. In fact this was how all the large *bals* in Paris were decorated. Despite its splendid situation just below Belleville, right at the junction of one of the liveliest stretches of the exterior boulevards and the main road between the north-east and the centre of Paris, the Folies *bal* was on the decline; its great neighbour the *bal* Favié, however, was at the height of its popularity.

At the Folies as in all the other *bals*, when the hall was hired for a meeting the space reserved for the orchestra was rapidly converted: the platform on the left, the committee in the middle and the authorities on the right. But here the superintendent and his stenographer were perched on a little dais which was lower than the one occupied by the speaker, the chairman and the assessors. This could be taken as being symbolic of this hall where between November 1868 and December 1869 there were 124 ordinary meetings and 31 election meetings, for here 'the working-class element dominates . . . the discussion in between different schools of socialism'. Inquisitive visitors in black suits and top hats were rare at the Folies: their presence would have been not only incongruous but, in periods of tension, suspicious. . . . A cashier from the rue d'Aboukir who had been with a group of friends at the meeting of 10 October 1869 was called as a witness for the prosecution at the trial which followed the affray: 'At the meeting people called us informers,' he testified, 'because we were well dressed.' At an afternoon election meeting, on a weekday, there was a large crowd: 'Everyone has deserted their workshops', explained the journalist.[6] Monday meetings got the largest audiences at the Folies (19.4 per cent), whereas in the halls in the centre this was a blank day (0.6 per cent at the salle Molière): the public meeting had become integrated with the old working-class custom of taking Mondays off. Workers came down in large numbers from neighbouring Belleville, but also from farther afield, from Ménilmontant, Charonne or la Villette, or even from la Roquette or le Faubourg: seven of the 25 signatories of a letter sent to the *Réveil* protesting about an incident at one particular meeting lived in the rue Saint-Maur and its immediate vicinity.[7] In fact the 11th *arrondissement* was poorly endowed with halls, and the Folies were used several times in May and June by the electorate of the 5th constituency. Thus the catchment area of the hall was as wide as the composition of its audience was narrow.

'The Social Commune', 'Wage-earning and Privilege', 'Mutualism and Communism', 'Socialism and Poverty', 'Emancipation of Labour' . . . the Belleville agendas were in keeping with the place and its audience, which was 'very impressionable and easily excited', and among which there were always a lot of women and children, mingling among the men who kept their hats on and smoked. An audience like this would not be there to pluck the flowers of rhetoric. A radical candidate is reported as saying in 1869 that 'Belleville is like l'Ambigu, it's always got to be noisy'. But neither demonstrations of excitability, nor the place of dramaticised speeches at the Folies should be exaggerated: most meetings were conducted in a passionate silence with a highly attentive audience. Jibes thrown at speakers were criticisms in the form of a witty repartee. The level of closures was only just higher than at the salle Molière (13 out of 124): behaviour was freer, but things were just as serious. If someone interrupted speeches that went on too long by making animal noises, the chairman could call him to order just as at the Vieux-Chêne, saying: 'People don't imitate cock crows at a serious meeting.'

On 13 December 1869, whether through fear of seeing a repetition of the incidents of October, or as a result of new pressures, Desnoyers the proprietor cancelled all engagements and announced 'that he wanted no more socialism' in his hall. Thus the Folies was no longer available for meetings, but since new halls had recently sprung up and had taken a solid foothold in the *faubourgs*, the harm was not too serious.

We have already emphasised how difficult and uneven was the history of the halls of the periphery. Before the May–June elections of 1869, putting to one side a large number of relatively unimportant halls which never housed more than half a dozen meetings apiece, there are a few places which clearly topped the list; we know these already: the Jeune-Gaule, the salle Robert, the halls along the boulevard d'Italie; let us also add the Jardin de Paris, a *bal* in Montparnasse, rue de la Gaîté. They began around February or March, and their reign was very ephemeral: two months, three at the most. But after September–October, a new generation of halls was ready to take over; they never assumed the importance attained by the Folies, but until the end of the period under study they all made it possible for the word 'socialism' to survive in the populous *quartiers*. In reality the history of the well-known halls which played an important role during the Siege and the Commune begins here. Thanks to them, during the last part of the Empire, the public meetings, their meanings and their ideas, began to take root in the working-class *quartiers*.

Like the first-generation halls, most of these were still situated along the line of the old barrier, where the very largest of the *bals* of the periphery had been. Thus, the place of the Jeune-Gaule was taken by the bal de la Chaumière, boulevard de Charonne, and the salle du Concert, passage du Génie, a *café-chantant* near the place du Trône. In the 18th *arrondissement* the *bals* which lined the boulevard continued to play host to numerous well-attended meetings: the salle Robert was replaced by the salle des Martyrs, 2 boulevard de Clichy, and the Grand Salon Poissonnière. Of course a certain public from the bourgeois *arrondissements* may have occasionally wandered into these places, but they would have been completely swamped by the crowds 'down from' Montmartre. The audience here was as working-class as the premises, for the halls of the boulevard de Clichy or the boulevard de la Chapelle were a far cry from the gilt and stucco columns of the Folies-Belleville. What was the salle des Martyrs like, for example? It was over a wine shop, with the entrance at the top of a steep, narrow ladder, a genuine rectangular atic 20 metres by 10, without windows, with tapestried walls covered in grime. Only the members of the committee and the superintendent had seats. 'What a hall!' exclaimed Molinari, who never went back a second time. At the Grand Salon, meetings normally took place in semi-darkness, as the decidedly exemplary proprietor wanted to economise on gas. These makeshift halls were crowded and stuffy. But for people who had made the effort to get to them, as Lissagaray said at the Plebiscite meeting in the salle Lévis at Batignolles, a large *bal* of a similar kind, 'the sweat of public meetings is every bit as healthy as the sweat of the workshop'.

One important consequence of these new halls opening was that meetings became more effectively established on the Left Bank, which hitherto had been largely ignored by the organisers. Before the elections its strong points were the 7th *arrondissement*, with the Pré-aux-Clercs, and the 5th with the halls of the Montagne-Saint-Geneviève; during the period which followed, there was a marked shift in favour of the *arrondissements* in the southern periphery. In Grenelle in September 1869 the salle Chaput, a *café-concert* where 29 meetings were held until April 1870, was inaugurated; a small hall was opened in the heart of Javel. In the 14th a hall in Plaisance and a hall on the place d'Enfer (Denfert-Rochereau) took over from the Jardin de Paris. In the 13th, 14th and 15th *arrondissements* the total number of meetings from the one period to the other rose from 68 to 94, and for the 5th, 6th and 7th it went down from 70 to 15.[8]

This new upsurge in meetings in the highly proletarian sector of the new Paris took off principally in the 13th *arrondissement*. Beyond the barrière d'Italie, Nostag's salle de la Fraternité had not been the first to open: a *bal* at no. 31 rue Nationale, the Belle-Moissonneuse, had opened a good month earlier. After a three-month gap, the Belle-Moissonneuse opened up again in August, just as a new hall was opening at 190 avenue de Choisy, the Alcazar d'Italie. We have little information about these premises, which during the Siege were to become the headquarters of the Blanquists in the *arrondissement*: by the end of 1869 it was already a leading venue for political meetings. Its name suggests that it was a recently installed *bal*, an imitation-marble replica of the luxurious *bals* of the centre.

In contrast the Belle-Moissonneuse was an old *guinguette* from the time of the former barrière des Deux-Moulins, which had become successful thanks to the 'tanners, rag-and-bone men and horse dealers' of the *quartier*: it was in the main shopping thoroughfare of the Gare *quartier*, probably the poorest district in Paris. Here too the entrance to the meeting hall was up a ladder, guarded by two ushers in *blouses* with red armbands; on the right stood a large counter made of tin, with a bust of the Emperor over it (people who hire places must be prepared for such humiliations. . .). '*Blouses* are in the majority. Not a hat to be seen, except the superintendent's and his assistant's.' This was the hall in which Budaille brandished his *bonnet rouge* on the platform, one evening in May 1869: 'I take it off to the people.' Many of the impromptu speakers here were workers. One took the floor telling the audience that the education he had not received would not enable him to speak like Jules Favre; in any case, he added, deputies and priests 'came out of the same hole as everyone else'. Applause, a warning from the superintendent; someone shouts: 'That was a good one!'

A working-class audience, therefore, but where did it come from? As regards the Belle-Moissonneuse, its closures enable us to have a relatively precise idea. 104 of the 2,000 to 2,500 people who had attended the ill-fated sessions of 14, 18 and 21 August 1869 signed the protest lists which were displayed in a wineshop immediately after a meeting was broken up. They lived in the following places:

the Gare *quartier*:	56
the rest of the 13th *arrondissement*:	15
the 5th and the 6th *arrondissements*:	13

centre Right Bank:	7
periphery Left Bank:	1
periphery Right Bank:	12

Therefore the hall recruited a large part of its audience from its immediate human environment: the rue Nationale, the avenue d'Italie, the avenue de Choisy, the rue de Chevaleret . . . are the most frequent addresses. But a good quarter of the signatories also came from Saint-Germain-des-Près, the Latin Quarter and the Montagne-Sainte-Geneviève: lawyers, journalists, students . . . a large contingent also came from Belleville and the *faubourg* Saint-Antoine (almost 10 per cent), whereas the 14th and 15th *arrondissements* were not represented; similarly, in the remainder of the 13th, people came from Croulebarbe rather than from la Glacière or la Butte-aux-Cailles. Thus it is clear that the hall drew its audience specifically from a north-south axis on the Left Bank, with fewer clients from the other side of the Seine, except for the large working-class *quartiers* on the Right Bank. There were two reasons for this: on the one hand the way the periphery had been partitioned and fragmented into *faubourgs* which had few social or economic contacts between one another; on the other the existence of a fringe group of passionate devotees who thought nothing of making the journey and who attended all the important meetings. Given the nature and the limitations of our sample, it probably exaggerates the real importance of this itinerant audience, but it still allows us to understand better the role and the catchment of the halls of the *faubourgs*: managed by local leaders and organisers, they gathered together people who were already regulars, militants who came a long way to attend, Democratic bourgeois who lived in the nearest of the centre *quartiers* and above all locals who made up the majority. These halls were like a series of isolated socialist fortresses encircling the centre of Paris.

Another proletarian *arrondissement*, virgin till now, was about to give birth to meetings: the 19th, la Villette to be precise. The salle de la Revolution, a *café-concert*, 128 rue de Crimée, which had just filed for bankruptcy, was inaugurated for election meetings. In September and November 1869 17 sessions were held on the subject of 'association' and 'the practical means for socialist action'; the premises were still used for Rochefort's candidature during the November by-elections, but closed down soon after. Its place was taken by the most famous of the *faubourg* halls, the Marseillaise, 51 rue de Flandre. Rochefort's triumphant election and the launching of the homonymous newspaper were ultimately linked with the opening of this hall, where the first meeting took place four days after Christmas 1869. In effect Rochefort had announced at an election meeting that once he was elected 'he would hire a hall where he and his electors could meet every week'. In his *Mémoires* he states explicitly that he was personally responsible for hiring the premises, and when he went there for the first time on 1 February 1870 to chair a meeting, the *Marseillaise* talks about 'the inauguration' of this 'vast hall which Rochefort has supplied for meetings with his electors to discuss the relation which must always exist between a mandatory and his voters'. Therefore this hall was officially conceived as the necessary instrument for the real exercise of an enforced mandate; or rather let us say that it was one of the weapons with which the socialists and the implacable enemies of the regime equipped themselves at that time: a man, a newspaper, a hall.

On the first floor of a vast warehouse, the premises looked like 'an immense shed, with a tiled floor and a roof supported by posts and beams divided into three naves, with no ceiling'. The meetings at the Marseillaise would ordinarily attract 2–3,000 people, and there were many more of them than extant lists would indicate, for these only take account of notified meetings (12) and not of the many private ones held in February or March 1870.[9] In effect this hall was heir not only to the rue de la Crimée but above all to the Folies-Belleville, as beneath its roof it gathered together both the local audience of a *faubourg* hall and the mass of regulars in the vast zone from la Chapelle to Charonne for whom this was the only large premises available. The unnotified meetings held in the rue de Flandre have an important significance: the hall was only partially under the control of the authorities. But when the superintendent was present, the law prevailed: of the nine public meetings held in April, five were broken up. It is true to say that at this time the la Villette meetings 'had become the best-attended and the most tumultuous'.

But if the meetings in the periphery of Paris were increasingly successful, those in the *banlieue* were on the point of collapse. They had played a major role in the movement between June 1869 and April 1869, exclusively within the industrialised communes in the north, the *arrondissement* of Saint-Denis, the salle Merot in Saint-Denis proper, and the Théâtre Loiseau and the quai Imperial in Puteaux. During the May–June elections a quarter of all meetings were held in the *banlieue*: even if we are a long way from the crowds of Paris, the proportion is still remarkable. Then the *banlieue* began to lose its meetings: six after June, as opposed to the previous 37. Thus the militants and organisers of the *banlieue* (led by Benoît Malon) were withdrawing into Paris: doubtless this meant a concentration of efforts, but it also meant the failure to establish a foothold within a milieu which was still deeply rural in its structures and mental outlook. Thus, in September 1869, the attempt by a committee chaired by Lazare Tixier to arrange some meetings for 'the inhabitants of Saint-Denis, and more especially the inhabitants of the countryside near Saint-Denis' with a view to 'make the taste for freedom of speech more widespread' fizzled out after a few pre-election lectures. More than ever everything was concentrated on Paris.

The 94 Plebiscite meetings which were held between 26 April and 2 May 1870 allow us to take stock of the successive transformations which took place at meetings at the end of the period under study. For the purpose of the campaign, 6 halls (16 meetings) were used for the first time: occasional premises, except those at 23 rue d'Arras (seven meetings) which during the Siege became one of the main Red Clubs, five other halls (eleven meetings) had been used previously during election periods: practical premises, such as gymnasiums. Several premises from the first period made another appearance, notably the Pré-aux-Clercs, but it was a limited resurrection: four halls, twelve meetings, the salle Molière continued its career with three meetings. But it was the post-election halls which played the crucial role: nine halls, 59 meetings. In the rue de Lyon, the passage du Génie, the boulevard de Clichy, the avenue de Choisy, the rue de Flandre, in all the *faubourg* halls, it was one meeting after another. It was above all in la Villette (salle de la Marseillaise), Montmartre (salle des Martyrs) and the *faubourg* Saint-Antoine (salle du Concert) that the meeting public proved itself the most faithful, sometimes up to the very end, to the revolutionary call for abstention. Therefore the anti-Plebiscite campaign became linked to the socialist meetings of the second period and the defeat of the Empire in Paris on 8 May 1870, and cannot be understood without them.

When the effects of Haussmannisation were beginning to be felt, free speech had succeeded in carving a place for itself in Paris. Meetings began first of all in the centre, taking root there and attracting a disparate audience, 'grands' and 'petits' bourgeois at the Capucines or the salle Molière, intellectuals in the halls on the Left Bank, workers in what was left of the old *quartiers*. . . . But they soon spread into the new *faubourgs* where workers, recently arrived in Paris or deported from the centre, made up the majority of audiences. At first the *faubourg* meetings were a working-class reaction against the deterioration of living conditions in the city. When Héligon was giving forth from the platform of the Vaux-Hall about female labour, and declared 'How much time is lost simply travelling! We've been thrown out of the centre of Paris, and we know all about it,' he was greeted with thunderous applause. In November 1869 Rochefort was given a standing ovation at the salle Lévis when he concluded a speech on Haussmann's great transformations with: 'The government has moved the workers out of the centre so they won't be so close.' The working-class feeling of dispossession, already very much in evidence in the reports at the Exhibition delegates, was frequently expressed by speakers at meetings. Tony-Molin, for example, at the salle Robert:

> What the administration want to do is to destroy anything that might recall the past. They are making every effort to turn Paris into a cosmopolitan, Imperial city, and it amazes me that Paris . . . which has guillotined kings, is still called Paris. Its real name should be Napoléon-Ville.

But people were not content with simply crying over broken stones: exile to the periphery was one more reason for fighting the Empire and the compulsory purchases of the bourgeoisie. Quite naturally the clubs took up this critical theme during the Siege, but thanks to the new balance of political power, adding a new element: an attempt at popular control of the *quartiers*, starting with the question of rents, subsistence and National Guard dodgers. But in 1868 things had not reached this point, and we must now return to the meetings to get to know the men who organised them and the ideas which dominated them.

Notes

1 This outburst tells us that the premises were also used as a fencing school.
2 The Reine-Blanche was later replaced by the Moulin-Rouge.
3 Place du Trône, now place de la Nation.
4 The building is still standing. It is now a packaging firm.
5 In Deschanel, *Les Conférences à Paris et en France*, 1870, pp. 47–49, 68–71.
6 *Le Réveil*, November 17th 1869.
7 *Ibid.*, 30 September 1869.
8 Nevertheless taken as a whole the Left Bank remained of limited importance: 26.5 per cent of meetings for the entire period.
9 Therefore our map seriously underestimates the importance of the *Marseillaise*.

5
Socialism and Revolution

ALAIN DALOTEL and JEAN-CLAUDE FREIERMUTH

Yesterday's Utopia will be tomorrow's reality: let us be Utopians by willing the betterment of the workers, the emancipation of all and the abolition of all castes.

(Paule Minck, boulevard de la Chapelle, 12 January 1869)

The public meetings were revolutionary not only because they were impregnated with messianism, but also because their dominant discourse combined:
- plans for a society which would break with the established order
- practical propositions for means of revolutionary action.

A   Revolutionary messianism

As early as the first months of 1869, revolutionary prophesying was a daily phenomenon at public meetings among speakers convinced that a deep and violent social movement was at hand. This proletarian revolution which was soon to explode took the form of the Commune. One of its most convinced heralds was Ferré: 'The force which oppressed us today can be our tomorrow, and we will crush the bourgeoisie beneath our feet' (6 January 1869, salle du Vieux-Chêne).

Bachellery summoned his audience to 'revolt', predicting that: 'The light we can see growing like the dawn is freedom on the rise. Let us bow to her authority and prepare ourselves to struggle on her behalf' (12 January 1869, boulevard de la Chapelle).

Humbert went even further: 'We are on the eve of great political events' (9 October, boulevard de Clichy).

Chauvière thought the same: 'The time is near, and we'll be there! It's not far off. Me, I see it clearly!' (24 January 1869, la Redoute.)

In the minds of most of the speakers, this revolution which was so near would inaugurate the power of the people – Geoffroy says that 'the time was not far away when the people would govern themselves' – and of the proletarian, that *honnête homme* for whom Peyrouton announced 'a glittering revenge'. A Blanquist, he warned the moneyed class: 'You are deaf to this social revolution which is rumbling all around you and which will engulf you, along with your possessions, and you do not realize that it is getting ever nearer, and that it's time you opened your eyes.' It was therefore the social revolution which was threatening. 'The time is near when everything will be put back in its rightful place,' said an unnamed speaker at the salle Robert on 3 March 1869 during a discussion on 'Work and Unemployment'.

It was claimed that the dates had been decided. 26 October 1869 was to be 'the revolutionary day of reckoning'. Millière spoke to his over-excited Belleville audience of 'great events being prepared'. We should explain here that the fatal date of the twenty-sixth was the day the new Chamber elected in May and June was due to meet; however the Executive seemed to want to postpone it, a tactic which was scarcely appreciated by the opposition in general and the public meetings in particular. Halls were rife with slogans. If the government failed to do its duty, there was to be a demonstration in the place de la Concorde. 'At the public meetings, everyone urged everyone else not to miss it.' How can we fail to be reminded of what was to happen in January 1870, the day of Victor Noir's funeral, and again on 4 September 1870? The calls to insurrection were becoming less and less abstract.[1]

After the crime of Auteuil [Noir's murder – eds], speakers were virtually inviting the people to have a revolution. On 18 January 1870 Lacord declared that 'the Chamber must be dissolved'. Vertut did not mince his words: 'Since we've got to sweep up all the filth that other people have made, let's sweep away the biggest piece of filth of the lot.'

In April 1870 there was a new upsurge of messianism. In a more or less distant future, one day would suffice to overthrow the regime. It would happen in the streets: 'The moment has not yet come to begin the struggle, but when it comes it will be outside rather than indoors' (Vertut). Authority would collapse; 'not even chassepots will be able to stem the popular flood when it smashes against the dyke which is holding it back', was the Blanquist Serizier's joyful prediction (he was supposedly drunk at the time). In the same hall in the avenue de Choisy, his crony Leo Meillet also exclaimed that the republican motto *Liberté-égalité-fraternité* 'would soon reappear'. Although at that moment in time Paris was involved in the Plebiscite, at public meetings the subject was revolution. 'They're trying to replaster a worm-eaten building', said Roullier, referring to electoral consultation. 'What we want is to throw our tyrants and our despots out' (we will notice the use of the plural). During the same session, when Passedouet, the future mayor of the 13th *arrondissement* during the Siege of 1870, and after a leader of insurgents during the Commune, spoke in the name of the International, he enables us to capture the state of mind of that organisation; it too was waiting for the right moment to present itself: 'In the opinion of the Paris section of the IWMA we should respect the law as far as possible until such time as we feel strong enough to break it.'

Faced with this avalanche of predictions, we are tempted to praise the militants' clairvoyance. In effect, the Commune was to prove them right. But nevertheless we should not be too impressed. For a start we should not forget that messianism is endemic to revolutionary milieus which live in the hope and conviction that the revolution is always about to happen. Then again at public meetings there were certain militants who, if ready for the supreme struggle themselves, considered that the masses still had something to learn. Once all had been prepared, the triumph of the cause was inevitable. Montel, for example, while wishing for 'the Revolutionary Commune', was less impatient than his colleagues, and predicted it for 1900! 'For the Empire will have fallen by then.'[2]

Nevertheless let us remember that the announcement of a great change about to take place was almost a cliche for the audiences at the public meetings. If an agreement was reached on its timeliness, this was not the case in respect of the goals to be aimed at and the methods to be used to attain them.

B   What objectives?

1   Democracy: a springboard

The demand for the rights of the people, even for a Party of the People, resounded through the public meetings; at the Maison-Dieu, Mme Désirée demanded: 'that women should have as many rights as men'. In contradiction she emphasised the defence of these rights as much as their conquest. Of course what we might call a legalistic ideology resulting from the legacy of the Democratic state of 1848 is apparent in some of these speeches – a frequent theme is that of the necessary defence of rights. Thus Lefrançais, contrary to Vermorel, claimed 'the right to fight a duel', which would be 'reclaiming a violated right'. But in general in so far as to obtain and enjoy democratic rights would be to foster the development of the revolutionary struggle, it would be inaccurate to reduce the battle for these rights to a mystification.

To affirm, like Ducasse, the 'primordial' right of speech despite 'those who wish to gag the people' (Budaille), the 'right to hold meetings' despite police tactics, and the 'right to work and to organise it' was to militate for the possibility of continuing revolutionary propaganda and also to pose the question of unemployment. Let us not forget that this was an era in which the dominant – bourgeois – ideology was teetering, and when the Constitution – the source of the law – was despised. Thus there were certain rights which were strongly challenged by public meetings, like the right to punish . . . in the name of Fourier! 'Passions should not be repressed, they should be channelled.' Repression must be eliminated, said Delattre, for 'it starts with a fear of the whip, then the bogeyman, then the devil, then the gendarme'.[3]

In principle, the Republic triptych of *Liberté-égalité-fraternité* should have been one of the war cries of the public meetings. If we make a list of everyone who, like Leval, cried: '*Liberté, égalité, fraternité*! Only socialism can be the consequence of this noble motto!' (24 April 1869, at the Folies-Belleville), who, like Humbert, wanted 'to win back our vanished freedoms', or who, like Passedouet, made the winning of 'the freedom of the press, freedom of assembly, freedom of association'[4] a prerequisite of any action to emancipate labour, we will realise that the people who recalled these 'revolutionary principles' were generally the least socialist. The 'great revolutionary motto *Liberté! égalité! fraternité!*' was only well thought of among radicals who saw it as an alternative to the *ancien régime*. When talking of the subject of 'freedom of association' for mutual aid societies, Lavertujon even seemed to be making an effort to convince his audience that 'the only way you will get freedom of association for mutual aid societies will be by replacing the Monarchic regime with a republican one'.

The public meetings and their most popular speakers were very suspicious of high-sounding slogans. The grandiloquence of 1848 was no longer acceptable. Passedouet, for example, advised his audience to be wary of 'watchwords'; Chemalé, another member of the International, also saw through the verbal magic so dear to the bourgeois republicans: 'Who exactly are these people who never stop telling us about the principles of 1789? They are people who have already shot us down three or four times.'

The only way in which the socialists were prepared to discuss these great 'watchwords' was in terms of their possible 'social application'. The sole principle they espoused was equality, doubtless because they saw it as being the most subversive. In effect it was not difficult to demonstrate that 'equality before the law' did not exist (Vertut). Thus there were a number of speakers who used a wide range of themes to argue in its favour. Lombard and Mme Désirée wanted 'the recognition of the equality of men and women'; Gaillard claimed it for all children legitimate and illegitimate, etc. This egalitarian spirit was the most remarkable characteristic of the communist movement, and we will return to it. For the moment we would rather emphasise the sceptical attitude of the public meetings towards the democratic values inscribed in the Constitution and preached by the radicals. The moderate republicans were shocked by it, since their policy was in essence to develop freedom.

For a great many revolutionaries, this famous freedom was nothing but a mirage which had always been used to deceive the people. It was Henri IV's 'chicken stew', which 'had always been promised but never provided'. Vertut launched an attack on the freedom of 1848 and the 'freedom of the Empire'. If 'individual freedom' was mentioned, it was to show that it did not exist, a demonstration at which the lawyers Falcet and Lafferière excelled. At the salle de la Marseillaise, Falcet wanted to make Rochefort and Megy honorary chairmen, because 'one stood for freedom to write and the other for individual freedom'.

In April 1870 the liberal Empire was very much the enemy of the very freedom it purported to re-establish. 'Individual freedom', exclaimed Vertut, 'means shutting Rochefort up in Sainte-Pelagie, it means my arbitrary arrest and preventative detention'. The regime could not give back the freedoms it had ravished. All it did was to make 'vain promises'. It was completely logical for the militants to consider that revolution was needed first and foremost if the freedom with which official propaganda, in an effort to gain time, was pounding their ears was really to be achieved. On 21 October 1869, first Vermorel, and then Decouvenance, asked 'what is the point of repeating the word freedom! freedom! day after day, since we haven't got it. There is only one way left to get it, and we all know what that is. Right?' Falcet was even more transparent: 'We will only have freedom,' he shouted to the salle Molière, 'when we can dance the carmagnole on the last of the despots.'

In the end the observer begins to realise that despite certain appearances, the revolutionaries were more concerned with liberation than with freedoms as such: 'the conquest of freedom' was indeed 'the present aim' (Passedouet), but, as Briosne explained, because it 'will give us all the secondary means of action, and that's the main aim'. There is no doubt that the socialists considered public freedoms and democratic rights as nothing but a springboard for revolution. Outside the public meetings, doubts were expressed about the sincerity of their affection for freedom; in his pamphlets, Vitu was the first to try to demonstrate, admittedly with his own ends in mind, that the revolutionaries were adversaries of democratic principles, 'totalitarians' before the name existed. According to this Bonapartist, these people wanted to install a dictatorship of the type created in the Year II. Extrapolation? A crafty montage of quotations? It was not simply that, because it reproduces the speeches accurately. Liberalism was clearly denounced by the public meetings. Ranvier, at Belleville on 17 January 1869, then Humbert at Ménilmontant on 27 November 1869, just to mention two, knew who the so-called friends of freedom were: the Church, the bosses. 'It is freedom that turns working-class women into prostitutes' (Ranvier).

> Without equality in political matters, freedom is the right of some to tell others what to do. In social matters, it is the right of some to speculate on labour, and the right of others to be destroyed by hard labour. (Humbert)

Therefore there was opposition to state-backed, clerical education[5] and 'freedom of worship' (Désirée, Peyrouton, Rigault). Certain outbursts inspired by the public meetings seem to have prophesied a people's dictatorship in the event of seizure of power. It would have been exerted over the bourgeoisie, as an orator, Lafayette, indicated when he admitted that 'Yes, we are despots'.

What Lebeaume wanted was 'the tyranny of the people'. Vitu went a bit far when he alleged that at the Pré-aux-Clercs on 2 January 1869 Briosne admitted that he wanted to subordinate 'freedom to communism'. However – and the Commune was to prove it – if the revolutionaries believed less and less in the effectiveness of lofty slogans, they were more and more convinced of the necessity for a dictatorship of the workers. (In this perspective Desprez's outburst at the lack of response at the meeting at the Maison-Dieu on 31 December 1869 – 'You are all unworthy of the freedom you demand' – takes on its full meaning.) In this field the class struggle line had triumphed, much to the regret of the Humanists. D'Ulbach joined forces with Ducasse in a polemic deploring the views of the public-meeting militants. Their 'freedom' was uncivilised, their equality 'scornful', their fraternity 'bitter'.

Therefore there was a break with the radical democrats. This also involved an anti-parliamentary stance, since the Republic which the public-meeting militants wanted to install was not the

Republic of 1848. If the public meeting militants were happy to recall the First Republic, which had retained all its appeal, they would never miss an opportunity of belittling the republican and parliamentary opposition of the Second Empire, the ex-supporters of 1848, whom they all too willingly identified with the shameful regime of December. June 1848 had created an unbridgeable gap. Ducasse rejected 'this fat, bourgeois democracy with its unhealthy obesity, which on 15 May and 14 June shot the people down'. Sérizier cultivated his memories of the anti-worker repression: 'They shot us in '48. . . . Let us forget the shootings, but not the people who ordered them.'

The names of Eugene Cavaignac, 'the victor of June! the assassin of the people!', of Marie, of Jules Favre, of Garnier-Pagès, those 'old criminals', (of 1848) were invoked time and time again whenever the counter-revolution was mentioned. Garnier-Pagès, the deputy for the 5th constituency, which included the *faubourg* du Temple and the *faubourg* Saint-Antoine, was the most reviled of them all, as he was the archetypal representative of the 'honest and moderate Republic' and of the old fogeys of 1848 whom nobody wanted any more.

The 1869 elections were to give the revolutionaries an occasion to mount an exceptionally violent attack. There were as many as twelve candidates challenging Garnier-Pagès, the most famous of whom were Raspail, Broisne and Baudin, brother of the representative killed on 3 December 1851. The various socialist and Jacobin groups[6] were to conduct a campaign of unprecedented viciousness – for Garnier-Pagès the 'outbursts' of 17 and 30 May at the Théâtre Parisien were veritable nightmares, among the most uncomfortable episodes in his life.[7] It was during these they succeeded in uniting to support Raspail, who was narrowly defeated. We will return later to this significant campaign, since at every subsequent election the same collision between the militant *habitués* of the public meetings and the representatives of the bourgeois democracy was to occur. These particular elections were to give the opportunity for a complete denunciation of the deputies of the Left and of the opposition. In the longest chapter in his pamphlet against the public meetings, *Les Clubs et l'opposition*, Vitu emphasises their propensity to criticise the legal opposition: 'Nor are the speakers and writers of the opposition shown any respect. Their doctrines and newspapers are ridiculed and thrown to the mercy of the most brutal hatred.'

The *Siècle*, the *Cloche*, the *Temps*, the *Journal des débats* were called into question one by one for their 'wishful republicanism' (Ducasse), their petit-bourgeois readership – (Budaille considered the *Siècle* to be a small property-owners' paper), but above all for their unswerving affection for legal formality and parliamentarianism. Had not the *Siècle* and the *Cloche* shown their scorn for the public meetings? Gaillard 'put the *Cloche* and its editor, that wretched slanderer D'Ulbach, on the blacklist'.

Already violently polemical in 1869, this campaign was to grow and flourish throughout 1869 up until the moment of the Plebiscite. The pusilanimous attitude of the Left at the time of the Rochefort affair strengthened this anti-parliamentary trend even more.

When the salle de la Marseillaise was inaugurated on 1 February 1870, Flourens attacked the Empire and the democratic opposition:

> He criticised M. J. Favre, the deputy for Seine, calling him a
> scoundrel and a wretch, and accusing him of feigning emotions
> he had never felt and of preaching to others what he would
> never practise himself. He attacked Bancel in the same way and
> said that it wouldn't be long until we would be sending all
> these wretches to the devil.

The public meeting militants were tired of hearing about these so-called democrats. On 7 April 1870 in the salle Molière a speaker 'who had tried to praise Jules Simon and Pellétan was greeted with boos and whistles'. This reaction tells us how much the popularity of the parliamentarians was in decline. In 1869 Jules Simon was still able to win a certain amount of applause at public election meetings in the 8th constituency. But now the deputies could no longer fool anyone: Vertut compared them to the members of the Convention during the Revolution, suggesting that 'times have changed . . . the giants of '90 have been replaced by the pygmies of 1870'.

It seemed more and more doubtful that they could be capable of 'leading the people towards a common happiness' and the much-vaunted new-style Republic. Parliamentarianism was not only powerless – Leo Meillet recalled that the only thing to come out of the law on coalitions had been the massacres at Aubin and la Ricamarie – it was also dangerous, and once in power it could well turn against the people. Laurier put the people on their guard: 'I am a liberal democrat and they say I'm a parliamentarian, but I can remember that it was under a parliamentarian regime that the assassins of freedom brandished their bayonets' (30 October 1869, rue de Crimée).

Having said that, we should add that the public meetings tended to build up new idols for adulation. While some of these personalities deserved this popular infatuation, like Flourens, Raspail and Megy, others were more dubious, after the fashion of Rochefort. Nevertheless one or two voices were raised which expressed disquiet at this cult.[8] The future was to prove that Rochefort was not the knight of the social revolution that some people had imagined. In 1870 he enjoyed unique prestige, despite the fact that his punctuality left much to be desired. On 1 February when he and Flourens arrived late for a meeting he himself had organised in the salle de la Marseillaise, he had the audience grumbling.

It is true that by and large audiences would not tolerate being treated in a cavalier fashion: 'They made their displeasure apparent, it must be said, in very energetic terms', observed a journalist from the *Rappel* when Briosne, 'the only speaker on the programme', failed to turn up at a meeting on association in October 1869, at the place d'Enfer.

More than mere passing pique, these skirmishes were the first outlines of the idea of the sovereignty of the people which was to triumph during the Commune. Even the leaders of the public meetings had to reckon with a rank and file that became more and more hard to please which was more and more in control of its own affairs. The opposition deputies, against whom the extreme Left had already launched the battle which was to rage during the Siege of Paris and the Commune, had also become the Aunt Sallies of the public meetings. We can scarcely share the surprise of the author of NA 155 when he notes that 'although they had been invited by their voters, the deputies of Seine showed a visible repugnance at the idea of going among them'.[9] At the time of the Plebiscite, despite a new upsurge of the political struggle at the heart of the republican camp, they took advantage of the relative defeat of the abstentionist lobby – the most progressive of the public meeting militants and their avowed enemies – to bring off a turnabout among the mass of the electorate. It was a complex and provisional victory, more apparent than profound, as we shall see.

Over and above regularly-arranged political occasions the anti-parliamentarianism of the progressive elements in the public meetings was to persist until it reappeared with renewed vigour during the Siege of 1870. Its motives were as political as they were social. Chalain put it well on 29 April 1870 in the rue de la Maison-Dieu: 'To vote No is to vote for the return of the bourgeois Republic, and we are for a socialist Republic.'

As far as the public meetings were concerned the bourgeoisie, even the republican bourgeoisie, had had its day. A socialist society was the order of the day.

2   A socialist society

The supreme goal in the dominant discourse of the public
meetings was 'the emancipation of labour', in other words, 'the
emancipation of the workers'[10] which some referred to as 'social
reform'. In any event, this essential objective which the public
meetings sought distinguished them radically from any of the
bourgeois movements. At a Belleville meeting where a 'plan for a
general association for the emancipation of labour' was on the
agenda, Passedouet, a member of the First International, was
careful to distinguish himself from the 'parasites' by railing against
exploitation, for 'the pleasures of a few . . . are paid for by
everyone else's labour'. And nobody should make the mistake of
thinking that it was a question of the speakers not having to work
any more, on the contrary! If Mme Piré advocated 'the
suppression of the slavery of work' in the name of this
association, it was to 'be free through work', for 'the best society
will be one in which everyone will be subjected to work. That is
the basis of equality itself'.

However such a total transformation of society so that the
proletariat would be the fundamental element implied a political
struggle. Nowadays we may find this self-evident. But at the end
of the Empire, when people were still being seduced by the
experience of co-operatives, it was an imperative which had to be
strongly affirmed, a task undertaken by Bachellery, among others:
'Come on now, a social revolution entails of necessity a political
revolution, and that's what I want. We are all agreed upon a
political revolution, I'm sure.'

In effect, hindsight allows us to share this optimism, for the
consensus at the public meetings was that this dual upheaval of the
political and social systems was necessary. However there were
several plans for a socialist-type society, and consequently some
serious differences of opinion between meeting *habitués*.

Despite everything, socialism was the common goal. The new
society advocated by the public-meeting militants would be a
'system' governed by the 'social revolution'; it would be a 'social
liquidation', since the 'revolution' was the common denominator
whatever the subject under discussion, and therefore it would be a
socialist society. It would be the logical conclusion to republican
principles: '*Liberté-égalité-fraternité*'. 'Socialism alone can be the
consequence of this noble watchword' was what Seval threw in
the face of the superintendent at the Folies-Belleville.

For most of the time this notion of 'socialism' formed the basis
of agendas. Discussions would be organised on 'The Future of
Socialism in France' or 'The Principles of Socialism'. The terms

'socialism' or 'socialist' offended no one. Who wasn't one? The Head of State himself believed he was one. Vermorel, who used his commentaries on Proudhon to 'preach' socialism, 'said that at the present time everyone was a socialist, even the state's most important civil servants'. Sometimes the term became so vague that just about anyone could be called a socialist: Yves Guyot chose the subject of 'Danton the Socialist' for a speech he gave at the boulevard de Grenelle in April 1869; Ledru-Rollin (a notorious anti-socialist) was elected honorary chairman of a meeting in the passage du Génie which was devoted to the question 'Instruction and Education according to Socialist Principles'.[11] Imprecise wordings like this were not always accidental. When a speaker like Briosne made a regular point of trying to keep a balance between the various schools of thought, he only succeeded in confusing everyone (audience and policemen alike). Briosne always tried to bring differing points of view closer together. When he spoke in favour of 'the suppression of the right of inheritance' he said it was because 'the socialist schools are all in agreement' on the subject.

In spite of such obscurities, we can nevertheless come to the conclusion that the public meetings tried to weld revolutionary union onto the base of 'socialism'. It was an aim which Allix welcomed joyfully during a meeting at Belleville:

> Allix was delighted to affirm that different Socialist systems had developed and that the misunderstandings that had existed between them had been resolved. He concluded by saying that it was good hygiene to cut out a disease at the root.

He was followed by Amouroux who demanded 'the union of all the schools of socialism to reach a common goal'. The will to achieve this goal implied a commitment by the public meetings to the class struggle – 'Socialism and Strikes' are on the agenda at Budaille's hall in the place du Trône – along with a consideration of the 'practical means of action'. For two whole years patient and didactic speakers applied themselves to the task: Amouroux, for example, or Allix, Delorme, Oudet at Belleville, with topics like 'Socialism and Poverty – Pathways and Means of Action for Socialism' on their agendas.

In these meetings, as in the others, cleavages became apparent. At the outset discussions developed a progressive image of socialism. Certain 'socialists' were challenged and their demagogy laid bare. Thus, at 190 avenue de Choisy, 'Paulet wanted to talk about socialism, but it was pointed out to him that he was not a socialist and that he had been given a study on the subject to take care of and he had passed it on to M. E. Pellétan.' And yet Paulet had been quite prepared to defend 'the emancipation of the workers' in halls in the popular *quartiers*, fighting notably against Horn's capitalist theories. Next, discussions turned to the task of recognising the different branches of 'the tree of socialism' (Chamaillard). In 1870 speakers talked about the different currents within socialism ('Socialists Today', 23 April 1870, salle de la Marseillaise).

In 1869 their approach was rather more allusive. If the haze which surrounded the various denominations – socialist, communists, mutualists – at the start of 1869 soon began to clear, we should not be too hasty in trying to label each speaker precisely as a 'socialist', a 'communist', a 'Fourierist' or a 'Saint-Simonian'. In fact the speakers rarely labelled themselves, preferring the apparent clarity of certain fixed objectives – like Lacatte in the salle Molière: 'The goal of the economic revolution should be the abolition of bosses'. If they did assume labels, they often couched them in rather enigmatic terminology: Amouroux: 'I am a radical socialist, I want revolution.' Roullier: 'In 1848 I was a communist, today I am a revolutionary socialist; I want social liquidation and I want it now.' Brille: 'They call us revolutionaries! Do they realise that this is what we pride ourselves for? A revolutionary is someone who rises up against the yoke of the oppressor and the despotism of his government.' Theodore Brisson, a sculptor, considered himself a 'radical socialist and an atheist'. Sébille 'was a democrat even before he was born'. Cantagrel was renowned for his Fourierism – maybe we could expect him to be more precise about the kind of socialist he was. At one moment it looked as though he might be, on 4 November 1869, for example, when he pointed out the limitations of Rochefort's 'incomplete' programme to a gathering of voters in the 1st constituency, 128 rue de Crimée:

> He would like to add direct legislation, that is to say deputies given sole responsibility for elaborating laws which the people would then be obliged to adopt or reject. In other respects the programme is not explicit enough on socialism. The elimination of wage labour is not included.

Urged by Gaillard to give way to Rochefort, he continued:

> It was up to the people alone to choose between him and Rochefort. Now, if he is questioned about this socialism he will reply that he owes his best ideas to Charles Fourier, the greatest socialist of modern times; however, he has some

reservations and has no intention of swearing allegiance to any one man.

We are left unsatisfied. In any case at that particular moment Cantagrel had to mute his socialist declarations of faith in order to assert that he was a republican, for despite Tolain's advice[12] it really does seem as though the socialists preferred 'men of action' (Vermorel) to doctrinarians. Collot says that he respected Cantagrel, 'but he thinks that his Fourierism would not stop him from making the odd little concession to absolute power', for was he not 'one of the men who in '48 let them confiscate our freedoms?' (Geoffrin.) Should we go along with Vitu who maintained that the 'three political groupings' (sic) in the public meetings, the communists, the revolutionary socialists, and the progressive socialists, were all intent on 'a more or less open communism'? Certainly not, because the socialists and communists agreed neither on their plans for society nor on the means of action for achieving socialism.

C   Divergences and points in common

1   Two contradictory projects

As we have seen, the public meeting speakers cannot be crudely categorised. In any case it would be anachronistic to try to establish perfectly defined 'parties'. Certain Proudhonists, after the fashion of Lefrançais, were involved in the process of evolving[13] towards the Left, which was something the policemen did not always understand. One superintendent found him 'not very clear', for, as the worthy but rather bewildered officer of the law put it, he 'attacks certain of Proudhon's doctrines which he himself quotes every other minute and then approves other doctrines of the self-same Proudhon'.[14] Some seemed to go in the opposite direction. Abel Peyrouton, openly a communist in 1868, was able to tell the judge at the Court of the First Instance in Marseille in 1871: 'I am a republican and my political and social doctrine places me under the flag of that old party and well known under the name of the Jacobins'.

The will for union also led many speakers to keep quiet about their political tendencies, and even to adopt labels which were not in keeping with their basic convictions. Brisson did not reject the adjective 'communist' and Briosne spent as much time defending individualism as he did communism. Some speakers affected rather neutral denominations: they would be 'materialists', or 'materialistic atheists' (which is when the Jacobins protested).[15]

But none of this could prevent the political struggle from exploding at the very heart of the socialist camp. It was generally when communism was being discussed that it became apparent, since the socialists were eager to distinguish themselves from the communists.[16]

Quarrels took over the stage. On 14 February 1869, in the place du Trône, Garraud, 'although he was someone who could command an audience's attention, was booed when he attacked communism'. Observers noted that 'the meeting lapsed into a rather lively fight between the communists and the socialists'. Low profiles were no longer possible. At Ménilmontant, Langlois recalled his friction 'with my friends the communists'. Now all the cards were on the table. In Belleville, Montel 'admits to being an authoritarian'; at the Pré-aux-Clercs, Lefrançais confessed to being 'a Communist'; and Labove admitted that he was 'totally opposed to the idea of communism'. A meeting was organised at the Folies-Belleville to 'discuss the question of the communists and the individualists'.

Certain topics, such as the French Revolution, were liable to exacerbate these divisions. In Belleville on 17 January 1869 the neo-Jacobins clashed violently with the neo-Hebertists. Ducasse, who idolised Robespierre – he called him 'The Great Man' – made an unrestrained attack on the Hebertists, by implication the Blanquists, calling them 'muddleheaded', and on the partisans of 'the Goddess Reason' (Lefrançais was to have some harsh things to say about Ducasse the theologian). Lemay qualified the Hebertists as 'zealots', which outraged the chairman and a section of the audience. A scuffle broke out. Vitu, as ignorant as ever about revolutionary trends, was flabbergasted. Certainly we may be tempted to join the militant Guilhar in deploring these divisions 'about these great men' which had infiltrated the meetings, but on the other hand we know that it was a confrontation which resulted from irreconcilable political choices which were to surface again with added vigour during the Commune. It was by virtue of these choices that people split themselves up into socialists or communists, idealists or materialists.

One exception might be the extremely violent quarrel which pitted the Blanquist student Rigault against the trio Héligon-Gaillard-Mme Désirée, in agreement for once. It was Rigault's social background and his well-known escapades, which seem to have gone down badly in Belleville, that sparked it off. They called poor Rigault a 'toad', a 'brothel creeper', a 'son of a bourgeois' and a 'snotty-nosed ragamuffin'. But this was simply a passing incident.

More important were the differences in social projects which might offer an explanation for the quarrels between the socialists and the communists we have described above. Let us examine these plans more closely.

A) 'PROUDHONIST' SOCIALISM

To begin with we should make a distinction between the Proudhonist ideas which penetrated the masses and 'Proudhonism' and the 'Proudhonists'.

As one would have expected, Proudhon is the author who is the most frequently mentioned. Langlois, one of the executors of his will, who called himself a 'mutualist socialist', was one of his inexhaustible epigones. The author of NA 155 notes that at the salle Molière Langlois 'took up again, not without some clever rhetorical touches, the idea of the people's bank', for, he said, 'the model bank is Proudhon's bank'. He was not the only one to make references to the social reformer from Besançon. Apparently a certain Pinet went on at length about Proudhon on 18 September 1869. However, and it was a sign of the times, some of Proudhon's theories were reprocessed by the economists. Courcelles-Seneuil used them to refuse 'collective property', Sabatier used them to justify the interests of capital, etc. Nevertheless we should recognise that if the writings of Proudhon were a godsend to the economists because of their technocratic aspects – they talk of cash, banks, credit – they were also appropriated by the Socialists (Minck, Longuet, Howert, otherwise known as Charpentier). His simplest idea, which Marx admired, 'property is theft', was widely taken up again; during the row between the economists and the socialists, Paule Minck justified the concept historically:

> Proudhon said: 'Property is theft' (and quite right too). I agree with him. It's even more than that, it's murder, it's an ever-increasing disgrace [*cheers*]. As examples she quotes the conquests, the pillage and the knights of the Middle Ages, Louis XIV, Louis XV, and the thefts committed by those monarchs. Capital is the result of ignomiy; if it is passed on, it is theft. She recalls slaves, serfs, vassals, and the inspiration of 1793 [*cheers*], but as capital still retained all its potency, the proletarian was turned into a convict.

Proudhon's shock formula was tirelessly repeated: 'It is by theft that property is established', insisted Budaille at the place du Trône on 7 February 1869. 'Property is theft,' cried the young worker Laime at the Redoute. On 18 December 1868 in the same hall, Bouille proclaimed: 'As Proudhon said about property, legitimacy is nothing but a continuous theft [*Prolonged cheers*].' Briosne said that at 'the origins of possession' was 'force', therefore theft, and Laviolette considered that 'property originated in despoilment'. Gaillard, although having 'the honour of belonging' to 'the communist class', defended the same idea: property 'comes from theft and murder'.

The public meetings likened property owners to bandits. On 14 November 1868 when the economist Villiaume was talking about Proudhon and insisted that 'he simply wanted to say that a large number of property owners were thieves', the audience replied: 'All of them! They all are!' a conclusion Briosne was to put in his own words at the Pré-aux-Clercs on 2 January 1869 when he made the harangue: 'In reality, you are thieves.'

But we should be quite clear about the fact that Proudhon's oft-repeated sentence: 'Property is theft', cannot be used by itself to categorise the Proudhonist or socialist movement. For people were not content merely to venerate the master's memory, they also tried to resolve the social question in his manner. It is here that we are able to discern several differences in doctrine between the Proudhon-impregnated socialists and the communists. The split comes over the questions of property and capital, but also over what dynamic principle should preside over the running of society.

In effect the Proudhonist speakers defended individualism and the legitimacy of a certain amount of property. Although they were co-operatists, they were nearly always opposed to collectivism. Dubosc, one of the chairmen of the meeting on female labour, an admirer of the Jacobins and a fanatic for Victor Hugo, wanted Co-operation, of course, but only if it was driven on by individualism: 'Everything for the individual, nothing for the state', he specified on 11 October 1868. Briosne, who occasionally put the case for collectivism during one of his polemics[17] desired co-operation for the ways it could help the individual to develop. 'On 30 September 1868 he proposed that women should have what already existed for men: co-operative labour associations. He saw in the grouping together of workers the birth of the individual and the development of intelligence (*applause*].' This solution for the social question would suppress the employers while at the same time guaranteeing 'the independence of the individual . . . against communism'.[18] One thing is certain. Although he rejected 'individual property and the right of inheritance', this artificial flower maker was a fervent believer in the spirit of enterprise:

For the time being we must be careful not to break individual
initiative. He [Briosne] does not want the group to dominate
the individual, nor does he want the individual to absorb the
group. Both elements must be protected and scientific means
must be found to resolve the problem.[19]

He was to return frequently to this theme, which became a
leitmotif right up until the Commune. Wishing for a society
where 'justice will reign in social relations, and harmony and
economy in production' he was tireless in his advocacy of the
principle that the productive class should take the initiative (singly
or in associations) in order to give capital back 'its true character
of an instrument of production'.

These ideas, which will be familiar to anyone interested in the
worker movement, were not really understood by the police
observers, who said they were strange 'theories'. They found
Briosne particularly obscure,[20] as they did everyone who, like
Mme Désirée, was inspired by Proudhon and who consequently
made concessions to the principle of property:

Citizens, I am a socialist, on the one hand I accept property and
on the other I don't. I do not accept that a parasite should own
property, I do not accept that someone who owns it through
the help of other people and of the workers should have it. In
those cases I believe that this property is a theft from society. I
understand property for someone who has earned it by his own
labour without the help of anyone else, and yet I am against the
right of inheritance.[21]

Here one can see the full measure of the fundamental split
between the socialists and the communists. If their common
rejection of the 'right of inheritance' brings them together, the
recognition of a certain kind of property which would be
legitimised by personal labour divides them. It was precisely the
idea that the proletariat could not accede to this property that
Duval was to develop. Therefore the socialists, or those who
called themselves socialists at a given moment, were to go so far
as to contest the right of inheritance while making it clear that
they were not 'communists'. Héligon, who proclaimed himself a
socialist and spoke proudly of belonging to the IWMA, made a
point of emphasising that he was not a partisan of collective
property.[22]

It was Héligon who defended the banner of socialism against
Bancel at the Redoute during the 1869 elections: 'I ask M. Bancel
if he would be prepared to come before you and defend and

propagate the principles of revolution he has just come out with were he on oath?'[23]

Therefore, in spite of their conviction about the value of individualism and of the validity of a small amount of property, the Proudhonists considered themselves revolutionaries. But they differed from the communists yet again in their analysis of capital, where they made certain concessions. The socialists, untiring and militant partisans of production and consumer co-operatives the creation and function of which would need extensive funding, admitted the organic need for capital. In fact many of them had participated in the venture for Labour Credit.[24] Funds were indispensable if they were to make their dream a reality. Thus Briosne, who furthermore was far from reticent in his criticisms of 'society today', wanted 'the spread of capital in the interests of all'. Although he declared himself to be opposed to 'financial feudalism' and the 'idle races', Limousin did not radically challenge capitalism; he went as far as to recognise 'the legitimacy of interest' (although he wanted to suppress 'the sovereignty of capital'). Langlois too admitted that 'given the state society is in today, capital interest is legitimate'. Some were to give a definition of capital which justified its existence. Limousin 'understands capital as meaning the accumulation of labour'. This extremely vague definition is no doubt some kind of allusion to the savings that the socialists thought possible.[25]

Thus the economists were manoeuvring with these beliefs and aspirations of the socialists in mind. 'We are all capitalists', said one of them (Frederic Passy) when proposing a Capital-Labour Association. 'Capital ought always to be united with labour', added Oriani. Horn maintained that 'unity through loyalty and without violence' was necessary. Just like certain socialists, the economists skilfully assimilated capital with labour in order to make it legitimate. In the words of Frederic Passy: 'We must respect capital, which is nothing but labour' (or 'accumulated savings' as Horn put it). From that, nothing was more logical than the conclusion that property is legitimate: 'Property is the product of personal labour, property is the economy of the worker' (Clamageran). We have come a full circle: capital = accumulation of labour = property = legitimacy of property.

The economists thus made every attempt to beguile the socialists into disassociating themselves from the communists. They tried to make them admit 'the necessity of capital', making it virtually synonymous with 'civilisation' (Courcelles-Seneuil), and occasionally they succeeded in doing so.[26] However, if a few of them, like Longuet, supported the right of inheritance, most of the time they rejected individual property, since although they accepted a certain amount of capitalism they were partisans of collective property in co-operation or association. The socialists disagreed with the economists on the notion of the legitimacy of interest,[27] since they wished for a People's Bank of the kind Proudhon had advocated.[28] They also disagreed with them in their conception of labour, which for them was the mainspring of the economy (for the economists the mainspring was interest, in other words profit, which they saw as being the only effective 'stimulant', since men were naturally lazy).

What did bring the socialists into line with the communists was firstly the dimension that several of them wanted to give to collective property – Paule Minck saw it being guaranteed by the state – and secondly their challenge of the right of inheritance (which Paule Minck called 'accumulated capital'). In the words of Brisson: 'We must attack capital in the shape of the right of inheritance.' It was doubtless for these reasons that in an article in the *Réveil* on 22 October 1868 bitterly attacking the Saint-Simonian economists, Ranc wrote that 'the socialists, with a very few exceptions . . . are all revolutionaries'.

In the meetings on 'Capital and Interest' the economists endured a swingeing defeat, and on 14 November 1868 they gave up trying. They had been opposed equally by the socialists (Cognet, Howert, Ulysse Parent) and the communists ('a *blouse*',[29] Napoléon Gaillard). However the break was not absolutely complete, since in 1869 we find that the call for the creation of a new Labour Credit Society brought socialists (Fornet, Gauthier, Rebierre, Kniep, Verdure, David, etc.) and the economists with radical tendencies (Clamageran, Ernest Hendle, Herold, Jules Simon . . .) side by side. By using very active democrat middlemen like Charles-Louis Chassin,[30] the socialists continued to frequent these bourgeois circles politically right up until July 1870.

B) COMMUNISM

In so far as many speakers defined themselves with reference to communism, as we have seen, we might have thought it possible to localise its militants easily according to the very clear-cut characteristics, and thus to study the content of their doctrine. There are two main reasons why this is not so: the dearth of source material and the weakness of certain communist speakers on the level of theory.

Sources are frequently not very explicit about the content of this communism. The police observers, the superintendents and their stenographers seem not to have always understood what its sectarians were trying to say. In fact, they could not have cared less. As far as they were concerned, all they had to do was to note the name of anyone claiming to belong to the communist movement, in other words, to single out the enemies of bourgeois society. On 9 March 1869, for example, at the place du Trône, they noted without much precision that 'Lacatte made a speech in favour of communism' and that Budaille 'also spoke along communist lines'. If any observers actually wrote down extracts from some of the speeches, it would be in order to stress the negative aspect of the communist discourse . . . and its success with the crowds. Thus, according to Vitu, Budaille supposedly said that 'this is the only conclusion we can arrive at: destroy and demolish. I myself have been a relentless demolisher: it's the same thing everywhere.' Notes like this are nothing more than snippets, and as far as the reports in the bourgeois republican press, (*Le Siècle*, *Le Rappel*), are concerned, they appear to us now like muffled and distorted echoes of the real discourse (now and again a speaker would write to the editors asking them to correct their version of what he had said).

Secondly, we are forced to admit that clarity was not the strong point of many of the self-confessed communists. In the front row are the uneducated ones whose professions of faith and whose references were without a solid basis, like Seval, for example: 'We only recognise one communism: the communism of revolution and the Jacobins who serve it.'

He even went on to quote Robespierre as having instituted the 'new' Cult of Reason! (Everyone knows that Robespierre was neither a communist nor a partisan of the Goddess Reason.) This kind of confusion was rife, Guihar also classed Robespierre, Saint-Just and Danton among the communists. Ducasse, who presented himself as a communist, was a fervent admirer of Robespierre. We should make it clear that not everyone was so uninformed about the realities of history, since at a meeting at the Redoute some known militants were of the opinion that Danton, Robespierre and even Marat 'were reactionaries'. In the second row, after the poorly-educated militants, came the manipulators. Budaille was one of them. This shadowy character presented himself as an intransigent propagator of communism. He 'does not want anything to do with individualism, that serpent coiled around society; communism alone can bring happiness to society'. He set himself up both as defender of the memory of Babeuf against the allegations of the Bonapartists' newspaper the *Pays*, and as a kind of prophet: 'Citizens, you can rest assured that we will achieve communism and that soon we will be able to issue a Code which will not be the Napoleonic Code but the Code of the People.'

Unfortunately, a letter Budaille sent to the editors of the *Réveil* at the beginning of 1869 reveals that his communism was not as pure as the above quotations would suggest. In it he gives a very long-winded explanation of how he intends to use the public meetings to effect a synthesis between the 'different schools':

> In 1789 our fathers took the cherished motto *Liberté-égalité-fraternité*; let us add another: individualism, socialism and communism. The first made us great and free, the second will give us happiness.

The only definition of communism he gives is that it is a 'poor *bête noire*, the individualist's nightmare'. Not much of a definition, we must admit. In a letter to the *Réveil* of 6 March 1869, H. Rondot wrote: 'He is a good speaker, and his ideas show plenty of radical thinking; he is witty, he is daring; as far as social systems go, he claims to be an apostle of Louis Blanc, while Ledru-Rollin seems to represent his political beliefs. All his socialist speeches begin with the word freedom.'

The Blanquist communists may be more endearing, but they too must be seen as tacticians. Thus we frequently find them playing the innocent. Duval insisted that he had no 'theories', and that he was 'neither a socialist nor a communist'; Rigault, after demanding 'the education of the nation by the nation', added maliciously that 'it may verge on communism, but I couldn't care less about that'. This was not a permanent attitude, however, for as Caria maintained: 'With communism, everything is possible.'

If we were to leave it at that, however, we would scarcely be any the wiser. It is therefore necessary to isolate the four major themes in their speeches which will enable us to define what the communist plan really was, namely: egalitarianism, the suppression of private property, its corollary dictatorship by the workers, and finally the challenge to the bourgeois family.

EQUALITY, THE CONDITION AND BASIS FOR COMMUNISM

At first sight, equality is never more than just one of the values of bourgeois democracy, even if it is a popular one. The radical bourgeoisie was prepared to have it on the agenda of their lecture meetings. Crude egalitarianism in itself is not particularly revolutionary. It was only when the quest for equality came up against the other values of 1789 and began clearing the ground for the subversion of the established system that it became corrosive. Therefore the communists used this idea, and indeed made it a fundamental principle, because it belonged to the logic of revolution. The version of civil equality according to the ideas of 1789 which we find in the speeches of the republican bourgeois of the 'liberal party' was challenged. At the rue de Flandre, Brissac put the view that 'education for all' would not 'be enough to create true equality', for there were classes – he uses the word 'caste' – which were linked by relations of exploitation, resulting in 'ignorance' and 'poverty'. 'Integral education' should lay 'the indestructible foundations of equality' (Flourens, Terrail). For the communists, equality was separate from the other values. Caria wanted 'justice' and 'equality', but was suspicious of 'fraternity'; he made a class analysis, and consequently he wanted to hate exploiters rather than love them: 'There are some people with whom fraternity is impossible,' he said, adding that these were the principles which had made him 'a communist and a man'. Vivier, another well-known communist, declared that 'without equality freedom will just be an empty word' (January 1870).

It is therefore proper to place the egalitarian ideas of these men in a revolutionary perspective. When invoking equality they adopted the tone of Babeuf, Sylvain Marechal and Buonarroti whom, like Gaillard at the Redoute, they defended vigorously. If it was a central theme at meetings, it was the communists who were usually the first to demand it. Like Humbert they rejected the accusation that they were demagogues:

> True communists are criticised for having too simple a
> doctrine. . . . But the people will always be on the side of men
> who make straightforward statements like: there will be no
> salvation without equality!. . . . We do not want inequality,
> not even intellectual inequality [*applause*].
>
> Ménilmontant, 27 November 1869)

For Johannard preaching equality meant agitating for 'true communism'. To exclaim like Bachellery at the Vieux-Chêne: 'I want complete equality', or to discuss 'the transformation of societies by means of equality' as they did at the rue de Charonne on 23 December 1869 was to attack the society of class in order to replace it with an alternative social organisation. At the salle Molière, Gaudoin was to demand 'the establishment of the egalitarian commune'. As for Lefrançais, he 'explained that the social organism must be based upon the right of equality'. He was 'struggling against individualism' and 'demonstrating that, far from breaking and destroying human equality as some people alleged, the revolutionary commune would develop it'.

But if this egalitarian society was to become a reality, then the first step would have to be the suppression of the causes of inequality, the result of man's exploitation of man. It was here that the communists became the champions of the attack against property and capital.

COMMUNISM AGAINST PROPERTY AND CAPITAL

This was also the way in which the economist Villiaume differentiated between them: 'There are two opposing systems, communism and the individual property which he advocates.'

Horn was to define communism as the system of 'collective property', and that was how it was generally understood. However there were certain militants who only advocated a share-out: 'Mme Désirée is a Communist. . . . She wants to be shared out', or even the right for everyone to own property. Budaille invoked Proudhon in encouraging tenants not to pay their rent, and he declared: 'Everyone living in lodgings ought to own them. . . . It's the first step towards communism.' These inaccuracies are possibly the result of defective witnesses or blundering speakers, and cannot be taken as representative of the doctrine. Briosne, a well-informed man, made it quite clear that communism had nothing to do with some kind of a diffusion of property ownership: 'We must not give anyone the opportunity of saying that we are in favour of sharing things out, because on the contrary communism wants to achieve collective property.' Before an audience at the Pré-aux-Clercs, after having invoked the memory of Babeuf at the Redoute, Lefrançais 'demanded that collective property be substituted for individual property'.[31] Beaufils thought 'that collective property should replace individual property'. The communists made a point of emphasising that for them this plan was absolutely fundamental. They thrust it forward passionately in all the *quartiers* of Paris. The young florist Louis Moreau chose the salle du Vieux-Chêne to put it across:

> I am a communist and I do not want individual property; the remedy we are proposing is not to destroy property, it is collective property, property for all and not property exploited by a few at the expense of all.

Bachellery was another exponent of this proposal. After having said of property that 'We want to suppress it completely', he asserted his plan which would resolve the struggle between the classes:

> The bourgeoisie is all-powerful in the social system in which it
> has landed property and the enjoyment of capital and credit. As
> for the people, they are too uneducated, they tremble and
> suffer under the yoke of the social system; their suffering is
> long; the cries, unanswered, turn to screams of rage . . . there
> must be a remedy, and that remedy is communism and
> collective property.

This claim enabled Bachellery to disassociate himself from
reformism. At Belleville, Leval asserted 'the principle of collective
property' and concluded with 'a violent outburst against
Proudhon', that 'false socialist' who had been a traitor in 1848.
Whenever a speaker's criticism of individual property was
accompanied with a proposal for 'collective property', then he
was a communist. It had been improper of Vitu to classify as
communists certain individualists who, like Briosne, criticised
individual property for being 'an obstacle to association'.
Sometimes the communists did not argue about the notion of
property but simply proclaimed themselves in favour of suppressing it. Thus Ducasse said that he wanted 'communism and the
suppression of property', as did Peyrouton, since he desired 'the
total obliteration of property'.
    Putting it another way, it was a question of expropriating the
expropriators. As early as 1 January 1869 Sébille chose the
Redoute for putting forward his demand for 'general expropriation . . . the suppression of capital and property which he called
two collective terms and the two causes of the evil'. If, for most
of the time, the communists were aiming at the capitalists, they
followed the IWMA in not neglecting the rural world. ('Camille
Adam, who spoke after [Clément], said that he agreed with those
who want to demolish everything that is worst about the present
social system, but that he would like to have something better to
put in its place. He wanted the expropriation of everyone with
possession for public usefulness, for in his view it was high time
the exploiters stopped being everything and the exploited
nothing.') Ducasse was loudly applauded at Belleville when he
stood up against 'the parcelling-out of property': 'What we must
do is to effect a general expropriation of land in the interests of
public usefulness.' Tony-Moilin was to say much the same thing
at the salle Robert when he proposed: 'that the state should
expropriate rented houses and land for reasons of public
usefulness' in exchange for a life annuity, a doctrine approved by
Vivier, 'who was proud to call himself a communist'.
    If the communists avoided idyllic descriptions of their future
society,[32] they were nonetheless ready to name the people they

wanted to do away with, that is to say, exploiters in all shapes and sizes. According to Bachellery: 'We must take drastic action and suppress the bourgeoisie' (8 March 1869 in the salle Robert).

As for Sabourdy, he considered that 'every parasitic being should disappear from society because they are no good for anything'. At the Redoute, Clément 'called himself a communist; he has had enough of parasites', that is to say, bosses and aristocrats, these exploiters. This aspiration went hand in hand with the idea of a clean-out – 'I wish I could prune away all these parasites; it's about time we stopped letting them fleece us,' threatened one speaker – which would prepare the ground for the construction of a different society. 'No more landlords, no more bourgeoisie, no more taxes of religion', was how Chamaillard put it at the Maison-Dieu on 12 November 1869. We can easily imagine how terrified the moneyed class must have been when publicists or pamphleteers reported remarks like these. It was effectively the very existence of their class and its system that was under attack.

Property and capital were more or less synonymous for the communists. Better than anyone else, Napoléon Gaillard spelled out at the salle de la Redoute this unresolvable opposition between capital and labour:

Citizens, I am a workman, work is man's only happiness; people who do not work are the most miserable creatures on earth, they are layabouts who lie in wait for the workers. He declared that he was a very advanced socialist, even a communist. The suppression of the interest on capital would not make the people any more happy. He made the comparison of a pair of scales: high up on one side, the rich, low down on the other, the poor. To bring the poor up, the rich must be brought down. It was not interest which had to be demolished, but capital in its entirety [*sounds of approval, murmuring*]; people who do not work should not be allowed to devour people who do. Returning to the idea of happiness of work, he said that an artist does not work simply for the money; that there were great workers who went to die in exile and that these men were not egotists. He concluded by saying that work should be everything, not money; the layabout who lies in wait for the worker must be destroyed, and the producer must become everything [*applause*].

The achievement of this objective – 'the working class emancipated from capital' – which for certain militants like Avet was their sole aim in life, would lead to the class struggle. If this

way were to triumph, it seemed to the communists indispensable
to advance class consciousness by eliminating bourgeois elements
from the workers' party, and one such element was the well-
known 'republican union' of the different classes advocated by
certain public-meeting organisers. As early as 1868 communist
propaganda aimed at inciting a direct struggle with capital began
to bear fruit. Avet, a representative of the 'new generation',
seemed to be pointing in that direction when he said: 'The people
must act on its own initiative. I've seen Roubaix and Charleroi.
There the masses are trying to liberate themselves from capital.'

The illusion spread by the economists and certain socialists that
there could be such a thing as a 'good capitalist' fell before the
remorseless attack of the communists. That way they were able to
contribute to the strengthening of class consciousness at meetings.
To Havrais's declaration 'People who have capital are incapable of
any generous feelings', a voice replied: 'We must split up the
classes' ('Female Labour', session of 11 October 1868).

To start with, the economists took note of how clear-cut the
communist discourse against capital was, and they tried to
neutralise it by classifying it as 'Utopian'. Without capital, they
said, there would be no 'stimulant' and therefore no production,
no progression. Thus, according to these liberals, communism
could only be achieved by 'angels on earth' – and we all know
what the bourgeois liberals thought about 'human nature' – or
even worse, by the state.

If it had remained on a theoretic level the anti-capitalist
discourse of the communist speakers would not have unleashed
terror among its opponents. What made it terrifying was the fact
that its propagandists envisaged a politico-social technique which
could be put into practice in order to achieve their goal, namely,
what would later come to be called the dictatorship of the
proletariat.

FOR THE 'DICTATORSHIP OF THE PROLETARIAT'

And yet this dictatorship was not simply a means to an end. On
the short term and for a while it was the organisational form
which society was to take. Sometimes communist speakers
wavered between pure dictatorial force – Ferré, 'I am enough of a
communist to want to impose communism' – and persuasion,
some even going as far as Johannard, who said: 'We must be
democrats, so let us be democrats'.[33] Sometimes they broached
the question from the social angle, sometimes from the political
angle. Witness Gonet in Belleville at the beginning of 1869:

In the question that concerns us there are two opponents, individualism and communism. Communism represents the future, it refuses to make any concession or compromise with our enemies. With them it's war to the death, war to the death and no quarter [*cheers*].

A complete reversal of class relations would make the disappearance of the capitalists a possibility. To achieve it, Peyrouton considered that the proletariat had to make itself into the dominant class, and he was paraphrasing Sieyes when he said: 'What is work? Work should be everything, but in reality it is nothing.' There had to be a radical change. 'We must scale the wall,' advised Ferrand, 'and once we're at the top, if our oppressors resist us, we all know, in the name of liberty, equality and fraternity, what we've got to do [*applause*].'

In effect, the communists were well aware of this. The workers should not overthrow the 'stingy' bourgeoisie in order to steal its privileges, nor should they indulge themselves in 'feelings of envy' (Peyrouton); not only were they above that, but moreover communism was in fact the means to fight against privileges (Bachellery). Therefore the workers should impose an implacable dictatorship upon the bourgeoisie.[34] Gaillard and Bachellery were the militants who spoke the most clearly on the issue. As early as 1868 Gaillard said that he was 'a very advanced Socialist, even a communist. . . . To raise the poor up, you've got to bring the rich down'. At the beginning of 1869 at the Redoute he repeated the offence by attacking 'individual property', saying that 'workers should be given the right of association or else the rich should be forced to put society into liquidation'. Without such a dictatorship, communism was not possible:

As long as the egotism of wealth exists, it will try its utmost to combat communism; but one day will come, and I believe that perhaps it's not far off, when the men who can handle a hammer, the men who produce, will have no difficulty in bringing the others to their senses, the others who are in the minority.[35]

Bachellery said virtually the same thing, although his dictatorship seemed to include more of the people, since it included rural labourers:

There are three million individuals who possess landed property or other kinds of property, and the remaining thirty-seven million are in the hands of the three million. Well now, what if we were to change this ratio. . .? What about putting the three million under the thirty-seven million, wouldn't that be better?[36]

It's all got to change; everything on the top must be moved to the bottom; and may everything at the bottom move to the top, so high at the top that no hand can be raised against it.[37]

Anyone who looks for long and exciting evocations of a revolutionary society ruled by a dictatorship of the proletariat in the speeches of the communists will be wasting their time. They had no room for Utopias. On the rare occasion when militants ventured along that uncertain path, like Bologne for example, it was to warn audiences that the class struggle would continue after power had been seized:

In a well-organised commune, every citizen should work for the public good, for the reorganisation of present-day society, with wives supporting their husbands in the struggle, encouraging them to fight social injustice, privilege, unfairness, and to sacrifice themselves if needs be in the interests of all.[38]

This reference to wives leads us to the last theme which distinguishes the communists from the socialists: their position in relation to the family and to women.

AGAINST THE BOURGEOIS FAMILY AS A SUPPORT FOR PROPERTY

There were a certain number of meetings ('Marriage and Divorce', 'The Child Born out of Wedlock', 'On Marriage and Cohabitation', 'On Divorce, Being Unmarried and the Family') during which the communists' challenge to the family was defined.

If this attack is to be understood, two important points must be borne in mind:
- the fight was in the name of atheist materialism; it was anti-Catholic and anti-religious;
- the suppression of the right of inheritance was one of the basic demands, for they saw it as being at the origin of property, and that inheritance and the family as an institution were one and the same.

The Catholics, whom we see speaking at the very first public meetings, were well known for being among the most pronounced supporters of the established order. Their position on the family was such a caricature that it could have been dictated to them by their opponents. Thus Recamier defined the family as 'the keystone of the social edifice', a magnificent metaphor blending family and property; Postel, on divorce, 'rejected it with all the strength he could muster because it is contrary to the family, which is society's image'; Gagne was against divorce through 'respect' of 'established law'; as for Frederic Faure, who also spoke against divorce, he defended 'property and wealth without which there can be no society'.

Faced with such pure and naive opinions, we will not be surprised to hear that the communist speakers should launch an attack on this bastion. We must emphasise that their position was not simply a negative one, for it resulted from a critical analysis of the family and offered a proposal for another way of life which would result in the creation of the true family.

For the communists, the 'family of today' advocated by the Church and the bourgeoisie could be defined in two ways. On the one hand it was at the origins of the state, and therefore reflected its authoritarian nature. Peyrouton talked of 'this awesome authority which has been passed on intact from the Head of State to the head of the family'. Therefore the struggle against the 'father' was the order of the day, since every family had its Napoleon III. This is why Rigault, backed by Caulet de Tayac and Kaufman, attacked 'the so-called rights of the father' in December 1869. On the other hand, the family was the expression of capitalism, 'the accumulation of capital in the same hands, a fearful misery, an imbecilic minority oppressing the majority'.

Certain socialists were to join the communists spontaneously in this struggle against the family; Briosne, for example, who on 22 September exclaimed: 'The family, it is crumbling, and I want to see it collapse.'

Under these conditions, it was inevitable that the 'holy institution' of marriage would be the target of some barbed communist attacks. For them, it was a union based on material interest. Peyrouton expressed this vehemently on 6 October when he maintained that 'greed and what are known in fashionable circles as the proprieties' were in fact 'the basis of marriage'. The result was a debauchery. If Briosne got called a communist, it was precisely because he developed the same kind of argument: 'In the eighteenth century we had the marriage of interests, moral hypocrisy, adultery tolerated through interest [*very enthusiastic and prolonged applause*]. 'Marriage of interests' meant women being sold off by their fathers.

Obviously the communists' opponents accused them of being immoral, of wanting the community of women, etc. But on closer examination we see that they were not simply attacking institutions, for what they wanted was the creation of a proletarian family. Like Ranvier, who 'wants the universal family . . . a family which will be as great as property will be small', their only argument with the (bourgeois) family was its legal hypocrisy, its economic-religious motives, and not its human structure as such. Against all expectations, they proclaimed themselves to be in favour of 'the true family'. Lefrançais, whose dream was a balanced, smooth-running family, since he was against divorce as being 'contrary to the family and to morality', had a range of solutions for resolving this 'disorder of the family' which was 'at its height'. Education was one of them. Reformed education would 'rescue women from the deleterious influence of the clergy and teach them their role as mothers in the family'. Thus this unexpected defence of the family took on anti-Catholic and anti-clerical overtones. The real destroyers of the family were the priests and the Catholics stigmatised by Cazenave: 'Yes, you are the enemies of the family; more than that, you are the enemies of humanity.'

If we look beyond the tactical alliances the communists made with the socialists and the Protestants in favour of divorce, for example, which they thought of only as a palliative, we see that the solution they advocated in meetings was cohabitation, which would form the basis upon which the true family could be built. Therefore it was not the 'hideous' or 'vile coupling' which Postel and Gagne rejected at a meeting on 'Marriage and Divorce' on 20 October 1868, but on the contrary the demonstration of egalitarianism and loyalty in the relationships between men and women. On 6 October Peyrouton had expressed this point of view well:

> No law is needed to consecrate the union of a man with a woman. . . . The only sanction this union needs is reciprocal affection. The triumph of this system . . . will mean the beginning of the revolution which will change society completely.

Anyone who reads about the meetings in the hope of finding debates on the sexual problems of the couple will be disappointed. Was this due to a certain puritanism on the part of the speakers and their audiences? Certainly Rigault's dissipations were poorly received, but then what are we to think of the laughter and the call to order which followed a speech by Moreau who looked at the question of marriage 'from the point of view of nature' and of 'the satisfaction of physical needs'? Could there have been taboos in these places dedicated to freedom of speech, or was it merely that the audience thought that he was giving too much importance to things which were self-evident? In any event, we know that the cohabitations which Lefrançais defended so warmly (followed by his friend Briosne) were in fact widely practised by the Parisian working class which formed the rank and file of the public meetings. More than a formal defence of freedom, cohabitation was the defence of a way of life which, by destroying the bourgeois family, was jeopardising the principle of property. That is why Moreau said: 'The results we are seeking can only be obtained by the destruction of property' (26 October 1868). Religion was equally threatened. It was precisely these charges that the 1871 Councils of War were to level against certain of the public meeting Communists such as Gaillard and Lefrançais. The second *rapporteur* of the 23rd Council wrote:

> Gaillard Napoléon, a shoemaker, aged about 55, lived for several years at no. 74 rue Julien-Lacroix, cohabiting with the girl *Clavelon* Augustine, aged 30. A fanatic, he was one of the best-known regulars at the clubs under the Empire, where he stood out because of his violent language and violent attacks on religion, family and property. One day he even shouted that marriage was immoral. He was prosecuted several times.

The Lefrançais dossier contains the same kind of accusations. The attacks on marriage and property of which he was guilty are closely associated. The Versaillais found Lefrançais's position all the more incomprehensible in that he was a schoolmaster with extremely domesticated habits:

> At a meeting at the Pré-aux-Clercs he had the gall to go as far as to advocate the theory of cohabitation as opposed to the institution of legal marriage . . . a father in the home and a revolutionary outside it, he denounced marriage as immoral and property as theft.

Another grievance the representatives of the established order were to have against the communist speakers as advocates of cohabitation was that they had been too supportive of women's initiatives or that they had been too indulgent towards them. For example the *rapporteur* of the 23rd Council wrote of Gaillard: 'His revolutionary ideas were admirably served, not to say over-excited, by his concubine, a fanatical woman who had a certain power over him.'

The communists were a driving force in the free thought movement and were extremely favourable to women's action both there and in the public meetings. On 13 July 1870 several of the well-known communist figures at the Paris meetings came to pay their last respects to Ranvier's companion, following her pauper's hearse from the rue Oberkampf to Père-Lachaise. This funeral gives us the opportunity to realise what the relationship between a public meeting communist militant who supported cohabitation and his companion might have been. A report in the *Cloche* says that this 'woman of the people', mother of six, was

> one of those rare and courageous daughters of the people who know how to fight against prejudice and social injustice and who encourage their husbands to agitate tirelessly for their rights, against the absolutism and the tyranny of despots. She was one of the first to demand rights for women, she involved herself whole-heartedly in every protest against social injustice and unfairness. She was able to shake off the stultifying yoke of religious stupidity and was truly worthy of the title of citizen and free thinker. A good wife and a good mother, she will be missed by everyone who knew her.

Over her grave, before two thousand people, Ranvier delivered a eulogy to his companion which was both emotional and political. Moreau, Mme Piré, Marly, Dumont and Briosne all spoke one by one. Need we add that Ranvier's children were to be communards?

These few characteristic examples give a good illustration of the fundamentally politico-social aspect of communist ideas on the notion of the family. Their attacks on the family were in essence a political and philosophical battle against the Catholic camp, and thus against the state which supported it; on the social level, it was the foundations of property that they wanted to undermine. Of course the moral aspect of their struggle may raise a smile, but as we have seen elsewhere the social criticism developed at the public meetings contained an ethical condemnation of the bourgeoisie. In 1871, during the commune, the anti-prostitution measures were to be inspired by this ideology. In this domain – this unflinching defence of the purity of the people in the face of the degrading practices of the moneyed class – the communists were supported by many speakers with different political persuasions. In effect, certain ideas bring the different schools together, and then unite them.

2 Two unifying themes

A) 'INTERNATIONALISM'

After this selection of comments on the nature of the socialism expressed at the public meetings by its various representatives, whether they called themselves Fourierists, Proudhonists, mutualists, socialists, collectivists or communists, we would now like to underline what seems to us to be one of the most important aspects linking these different tendencies: internationalism. Not only were many meetings organised by members of the IWMA, but it is significant to remark the almost complete absence of chauvinism on the part of speakers and audiences alike. The meetings were well aware of the enemy within. In October 1869 at the passage d'Isly, Taillardat, a mechanic, had this to say:

> I went to China to take civilisation to it. In that far-off land, where we were sent without having been asked for by the people, we machine-gunned the poor Chinese, who bared their breasts to us rather than flee death.

On 17 April, at a meeting on 'Social Interests during the Consulate and the Empire', colonial expeditions and repression were unequivocally challenged. Nathan spoke at length about the violent way the French soldiers had treated the Arabs.[39] On 6 April at the Alcazar ('The Colonies from the Commercial and Colonising Point of View') Paulet was of the opinion that 'the first time that France began colonising, it was in order to establish slavery. . . . Africa will only become prosperous if it manages its own affairs'. On 8 October 1869, also at the Alcazar, Vertut said that 'Algeria had been slaughtered but not colonised'. He also attacked 'the Mexico expedition' (14 January at the Maison-Dieu). Shortly after that Leo Meillet declared that he wanted to get rid of 'militarism and chauvinism as soon as possible, for they were the cause of parasitism and prostitution' (session of 25 January, 4 boulevard de Clichy).

European questions were not often discussed but when they were it was often from a similar angle. The public meetings agreed neither with the Empire nor with the republican salons. The Emperor's Italian policy – 'Mentana' – was denounced, and Paule Minck was heard to deliver a revolutionary paean to German unity which Marx would surely not have rejected:

> Mme Paule Minck was very violent. She spoke about the Germans, among others, saying that in her view they had done the right thing to submit themselves to the rule of a sovereign

because when the time came it would be easier to overthrow one tyrant than a dozen petty kings.[40]

In such conditions, the socialism advocated by speakers at the public meetings had nothing national about it, did not side with the Tricolour Republic of the radicals or the parliamentary and progressist bourgeoisie of the opposition, and refused to support colonialism without or class collaboration within.

'Socialism is the redemption of all peoples, it is everyone's salvation', maintained Vertut on 5 October 1869, avenue de Choisy. 'Let us raise the red flag again!' cried Chauvière the young Blanquist – he was about 17 at the time – right in the middle of a very violent speech on 2 February 1869, boulevard de la Chapelle. On this level the audiences at the public meetings were finely in tune with the speakers; on 23 April 1870, during a meeting on 'Socialism Today', the stenographer recorded the following:

> Mme Piré was very violent.
> Among other things she said that the socialist's flag was only one colour.
> The audience was carried away, and cried 'Red! Long live the Republic.'

Again, this unequivocal choice of flag for the proletarian revolution pointed directly towards the Commune.

B)   THE COMMUNE

As early as the first months of 1869, the 'social commune' was a revolutionary demand at the public meetings. It was unanimous, since people as different as J. Allix, Falcet, Mathorel, Montel, Amouroux and Mme Piré became its 'principal speakers'. The establishment of the commune – the dream of every public meeting militant – erased all differences of opinion. It was a project which allowed for transitions and alliances, as was shown by the speech given by the communist Millière at the Folies-Belleville:

> In a warmly-applauded speech, Millière broached the problem of the organisation of a commune, saying 'we must be concerned not with the goal to be achieved but above all with the means of action for transition. Co-operation is a fine thing but it is not enough. It is a stage in the preparation for integral association which the social commune must achieve. But this

association must not hamper the formation of free groups, for we won't transform humanity all in one go, overnight.'

He proposed that if communes still possessed any communal property it should be used as the basis for a new organisation of culture. He asked what the point would be of dividing it, splitting it up and alienating it. He concluded by inviting socialists of whatever shade or hue to give their assistance. (31 August 1869)

In the same hall Vésinier summed up the unitary aspect of this so ardently-desired commune well when he spoke of 'the ways and means of organising the social commune which will be the basis for the great democratic and social confederation' (beginning of October 1869). Every *quartier* was to have its meetings or digressions on the commune. From the salle Molière[41] to the boulevard de Clichy and passing along the rue Lhomond,[42] everyone could dream of this new form of social life by debating what 'the social commune' would be. No aspect was neglected: at the passage du Génie, the subject was 'On Taxes in the Social Commune'; salle Moliére, it was the origins 'of the establishment of communes in France according to Augustin Thierry'. Certain militants such as Jules Allix were veritable preachers for this famous commune 'which would look after its own affairs'.[43]

However, while we can assert that the Commune really was the essential project of the public meetings, we must recognise nevertheless that there were certain speeches which foreshadowed future differences of opinion about it. In effect – and one thinks of the events of 31 October 1870 and the internal conflicts of the communards between 18 March and 28 May 1871 – one senses that there were, and would be, different concepts of this universally-desired commune. The 'revolutionary commune' praised by Giot, and the 'egalitarian commune' demanded by Gaudoin were no doubt versions of the Commune of An II, which Vertut referred to when he recalled 'the blood shed in '93 for the cause of freedom', and which the neo-Hebertists, and especially Rigault, were intent on recreating. Was it the same Commune as the one envisaged by the gentle Allix? At this time – and it is something that emerges very clearly from NA 155 – the theme of the Commune consolidated energies while stimulating the imagination. A later note on NA 155 remarks of a session at 104 boulevard de Clichy where the topic was 'On the Organisation of the Social Commune': 'They were developing a project or organising the commune which was to be put into effect less than two years later.'

D The means of action for the revolution

There was a whole hierarchy of means of action for the radical transformation of society. Of course these were a function of the various socialist and Jacobin schools of thought. We should also note that the militants had to bear the repression in mind, and could not always speak about the means they would use to reach their goals as openly as they would have liked. Bologne, who proclaimed his support for production associations at the Folies-Belleville, added that he could not talk about the 'practical means of action' because of the rue de Jérusalem (where the headquarters of Pietri the prefect of police were). However, if everyone alleged – for there were some demagogues – that they wanted 'the emancipation of the workers', they were divided above all on 'the practical means of action' to achieve it.

Although we may find the occasional speaker who wanted to resolve the social question through reforms such as worker participation or gradual improvements in the law, most seemed committed to revolutionary means of action. 'We won't cure it [the social condition of poverty] by putting innocuous poultices on it,' cried Vertut at the rue Nationale on 23 October, 'but only by changing it completely.'

Nevertheless, as is to be expected, these proposals for means of action came up in speeches in a quite disorganised way. To make matters easier we have sorted them into groups:
1) proposals based upon economic and social solutions,
2) proposals based upon politics.
Of course, since means of action such as co-operation and strikes are not all that far removed from politics, this distinction must be an arbitrary one.

1 Economic and social practice

A) MUTUALISM – CO-OPERATION – ASSOCIATION

One of the great means of action proposed for the transformation of society was, once again, mutualism[44] and, above all, co-operation. In this field, the most active zealots were the Proudhonists, who enjoyed the patronising encouragement of the liberals and the radicals. They differed from the latter, however, in the passion with which they vulgarised and widened out Proudhon's criticisms of 'financial feudalism'. An attack on this mythical monster, ancestor of the '200 families', the 'trusts', or 'monopolies', was bound to satisfy all those who, when it came to naming class enemies, were not particularly worried about being precise. But it was also on the condition that they did not denigrate the enemy too specifically that it was possible to approach the capitalists to finance the workers' production and consumer co-operatives for which the French delegates at the IWMA Congress in Brussels in September 1868 had worked so hard. It was to be Tolain, the most competent spokesman for these co-operatists, but also a ubiquitous militant at the meetings, who most popularised this kind of method. With a pronounced taste for technical explanations, he laid down the economic conditions by which co-operation, which he called association, would be possible:

> He analyses the mechanism of the Banque de France and
> recommends that the workers should take it over in order to
> organise credit, and then production and exchange. He
> castigated wages as being immoral. He makes the following
> proposals for collectivisation:
> 1 mines, quarries, in a word, underground enterprises;
> 2 roads, canals, railways;
> 3 the Banque de France, insurance companies and the large
>   credit institutions.
> Finally he demands the right of association.[45]

Here we find again the decisions of the IWMA Brussels Congress on 'property', namely a sort of programme of nationalisation and 'Proudhonist' theories on banks which the Congress had recommended for study. It also represented the economic part of the IWMA's programme contained in the address: 'To the Electors of 1869'. We should underline the fact that despite the decisive progress the true revolutionaries had made, Tolain was not completely isolated at public meetings. Although he had no hesitation in attacking that celebrated 'financial feudalism', he also supported 'the individuality of property' for which he had made a case in September 1869 in Basel. The way he saw it, and the way the people who seemed to come into line with him saw it, it was by no means a question of holding a pistol to the heads of the real bourgeois. Faillet, who was accused in the press of having said at the salle Molière that 'the only way to resolve the social problem is to make the bourgeois give back their ill-gotten gains and to get rid of the Jesuits', reconstructed the exact thrust of his discourse. It was not a question of bosses, property owners or capitalists, but of mysterious companies, 'financial feudalism' no doubt:

French capital is for the most part in the hands of large financial
and industrial companies and in the hands of the Jesuits. Now
the problem which besets us would be resolved more
effectively than many people think the day when society makes
the big administrators and the Jesuits return their ill-gotten
gains and takes possession of the thousands of millions which
have been embezzled.

(*Le Rappel*, 11 October 1869)

Falcet, who at first had been confused with Faillet, was eager to
make it quite clear that as far as he was concerned he had never
been involved in this kind of disclosure. To be fair, we should add
that the Proudhonists were not the only ones to indulge in facile
attacks on 'financial feudalism', but for them it corresponded to a
kind of alibi for not fighting. Behind these words lurked the
completely capitalist compromise they had to agree to if their
great co-operative dream were to succeed.

At the public meetings the ideological course of co-operation
followed the same path as that of its apostles, the senior members
of the first bureau of the IWMA. Although these 'Gravilliers' did
not quit the arena of the public meetings, they were nevertheless
forced by the dominant trend to muffle their pro-cooperative
propaganda after the thunderous launching of their campaign in
1869.

During the first large series of meetings on 'Female Labour' at
the Vaux-Hall, the right-wing and the left-wing Proudhonists,
plus a few Jacobins and liberals, took advantage of the launching
of the meetings in order to reactivate their co-operative and
associationalist solutions.

Dubos from Lyon, who called himself a 'disciple' of Proudhon,
wanted to resolve the problem of female labour by 'the creation of
mixed associations';[46] Dubosc concurred. Briosne too supported
this type of association which he considered would allow for the
reconciliation of individualism and collectivism. This is why he
proposed 'the co-operative labour association. In the grouping
together of the workers he saw the birth of the individual and the
development of inteligence [*applause*].' This outpouring of
professions of faith blithely erased all the contradictions. It was
'the only remedy' (Fornet), and could be applied to any situation
and to any social or corporative group. For many people it was
the one remedy which could lead to the suppression of capitalist
exploitation. Combes maintained that it 'would suppress the
boss's profits to the benefit of the working woman'. It was pure
socialism. With great fervour Lemmonier of the IWMA 'said that
he is a socialist, that is, a co-operatist, given that co-operation is

the transformation of socialism'. He added that if women were educated 'they will march with us in the exercise of democratic and social co-operation'. We reach sublime heights when Paulet declared passionately that all that was needed was 'a single association with a bank and a vast general store for selling things'.

However, these lyrical flights of oratory could not be sustained, for the public meetings were not as compliant as the co-operatist press. In the meetings a left-wing opposition to co-operation was quick to develop. As we know it was inspired by Blanquism, which like Blanqui himself was very hostile to the 'deadly trap' of co-operation.

Co-operation was deemed harmful as much for its illusory character – for the Blanquists experience had proved that it was merely a pipe dream – as for the fact that it was addressed to an ultra-minoritarian egotistical elite and not the masses. In this period, which Blanqui defined as the period of 'criticism', one of the communist revolutionaries' main concerns was to develop the struggle against Utopias and Utopians. They saw co-operation as belonging in that category, and therefore their attacks pulled no punches. Poirier attacked Briosne's theories mercilessly: 'Co-operation is impotent, what we need is complete social renovation, by any means whatever,' but it was above all Ranvier who called the tune. He minced no words. For him the co-operativists were nothing more than new exploiters of the working class disguised as socialists:

He speaks of the worker who is nothing and should be everything [*applause*).
He protests at associations which replace the actual bosses by employer-societies.
Nothing can be achieved under the present regime [*applause*].

From the revolutionary point of view he came down resolutely in the camp of the opponents of this system: 'Starting from communist theories, he wanted no co-operative societies. They are privileges and he is against them.' Other people were to use this irrevocable condemnation to the same ends:

Havrais, who says he's a socialist, does not want co-operative societies: in such societies the more intelligent members profit from the others' lack of education.
The uneducated are always exploited; it's the history of humanity.
He spoke of a co-operative association founded at Cail's which hadn't worked. The manager took over sole ownership of it.

Certainly not all the speeches by opponents of co-operation were so clearly thought out, for many militants were still not ready to admit that their fine dream was nothing but the capitalist avatar the history of co-operatives has incontestably proved it to be. But doubt had crept in. Of course, some blamed the difficulties and failures of co-operative societies on the public authorities or finance. Leboucher recalled in particular the decree issued by General Castellane 'who had ordered the sale of objects belonging to one of these societies in Lyon and which had been confiscated'. Dubosc recalled that credit was 'today in the hands of the financial aristocracy which was born of the aristocracy of the past'. In any case there were many others, like the unnamed person who interrupted Horn with 'co-operation is impossible', for whom there was a whole range of insurmountable barriers, and who, like the worker Rouyer, wanted to know if the co-operation 'which we've been offered . . . can ever succeed'.

A new current was developing, formed by those who thought that co-operation was nothing more than a 'palliative', but that it could be used as a theme for the struggle in so far as it could provoke 'the union of male and female workers' (Tonio). In this case it lost its identity as an actual means of action and became a possible aid to the realisation of the need to do something more. It was nothing more than a simple stage on the path which led to revolution, as we have already seen with Millière.

Bit by bit the theme of co-operation disappeared, giving way to political questions of increasing interest to audiences both in Paris and the *banlieue*. In March 1869, in an attempt to make up for the audiences' increasing lack of interest in 'the social question', the public meeting organisers in Puteaux invited regular speakers from the public meetings in Paris.

This evolution reveals the general politicisation of the public meeting movement, its gradual drift away from Utopistic and economic solutions, and the retreat from Proudhonist ideology within the progressive section of the proletariat. There were even some spectacular rallyings to the communist anti-cooperative cause. In October 1869 Lefrançais, who on 11 October 1868 was still saying 'for some . . . co-operation is a way of finding a solution, for others it is just a means for transition', escaped from this impasse:

If the co-operative societies were to take control of capital and credit, the situation would be even more deplorable than it is today. They would form a caste of small industrialists halfway between the bourgeoisie and the proletarians. They cannot resolve the social question; all they can do is to perpetuate

poverty and the present struggle. (11 October at the Folies-
Belleville)

Taken in conjunction with the mediocre interest meetings
showed for questions about co-operation, this evolution reveals
the progress revolutionary attitudes had made in their aim to
overthrow the capitalist system en block rather than to nibble
away at it surreptitiously – and legally.

The worker aristocracy from which the co-operativists were
principally recruited no longer had a free field in the public
meetings. Now it preferred to treat the question more discreetly.
In 1870, when Baussard said that he did not believe in 'the
effectiveness of co-operative societies', no one contradicted him.

But by no means did this signify that the workers' movement
had given up its projects for co-operatives, and in fact they were
to resurface on a massive scale during the Commune, albeit in
different forms, but it could not, or would not, any more defend
them in the public meetings, where politics was winning the day.
The student of the co-operative movement would therefore have
to leave the public meetings and turn his attention to the hundreds
of co-operativist meetings which were held during this same
period. But that is not our task. The same is true of the history of
the workers' unions, which had been flourishing since 1868 and
which were organising resistance to capital in a more and more
radical direction. If these chapels were increasing in numbers and
quality – their Federation, a genuine branch of the IWMA, dates
from December 1869 – they were not the product of the public
meetings but of the workers' movement itself, spurred on by the
great militants of the First International. Nevertheless, the latter
sometimes also spoke regularly at the public meetings. Public
meetings rarely included unions on their agendas, but even so
they were frequently alluded to. The growing politicisation of
these unions was not unconnected with the interest they aroused
(in 1870 we are a long way from the time when Pindy saw unions
and political movements as opposites).[47]

During the session at the salle Molière on 26 November 1868
devoted to unions, the point was taken that although the union
movement caried out its activities elsewhere than in the public
meetings, it was not unaffected by the questions of a general
nature which were discussed there, including those which were
directly political.

In turn, the public meetings sometimes popularised certain
union ideas, particularly those concerning workers' associations of
all kinds as well as their modes of action.[48] However, they
considered themselves to be superior to such associations. Thus

Vertut felt able to maintain that while workers should form associations, 'the public meeting is the best association possible'.

In other words, this means that they were a forum in which every revolutionary opinion could be expressed, and where all the means of action for the triumph of the cause could be discussed. In this respect the solutions of the public meetings frequently coincided with those of the workers' movement. But they were discussed in depth. This was the case with strikes.

B) STRIKES

'The question of strikes' was broached very early on in the public meetings, notably at the salle Molière during a meeting where there were some conspicuous internationalists. People from the *faubourgs* were passionately interested in this subject, and this enables us to realise how important the proletariat was in the meetings. In fact, if there was such an interest in strikes, it is an obvious proof that this was a wage-earning milieu. The fact that strikes in other countries were greeted with interest and encouragement indicates once more that the militants had been won over in internationalism. Speaking on 'coalitions', Ducasse congratulated the Geneva typographers 'for having gone on strike and daring to stand up to their bosses'. As for Chalain, he was forever recalling 'the Charleroi coalfield affair'. Thus every strike was of interest to speakers and audiences alike, even if they broke out in sectors which hitherto had traditionally been strike-free, like the *grands magasins* sales assistants.

One of the problems posed was the question of what strikes were understood to be. Were they a simple form of resistance to capitalist exploitation? were they a revolutionary means of action for overthrowing the bourgeoisie? Here, as for other subjects, it would appear that the public meetings acted as a forum for clarifying the debate rather than as a headquarters for the workers' movement. With a few exceptions, everything that concerned strikes as such (their activation, their management . . .) was decided elsewhere. Discussions at meetings had the function of making people aware of their value and their meaning, and sometimes their results were assessed. The meetings were centres of information about the struggles between the bosses and the proletariat.

In so far as many speakers were worker militants, it was logical for them to use the opportunity of the meetings to inform a public which was itself revolutionary and which was thus sympathetically inclined towards anything which appeared to contest the prevailing system. This militancy in favour of strikes was aimed above all at strengthening the political consciousness of the Paris meetings, although to begin with the concern was with challenging the social organisation of society by attacking the bosses. This developed in close liaison with manifestations of working-class solidarity.

The public meetings were quick to condemn the bosses. As early as 1868 their supporters and small representatives were violently opposed by direct democracy; in other words, they were stopped from spreading their ideology by being refused the right to speak. In 1870 this uncompromising rejection of the employers culminated in the Le Creusot conflict which was considered exemplary for a number of reasons. Thus a certain Jacob incited 'hatred for the bosses by speaking about the Le Creusot strike'. On another occasion humour was used: the salle de l'Alcazar, where the topic was 'Mines and Mining Companies', invited 'M. Schneider, a deputy and the proprietor in Le Creusot, the Marquis of Campaigno, a deputy and the proprietor of Aubin, Desseilligny, a deputy and proprietor of La Ricamarie . . . to come and put the interests of capital in the presence of socialist theories' (*La Marseillaise*, 8 February 1870).

Working-class solidarity began to take shape through the collections which were a central part of the public meetings, and this in turn allowed for the development of class consciousness. In 1869 there were collections 'for the victims of Aubin', for the striking drapers' sales assistants and for the sales assistants in the Louvre department store. While in 1870 numerous collections for the Le Creusot strike fostered this solidarity. It could be seen in the passage du Génie, the salle Molière, the boulevard de Grenelle, the rue Lhomond, etc. The aim was to support 'our brothers in Le Creusot' (Crémieux), to whom 'fraternal greetings' were addressed (Albert May). This popular practice continued with increased vigour in April with the strikes in Fourchambault and Torteron and the second Le Creusot strike. On 7 April a collection was made at 190 avenue de Choisy during a meeting on *Cahiers du Travail*, and then it was the turn of the salle de la Marseillaise, where the topic for discussion was in fact 'Strikes', to collect donations 'for the families in Le Creusot'. We should also note the collections for the Fourchambault strikes which were made in the salle des Mille-et-un-Jeux and the salle du Concert-du-Châtelet, 54 rue Lhomond, where they were combined with the Le Creusot collections. In the passage du Génie, there was a collection in support of the strikes of Torteron and Fourchambault.

This active solidarity was frowned upon by the authorities who sometimes tried to oppose it. In Belleville on 9 October 1869 the police used force to stop the collection of 'subscriptions'. The authorities had understood that such actions were more political than social. Less and less of a distinction was made between the two. At the Maison-Dieu on 14 January 1870, Vertut 'proposed that contributions be made to the building of a monument to Victor Noir [the young journalist whose murder in a dual by the Emperor's brother provoked widespread popular protest – eds] and it was decided that half of the total collected would be given to the striking tawers'. When the strikes were discussed, the public meetings were eager to emphasise their political aspects; this explains why speakers harped on the repression of strikes during the Empire. What they wanted audiences to understand above all was the collusion between the government, in other words the Imperial state, and the bosses. Labour disputes were approached from the political angle rather than from the point of view of the workers' demands. This was how Amouroux described the Aubin massacre on 9 October 1869 in the salle Molière (and the superintendent issued him with a warning):

> Blood was shed, and I ask the authorities' representative if he can remain unmoved by such appalling events!
> At Aubin, some miners asked for a wage rise. The engineer refused. Carried away by violence, the workers ripped the engineers' clothes. When the sub-prefect turned up they gave him the same treatment. A moment later the chassepots were fired and ten workers fell beneath their bullets.

And this was how Vertut in the same hall on 13 October attempted to stir his audience up about the massacre:

> Why do we stop ourselves talking about such things? Surely you're all such good people that you can only do good deeds. Why be displeased when people talk about them? If you've done something bad, then it's time you were punished. You are the champions today, but tomorrow our turn will come.

The bloody confrontations between the forces of order (the army, the police) and the workers which accompanied large-scale strikes were events which the militants took advantage of in order to arouse the indignation of the people and to harden their positions in respect of the presence of the authorities in the halls – according to Falcet, 'when Rocher began speaking about the Le Creusot affair again, the superintendent intervened once more. Rocher replied that this intervention was unfair and that whether he liked it or not he would speak about Le Creusot and plenty of other things as well', as well as to demonstrate that dialogue with the regime was not possible, thus encouraging audiences to conclude that the situation could only be changed through force. Thus at the rue Lhomond a superintendent recorded that Larmier and Passedouet 'incited hatred against the government by speaking about the Aubin affair'. Speakers were to return time and time again to the fact that the bosses had the support of the army to break strikes. On 2 April at the passage du Génie, Jacob said that 'to get his workers back down the mines, M. Schneider called in a general whose only claim to fame was that he had pillaged the Emperor of China's Summer Palace. Dujardin also attacked M. Schneider'. The Le Creusot strike became the symbol of bourgeois and Imperial violence. More than a mere device to arouse strikers, as NA 155 alleges, it was a political object lesson. Debating gave way to popular anger, to 'enough's enough'. Discussions were becoming dangerously heated. (On 2 April at the passage du Génie, Geoffroy 'spoke very excitedly about the Le Creusot strike and of the part played by M. Schneider, and had to be warned three times', while at the Théâtre Parisien Vertut 'spoke in very violent terms about the events in Le Creusot'.)

All through April, revolutionary propaganda was to develop this theme. It was obvious that the Empire and the bourgeoisie were only surviving thanks to the violent actions of their army rabble. Speaking about Le Creusot, Camille Adam 'said that despotism and tyranny were being upheld with the help of chassepots'. Vertut attacked 'the rich' for using state violence for their own profit, as in Le Creusot (salle des Mille-et-un-Jeux, end of April).

The Le Creusot affair, like those of Aubin and La Ricamarie, won a place in the memory of the people in the same way that the death of Victor Noir had done. 'They will not stop us from celebrating the anniversaries of the Aubin massacre and the Auteuil murder'.[49] It was backfiring on the regime, since it encouraged insurrectionary tirades. At the avenue de Choisy, Passedouet considered that the Aubin and the Le Creusot affairs went beyond the pale: 'It is time', he said, 'to end these bloody saturnalias of tyranny and despotism.' The militants used the events at Le Creusot as a lever, like Nathan junior who tried to 'incite the audience' at the Pré-aux-Clercs on 12 April, where the topic for discussion was 'The Progress of Civilisation from the Point of View of the Law'. The point of no return had been reached. Conciliation had become impossible. The repression was playing into the hands of revolution. In April at the boulevard de Grenelle, Yves Guyot thought that the repression would baptise the strikers: 'They can shoot them, but for the men who keep on their feet it will prove to be a blessing.' The strike of the Le

Creusot workers had become a *chanson de geste*, and was seen in Paris as a revolutionary event which could serve as a model, for women as well as for men. When Paule Minck gave forth at length 'on the energy of the women in Le Creusot while M. Schneider's workmen were on strike', her aim was to rally Parisian working women to the red flag, for in her view, if they were to act like their sisters in Le Creusot, 'the revolution is achieved'. The model to follow was therefore a combination of organised resistance and street battles of the kind Paule Minck was referring to. At this point we should recall that on 2 April the workers' wives in Le Creusot had successfully attacked some policemen with stones to liberate three of their sisters who had been arrested. It was time to bring the regime down by whatever means possible. Everywhere speakers were conveying this message, which the events in Le Creusot had justified. The police had no illusions about this upsurge of insurrectionism. As soon as meetings broached the affair, the superintendents broke them up, as at the salle Molière:

> The superintendent: I remind you that the topic on the agenda is 'Capital and Labour'.
> Citizen Vertut: That's what Le Creusot is all about. In '89 our fathers demolished the Bastille. We, too, must demolish the Bastille of hunger and ignorance.
> The meeting was called to a close.

By their progress and their spin-off effects, strikes were therefore the means by which the workers were placed on the path to revolution. But for the meetings they were just one means of action among many. Strikes were revolutionary; they were not revolution. Robert Brecy's *Le Grève générale en France* is an excellent book, but in our opinion he is talking nonsense when his search for the precursors of the idea of general strikes as developed by the revolutionary unionists between 1880 and 1890 and then by their leaders Pelloutier and Briand in their famous 1892 pamphlet, leads him to attribute its initial formulation to the public meetings, and particularly to Vertut. The actual content of our quotation contradicts the idea that Vertut may have thought of a general strike as the fundamental means of achieving revolution, or even as revolution as such, as the union revolutionaries of the Third Republic were to believe and maintain. Here it was merely one means of action among many to fight capitalism, as we can see in what Vertut said in a speech on 'The Practical Means of Action for Socialism':

that strikes, association and co-operation are the means of action. Up until now strikes have not enjoyed good results because they have always been partial and not general. All workers should get together and declare that they are no longer willing to work for current wages, then you'll soon see the bosses going after the workers and agreeing to meet their demands.

If the mineworkers in all the coalfields had done that, the companies would have given in, and many an unfortunate event would not have taken place.[50]

If on the other hand Robert Brecy is right to emphasise that Vertut's words belong in a 'revolutionary situation', we ought to add that it is precisely for that reason that although this militant seemed to be recommending a general strike (on 13 October in the salle Molière he was still saying things like: 'It is no longer partial strikes that we need, but a general strike') he in fact championed the point of view that strikes are not enough to make revolution victorious. In our opinion these suggestions about a general strike were aimed at sustaining the widespread state of agitation. Vertut was not alone in this. In April 1870, for example, we see proposals of this kind being applied to a range of problems. They are rather more related to what we might call civil disobedience. Thus Passedouet suggested: 'a strike against conscription as well as a strike against taxes. He also wanted an election strike' (which would not prevent him from rallying with the 'noes' shortly after during the Plebiscite); Vivier appears to have followed in his footsteps when he spread 'propaganda in favour of a general strike', although at the same time he did not forget to add maliciously: 'Actually, I believe that demolition would be a better course of action.' Finally, the landlords were not forgotten, since Mme Désirée urged her audience at the avenue de Clichy to hold 'a general strike' against rent for April,[51] while Flageol, a foundry worker, whom a police note presents as 'an excellent workman, and chairman of a mutual aid society, but who frequents the public meetings', went around the 11th *arrondissement* sticking up posters and tracts on the doors of wineshops and the Piat factory which preached 'a general strike in Paris and throughout France' in order to obtain the dismissal of the army and the suppression of general taxes and city taxes before 10 April.

None of this should make us forget that the debate on the value of strikes was not over. The split which became apparent in 1869 seemed less in evidence. One observer at this time remarked that there were clearly two separate opinions; in a discussion at the boulevard de Grenelle devoted to 'Strikes, their Organisation and their Consequences' he noted that:

> Drouchon spoke about creating resistance societies and unions. Tolain attacked the bourgeoisie and the big landlords and urged strike action, while Héligon spoke against it.[52]

At that time the Blanquists were the most fanatical supporters of strike action, and in this they were in disagreement with certain Proudhonist co-operativists for whom strikes were a last-ditch measure.[53] For the Blanquist communists, however, strikes were the means for immediate action against capital. They were 'something everyone can understand; the idea is straightforward: resistance to oppression. Everyone is joining this cause.'

In 1870 the strike movement grew to an unprecedented size, and it became necessary to take stock of the situation. The Paris Federation of Working Men's Societies took the initiative of launching a series of public meetings at the passage du Génie on 'Diverse Social Questions'. On the agenda of the first of these meetings was 'strikes'. Just as at other meetings, the speakers theorised on the causes (a generally defensive standpoint) and the limits (the standpoint for an offensive) of strikes.

The debate was rather confused, for while most of the speakers recognised that strikes were on the increase, and that given the reasons behind them their necessity could not be challenged, Montel thought that 'it is poverty which produces strikes', and Leo Frankel gave a very pertinent reminder that wages had gone up much less than the price of consumer goods; on the one hand they were concerned with the organisational role they had to take as workers' leaders, on the other hand they were worried by the danger of the workers' movement ending up in a reformist impasse. Many speakers thought it would be preferable to launch an offensive of 'scientifically prepared' strikes rather than to rely on 'spontaneous reaction' strikes as recommended by Tolain, although some, like Montel, insisted that strikes erupted spontaneously 'and not as the result of the schemes of a few agitators' (he was doubtless referring to defensive strikes). Sérizier, who on 31 March exhorted his audience 'to hate their bosses and to organise strikes', and Varlin, who emphasised the need to 'prepare strikes', were among those who had been won over to the methods of the organised labour movement. But they were concerned above all with the place these strikes were to have in the revolutionary arsenal. This explains why Sérizier appears to have done an about-turn on the subject, regretting that 'strikes turn the workers round in a vicious circle', like his friend Beaufils who declared that 'strikes seem to be a bad means of emancipation, because they are aimed at increasing wages and not at eliminating the bosses'. Sérizier was afraid that through strike action and its resultant string of negotiations between the social 'partners', the workers would become socially integrated. Our leather dresser had doubtless understood that under certain conditions the workers' movement and the revolutionary movement was liable not to meet. Far-sighted as ever, Varlin suggested that strikes could strengthen practices of solidarity. There is no doubt that in his mind such a solidarity would work towards the birth or the growth of class consciousness. But Varlin had also understood the limitations of strikes as a means of action: speaking at the boulevard de Grenelle, 'he urged the workers above all to join the International Working Men's Association which was intended for their total emancipation'. Therefore for Varlin and for numerous other speakers it was a question of guiding the social movement towards a political horizon which was situated a long way from the rut of workerism.

The position is similar to the one expressed at the public meetings at that time, linking strikes with politics. On 25 April at the Théâtre Parisien, there was a joint collection 'for the strikers at Fourchambault and the anti-Plebiscite committees'; on 19 April at the salle de la Marseillaise a collection 'for the strikers in Fourchambault' was made to cries of '*Vive* Rochefort!'; when the striking sugar-refinery workers organised a meeting in the same hall, it was Rochefort whom they chose as honorary chairman. Therefore, for the public meetings, strikes, even general strikes, were not a panacea which would procure the downfall of the Imperial regime and the power of the bosses. Outside of the fact that they helped to foster the birth of a class consciousness which was as social as it was political, they were merely one means of action among many to launch the attack against the oppressors. As early as 1868 Paule Minck was able to say:

> The social edifice is being attacked from all directions. This edifice is based upon arbitrary rules [*cheers*]. There are hurdles on all sides. Let us try co-operation, strikes, and many other things as well.

No one could have summed up the opinion of the public meetings about the question of means of action better than this. In real terms only the goal was important. In 1869–70, the time for politics had arrived, and it was completely natural that speakers and audiences alike should turn towards specifically political means of action.

2   *Political action*

As with economic and social means of action, it is hard to separate ends from means, and the distinction between what was legal and what was revolutionary, except in the case of calls to violence, is very finely drawn. This is particularly true for the subject of instruction and education.

A)   SCHOOLS FOR THE PEOPLE

The first thing we should notice is the interest in everything affecting education paid by speakers and audiences of all political persuasions.

The first meeting on this subject was in 1868, when we see an agenda with the item 'Co-operative Schooling', a subject involving education which was to remain of general interest right up until 1870. The Catholics were the first to associate themselves with the question, giving lectures on the problems of childhood organised by 'The Society for the Protection of Children'. Like Postel, that 'detested' Catholic of the Pré-aux-Clercs who called for 'equal instruction for all', they never missed a chance to talk about this 'means of reform' which for them was preferable to the upheavals of socialism.

The radicals were the next to take up the cause. They were tireless in their advocacy of 'free and compulsory instruction', which was to be a basic element in their programme. Jules Simon, followed closely by people like Jules Ferry, Lavertujon and Brisson, was one of the most indefatigable spokesmen for this slogan, which was repeated religiously and *ad nauseam* from 1868 to 1870. Ferry was prepared to speak on 'The Foundation of Independent Secondary Schools' at the Grand-Orient, but that did not put into question their fundamental ideas on the issue, and neither did Jules Simon's or Arago's lectures on 'Technical Training' in 1870. The radicals were always ready to hold forth on 'The Aims' and 'The Programme for Democratic Schools' (Colfavru at the Folies-Bergère on 3 April 1870).

Many socialists joined in the chorus of 'compulsory free education' by adding the term 'non-religious', no doubt to make themselves more distinctive.[54] We find it high in the Belleville List of 1869 along with other typically radical ideas. Other more cautious revolutionaries avoided following the crowd but occasionally got involved in reformist dead ends such as: Let us create non-religious free schools.[55] Briosne qualified the idea as a 'chinoiserie'. Most of the time they never got beyond the debating and investigating stage. A meeting at the passage du Génie tried to

define a model of instruction and education 'in accordance with
socialist principles', which would be more progressive than the
principles which since 1868 had inspired discussion on the subject
(the statutes of the society for co-operative schools which were
drawn up on 30 July 1868 limited themselves to the definition of a
'non-religious', secular but moral system of teaching). At the salle
de la Marseillaise, after agreeing with Vertut that schools turned
out 'machines for exploitation', and with Mme Piré that they
produced '*almahs* and *bayadères*', the audience went on to listen to
Paule Minck speaking on 'The Influence of Education'. Therefore
a different kind of education was needed. Naturally Rigault turned
towards the 'plan for education presented by the commune of
Paris' which would represent 1793 and not 1789. Gaillard
proposed courses in civic instruction so that 'the catechism be
replaced by the philosophical history of nations, the Old and New
Testaments by the Civil Code. We want to create citizens, not
slaves.' Others, like the cardboard-maker Kauffman, suggested
taking inspiration from Prussia. Instruction and education were
regarded in the same way as many other means of action: unsure
of exactly where they were going, the revolutionaries were
seeking a solution which would be specifically theirs and which
would guarantee popular independence from the radicals. It was
Humbert who opposed Arago in 1869, expressing these reservations and suggesting the path to be taken:

> As far as the question of compulsory public education is
> concerned, does the citizen know who will foot the bill?
> Anyone who has studied social economics will know that
> nothing is free. Aren't taxes paid by the worker and by the
> proletarian? What we must do is to organise integral instruction
> and society in their entirety, using justice as a basis. What
> means of action did you use in 1848 to achieve that result?

In the end the revolutionaries discovered the school where this
integral education could be practised: the public meetings! Thus
Vertut could cry: 'We need them every day to instruct the people',
which was a rewording of Sébille's intervention at Belleville on 30
January 1869: 'We must keep these sessions going because they are
the people's school. The people need instruction. The authorities
would be only too happy to be able to close these meetings.'

B)   UNION

Many speakers, regardless of their political persuasions, advocated
unity as a revolutionary means of action. If in a number of cases

speakers remained rather vague about it, like Paule Minck: 'Unite in strength and they will fear you. Unite, be brave, and one day you'll be free', it is not difficult to see that this magic word implied some very different political and social options.

Given their political logic, the radicals, Jacobins and liberals were the most noticeable partisans of unity, for they did not want to make class struggle the basic principle of their action, since for most of the time they were themselves bourgeois. For them, the enemy was a political one: it was the Empire and not capitalism, and they disapproved of it merely in terms of its excesses. Therefore they made an effort to smooth down the differences between the political groups in order to channel their struggles against the common enemy, and tried quite skilfully to rally all the forces of the opposition in this direction. Falcet was an example:

> We must march forwards to conquer freedom; let us not be divided, let us join hands; let us no longer talk of socialism or communism. Let us have a single flag, and a single watch-word: Die fighting.[56]

This kind of impassioned phrase, which recalls the cries of the *canuts*, was liable to attract those most moderate or most crafty socialists who would be prepared to muffle their social and philosophical convictions if it meant that the Empire would be overthrown. Thus the militant worker Durand could propose that 'we do not want any authorities running our affairs. We must unite to overthrow them', and Flourens, frightened by the quarrels that were splitting meetings up, could plead with the Folies-Belleville audience to 'keep calm', demanding 'freedom for all opinions . . . in the interests of discussion'.

These ambiguous positions which came as a result of this wish for unity provoked some extremely confused speeches even from politically well-informed and conscious quarters. Millière moderated one of his speeches on 'social equality' so much that he went so far as to accept 'natural inequality', something he did not believe in at all. This was because he was being careful not to alienate people who did believe in it:

> Let's not tar everyone with the same brush. We must single out those people who in the end will realise that to apply the laws of justice will be to procure the common good.

To be fair we should add that Millière 'calls for unity among socialists' and not for the class unity of the republican front proposed by the radicals and Jacobins.

In a third category can be grouped those who supported either unity among the workers and peasants – Sabourdy proposed that 'if things go badly it will be our fault, we are too divided over the question which should be important to us all. If our friends from the country were with us, we could overthrow the entire armoury of the law' – or proletarian revolutionary unity. The latter was to introduce into the idea of unity a notion of class, in that the bourgeois, even the republican bourgeois, would be excluded, but that progressives who were sincerely in favour of emancipation for the proletariat and who would be able to fight for it would be accepted.

These different conceptions of unity as a means of action were to come into conflict above all during the voting periods.

C)   THE BALLOT PAPER AS A MEANS OF REVOLUTIONARY ACTION?

On three occasions the 'non-political' public meetings were turned into public election meetings. Under normal circumstances speakers never presented elections as a means of reaching their objectives. But during the election periods they were obliged to break this calculated silence. We have already seen how certain of their political characteristics stopped them in principle from compromising themselves in any demonstrations of bourgeois democratic feelings or in the machinations of the liberal Empire. It is therefore all the more interesting to study their attitude towards the 1869 elections – the general election for the Legislative Body in May and June and the by-elections in November and December – and the Imperial Plebiscite in April and May 1870.

THE MAY–JUNE ELECTIONS OF 1869

This is not the place to write a history of this election period which impassioned Paris from 2 to 17 May and from 29 May until 1 June, filling some hundred and fifty meetings with unhoped-for numbers. What we must do is to follow our *clubistes* carefully to see how they reacted to the prevailing institutions. The policies they supported will help us to identify their attitudes towards practical action. In other words, we will be able to measure the extent of their revolutionary spirit, of their socialism. This is all the more true in that the public-meeting audiences rgew in size and the political and social profile of the halls was modified by the influx of masses of voters and the disappearance of women and children [who were not enfranchised – eds]. Therefore the temptation to indulge in opportunism and demagogy followed the same curve. It would be an exaggeration to talk of an explosion, but nevertheless it is true that the period saw the emergence of differing behaviour patterns among the club-goers. Some came out in favour of the liberals from the very first day, while others exploited the situation in order to militate in favour of socialism.

In several constituencies the opposition candidates, the 'radicals', enjoyed the support of several well-known public meeting speakers. It is a privileged moment for us to measure just how far the latter were committed to revolution, or more exactly to perceive the form and type of revolution they aspired to. In fact, while a certain number of them allowed their neo-Jacobin convictions to shine forth – such convictions being in line with prevailing political policy – others who, in other respects, were undeniably socialist revealed themselves as people wanting social revolution, but wanting it without the expense of a civil war, and through introduction of reforms. We should add that certain militants who seemed in agreement with the latter only associated with them for motives of political expediency, intending to use elected representatives as 'agents' in the new assembly. This attitude was to crop up again during the legislative elections of February 1871, on the eve of the Commune.

This composite camp of radical supporters was bound together by the idea that the elections were nevertheless a means of advancing revolution. However, this could not be of a socialist kind. This was the case with the Gambetta campaign in the 1st constituency. J. Rougerie has already studied this, so we will not go into any details.[57] Suffice it to underline that although Gambetta accepted the famous *Cahiers* edited by the constituency 'radical committees' which were mainly composed of socialists, among whom we see public meeting leaders like the internationalists Sabourdy and Biette, some of the policy statements he came out with reveal his opportunism. For did he not declare to a deliriously enthusiastic audience at the Folies-Belleville, 'America, that's the model to follow'?

Of course, the socialist public meeting speakers who followed this difficult path were faced with disappointments. If a Jacobin like Falcet was happy to back someone like Gambetta, if people like Mathorel or Sébille could support someone like Bancel without any apparent embarrassment, militants like Allix or May and Héligon felt obliged to express their reservations about the policy statements of their candidates d'Alton Shée and Bancel. But they were repudiated and must have given in, since in the end they toed the line.

In the 2nd constituency, d'Alton Shée was standing against

Thiers, and was supported by Allix, the organiser of the 'Socialist Democratic Commitee' which had developed from the initial public election meetings. To help his cause the good Allix went so far as to maintain that radicalism was the same as socialism. It is true that on 6 May in the Triat gymnasium his candidate insisted 'that he had a radical, democratic and socialist programme. He wants the abolition of the Church budget, permanent armies, municipal commissions and a nominated *magistrature*' – something that was therefore very close to the Belleville *Cahiers*. But it went no farther than being a 'radical democratic' programme. In time, Allix was to sense this, and was repudiated by d'Alton Shée (sic) for having proposed that 'we must achieve socialism first, because only through socialism will we achieve freedom.' If he wanted the votes of the bourgeoisie in his constituency, d'Alton Shée could not very well afford to frighten them. It was an attitude which paid off, since on 16 and 17 May in Passy and at the avenue Montaigne he was adopted as candidate.

May and Héligon had the same kind of experience in the 3rd constituency. At the Redoute on 5 May they crossed a few swords with Bancel, but were taken in by the former people's representative whose support for property did not prevent him from advocating 'workers' association' (4 May, Théâtre Molière; 5 May salle Molière) and who, needless to say, took up old radical refrains such as 'the abolition of permanent armies', just the kind of honeyed words with which to catch a public greedy for such titbits. During his campaign, Bancel did not hesitate to invoke the revolution, but not the revolution which had been on the agenda nearly every evening since 1868. It was the Revolution of 1789 that Bancel was extolling, for he was against 'armed revolution' and in favour of 'democracy'; his policy statements were thus directed just as much to the Bonapartists as to the genuine revolutionaries:

> Democracy is holy and sacred . . . I am one of its children, I
> will be its defender and its apostle, but demagogy is nothing
> more than the path towards dictatorship and despotism. I am
> neither a Jacobin, a Montagnard, a Girondin, a Maratist or a
> Hebertist, but the devoted son of the Revolution and a lover of
> freedom.

This kind of declaration may have made conscious militants wince, but the majority of the electorate were blinded by their own prejudice and ignorance. A demagogue like Jules Simon was all the rage in the 8th constituency, particularly in the *faubourg* Saint-Antoine. On 8 May he was adopted 'unanimously' as candidate by an audience of 1,200 at 24 passage du Génie. It is true that Simon condescended to speak to the masses. He was the only deputy who replied to the invitations from the socialist and militant workers to go and address their public meetings. He did not even hesitate to go to Budaille's hall, even if it meant being forced to clarify his position regarding property: 'If anyone suggests that I have attacked property,' he cried at a meeting in Pantin, 'he's a liar.'

If Jules Simon was unable to pull the wool over everyone's eyes, this was not the case with the young radicals whose energy (and humour) was to prove extremely seductive. These men who were to sit in the government of 4 September stimulated the enthusiasm of the mass of the voters and even, let us not forget, of certain militants whose proverbial caution seems to have been lulled to sleep. Like Gambetta, men such as Jules Ferry, Ernest Picard and Rochefort seemed much more ready to fight than the Old Men of '48. Thus they were able to rally the support of known public meeting militants. On 14 May at 43 boulevard de Magenta Allix announced his support for Picard.[58] In the 7th constituency, Arthur Arnould the future Communard, Doctor Dupré, Raspail's friend, and the progressive, revolutionary students gave noisy support to the publicist Rochefort who at this stage was making no pretence of being a socialist; Jules Ferry scored a 'triumph' before an audience of three thousand people in the salle des Peupliers, 195 rue de Grenelle, although this particular hall was normally frequented by the IWMA and was thus not an easy target.

By reinforcing the radicals this election campaign provoked a shift to the Right. Audiences came out in support of peaceful revolution, even if they were largely composed of workers. Thus on 12 May at the salle Molière (3rd constituency), May could say:

There are two classes of revolutionaries:
1 those who are always ready to build barricades,
2 and those who are prepared to do everything possible to achieve reforms without tearing up paving stones and brandishing knives.
We are in the second of these classes, all we want is a social revolution.

Sébille added that he wanted 'a peaceful revolution, no more classes, nothing but one people'.

They were not repudiating socialism and the 'sociale'; indeed they went on militating for them, but they envisaged attaining them by a process of reforms and democratic freedoms in the manner of Allix who wanted them to insist upon the need to abolish 'all criminal charges brought against the press and free thinking'. This moderate policy resulted in some people attacking the socialists. Thus Sébille went to the meetings in the 5th constituency in order to oppose the friends of Raspail and Briosne. But as we shall see, he was merely returning a favour.

Unlike the neo-Jacobin speakers, the reformist socialists and those who despite their very progressive socialist views thought they could use the radicals, most of the socialist revolutionaries did not consider these elections to be a means of achieving revolution. Nevertheless, they used the election campaign for their own ends, namely as a good opportunity to spread socialist propaganda to the masses. It is in this sense that we should interpret the small number of socialist candidatures to win the support of the meetings during the first round, like Lefrançais in the 1st constituency, Vallès in the 8th and Briosne in the 5th. We should add that their programme, while frequently aimed at 'stirring up' the 'electoral mixture' and the 'political rabble',[59] was above all directed against the Old Men of '48, those tricolour 'murderers', although in the run-up to the elections some of the most intransigent communists had made violent statements about the same issue, rebelling against the initiative of the 'Proudhonists'[60] who had invited 'the liberal opposition deputies' to a meeting to discuss the social question, saying that 'the defeated men of June will not join in discussions with their own murderers'.[61]

As a last detail we should add that these socialist candidates had no connection with the 'worker' candidates who were so popular with audiences.[62] In the 4th constituency, Lefrançais tried hard to turn debates in the direction of socialism. It is obvious that the election itself was of no interest to him. As he said at the Alcazar on 11 May to an audience of 2,500:

Twenty years ago, after Proudhon, Cabet and Pierre Leroux were elected, it seemed that the revolution had finally triumphed!
Today you know that the reverse is true, and we must begin the struggle all over again.
I stand as the candidate for turning 1869 into 1849.

He knew that no government, Imperial or republican, would be able to satisfy the socialists: 'For any government to grant all the freedoms we demand would be suicide,' he said laughingly at 43 boulevard de Magenta.

Lefrançais, who was roughly treated by the conservative press, had some difficult moments. But they were nothing compared to what his comrade Vallès had to put up with. Selected by the electorate of the barrière d'Italie (8th constituency)[63] 'where the movement of attitudes is very active', Vallès also stood as a 'revolutionary socialist candidate', promising to stick Jules Simon's head in 'his own political filth', as Lefrançais was to write afterwards. Courageously, Vallès was to cross swords with Simon in many halls, including the one at 12 rue de Lyon, where despite the cheers in support of his philosophical opponent he dared to call himself 'an even more radical candidate than Simon' before being jeered. If Vallès was 'coldly received', Simon was cheered by the workers as he left. In *L'Insurgé* Vallès paints this campaign in a few biting pages, recalling in particular the problems he encountered in the salle du Génie and in Boulogne, where he was actually physically attacked. What he does not write about is the avalanche of second-rate polemics against him that the conservative press poured out insultingly for its delighted readers. A pamphleteer spat out:

> We will not mention that literary rag-and-bone man, that street lounger and communist, the obscure and long-haired Vallès.
> He has nothing and will always have nothing, since he has no idea of how to behave and he hates work.

One columnist added scornfully that Vallès 'cannot seem to understand that it would be quite enough for him to be clever enough to write journalism'.

To sum up, in this constituency Vallès and the regular public meeting *habitués* who had chosen him to defend their flag were submerged by a mass of frenzied voters.

In the 5th constituency Briosne had fewer problems, for here there were a larger number of candidates standing against the outgoing deputy Garnier-Pagès. While Tolain[64] and the 'socialist democratic' committee supported Briosne, other public-meeting speakers spoke in favour of Raspail, either as individuals (Humbert, Ducasse, Lermina) or on behalf of a committee (Raspail's committee had members such as Banet-Rivet). The choice of Raspail as a candidate was made at a meeting at Chatelain's which Vallès had attended. For the record we should also mention Georges Baudin's candidature. The brother of Alphonse Baudin, who had been killed on 3 December 1851, and a lawyer by profession, he had recently arrived from Nantua, and although he was standing on a 'democratic and socialist' ticket with full-blooded backing from the *Réveil*, he collapsed as early as 11 May at the very first attack by his rival Ducasse, a Raspail supporter. Not colourful enough for the sharp audiences of the

Folies-Belleville, he had to make do with a minor role. Nevertheless his presence helped to conjure up the spectre of Bonaparte's coup d'état. It is by taking into account all these various candidates and the militancy peculiar to these *quartiers* in the east end of the city which the campaign fomented that we can understand its revolutionary aspects. Here, in the 5th constituency, flanked by the *faubourg* du Temple and the *faubourg* Saint-Antoine with Belleville and Ménilmontant at its limit, the public meeting militants were not isolated, since their supporters made their presence at meetings known and imposed the techniques they used. A firework display was inevitable, with rockets bursting in all directions.

At various meetings in the first round, Briosne specialised in socialist pedagogy; Raspail and his supporters devoted their energies to criticising the Old Men of '48. A few of Raspail's supporters used the election campaign and Raspail himself to spark off the passionate feelings endemic in the *faubourgs*, spreading propaganda and agitating for the change that was imminent. On 11 May at the Folies-Belleville, Briosne opened his speech with 'a vivid expose of the suffering of the people. . . . He said that society should be reorganised and that the workers should be given their true place'.[65] On 16 May in the Grand Théâtre Parisien he took up the theme again, while at the same time declaring that he was fully prepared to stand down in favour of Raspail. He said the same thing the next day at the Folies-Belleville in a policy statement based upon two main points, namely 'from the political point of view, representation of minorities, from the social economics point of view, emancipation of labour through freedom of association', an idea that the *National* called 'a pretty obscure theory of socialism'. In any event, he seems to have enjoyed 'an immense success as a speaker',[66] which must be translated as meaning that his socialist propaganda was reasonably successful. Now that his goal was achieved, Briosne declared that 'he would step down in favour of Raspail if people thought that he was a candidate opposed to the past'. The intelligent Belleville audience had understood and the meeting dispersed to the cries of '*Vive* Briosne! *Vive* Raspail!'

And in fact, from the political point of view, support for Raspail the club-goer of 1848 and one of the active figures in the bloody events of 15 May 1848 meant reviving the tradition of class struggle which had led to the public meetings of 1868–9 by way of June 1848. By now Raspail was 75, and had somewhat watered his wine. His programme was reformist rather than socialist, and his ideas and his justification for them were drawn largely from the past, but nevertheless he remained inveterately anti-establishment and an irreconcilable foe of the men of 1848. This 'crazy old man of the *Montagne*'★ persisted in denouncing priests, policemen and informers, a frequent public meeting theme. The real political hue of his candidature is revealed by his committee, which was made up of socialist co-operativists and free thinkers. They were to form the bulk of the revolutionary cadres in the 11th and 20th *arrondissements* during the 1870 Siege and the 1871 Commune.

Compared with Raspail, Garnier-Pagès was the symbol not only of the bourgeois republican reaction of 1848, but also of the ambiguities of the parliamentary opposition of 1869.

The revolutionaries were not to forgive this businessman and financier for his policies as member of the provisional government of 1848, be it as Minister of Finance – the 45 centimes tax had helped to reduce the popularity of the Republic in rural areas – or in respect of his attitude towards the Paris workers who rebelled in 1848. At that time he had been in favour of the repression and the abolition of the National Workshops, and it was he who first said: 'All this must be stopped.'

Although he was elected by the 5th constituency on 20 March 1864 to replace Jules Favre, and despite the fact that he was a fairly active member of 'the small democratic opposition group' of 1864 (it met in his house), he was an uncompromising adversary of the extreme Left. Early in 1868 he denounced the public meeting militants to the Legislative Body, calling them *agents provocateurs* 'in cahoots with the Empire'. He was to be member of the 1870 provisional government and at Versaillais in 1871.

Therefore when the public meeting speakers went for his throat they were not trying to settle old arguments but were anticipating the struggle to come. They re-established the facts and experience of 1848, and drew their conclusion. For them, the Empire and the bourgeois republic were the two faces of a capitalist Janus. Their condemnation was political, but it was pronounced by and in the name of the class conscious proletariat (because even so there were some workers who supported Garnier-Pagès[67]). On 17 May when Garnier-Pagès made an appearance at the Grand Théâtre Parisien, 12 rue de Lyon, it was a head-on collision between bourgeois democracy and the supporters of proletarian socialism. Jules Lermina, who from the outset of the campaign had devoted himself to tearing Garnier-Pagès to pieces, was there surrounded by his public meeting cronies, waiting to welcome him. His demolition act, perfected on 11 May at the Folies-Belleville and 16 May at the Grand Théâtre Parisien, made him one of the

★ An allusion to the Robespierristes.

proletariat's most implacable prosecutors. This was real class-struggle territory, for by rummaging remorselessly through Garnier-Pagès's recent or distant past,[68] Lermina was able to unmask (winning himself laughs in the process) the anti-working-class practices of reactionary bourgeois who had disguised themselves as republicans. This is what transpired on 17 May:

> *Garnier-Pagès*: The banner I've fought under all my life . . .
> bears three things: '89 Revolution, 1830 Revolution, 1848 Revolution.
> *A Heckler*: Enough fancy phrases! What you ought to do is explain the way you voted in 1848! [*Commotion*]
> *Garnier-Pagès*: And each of these revolutions can be summed up by the watchword: *liberté, égalité, fraternité!* . . . [*applause*]
> *From the Floor*: That's fine! Answer the question! Keep to the facts!

Try as he might to escape behind the work of February 1848, he was not to succeed in achieving the amalgam, the symbiosis of the people and a provisional government. 'Those ever-glorious days' were swept aside remorselessly by Lermina, his public prosecutor, whose task it was to refresh his memory concerning his 1848 Ministry. A militant, Lermina represented the 'insurrectionaries' of June 1848 and their heirs, the people who for almost a year had been regularly attending the public meetings. Garnier-Pagès, driven back on his defences by Lermina's indictment,[69] became very agitated, and 'spoke about the events of the June Days, calling them a reactionary plot'. This was exactly what his opponents had wanted him to say. Revolution was in the air:

> 'Why are we acting in this way?' exclaimed Lermina. 'It is because the situation has changed since 1863. Tomorrow circumstances may arise which will call for strong and valiant hands to keep the flag of radical democracy flying'.

How could Garnier-Pagès be the standard-bearer of the oppressed classes? Had not his hands been steeped in the blood of those 'agitators' the workers of June, had he not spoken out against the public meetings of today, had he not always used his vote or his abstention to collude with and to champion the cause of law and order and the bourgeoisie?

> 'If the moment came, M. Garnier-Pagès would not be worthy to carry the flag of democracy', cried Lermina, 'He is not the

man for us; we cannot propose him' [*several moments of prolonged applause*].

It is obvious that the deputy had not expected such large-scale opposition. Despite his own prodigiously skilful oratory, his opponents were merciless. Enemy of the workers in June 1848, passive by-stander on 2 December – these were the taunts hurled at him by one heckler.

However, although for Garnier-Pagès this must have been one of the most uncomfortable evenings he ever spent,[70] some commentators agree that he succeeded in limiting the damage, since the meeting failed to reach a unanimous decision. This is not really important, for in fact this public confrontation was a prelude to the Commune. There are definitely two sorts of republic: one conservative and parliamentary, the other social and revolutionary.

The third aspect of the campaign – Raspail's nomination means revolution – was developed by two stars of the public meetings, Felix Ducasse and Alphonse Humbert. For them, the meaning of the choice of candidate was simple. The task was to advance the idea of 'socialist' revolution in the 11th *arrondissement*:

It is essential that these two great homes of Democracy, the *faubourg* Antoine [sic] and the *faubourg* du Temple, should elect Raspail and assert their hatred of arbitrary rule and fanaticism, their steady resolve to achieve social regeneration by whatever means possible. Their vote must be unanimous, demanding the right to work, absolute equality (of all citizens), abolition of wage labour, disbanding of the army, expropriation of the convents, etc!

For Ducasse and Humbert, there was no possible equivocation:

Garnier-Pagès, Raspail; two principles rather than two men. On the one hand capitalist reaction, on the other the demands of the common class.

During the second round they were to have a large following for this policy, for all the speakers from the Blanquists to the Proudhonists, rallied in support of Raspail's candidature, and agreed with Raspail's campaign committee that the people's doctor was 'the veteran of socialism', and with Ducasse that 'he is the man the people need, the martyr of every government, who has never acted contrary to true radical democracy and socialism'.

The bitterness of the election struggle and the riots led to heated attitudes and distorted discussions. Garnier-Pagès's outbidding tactics had to be answered (his son-in-law Dréo called him a 'radical and socialist candidate'), one had to be seen to be more red than he was. While continuing to be against the executioners of 1848, Garnier-Pagès, Jules Favre and Clément Thomas (Raspail-Lermina), and the 'vanishing act with 1848' (Banet-Rivet), the campaign for Raspail's candidature took on a more revolutionary meaning, apart from the odd reservation. There was a change in perspective. On 30 May Lermina 'concluded that Raspail should be elected with a view to the possible revolution to come'.

One unidentified speaker indicated the ultimate goal over and above the elections themselves: 'We must destroy the Carthage of parasitism and exploitation.' Therefore Raspail should be sent to the Chamber 'to carry the flag of socialism' (Vermorel) and as a living protest. His very presence would be an insult to the authorities for he was the symbol of a certain kind of universal revolution. Lermina was very outspoken (he was to be arrested for it) and during a private meeting held at 116 *faubourg* Saint-Antoine on 3 June he made the following outburst: 'Raspail will lead the people against the Tuileries, and if he is too old to walk, we will carry him on our shoulders.' His election 'will be a step towards revolution', since it would excite attitudes in the *faubourgs* in that direction and bring the possibility of the emancipation of the workers nearer (Storme, 4 June, 116 *faubourg* Saint-Antoine).

These few examples of public meeting speakers standing as candidates does not exhaust the question. In fact, during this period these candidates moved around a lot, helping each other or criticising the official or the liberal opposition candidates publicly. Those two old cronies Lefrançais and Briosne frequently exchanged favours. On 5 May Lefrançais attended a meeting at the Folies-Belleville in the 5th constituency in order to launch a 'rip-roaring' attack on Garnier-Pagès; Briosne returned the favour by going down to the Alcazar in the 4th constituency to accuse Picard of being an Orleanist. Then on 13 May Lefrançais and his friend were at the Cirque Imperial where after listening to Raspail they threw out the Bonapartist Hugelman. Lefrançais had already publicly dissented with Bancel on the 5th at the salle Molière. As for Briosne, his intervention at the Théâtre Dejazet on May 9th stirred up the audience so much that the meeting had to be broken up. When Jules Simon went slumming at Budaille's, these two accomplices joined forces again, this time surrounded by old comrades of June 1848, to remind him of his 1848 votes and decoration. Lefrançais went as far as to grab him by the waistcoat to show the audience the empty buttonhole where Cavaignac's decoration had been.

We will find this kind of intervention in all the constituencies. In the 2nd it was Millière who drew attention by his attacks on Dewinck, the official candidate, and on Thiers, the counter-revolutionary, that 'assassin' of freedom; he was joined by Delbrouk, who recalled the 'massacre of the église Saint-Merry'. In the 7th, where the meetings could be very rowdy, it was the Blanquist Adrien Regnard, a well-known figure in the Latin Quarter, who vigorously opposed Favre. On 30 May, led by Humbert, the trio Briosne, Joffroy and Lefrançais rallied to his support at the Cordelières Saint-Marcel. The previous evening at the Sorbonne gymnasium, Lermina also set on Favre. We could go on listing examples, but the time has come to evaluate the actions of the public meeting speakers in response to the elections, the first since the law of 6 June.

The very first thing we notice is that in spite of a certain degree of success in the 1st, 5th and 7th constituencies, the obstacles were not really overcome. Even the most seasoned speakers were purely and simply swept aside by a crowd of voters who did not usually attend the meetings. For example, on 14 May the brio of Lefrançais and Briosne was not enough to win the day against 3,500 voters who had thronged to the Alcazar. They were not even able to make themselves heard. We have already seen what misfortunes Vallès suffered. We could give other examples. The explanation for this relative defeat could well be found in the lack of strategy on the part of the public meeting militants, whose onslaught was quite unconcerted. As we have seen, some of them went straight to the support of the radicals, either through conviction or expediency;[1] others, the purists or the hard-liners, may have been divided to start off with about how to combat the official Left, and in any case were convinced that these elections could not possibly be a means of attaining socialist revolution, but nevertheless they became involved by redefining the nature of their support for the most progressive radicals, even to the extent of rallying the men they had denounced as the worst enemies of the people. After having backed Vallès in the arena of the 8th constituency only to abandon him, Passedouet finally came out in support of Pellétan in the 9th! Lacatte followed suit!

The elections had their own logic. It was not the same logic that prevailed in the usual public meetings. Most voters only agreed with progressive speakers who were 'in', applauding men like Simon and Picard when they concluded, as the latter had done, 'that the application of socialism is a Utopia'. No doubt we should also emphasise the financial and organisational strength of the bourgeois democratic committees, their political coherence and the attraction they held for the militant socialists, but this would lead us away from our chosen area of study. In any event the game was not yet over, even as far as the elections were concerned, for certain themes had been barely touched upon, in particular those contained in the thirteen reforms specified in the IWMA address 'To the Voters of 1869' which included democratic demands (to extend and obtain 'freedom'), and proposals for social reforms (nationalisation of the big financial companies), as well as for political reforms, among which the abolition of the permanent army and the arming of all citizens, the separation of Church and State, the overall reform of the legal system, compulsory non-religious instruction for all and the introduction of a graded tax system were the most prominent. In this programme, which Briosne supported, was also the idea of the sovereignty of the people with the corollary of the recallable mandate.

A great many of these themes matched up with the concerns of the radicals, and they were to be brought up again during the November-December by-elections, notably those questions relating to representation and criticism of the army.

THE BY-ELECTIONS (NOVEMBER-DECEMBER 1869)

The new election period which opened on 31 October 1869 – the deputies for the 1st, 3rd, 4th and 8th constituencies having opted to stand in the provincial elections (Gambetta, Picard, Simon and Bancel) – began in an overheated atmosphere, particularly in the 1st constituency (Belleville, Batignolles, Montmartre . . .) There were to be 110 election meetings and their liveliness (several were broken up and there were several examples of proprietors refusing to rent out their premises) indicates a much more effective participation on the part of the usual public meeting speakers, some of whom were standing for the second time (Allix, Sébille, Laferrière, but also Cantagrel, Laurier, Floquet and Brisson). Once again there were three themes in particular which were fought over in the meetings. The first of these, 1848, split the republican camp; the second, criticism of institutions (the army, the Constitution) united it; the third, 'enforced mandates', continued to progress. As in the May-June period the subject of the 1848 Revolution split the public meeting speakers into Jacobins and socialists. The former pleaded the cause of the Assembly, the latter the cause of the June workers. In the salle Molière, Laferrière recalled his sympathies with the 1848 government and spoke about 'our great citizens of '48', while his crony

Falcet went on to present an extremely clever defence of the old-
timers Raspail, Ledru-Rollin, Felix Pyat, Louis Blanc, Barbès and
Victor Hugo (the combination is significant) and a rude attack on
the June insurgents. 'During the June Days, some insurgents were
found to be carrying English gold'.[72] The delighted radicals
approved this rejection of violence unreservedly. Hérold (another
4 September man) went so far as to boast that in June he had
demanded 'the indictment' of those responsible for the riots.[73]
This condemnation of insurrection as a means of action coincided
with the rejection of socialism. Laurier, who called himself a
'radical' and claimed to follow 'radical policies (. . .) of the kind
which derive from the Republic of Danton, Vergniaud and Saint-
Just', rejected socialist systems which would be nothing but
'absolutes', doubtless contrary to the kind of freedom he was
advocating. Like Hérold, the Jacobins and the socialists 'skirted
the social question' without ever actually broaching it. Occasionally
there were meetings which the radicals dominated where even the
future struggle against the revolutionaries was brought up.
Emmanuel Arago, one of the most cunning amongst the radicals,
slipped this into the middle of a reformist hotch-potch:

> As for the functioning of universal suffrage, the speaker is in
> favour of it, but he is above all a revolutionary [sic]. He will
> become a Conservative [sic] when he is no longer confronted
> with a crowned head.
> (Meeting of 3 November, 290 rue de Charonne)

It is not difficult to imagine how the revolutionary socialists
reacted to speeches like this. In fact their reaction was sometimes
even more violent than it had been in May and June. As it
happens, some militants, like Allix or Passedouet, had moved
farther to the Left. When he stood as candidate at the Folies-
Belleville, Allix declared:

> This is what I believe in . . . to start off with, the Legislative
> Body should be abolished. I will fight to the last breath for the
> rule of law against rule by force, until the government we all
> love is triumphant.

This was not the government of the Men of '48 and their heirs,
whom the socialists roundly condemned. Picard was bitterly
attacked by Lombard and Ferre. Paulet 'made a violent attack on
the Men of '48; he accused them of murdering the Republic.'
Chatelain, another candidate in the 2nd constituency, made the

following statement in full assembly at the salle Molière, lair of radicals:

> I am a new man. The old men have had their day! [*A heckler*: There's life in them yet!] They were responsible for the June Days, the transportations, etc. [*Interruptions*]

However, at the Redoute (3rd constituency), that Mecca of Jacobinism, Sébille was also able to speak out against the Bourgeois republicans:

> The speaker spoke about the June Days, and in reference to citizen Pascal Duprat's candidature, exclaimed: 'There's one man standing who proclaimed the state of siege, he's a candidate whose hands are streaming with blood.' [*Commotion. Shut up! Put it to the vote!*]

The orators spoke out loud and clear against the Left in the name of their movement. Emmanuel Arago was challenged by Humbert to justify the so-called socialist convictions he had been professing for the last twenty years:

> Citizen Humbert asked under what circumstances citizen Arago had ever proved them, and what solution he proposed to resolve the question of the proletariat and poverty.
> Have you ever participated in our public meetings? If you had studied social questions, why did you not deign to attend our public meetings before the elections to let us know your solutions if you have any or discuss ours if you haven't?

To attack 'formalist republicans' was the order of the day. Gaillard, always very active, even tried to bring all five candidates together at the Folies-Belleville on 8 November with the explosive topic of 'Men and Principles'. Together with Flourens, Humbert and Albiot he was to draw up a counter-manifesto in reply to the Left's election manifesto, which several meetings voted to accept. Lermina drew his conclusions about the inactivity of deputies during the repression of June 1869. Raspail was the only one he looked on favourably while he denounced Garnier-Pages, and also Gambetta whose popularity in Belleville seems to have waned (Gaillard took him to task in particular for having compared Marat to Caesar).

Rochefort, who was applying for Gambetta's seat, accepted the famous Belleville *Cahiers* as his predecessor had done, but he still had to prove that he really was 'a red'; thus he stood on a 'socialist revolutionary' ticket and insisted that he regretted that there had been no demonstrations on 26 October, etc. In spite of the voters' enthusiasm, it was only *in extremis* that he enjoyed the benefit of the Blanquists' support when they rallied to him rather than to the pseudo-liberal Carnot.

It is scarcely worth saying that this mistrust was justified, so we will simply underline the fact that Rochefort's candidature was thought by his supporters to have a clear revolutionary significance. This election was seen as being a step forward for revolution, and this was so not only at the Folies-Belleville where Bachellery justified his choice by exclaiming: 'We must bring back those great days when revolution ran through the streets, showing freedom the way', but also at the boulevard de Clichy where before a packed hall Thomas gave it an anti-Constitutional turn: 'No more parliamentarianism. A vote for Rochefort is a vote for revolution.' But criticism of institutions was rather to have the effect of making candidates more united. In effect, Laferrière's attack on the Constitution was almost as strong as a man like Allix's, whose campaign was based upon the wish to abolish the 1852 Constitution. He wanted to go even farther than the Belleville voters who were calling for the revision of article 291 and the abolition of article 75. 'It's no good changing the odd article; it's the Code and the Constitution which need changing.'[74] As we have seen, this theme was to be vigorously taken up again in 1870 during the Plebiscite campaign.

The same applies in respect of the attack on the standing army, which united the entire republican camp, from the radicals who, like Gent, considered that 'the army is a breeding-ground for idleness where strong young men specialise in learning the art of killing and even of killing French citizens, like in La Ricamarie, like in Aubin' [*applause*], to the socialists, who signed the Belleville *Cahiers* and who wanted 'the abolition of standing armies', and including Chamilliard, the workers' candidate, who also wanted 'the abolition of the standing army'. Like criticism of the Constitution, this anti-militarism would go on uniting the republicans in 1870, allowing the ever-dynamic Gent to advise reconciliation (4 November at the passage du Génie):

He said that the word 'democracy' covered everything: it must be understood that even noble-hearted men have separated the two words 'democracy' and 'socialism'. We must study this social question which neither 1830 nor 1848 managed to resolve.

and permitting the ever-scheming, Mephistophelian Lissagaray to tell his revolutionary comrades who had written the document attacking the Left:

> We must put off the publication of this counter-manifesto until later. What's the point of blaming the Left at this moment in time?
>
> (*Le Rappel*, 22 November 1869)

The theme of the 'enforced mandate', which was inseparable from the conception of a direct democracy as advocated by all the socialist groups who thus revived the traditions of An II and determined what the modalities of the relationship electorate/elected would be once the revolution had come, was everywhere to be seen. In 1871 these ideas were to triumph along with the Commune (even though they would not always be put into practice). The 'enforced mandate' was discussed everywhere. Sometimes audiences insisted upon it. Rochefort accepted it, and so did Gent. In spite of an animated election campaign marked by bitter polemical exchanges, the results of the by-elections of November and December 1869 were no different from those of May and June. However, the public meeting speakers and the revolutionary socialists had shown a more homogeneous attitude. Not only could they claim credit for the victory of Rochefort, who was thought to be a genuine 'redder than red' socialist, but also their unflagging militancy pressurised the radicals into being more sharply critical of the Empire and its institutions. This small shift to the Left on the part of the republicans prefigured the 1870 Plebiscite campaign. Although the social ambiguities which characterised the republican camp had not yet been resolved – something which continued to work in the radicals' favour – subversion continued to advance on the level of ideas, if not on the level of the electoral verdict.

THE PLEBISCITE

As early as 21 April it was announced that the Plebiscite would be held on 8 May 1870. A decree was issued on the twenty-third permitting public election meetings to begin on 24 April.

As everyone knows, the object of this ballot was a revision of the Constitution in a Liberal direction which would at the same time justify the Imperial 'democracy' that the Emperor had tried to introduce along with universal suffrage.

The rival trends were to dispute the votes of the public meeting audiences. One advocated abstention or a blank or spoilt ballot paper ('people should write "Long live the social and democratic

Republic!", "Long live the '93 Constitution!" or "Long live the
social revolution!" on their ballot paper, or things of that kind –
let us say "Cambronne's word" (merde) to them'.★ suggested
Victor Civelle at the salle de la Marseillaise on 26 April); the other
advocated a 'No' vote. In principle, the socialists favoured
abstention[75] or blank or spoilt ballot papers. In this way they were
following the orders of the *Marseillaise* (which had published a
letter from Rochefort which was to be read in halls over and over
again) and the International, the Paris sections of which had joined
forces with the Federation of Workers' Societies as early as 22
April in recommending abstention. The following day a central
republican committee was set up composed of press delegates,
election committees, workers' associations and sections of the
International. It met again on Monday 25 April to co-ordinate the
abstentionist attack. The abstentionist lobby could also rely on the
powerful Raspail committee in the 5th constituency which
regrouped around Poirier on 26 April to advocate blank ballot
papers. Among these forces we should not omit to mention the
Blanquists who were to champion abstention wherever they
spoke (Bachellery, rue de Lyon, on 25 April). Among the ranks of
the abstentionists were the most popular of all the public-meeting
speakers: Clément, Bachellery, Lermina, Chalain, Avrial, Bony,
Malon, Dupas, Roullier, Delahaye, Verlet, Vivier, Roussel,
Johannard, Humbert, Casse, Sérizier. Geographically, the abstentionists were particularly strong in the 18th, 12th, 19th and 15th
arrondissements, since they dominated in the collective votes, at
least until 30 April, at 4 boulevard de Clichy, the passage du
Génie, boulevard de Grenelle, and the salle de la Marseillaise.
Only the latter was to remain abstentionist right up to the end.
The abstentionists' argument was simple. The socialists had two
enemies: The Empire and the bourgeois Republic. A 'No' vote
would mean recognising the former and joining ranks with the
latter. As Bauer then said:

> Among the 'No' voters will be the reactionaries: we mustn't
> unite with people like that; we must abstain, voting 'No'
> would legitimise the Empire.

Moreover, involvement with the Left of '48 was to be avoided.
On 29 April at the rue Dieu, Pichon riposted bitterly to Pascal
Duprat:

> You've got no right to take the Empire to task for its crimes,

★ Supposedly Cambronne's last word.

for you've got your own crimes on your conscience. Unite with you! How can murderers expect to be united with the people they've murdered?

Therefore, from the proletarian point of view, separation from the Left was necessary. Clément was among the speakers who insisted upon this:

We must vote 'No', because above all we must make a break with our bitter enemies the formalistic republicans. Let us remember the June Days.

(27 April, 142 boulevard de Grenelle)

The return of their Republic would mean victory for the bourgeois reaction. It would be an over-simplification to deduce from such speeches that the revolutionary socialist speakers were simply being divisive, and that effectively they were playing a power game, for in fact they were in favour of unity, but not the same kind of unity as the liberals, the radicals and the Jacobins were offering:

'Unity, that's fine', exclaimed Humbert in reply to Pellétan on 28 April at 142 boulevard de Grenelle, 'but let's be clear about it. You helped 1852 to happen by attacking the socialists, so don't you talk about it.'

They advocated revolutionary unity in the manner of the abstentionist Henri Bauer, who told the salle de la Fidélité about the Young Students' Manifesto 'which is aimed at uniting the workers and the students against the common enemy, the Empire, in order to serve the Republic more effectively'.[76] On 30 April at the passage due Génie, one worker, Dumont, was to reply positively to this invitation to abstentionist unity: he held out his hand 'in the name of working-class youth and the students' and 'proclaimed himself an abstentionist'.

It was on the Left that the real divisive forces were to be found. Alfred Breuille 'proclaimed himself in favour of abstention and made a forceful attack on the way the Left was behaving',[77] and in the rue d'Arras Ducourdray and Brissac 'were forced to admit that the alleged split in the republican camp was an invention of the Left, whose initial decision had been taken without any consultation whatsoever with the working men's committees' (meeting of 29 April).

More generally, certain abstentionists maintained that the Plebiscite was useless. For Delarue 'whatever the vote is, we'll be

Arrondissement

	Eligible voters	Voters		Yes		No	
		Number	%	Number	%	Number	%
1	17 016	14 286	83.86	7 370	43.31	6 434	37.81
2	14 962	12 012	80.28	5 240	35.02	6 355	42.47
3	23 459	17 952	76.53	6 107	26.03	11 390	48.55
4	20 250	15 587	76.97	6 280	31.01	8 869	43.80
5	19 981	15 993	80.04	6 271	31.38	9 118	45.63
6	21 798	17 741	81.39	8 842	40.60	7 991	36.66
7	16 770	13 833	82.78	8 665	51.67	4 662	27.20
8	13 346	11 011	82.50	7 662	57.41	2 946	22.07
9	20 031	15 495	77.36	8 570	42.78	6 222	31.06
10	25 013	19 364	77.42	6 967	27.85	11 813	47.23
11	29 332	23 733	80.91	6 520	22.23	16 704	56.95
12	13 777	11 516	83.59	3 472	25.20	7 825	56.80
13	9 034	7 460	82.58	2 207	24.43	5 043	55.82
14	13 386	10 574	78.99	3 612	26.98	6 712	50.14
15	12 595	9 701	77.02	3 616	28.71	5 854	46.32
16	7 252	5 916	81.58	3 434	47.35	2 292	31.61
17	14 766	12 278	83.15	4 977	33.71	6 939	46.99
18	22 418	17 684	78.88	4 618	20.60	12 257	54.67
19	14 493	10 428	71.95	3 040	20.98	7 157	49.38
20	16 333	13 397	82.02	2 933	17.96	10 177	62.31
Total	346 012	276 011	79.77	110 403	31.91	156 760	45.30

8 May Plebiscite in Paris.

no nearer to revolution'.[78] It was therefore appropriate to behave as though nothing were happening; the proletariat had nothing to win. At 4 boulevard de Clichy 'Citizen Seyma said that poverty is forcing workers to tighten their belts while at the same time the government is gradually squeezing their throats. . . . On polling day you must stay home.' However, the abstentionists were able to use the campaign in order to challenge the Constitution. On 1 May in the chaussée du Maine, Chatelain waved it in the air, ripped it in two and threw it to the ground amid much applause. That same morning at the Pré-aux-Clercs Loriot had said that 'the 1870 Constitution was not perfectible', and the only way to destroy it was by revolution'. While certain abstentionists were convinced that abstention was the only valid course of action, and that the Paris electorate would be well aware of it, they felt it necessary to recommend a 'No' vote in rural areas. This is what Sérizier did at 190 avenue de Choisy. Then again the absten-

Abstentions		Blanks		Don't know		Protests	
Number	%	Number	%	Number	%	Number	%
2 730	16.04	345	2.03	53	0.31	84	0.49
2 950	19.72	314	2.10	23	0.15	80	0.53
5 507	23.47	309	1.32	141	0.60	5	0.02
4 663	23.04	285	1.41	90	0.44	63	0.31
3 988	19.96	438	2.19	166	0.83		
4 057	18.61	694	3.18	3	0.01	211	0.97
2 937	17.51	356	2.12	26	0.16	124	0.74
2 335	17.50	255	1.91	57	0.43	91	0.68
4 536	22.34	512	2.56	8	0.04	183	0.91
5 649	22.58	375	1.50	109	0.44	100	0.40
5 599	19.09	285	0.97	94	0.32	130	0.44
2 261	16.41	129	0.94	16	0.12	74	0.54
1 574	17.42	76	0.84	134	1.48		
2 812	21.01	145	1.08	21	0.16	84	0.63
2 894	22.98	157	1.25	26	0.21	48	0.38
1 336	18.42	140	1.93	50	0.69		
2 488	16.85	232	1.57	130	0.88		
4 734	21.02	632	2.82	87	0.39	90	0.40
4 065	28.05	143	0.99	31	0.21	57	0.39
2 936	17.98	170	1.04	117	0.72		
70 053	20.25	5 992	1.73	1 382	0.40	1 424	0.41

tionists admitted that it was possible to show one's opposition in a variety of ways. On 1 May, at the salle Molière, Roullier maintained that a 'No' vote, an abstention or a spoilt ballot paper were 'one in the same thing'.

As for the 'No' supporters, in principle they recruited from among the non-socialist republicans. On 19 April the Left and the delegates of the democratic press adopted Gambetta's and Jules Ferry's definitive manifesto without discussion. After recognising that all attitudes of opposition were valid, this document concluded by recommending a 'No' vote. It was signed[79] by a group of deputies from the Left and their journalist supporters who as we know were opposed to the usual public meetings. In this group we will find most of the men who were to make up the government of 4 September. These radicals were to reconstitute committees which were highly reminiscent of those which had been formed during the 1869 elections. Their policy was to open up the political spectrum, and in particular they made every effort to attract part of the extreme Left. Therefore it is not surprising to see radicals like d'Alton-Shée, Mathorel, the lawyer Coulon and Jacobins, even left-wing ones, coming out in favour of a 'No' vote. This political manoeuvre even found success among the extreme socialist left. This is why Passedouet, a leading Internationalist, was for abstention in theory, but advocated a 'No' vote from the very outset of the campaign. We should also add the names of Vésinier, who recommended a 'No' vote in the name of the International (at the Folies-Bergère on 2 May). Vertut at the rue de Lyon, and Lermina, also at the Folies-Bergère. This position, which had the advantage of being simple, was easily confused with the simplest republican credo and could thus convince the average voter. Although by no means the largest contingent at the outset of the Plebiscite meetings, some workers in the rue d'Arras or the avenue de Choisy lost no time in declaring their support for a 'No' vote.

However, while many republicans with Jacobin tendencies, like Ducoudray at the rue d'Arras or Flacet at the salle Molière (26 April), announced their intention to vote in favour of a 'No' vote right from the start, a group of them were aware of the power the abstentionist organisers wielded within the meetings, and limited themselves initially to advocating unity, like Ulysse Parent and Ducoudray, or the 'social republic', like Lissagaray at the Folies-Bergère on 25 April.

Geographically the 17th *arrondissement* (rue de Lévis), the 3rd (salle Molière), the 5th with its hall at no. 3 rue d'Arras, along with the 6th with the salle du Pré-aux-Clercs were won over to the 'No' vote. After 30 April we may add the salle des Mille-et-un-Jeux in the *faubourg* Saint-Antoine (12th). It was the salle du Pré-aux-Clercs, with Sicard, that was the most fiercely in favour. On 1 May the meeting approved a letter demanding that Rochefort go back on his decision and 'align himself with the "No" voters'. Such political pressuring was not to everyone's taste. At the boulevard de Clichy (18th) Joffrin was to protest about the Pré-aux-Clercs decisions as early as 2 May.

The result of the elections was to go far beyond the hopes of the 'No' – vote supporters who had won the day in the 11th, 12th, 13th, 14th, 18th and 20th *arrondissements* which encompassed most of the working-class *quartiers* and a great many public meetings. Their main argument was the rural vote. Here abstention would be too arbitrary, and so the 'No' vote – or as it was sometimes called, in the words of Frédéric Morin (rue d'Arras, 1 May), the 'tactical' vote – had to be adopted.[80] Craftily, they emphasised a letter of Raspail, as Ducoudray did at the

Cordelières-Saint-Marcel. However the tone was not always diplomatic. The 'No' supporters went so far as to insinuate that the abstentionists had betrayed the republican cause[81] and that possibly the sugar-refinery workers, who were engaged in a very untimely strike, were being manipulated in favour of a 'Yes' vote. That would really have been playing into the government's hands!

The mood was in the abstentionists' favour up until 30 April, as the following table showing voting intentions during the Plebiscite campaign reveals. We have established it mainly from the *Marseillaise*, and therefore it reflects the newspaper's *partipris* for abstention. Its journalists preferred to listen to people who came out in favour of that solution. However, it was infinitely more objective than its sister the *Rappel*, which favoured a 'No' vote. The *Rappel*'s descriptions of meeting committees were imprecise, and it habitually altered certain speeches, always emphasising their criticisms of the Empire and eliminating their socialist criticisms of the Left.

Voting intentions of the public meeting speakers

	Number of meetings	Absten-tion	No	Blank	Spoilt	Unde-cided	Yes	Total
25 April	4	3	13	—	5	2	—	23
26 April	12	25	26	—	—	2	1	54
27 April	15	27	26	2	3	5	—	63
28 April	16	37	32.5★	—	5.5★	8	2	85
29 April	16	29	30		4	25	1	89
30 April	24	31	36	1	1	24	4	97
1 May	44	28	49	1	2	40	4	124
2 May	16	7	33	—	—	46	4	90
	147	187	245.5	4	20.5	152	16	625

★ On 28 April at the salle de la Marseillaise, Carteret advocated 'No' votes and spoilt ballot papers. As a result, 32.5 per cent voted for 'No' and 5.5 per cent for spoilt papers.

The number of meetings listed above is higher than the figure given in the *Marseillaise*, which published all the voting-intention statistics except the very vague numbers for 25 April, which are taken from the *Rappel* (there were several abstentionist speakers at the rue d'Arras, but the *Rappel* gives neither their names nor the details of how many they were). The *Marseillaise* published reports on 11 meetings on 26 April, 13 on the twenty-seventh, 14 on the twenty-ninth, 13 on the thirtieth, 19 on 1 May and 12 on 2 May.

What we see in these voting intentions is above all militant propaganda, vanguard action which in this period of increased attendance at the public meetings was not necessarily in tune with current opinion. It was not because the speakers in halls which favoured abstention were more numerous that audiences followed them. And yet from 25 April to 30 April the abstentionists, who were usually the driving force behind these halls, were able to maintain the advantage in favour of their adopted stance.[82] So there were 173.5 who intended to abstain or to submit blank or spoilt ballot papers, against 163.5 in favour of a 'No' vote. During this period many 'No' supporters followed Lissagaray by not openly stating their intentions, being content simply to criticise the Empire.

The repression which was directed towards the abstentionists, thinning out the ranks of their most influential speakers (we will study these arrests and the Empire's aims later) modified the overall profile of the meetings. While some abstentionists kept angrily to their standpoint – Lefevre (1 May, boulevard de Clichy) said 'that the question of the Plebiscite is a trap. . . . The Emperor is making Sir Chassepot his patron saint', Chatelain trampled the Constitution underfoot (Maison-Dieu) and Vogt (mille-et-un-Jeux) maintained that 'he would abstain, even if he were alone in doing so' – many who began took a step back and began to retreat towards the position of the republicans, limiting themselves to criticising capitalism and the regime. The discussion was focussed on the social level, although at this time the workers' movement had difficulties expressing itself. On the level of dominant discourse it was a reversal of current trends. Pressure from certain abstentionist organisers could not prevent a veritable collapse, apart from in a few halls (passage du Génie, the Marseillaise, the boulevard de Clichy) where their influence was particularly strong. In particular they lost control at the boulevard de Grenelle and as a result many militants rallied to the 'No' vote. Were they frightened of the repression? Possibly. Even so we should note that on 5 May the powerful Raspail committee, which was the seedbed of worker militancy in the 5th constituency and which had advocated blank ballot papers, called for a resolute 'No' vote. The next day the *Marseillaise* explained this new resolution as a desire to respond to the proclamation that the Empire had distributed en masse direct to voters' homes. The Raspail committee's main argument was the same as the one held by everyone who had rallied to the 'No' vote: abstention, 'the only possible response to the Plebiscite', was 'impracticable' for 'clerks, country folk and soldiers', who were too closely under surveillance. At the passage du Génie Harlant rallied to the 'No' vote on

4 May and so did Moreau on the fifth. Similarly Barriot 'recognised that action was necessary' (Pré-aux-Clercs, 1 May). Gayet also followed suit. On 1 May, at the passage du Génie, Bauer preached 'agreement and support for a "No" vote', and on 2 May, at the rue Dieu, Bibal rallied to the 'No' vote in the name of reason and revolution as did Amet at the rue d'Arras on the same day . . .

The halls followed a similar path and rallied to the 'No' vote on 8 May, the 12th *arrondissement*, where the salle des Mille-et-un-Jeux had long been abstentionist, scored highly on the 'No'-vote scale (56.8 per cent as against 16.41 for abstention). This had been possible because while the campaign was actually under way the different political currents had had several standpoints in common: criticism of the Empire, the wish for revolution, a common practice for matters concerning the army.

As we have had occasion to say many times, criticism of the Empire was a unifying theme. Of course, there was a difference in nature between the criticisms of the revolutionary socialists and those of the Jacobins and the radicals. The former were above all concerned with the links between the regime and capitalism. What they could no longer accept – Hourriez said that he had 'had enough of it' – was the politicosocial oppression by the Empire which, in the words of Roullier, 'not content with stuffing itself with wealth, is crushing the workers, abusing them and beating them'. The Jacobins and the radicals put more weight upon the fact that this political regime was in contravention of the law of the legitimate Republic, namely the Montagnard Republic of 1848 (on 1 May at the rue d'Arras Pasquet was proclaimed chairman because he was 'an old republican from 1848') which had been put to death by the 1851 coup d'état; Ducoudray defended the 'No' vote, Eugene Tenot's book in his hand. As far as the radicals were concerned, 1848 was the only date they wanted to know. This led men like Lissagaray to maintain in the face of the facts that: 'It wasn't the Republic which shot the workers, it was the Empire.'

The 'liberal' Empire's repression reinforced the idea of a common enemy, for if the progressive militants refused to be silent about June 1848, the majority did not really feel concerned about it, either because it was something that had happened more than a generation ago and they had forgotten about it, or because the new Parisian populations had not lived through it. On the other hand, the new working class could judge the present benefits, acts of violence and arbitrary behaviour of the Empire on a day-to-day basis.

It was rather on this basis that the growing awareness of the Paris masses developed. To a certain extent this also influenced the way revolution, that other factor for unity, was perceived.

Undeniably there was a will to revolution. In April and May of 1870, nobody seemed to be against this much-vaunted evolution any more. Many speakers even considered that this was the real point of the Plebiscite. However, it is not difficult to realise that such speakers were talking about a political revolution and not a social one. Even worse, some more or less realised this, but expressed with satisfaction that it was the Empire itself which was putting revolution to the vote:

> 'If it's revolution', exclaimed Billete on 30 April at the rue d'Arras, 'we won't have asked for it, but given the position we've been placed in we'll accept it!' [*Prolonged cheering*]

This revolution would simply be a return to a unitarian republic of the 1792 type, which Lissagaray was referring to when he said:

> The army and the people would unite and march together beneath the glorious banner of revolution. (1 May, passage du Génie).

It had to be conducted sensibly, reasonably. On 2 May at the rue Dieu Bibal, a 'No' supporter, asked 'that at long last people should call upon the genius of the revolution which is Reason'. Therefore it was no longer a question of barricades or bloody confrontations. Now revolutionary combat would consist merely of peacefully placing a 'No' vote in the ballot box. Vertut was one of the speakers who presented this point of view at the rue de Lyon on 28 April:

> If you had to take up arms to fight tomorrow, would you abstain? No! Well then, the electoral roll is calling you, be logical and fight!

Revolution and civil war were opposed, because violent means of action were thought to be a thing of the past, unworthy of republicans and fit only for the Empire:

> 'The Empire is a continuous civil war,' said Vertut at the Saint-Mande gymnasium on 2 May. 'The republican is revolution waged in the full light of day, bravely, hands without weapons and breasts bared.' [*Enthusiastic applause*]

It is possible that the content of the speeches was influenced above all by the repression. This is certainly what is suggested by Leo Meillet's words on 6 May before an audience of 1,000 people at 190 avenue de Choisy: 'He believed that revolution was imminent and that it would surprise everyone; the important thing was not to fall into the trap the authorities had laid.' Blanqui's phrase – 'Your rifle is your ballot paper' – was not completely reversed, as Poncet, also a 'No' supporter, demonstrated on 2 May: 'The ballot paper is a more powerful weapon than the chassepot, we should use it to overthrow bad institutions.'

Thus the elections were becoming the privileged means of obtaining revolution. At least, this is what the 'No'-vote victors in the public meetings were to win agreement for. Dumont 'protested against the fact that citizen Vertut had suggested that he had spoken in favour of violent revolution. He had done no such thing'; on 1 May in the salle du Génie, 'a worker declared his opposition to violent revolution'. We could ramble on endlessly about what appeared to be a legalistic and electoralist tidal wave, hurling down insults from the tribune of history on the heads of the reformist republicans, those propagators of bourgeois ideology, but that would be to forget that a great many socialists rallied consciously to this attitude. Perhaps in those times of repression they thought it preferable to be discreet about their real convictions. In any event they had not given up completely: 'Despite all this the revolution will triumph', affirmed Dubuc at the passage du Génie on 1 May, while at the Pré-aux-Clercs Loriot recalled that the real way of resolving the problem had not changed: 'Since the 1870 Constitution is not perfectible, the only way to destroy it is through revolution.'

In the final analysis, as we all know, it is material relationships of strength which decide everything. Now the public meetings had developed their propaganda with a view to winning over the soldiers, and in fact this was the most dynamically unitarian factor in the anti-Plebiscite campaign. We should emphasise that this action, which had its source in Flourens' initiative and which was to bear fruit in 1870 and 1871, was without a shadow of doubt one of the most revolutionary in the political history of the period. To talk to ordinary soldiers with the purpose of attracting them to the public meetings was on the one hand to undermine the last rampart of the Empire and capitalism, and on the other to export revolution into the rural areas.

The 1870 Plebiscite ended in confusion, both in terms of its direct consequences, the repression and the disturbances between the 8 and 11 May which we will examine later, and in terms of what the campaign and its result really signified.

Did the revolutionary socialists really believe that by abstaining they were acting for their cause? Was it a deliberate act with a directly political aim, or more a scornful rejection of institutions in which they were no longer prepared to participate? The authorities hit them hard, which suggests that they may have been afraid of the influence their voting instructions might have had. It would seem that such a fear was misplaced, since the results showed this influence to be rather weak, with the exception of their frequently very relative successes in the 3rd, 4th, 9th, 10th, 14th, 15th, 18th, and, above all, the 19th *arrondissements* (where the salle de la Marseillaise had played an important part) in which abstentions were a record 28.05 per cent. In the final analysis, we can say that if the revolutionary socialists rejected the Plebiscite as a means of emancipation, they used the campaign period to develop their propaganda.

The 'No' supporters frequently behaved in an identical fashion and did not sniff at the opportunity they were given to address the masses who for once were there to listen. More than the socialists – we will refrain from returning to the political breakdown between abstention and a 'No' vote – they thought that their action during the Plebiscite would advance the revolution. For them, the ballot paper was a weapon equivalent if not superior to a rifle. Unfortunately the revolution which a success in the Plebiscite would permit would only mean a different regime and not a complete social change, for it could only come about on the basis of a union between different classes. This explains the veritable crow of victory from the radicals when the public meetings rallied to support their methods. It was almost indecent. Frédéric Marin of the *Rappel* saw in it the expression of the maturity of the people: henceforth the halls would be responsible, democratic, and would no longer echo the usual 'imprecations' of the extremists, that 'supreme resource of novice speakers' or . . . of *agents provocateurs*; the people, *admirable*, would transform themselves into a great *force tranquille*:

We must not be afraid to say that everywhere or almost everywhere the best-applauded and most numerous speeches have doubtless been remarkable for their republican energy, but also for their wisdom, common sense and moderation. And last week the public meetings not only displayed a spectacle of moderation and the obvious desire for harmony between all classes, but also (something which is infinitely rare in such assemblies) they displayed a marvellous tolerance towards people who opposed their closest-held convictions.

Happily, this was wishful thinking on the part of Morin and friends, who were eager to confuse circumstances and evolution. Their burial of the revolutionaries was premature (unless they were acting in bad faith, and what was to follow would prove that they were). Also, maybe they sensed that social revolution was imminent and were trying to convince themselves that class struggle was at an end in order to remove the danger. Careful study of the results seems to justify this fear. In effect, the 'Noes' prevailed in the popular and working-class *arrondissements* like the 3rd, 5th, 10th, 11th, 12th and 13th, achieving an absolute majority in the working-class centres, 56.95 per cent in the 19th (sphere of influence of the Raspail and Garnier-Pages committees), 55.82 per cent in the 11th (we have noted Passedouet's stance here), 56.95 per cent in the 13th which included part of the *faubourg* Saint-Antoine, and above all the 62.3 per cent in the 20th, which, as it happens, was known as the most revolutionary *arrondissement!* The meaning of the 'No' vote was maybe not the same in *quartiers* where the public meetings flourished as it was elsewhere. We should note that a percentage of 'No' votes higher than the Paris average was frequently accompanied by a higher-than-average percentage of abstentions: this was the case in the 3rd, 10th, 14th, 15th, 18th and 19th *arrondissements*. There is therefore no doubt that attitudes towards the Plebiscite did not cover the full range of political means envisaged by many Parisians, and in particular by the regular public-meeting militants.

D)   VIOLENCE

The public meetings were a milieu in which violence and proposals of violence as a means of action were almost a day-to-day thing. Apart from some extremely rare exceptions – on one occasion Drouchon presented violence and the public meetings as opposites – nobody at the meetings rejected them. According to their own political persuasion, critics of the public meetings saw this in terms either of stupid demonstrations or of an inclination towards terrorism. For him, the violent and thoughtless speeches of the public meetings clearly played into the hands of the Empire of 1870, for they prevented the formulation of a republican front composed of workers and bourgeois:

> The failings of personal government had placed it in a difficult position. The bourgeoisie was beginning to detach itself from it. . . . All that was needed to bring it gradually round to the Republic was for the republican party not to forget the lessons it had learned, and to make the effort not to frighten anyone

off. But this was not to be. The platforms of the public meetings never stopped resounding with threats and sabre rattling, that stock in trade of prattlers who pretend to be socialists without really knowing what a social question really is. If the public meetings of that period failed to reveal a single orator, a single tribune, on the other hand they teemed with people bragging about Jacobinism and social liquidation. To calm the fears of the bourgeoisie it was not enough to disown people of that kind, what was needed was to prove that if there were to be a republican government, it would be strong enough to contain them, and if needs be put them down.

Vitu and his fellows brought back the juiciest morsels from the meetings to reactivate the fears of 'decent folk' in town and country with 'the red spectre', and tried to suggest a continuity between the terrorism of 1793 and the public meetings. Our task will be to relocate this terrorist and insurrectional discourse in an overall logic. Reminders of the ups and downs of the Great Revolution, of its heroes from the Convention or the tanks of the sans-culottes, were not indications that a kind of collective memory was emerging (since, in any case, reminders tended to be of 1848) but more a technique for exalting revolution and revolutionaries in general. More than a model, An II was a point of reference, just as June 1848 was. To praise the regicides of the Convention was the same thing as justifying the revolutionary actions of the enemies of Imperial absolutism; to come back time and time again to the September massacres and 1793 was to invite the people and the proletariat to autonomous action. Threatened by closures and prosecutions, speakers could not always call their political enemies by name, but nothing forbad them to talk about history. To choose people condemned by the dominant political ethic as one's heroes was a way of coming back to politics and of suggesting to audiences that if the practices of the men of 1793 had been good for the eighteenth century, it was quite possible that they might not have lost all their qualities in terms of the present day. Thus halls were to echo to apologies of the 'blood drinkers' of 1793. The big stars came first. Vertut gives as examples 'the characters of Danton, Saint-Just and Marat'; Merot demanded 'respect for Marat, Robespierre, Saint-Just', whom Lemaitre exaltedly called 'the greatest geniuses of the Revolution'; Vinot was to name Danton, Robespierre and Marat, the three men who symbolised what, on 28 November 1868, at Menilmontant an unnamed speaker called 'the true Convention'.

It is incontestably the names of Robespierre and Marat which return the most frequently. Debeaumont was always ready to admit his admiration for Robespierre; Robespierre's bust adorned Falcet's home. The radical Floquet, who was often more or less disguised as Robespierre, a detail Lefrançais was to make fun of in his *mémoires*, won applause by recalling and condemning Marat's assassination. Marat was the hero of whom Budaille made the apologia on 23 February 1869 during a session devoted to 'The Struggle of Man in Nature'. More than anyone else, the Friend of the People was invoked as a model. On the question of the September massacres, to which we will return, it was still around his name that 'memories' crystallised. Ducasse said notably: 'Thus I pay homage to the energy devoted in those circumstances by Jean-Paul Marat, the Friend of the People so cravenly murdered by a common whore.'

The choice of characters was not an innocent one. If the name of Maximilian Robespierre was always on the lips of the neo-Jacobins, the neo-Hebertists swore by *Père Duchêsne* alone – Herbert, whose newspaper Rigault used to read aloud from the platform. With a very few exceptions, they all conjured up 1793. Vitu was careful to record that everyone agreed 'to make 1793, the date of the Terror, the vintage year of revolution'. There were a few other speakers who praised 1789, such as Durand, but the meetings gave them no support. When De Pressensse spoke about 1789: 'he was heckled from all corners of the hall: No, no, not 89! 93!' (The Pré-aux-Clercs, 9 November 1868). It was in this same spirit that Paule Minck 'had no intention of being satisfied with the principles of '89'. No one wanted that bourgeois revolution again. What people desired was 'the 1793 Republic' (Floquet) or rather 'the 1793 Revolution' (Casse).

It is difficult for historians and scholars not to smile condescendingly at the illusions the public meetings had about An II, for it is true to say that they saw the sans-culotte movement as a proletarian struggle. This is why Paule Minck missed 'our dear, beautiful France . . . the France of '93'. Like Theopile Ferré, she thought that the 'glorious' years of 1792 and 1793 had seen the advent of the power of the proletarians. The Blanquist Ferré went so far as to say: 'The Revolution of '93, which was the second Revolution and the genuine article, gave the workers employment.' His comrade Chauvière made no distinction between the 1793 sans-culottes and the workers of June 1848, whose ghosts were now risen to settle accounts with the bourgeoisie. To swat up 'the catechism of 1793', as Ducasse suggested that young people should do, would be above all a means of suggesting revolutionary violence to the masses. Revolutionary violence was the necessary answer to Imperial and bourgeois oppression and to the violent actions of the clergy and the police.[83]

The dominant classes and their representatives had been judged and deserved only the supreme punishment. This is the perspective in which we should see the speeches invoking the September massacres which led from the public meetings of 1868–70 to the people's execution of the political hostages of the Commune during the Bloody Week. To the great indignation of their opponents the public meetings sang paeans of praise for the actors of September 1792 who had solved the problems of the prisons on the eve of Valmy. Ducasse declared:

> I applaud the energy of the men who said: if we go to the
> frontier, we must not leave murderers behind us to kill our
> wives and children.

The September massacres had not only been necessary – Ducasse suggested that they had 'asserted freedom' – but they were just, for it was a 'struggle by people crushed beneath fifteen centuries of oppression' and 'the people had sixty generations of victims to avenge' (Mme Paulmin). Even Briosne, who was hardly a bloodthirsty tiger, defended them against Pressensse's attacks by calling them 'one of the most glorious events in our history'. Regicide was an object of delight for the public meetings. There were speakers like Terrail and Vertut who made 'the apologia of Louis XVI's execution', that 'act of popular wisdom'. Even Floquet was not above recalling its merits. It was too good a line of argument to abandon. Unlike the Humanists of 1848, the speakers cherished the cult of the guillotine and political executions. It was proposed that they be employed for priests and policemen. When André Rousselle suggested with all the logic of a radical that the Jesuits be thrown out, the audience cried: 'They ought to be guillotined!,'[84] an opinion which was echoed by Vertut, who thought that 'to suppress the Jesuits, Danton's and Robespierre's methods were the right ones'. The audience of the salle Molière wanted to lead the police superintendent to the guillotine. Like their guides (Gaillard, Rigault, Ferré) they were therefore of one accord when they let out the seditious and terrorist cry of 'Vive la guillotine!'.
   Thus the audiences had probably been won over to using methods of force to decide the fate of their social and political enemies. The salle de la Marseillaise, stirred up by Flourens against Schneider the master of Le Creusot, cried fervently: 'Let's hang him!' Such cries and opinions are only meaningful in so far as they reflect the awareness:
– that the political and social struggle was implacable,
– that it was not possible to evade the question of material

relationships of strength which in the final analysis decide everything, and that consequently verbal criticism could never replace armed criticism, that is to say, the use of force.

In a word, the public meeting revolutionaries were not convinced that democratic change was possible. Above all they militated to win minds over to their cause, which could only triumph through armed struggle. If they believed only in violent solutions, it was because they had learned from previous democratic and liberal experiments, especially 1848. Regretting the failure of the June Days, Paule Minck concluded one of her speeches by saying that 'only force can bring rights and freedom', and when Ferré was forced to accept the arbitrary closure of a meeting he was chairing, he exclaimed:

> If we had the force, we would go on with the discussion despite the authorities, and then there wouldn't be any more authorities.

What is remarkable about these attitudes is the fact that so many people had escaped being taken in by the trap of the public meetings and the mirage they offered of freedom of speech. They had understood that this supervised freedom was nothing but a pitfall, and that it would never allow for the resolution of the social question. In the words of Ducasse, it was a 'half-measure'. Thus the violence of exploitation had to be countered with the violence of the people. Even Bisson recognised that social wounds could only be cured 'with fire and the sword'. If weapons were lacking, they would hopefully become available and put into use at the earliest opportunity. It was the Blanquists who awaited this blessed moment with the most resolution. As early as 6 January 1869, Duval told the audience at the Vieux-Chêne that:

> Me, I agree with citizen Jacquelard, the communist radical who said at one of the Redoute meetings: 'Our turn will come; the force which is oppressing us today can be ours, and we shall crush it beneath our feet!'

And on 3 March at the salle Robert, Bachellery exclaimed: 'The force of arms shall be ours!'

This call to force used the memory of the popular past to find its models of energy. Once again An II is quoted. Chauvière bellowed that

> The worker can only save himself by the same means as he

used to save himself in '93 [*cheers*],[85] but also in June 1848 and December 1851.

While Rigault, Ducasse, Sérizier and Clément harped on the June Days (Sèrizier referring to his personal involvement[86] as did Clément who warmly remembered the June Days of 1848, waged in the name of the communism for which he is an apostle), Banneloche, a carpenter, declared his support for immediate armed struggle, speaking of the coup d'état and 'the misfortunes of the corporation in 1851, that fatal year in which everything I loved most was wiped out. I fought for it on the barricades, we lost it, but I'm ready to fight again to win it back.'

Revolts, insurrections and resistance like this were an integral part of the life of the worker. The worker, said Chauvière at Belleville, when pushed irresistibly towards hunger, 'will take up whatever weapon he can find and will go off to be killed on the cobbles of the *faubourg*'. Peyrouton was not so sure of this, since in fact he called for education to train 'men who are capable . . . of dying when needs be [*Thunderous applause*].'

Very frequently speakers alluded to an armed struggle while presenting themselves as future victims. Thus Briosne on 9 January 1869 at the Redoute:

The struggle begins today and we will only stop when you have laid us in our graves! [*Even louder salvos of applause*]

Speakers often gave their audiences a nod and a wink. 'You know what I mean', said Clément to the audience at the Redoute on 29 November 1869. On 1 October 1869 at the route de Choisy, Larmier was given a warning for having asked 'whether we didn't ought to use those little tools which have done the trick before to convince you-know-who'. Recalling the bourgeois manhunts during previous repressions, Ranvier concluded: 'In future the roles will be reversed and the hunted will have their chance to enjoy being hunters. [*Enthusiastic applause . . . the chairman and Rigault the assessor clap with the rest*]'

Laubin shouted: 'No more exploiters!' and suggested the means: 'We must demolish the block which is barring the way to democracy, we must . . . and it it this: Live free or die fighting. [*Bravos, stamping of feet, prolonged cheering*][87]

As one can imagine, all these references to revolutionary events, all these calls to the use of violence did not stay merely platonic. To begin with waiting was no longer possible. 'We need another '89,' said Mayard, 'not eight days from now but right away.'

At the beginning of 1869, the observers noticed an increase in insurrectional speeches. At la Chapelle as early as 11 January Bachellery was calling for revolt. As we have seen, the authorities attempted to smother revolutionary propaganda by repression (closures and prosecutions), and at one time even considered postponing the meetings scheduled for 24 February, the anniversary of the 1848 insurrection, but they had second thoughts and only took measures 'to suppress all disturbances on the public highway'. This agitation reached its peak in March with several calls to insurrection which were actually addressed to meetings. Garreau, a locksmith and the future manager of Mazas during the Commune, invited the regulars at Budaille's to overthrow bourgeois society;

> I want to murder the bourgeoisie, the capitalists who devour everything . . . I want us to go into the streets fully armed, not tomorrow, but right now.

The Blanquists took advantage of the noisy meeting on unemployment at the salle Robert to cry out an insurrectional slogan. Already on 10 March 'people wanted to resist, they started singing the Marseillaise. *Aux armes, citoyens!* Everyone was highly excited, and wanted to go and get the audiences from other meetings in Paris.'

On 23 March the organisers of the meeting thought the time was ripe. Ferré (Chairman) and Bachellery had already laid plans with their comrades to resist the authorities' injunctions, and after a stinging attack on Napoleon I's anti-working-class regime, Bachellery exclaimed:

> Believe me . . . the question of unemployment can only be resolved by force of arms, and so it's a call to arms that I'm making.

As soon as the meeting was pronounced closed, the speaker repeated his call to the noisy approval of the audience: 'Yes! Yes! by force of arms.' He was sentenced *absente reo* by the Sixth Chamber for 'incitement to crime', despite the fact that his over-spontaneous call to armed struggle was not followed up in practice.

The audience of the salle Robert was to continue in this insurrectional spirit. Once again, on 30 March, when the closure of the public meetings was brought up, someone in the audience threatened that: 'If they are closed down, we'll use force to start them up again'. Now and again there were to be other calls to insurrection or revolution.

The great riots of May–June 1869 and May 1870 and the February 1870 insurrection were the fruits of this incessant propaganda in favour of violent means of action. If the public meeting militants were not always agreed about the best moment to use insurrection[88] – a question we will return to later – they were not against it in principle. Flouren's wild escapade on 7 February 1870 was not criticised in the popular meetings.[89] Need we add that the meetings did not always mince their words? On 17 April 1870 at the salle de la Marseillaise, Giot said that 'we must send the b..... exploiters and parasites packing'.

We have studied the revolutionary personnel of the public meetings and their evolution towards a coming together, a symbiosis, of their most left-wing elements, namely the elements whose aim was to overthrow the regime and transform society. On the level of means of action we have seen that they were all considered, including the most violent. And yet when the riots of 1869 and 1870 broke out, the speakers, who had been exhorting the people to action, hung fire, even going so far as to condemn them: it is a contradiction which cannot be passed over without comment. It was one of the realities of the public meeting movement.

Notes

1 See Allix's, 23 March 1869, at the Pré-aux-Clercs: 'Rights and Duties' (NA 155, p. 326).
2 NA 155, p. 776. Meeting of 17 April 1870, 142 rue de Grenelle. At Belleville Brisson had been in much more of a hurry: 'We want freedom, but by the quickest and most radical way' ('On the Education and Instruction of Children', NA 155, p. 147).
3 NA 155, boulevard de Clichy, 3 October 1869: 'On Fear and Ingratitude in Education'.
4 Ibid., pp. 570–1: 'Plan for a General Association for the Emancipation of Labour'. Passedout concluded: 'To win freedom, that is our present aim'.
5 Qualified, however, since Passedouet attacked state education for inevitably 'violating freedoms' (sessions of 14 August 1869, rue Nationale, 'Child Education', NA 155, p. 488).
6 The Raspail committee, breeding ground for militants, workers and revolutionaries; the Democratic Socialist committee led by Tolain, Demay, Briosne . . . the best known public-meeting speakers: Ducasse, Humbert, Lermina, Lefrançais; the Blanquists, either in prison or at liberty; Victor Hugo's newspaper Le Rappel and Delescluzes's the Réveil . . .

7 He had another rather unenviable evening during the October insurrection of 1870 when, as a member of the Provisional Government, he was held prisoner by the insurgents who had invaded the Hotel de Ville to proclaim the Commune.

8 After the salle de la Maison-Dieu had elected Rochefort as honorary chairman on 27 April 1870, Limousin 'accused the assembly of creating idols for itself' (*La Marseillaise*, 29 April).

9 NA 155, p. 734. On 27 March Jules Ferry preferred to say he was ill rather than to go to the Grand Orient to give a talk on 'The Foundation of Independent Secondary Schools'.

10 BHVP NA 155, p. 601; Paulet, 10 October 1869 at the Folies-Belleville; Vertut wanted to shake off 'the chains from within' at the Alcazar in October 1869.

11 NA 155, p. 531. The same topic was discussed at 190 avenue de Choisy where Ledru-Rollin was made honorary chairman along with Rochefort, Barbès and Millière.

12 He emphasised 'the need to choose socialist candidates', Folies-Belleville in the 4th constituency (*Le Rappel*, 7 November 1869).

13 During the session on 26 October 1868 ('Marriage and Divorce') he replied to an opponent that Proudhon 'was as capable of making a mistake as anyone else'. (45 AP6)

14 *Ibid.* Session of 18 August 1868: 'Female Labour', the Vaux-Hall.

15 However, in September 1869 Ducasse was to defend the materialist stance at the meetings on 'The Right to Punish' (NA 155, pp. 504, 505, 507).

16 *Le Rappel*, 7 October 1869. Joly was explaining his ideas in respect of 'the coming of women'.

17 Did he stand up for 'communism' against Laviolette (NA 155)? In fact Briosne became very skilled in his presentation of the different tendencies. He did not agree with 'the agrarian law', despite Ruisseau's accusation ('Marriage and Divorce'), nor did he have the 'Icarian Plan' the Institute Librarian Lenormand reproached him with ('Marriage and Divorce', 6 October 1868). On the other hand we hear him praising 'individual initiative' ('Marriage and Divorce', 22 September 1868).

18 Session of 11 October 1868.

19 'On the Organisation of the Social Commune', *Le Rappel*, 5 January 1870.

20 45 AP5. See the remarks made by superintendent Pezeret in the minutes of November 8th 1868: 'Monopolies'. Another informant in NA 155 admits to not having grasped his 'abstract and philosophical . . . demonstration. . . . He said he was a Collectivist, which was another word for Communist'; the superintendent at the meeting on marriage and divorce reported that on 22 September 1868, Briosne 'defined communism and individualism in a very confused way'.

21 NA 155, p. 173; Paule Minck at the Pré-aux-Clercs, 12 January 1869, 'Heredity'.

22 *Le Rappel*, 11 October 1869. Letter from Héligon about Molinari's criticism in the *Journal des debats* of one of his speeches at a meeting on

'Wages and Unemployment' at the boulevard de Clichy.

23 *Le Rappel*, 6 May 1869. The newspaper recalls that Héligon is 'known for his socialist opinions'.

24 This People's Bank, started in 1866 by Beluze, Cabet's son-in-law, and which grouped together 'all the capital that was sympathetic to workers' associations', had as many as 2,000 associates and 1,000,000 francs capital before it went bankrupt in November 1868.

25 On 17 October, Murat said notably: 'The worker should try to put some funds by and deposit them wherever he likes so that he'll have something to retire on later.'

26 On 14 November 1868 a certain Cherlowski, a confirmed socialist rejected communism as a 'backward system' which would turn the clock back to the times of 'savages and monks'; a similar observation was made by the economist Oriani on 17 October: 'It is retrogressive to attack capital.'

27 See Cognet and Howert (known as Charpentier), 14 November 1868, among others.

28 Landrecht, 31 October 1868.

29 It was an unnamed man in a *blouse* who as early as the second meeting had demanded that the speakers should say in advance whether they were for or against the legitimacy of interest.

30 They played a part in the launching of the newspaper *La Démocratie*, either as shareholders in its limited company or as members of its board of directors. We may note the following names: Allix, Verdure, Flourens, Andre Leo, Paule Minck, etc. (and even both Gaillards!).

31 Vitu, p. 45: session of 29 January 1869. See also Gaillard's attack on individual property on 30 January 1869 (NA 155, p. 142).

32 In October 1869 when he put forward 'the theory of collectivism' Paulet was very vague when he 'supported the idea that this was the only system which could give every worker the integral product of his labour' (session of 11 October 1869 at the Folies-Belleville, 'On Wages', *Le Rappel*, 13 October 1869).

33 *Ibid.*, p. 448, session of 9 April 1869, rue de la Folie-Merincourt, meetings about the family. However, that day Johannard did make it clear that 'everyone must work'.

34 They were to be denied all freedom of expression. Camille Adam: 'We've been gagged for long enough. Maybe the day will come when it will be our turn to gag the others' (NA 155, p. 680, rue de la Maison-Dieu, 21 January 1870: 'The Eradication of Pauperism').

35 Archives of the Seine, D3 U9, judgment on appeal, 18 February 1869 for the session of 30 January 1869, salle due Pré-aux-Clercs.

36 13 January 1869, salle du Vieux-Chêne.

37 19 January 1865, boulevard de la Chapelle.

38 *Le Rappel*, 9 October 1869, session of 7 October at the Folies-Belleville devoted to 'The Social and Agricultural Commune'.

39 BHVP NA 155, p. 754; on 21 April 1869 at the salle Molière Tolain spoke of how 'the French had brought that country not civilisation, but suffering and servitude' (pp. 453, 454).

40 *Ibid.*, p. 694: 'The People, What they Have Been, What they Are and

What they Should Be From the Social Point of View'.

41 NA 155, p. 542, October 1869: 'The Social Commune – Ways and Means of Effecting It'.

42 *Ibid.*, p. 642, 'On the Organisation of the Social Commune'.

43 *Ibid.*, p. 683, 22 January 1869: 'The Social Commune – Ways and Means of Effecting It'.

44 Tolain was one of the most conspicuous propagandists for 'the mutualist system', for, as he said, 'only we the socialists can rebuild society, with the help of our principles of mutuality'.

45 *Le Rappel*, 13 October 1869: meeting of 11 October 1869 at the Folies-Belleville: 'On Wages'.

46 AN 45, AP 6; session of 30 September 1868; on 11 October he added that there would be no more bosses, and that co-operation 'will guarantee the independence of the individual . . . against communism'.

47 Vitu, p. 111; hearing of 4 February 1869 in the Sixth Chamber: 'Pindy protested that he had never intended to make any calls for violent action in support of his ideas, but that he had merely proposed peaceful means for the workers to emancipate themselves from the employers by the creation of unions'.

48 45 AP 6. Havrais 'knew only one remedy for the situation: resistance funds and societies' (session of 11 October 1868); as for Heurtebise, he advised women workers 'to strike over working hours . . . you should set up a resistance fund' (session of 14 October 1868).

49 NA 155, p. 772: meeting of 6 April, 142 rue de Grenelle: 'The Principles of Socialism'; elsewhere it was Labroye and Beaufils who 'protested vigorously about the Aubin massacres and the autumn convictions'.

50 *Op. cit.*, pp. 14–15: meeting of October 1869, rue de Crimée. Quoted from *Rappel*, 22 October 1869.

51 NA 155: meeting of 7 April 1870, *Cahiers du Travail*. On 14 September 1869 at the avenue de Choisy the shoemaker maintained that there should be a rent strike: 'We are fed up with paying interest on capital.'

52 NA 155, pp. 525–6. Gustave Drouchon was not only a free thinker and a public meeting organiser, but also a militant and a member of the IWMA. On 11 October 1868 Havrais was already saying the same things as Drouchon: 'He only knows of one way of remedying the situation: resistance funds and societies' (AN 45, AP 6).

53 Samuel Bernstein: *Auguste Blanqui*, pp. 278–80; Testut, *op. cit.*, p. 51. The second question at the Brussels Congress related to 'Strikes, Federation between Resistance Societies, and the Creation of Councils for Arbitration in the event of Strikes'.

54 NA 155, pp. 374–87; meeting of 20 March 1869, salle Robert. On the other hand Briosne kept to the radical theme, which he traced back to the Convention, for in his estimation 'free compulsory education' was enough: his children could choose their own 'faith' (atheism would be one of them!) when their intelligence was sufficiently developed (NA 155, p. 443; meeting of 6 April 1869: 'Rights and Duties', at the Pré-aux-Clercs). See also p. 414, session of 10 April 1869, salle Robert.

55 *Ibid.*, p. 273. Bretonneau wanted to start one in Belleville; see Briosne's comments p. 529; see also Masse who attacked the term 'compulsory' because it reminded him of the Imperial government (session of 5 October 1869, avenue de Choisy).

56 NA 155, p. 616; meeting of 7 October 1869, 4 boulevard de Clichy. In 1870 at the salle Molière, Falcet was one of the most fervent advocates of unity: 'We must unite; Concord is all' (*La Marseillaise*).

57 'Belleville' in *Les Elections de 1869*, pp. 3–36, vol. XXI, Bibliothèque de la Société de 1848.

58 AN 45, AP 5. Did Lermina, who had attacked Garnier-Pages and Jules Favre so remorselessly, follow suit? The sources are contradictory: according to *Rappel* of 9 May 1870, he announced his intention to vote for Picard at the Alcazar on 7 May; according to Vitu, he opposed Picard (*op. cit.*, p. 68).

59 Lefrançais, *op. cit.*, p. 349.

60 *Ibid.*, pp. 274–5: listed are Chemalé, Andre Murat, Lefrançais, Briosne, Tolain, Demay, Bibal, Combes, Longuet, Denis, Langlois.

61 APPo, BA 362–1. Among others, signed by Rigault, Chauvière, Ducasse, Humbert, Breuille, Gaillard, Fortin, Bologne . . .

62 Henry was rejected by an audience of 3,000 voters on 9 May at the Folies-Belleville; in the same hall on 11 May Demay's speech provoked laughter and jeering; on 14 May rue de Lyon, Stenson's attempt to stand as 'the candidate of the working class' was ruled out of order (45 AP 5).

63 Passedouet and the men of June 1848 were behind his candidature (cf. *L'Insurgé*, p. 76).

64 In the 1st constituency Tolain supported Gambetta.

65 *Le Réveil*, 13 May 1869, 45 AP 5: Briosne 'presented the socialist system which he has already elaborated on so often in public meetings'.

66 *Le Figaro*, 19 May 1869.

67 Jules Mallarmet, a bronze fitter, ex-member of the Luxembourg Commission in 1848, ex-communist, ex-clubgoer, and who was in the forefront of the initial public meetings in 1868, was on his committee; the other bronze fitters followed suit.

68 On 16 May he analysed his recent career as a deputy, concluding that his main principle in life seems to have been not abstention but absence.

69 *Le Figaro*, 19 May 1869, reported Lermina's 'biting indictment' and the 'series of votes which must have been highly unpalatable for the ex-member of the provisional government'.

70 He was to experience another unenviable evening during the insurrection of 31 October 1870.

71 We note that when d'Alton-Shée visited Briosne's electoral stronghold on 30 May, the latter failed to attack him.

72 *Le Rappel*, 5 November: meeting of 3 November in the 2nd constituency; *Le Rappel*, 6 November: Falcet repeats this analysis at the salle Molière (4th constituency).

73 *Le Rappel*, 12 November 1869: meeting of 8 November at Asnière (8th constituency).

74 *Le Rappel*, 7 November 1869: meeting at the salle des Folies-Belleville, 4th constituency. See also the meeting of the fourth, salle Molière, where Allix said: 'The Constitution originated in the crime of December' (the superintendent announced that the meeting be closed).

75 They also favoured 'active abstention', which consisted of withdrawing one's voting card. See Parent, salle de la Fidélité, 22 May 1870 (*La Marseillaise*, 4 May); *idem* Dupas, 28 April, salle de la Marseillaise (*La Marseillaise*, 30 May).

76 *Le Rappel*, 1 May 1870, does not mention this in its article on Bauer's abstentionist convictions.

77 *La Marseillaise*, 3 May 1870; chaussée du Maine, rue Maison-Dieu, 1 May.

78 *La Marseillaise*, 2 May 1870; passage due Génie, meeting of 30 April.

79 *Le Rappel*, 22 April 1870. It was signed by Arago, Bancel, A. Crémieux, Disseaux, Dorian, Esquiros, Ferry, Gagneur, Gambetta, Garnier-Pagès, Girault, Glais-Bizouin, Grevy, J. Magnin, Ordinaire, E. Pellétan, Jules Simon, deputies; Deléscluze, A. Duportal, Louis Jourdan, Andre Lavertujon, Pierre Lefranc, A. Peyrat, Louis Ulbach, Eugene Véron, delegates from the 'democratic press' of Paris and the departments.

80 Passedouet, Bionne, 26 April, avenue de Choisy.

81 Gonez, 29 April, rue de la Maison-Dieu (*La Marseillaise*, 1 May).

82 Sometimes their methods were rather undemocratic: witness the meeting where Jules Vallès, the committee chairman, was clever enough to sense the way things were going and managed to stop a vote being taken at the end of the session.

83 NA 155, pp. 281, 403. Félix took the Pope to task for opposing 'our demands for our rights', a reference to the Syllabus of Errors, and thus forcing him and all workers to use violence (11 February, 27 rue de la Gaîté: 'Wage Labour and Pauperism'); at the place du Trône, it was alleged that the police had set the people up 'to incite them to revolution' (session of 9 March 1869).

84 Vitu, p. 59, NA 155, p. 163; session of 8 January 1869, salle du Vieux-Chêne: 'The Society of Jesus as a Teaching Body'. 'You kill vipers,' Marchand pointed out after comparing the Jesuits to those reptiles (session of 8 January 1869 in the Vieux-Chêne, NA 155, p. 160).

85 Vitu, p. 61, NA 155, p. 6212. Legrand: 'remember the group of the Marseillaise on the Arc de Triomphe which seems to be crying: "To arms!" ' (session of 30 October 1869, 128 rue de Crimée: 'Socialism and Practical Means of Action').

86 'I fought in 1848. I was only 14 and I carried a rifle like a man; the workers nowadays are not capable of doing as much' (NA 155, p. 730; avenue de Choisy: *Cahiers du Travail*).

87 Vitu, p. 62, Belleville, 11 December 1868. Chauvière also recalled the *canut*'s struggle and their watchword.

88 NA 155, p. 726. Passedouet demanded 'the right of insurrection' as in
    1793 (meeting in March 1870, avenue de Choisy: *Cahiers du Travail*).
89 *Ibid.*, p. 754. On 7 April at the Théâtre Parisien, when Falcet spoke 'in
    veiled terms' about Flouren's attitude at Victor Noir's funeral, 'the
    assembly understood what he meant, and cried "*Vive* Flourens!" '

Bibliography

Agulhon, Maurice, *La vie sociale en Provence intérieure au Lendemain de la révolution*, Société des Études Robespierristes, Paris, 1970

Agulhon, Maurice, *1848, du l'apprentissage de la république 1848–52*, Seuil, Paris, 1973

Agulhon, Maurice, *Les Quarante-huitards*, Archives-Gallimard, Paris, 1975

Agulhon, Maurice, *Une Ville ouvrière au temps du socialisme utopique Toulon de 1815 à 1851*, Mouton, Paris, 1977

Agulhon, Maurice, *La République au village*, Seuil, Paris, 1979

Cobb, Richard, *Les Armées révolutionnaires*, 2 vols, Mouton, Paris, 1961–3

Cobb, Richard, *The Police and the People: French Popular Protest 1789–1820*, Oxford University Press, 1970

Cobb, Richard, *A Second Identity*, Oxford University Press, 1969

Cobb, Richard, *People and Places*, Oxford University Press, 1985

Faure, Alain and Rancière, Jacques (eds), *La Parole ouvrière 1830/1851*, Paris, 1976

Gossez, Remi, *Les Ouvriers de Paris, livre une: l'organisation 1848–1851*, Bibliothèque de la Révolution de 1848, vol. 24, La Roche-sur-Yon, 1967

Johnson, C. H., 'Economic change and artisan discontent: the tailors' history, 1800–1808': in R. Price (ed.), *Revolution and Reaction: 1848 and the Second French Republic*, Croom Helm, 1975

Rancière, Jacques, *La Nuit des prolétaires*, Fayard, Paris, 1981

Rougerie, Jacques, *Procès des communards*, Julliard, Collection Archives, 1964

Rougerie, Jacques, *Paris libre*, Seuil, Paris, 1971

Rougerie, Jacques, '1871', in: *La commune de 1871*, Les Éditions Ouvrières, Paris, 1971

Rougerie, Jacques, 'L'A.I.T. et le mouvement ouvrier à Paris pendant les événementes de 1870–1871', *International Review of Social History*, 1972

Schulkind, Eugene, 'The activity of popular organisations during the Paris Commune of 1871', *French Historical Studies*, 1960

Schulkind, Eugene, *The Paris Commune of 1871: the View from the Left*, Cape, 1971

Schulkind, Eugene, 'Socialist women during the 1871 Paris Commune', *Past and Present*, 100, 1985

Scott, Joan, 'Men and women in the Parisian garment trade: discussions

at family and work in the 1830s and 1840s': in P. Thane (ed.),
Festschrift for Eric Hobsbawm

Sewell, William, Jnr., 'Social change and the rise of working-class politics in nineteenth-century Marseille', in: *Past and Present*, 65, 1974

Sewell, William, Jnr., 'The working class of Marseille under the Second Republic: social structure and political behaviour in workers in the Industrial Revolution': in *Recent Studies of Labor in the United States and Europe*, Stearns, Peter N. and Walkowitz, David J. (eds), Transaction Books, New Brunswick, 1974

Sewell, William, Jnr., *Work and Revolution in France: the Language of Labour from the Old Regime to 1848*, Cambridge University Press, 1980

Thompson, E. P., *The Making of the English Working Class*, Gollancz, 1963

Tridon, G., *Les Hebertistes – plainte contre une calomnie de l'histoire*, second ed., Paris, 1871